The Principal Navigations, Voyages, Traffiques and Discoveries of the English Nation — Volume 04

Richard Hakluyt

Alpha Editions

This edition published in 2024

ISBN 9789362513922

Design and Setting By
Alpha Editions
www.alphaedis.com
Email - info@alphaedis.com

As per information held with us this book is in Public Domain.
This book is a reproduction of an important historical work.
Alpha Editions uses the best technology to reproduce historical work
in the same manner it was first published to preserve its original nature.
Any marks or number seen are left intentionally to preserve.

Contents

VOL. IV	- 1 -
NORTH-EASTERN EUROPE, AND ADJACENT COUNTRIES PART III	- 2 -
THE MUSCOVY COMPANY AND THE NORTH-EASTERN PASSAGE SECTION II	- 3 -
NORTH-EASTERN EUROPE.	- 4 -
END OF VOL. IV.	- 263 -

VOL. IV

NORTH-EASTERN EUROPE, AND ADJACENT COUNTRIES
PART III

THE MUSCOVY COMPANY AND THE
NORTH-EASTERN PASSAGE
SECTION II

Navigations, Voyages, Traffiques, and Discoveries in

NORTH-EASTERN EUROPE.

The Priuiledges graunted by the Emperour of Russia to the English merchants of that company: obteined the 22. of September, Anno 1567. by M. Anthony Ienkinson.

One onely strengthener of all things, and God without beginning, which was before the world, the Father, the Sonne, and the holy Ghost, our onely God in Trinitie, and maker of all things whom we worship in all things, and in all places, the doer and fulfiller of all things, which is the perfect knowledge giuer of the true God, our Lorde Iesus Christ, with the comforter the holy Spirit, and thou which art the strengthener of our faith, keepe vs together, and giue vs health to preserue our kingdome, thou giuer of all good fruites, and helper of all Christian beleeuers.

We great lord by the grace of God, and great duke Iohn Vasiliwich of all Russia, Volodimer, Mosco, Nouogrod, Cazan, Astracan, Plesco, Smolensko, Tweria, Yougorie, Fadika, Bulgar, Sybier and others, Emperour and great duke of Nouogrod of the lower land of Chernygo, Rezan, Polotski, Rostoue, Yereslaue, Bealozera, Oudoria, Obdorio, Condensa, and lord of many other lands, and of all the North parts, commander and lord of Lifland.

Whereas our sister Queene Elizabeth, by the grace of God, Queene of England, France and Ireland, hath written to vs her letters, that wee would graunt her merchants, William Garrard, William Chester, Rowland Heyward, Lawrence Hussie, Iohn Marsh, Anthony Ienkinson, William Rowly, and their company of England, to come in ships into this kingdome, and those merchants, William Garrard and his company haue required of vs that we would graunt and licence them to come into our countrey of Dwina, with all kind of wares at wil, to our City of Mosco, and to all our castles in our kingdomes, we for our sisters sake Elizabeth, by the grace of God, Queene of England, France and Ireland, haue licenced her merchants, William Garrard and his company to passe in ships to our kingdome of Colmogro, and to the land of Dwina, and to all other our inheritances in the North parts, with all kind of wares to our city of Mosco, and to all castles and townes in our kingdome. And sir William Garrard and his company desired of vs, that we would graunt them licence to passe to our inheritance of Cazan and Astracan, and into our inheritance of Nouogrod the great, and to our inheritance of Lifland to Narue and Dorpe, and to other our castles and townes of Lifland, with all kinde of wares, and the trade to be without custome, which request we haue graunted to sir William

Garrard and his company, and haue giuen them licence to passe to our inheritance of Cazan and Astracan, and Nouogrod the great, and into our inheritance of Lifland, Narue and Dorpe, and other places of our inheritance in Lifland with all kinde of wares, to buy, barter and sell at will, without custome: and what wares soeuer they bring out of England, or out of any other countrey, needfull or necessary, that they shall bring all those wares needfull or necessary to our treasury, and those wares there to be opened, and then to take out of the same such wares as shalbe needful for our treasury, and the rest being deliuered againe, to sell and barter at their pleasure, and to sell none of the fine wares before they be seene of our chancellers, except sorting clothes, and other wares not meat for our treasury: and when our chanceller will send our treasure out of our treasury with them, they shall take it with them, and so sell and barter it for wares meet for our treasury, and bring it to our treasury, and they to take no other mens wares to barter or sell with them, nor yet our people to buy or sell for them their wares: and if those English merchants do desire to passe out of our kingdome of Astracan to Boghar, Shamaky, Chaday, or into any other countreys, or els go into their owne countrey, then they to take their treasure with them, and to barter and sell it for wares necessary for our treasury, and to bring it and deliuer it to our chancellor, and when they come backe againe to our inheritance of Cazan and Astracan, or to any other of our castles and townes, that then our captaine of Cazan and Astracan, and all other our people of charge shall not holde them, but with speed let them passe without taking custome of them or their wares, and without opening or looking vpon them in any wise: and when they haue not our treasure with them, that then likewise no custome shalbe taken of them nor their wares to be seene of any man.

And likewise we haue granted them to buy and sell in all our kingdomes and castles, with all kinde of wares: and we haue also licenced them, that when those English merchants do desire to buy and sell with our merchants wholly together, that they shall haue liberty so to do wholly together: and they that do desire to sell their owne wares by retaile in their owne house, that then they sell it in their own house by retaile to our people, and other strangers, as they can agree: and weights and arshnids to be kept in their house with our seale, and they themselues to barter and sell their owne wares: and no Russe merchant in Mosco, or any other place in our kingdome to sell for them any wares, nor to buy or barter any wares for them, nor couler any strangers goods. And whereas those merchants of England, sir William Garrard and his company do desire to sell their wares at Colmogro, Dwina, Vologda, Yeraslaue, Costrum, and in Nouogrod the lower, Cazan, Astracan, great Nouogrod, Plesko, Narue, Dorpe, and in other our townes and castles, they shall haue their will to sell it: and of their wares of England and Russeland no custome shalbe taken, neither they nor their wares shalbe stayed in any place: and when they depart out of Mosco, to aduertise our chancellor thereof, and not to giue any note or inuentory of any kinde of their wares they cary away: and when the English merchants, sir William Garrard and his company do come vpon the sea, and by misfortune haue their ships cast away vpon those coasts of the North parts, then we will their goods to be sought out with trueth, and to be deliuered to sir William Garrard and his company, which as then shall be found in our countrey: and if that sir William Garrards company be not in the Mosco nor in our countrey: then we will and command that those goods of theirs shall be layd vp in a place of safegard vntil such time as the said sir William Garrard or his company come to demand the same: and then at their comming we will that it shall be deliuered. And whereas heretofore we haue giuen sir William Garrard and his company in this our kingdome of Mosco the new castle by the church of S. Maxim behinde the market, they shal there stil holde their house as heretofore we haue giuen them, paying no custome for the same: and we also do licence them to keepe one Russe porter or two or els of their owne countrey, and those porters shall dwell with them, and not sell for them, nor barter, nor buy for them: And also I haue granted them to buy a house at Volodga and at Colmogro, or in any other place where they can chuse for them selues any good harbour, and there they to set vp those houses in those places at their owne charges: and in Vologda or the other houses to keepe two or three porters of their owne, or else two or three Russes, and their wares to be layed vp in those houses, and to sell their owne wares at will: and the porters without them to sell none of their wares, neither yet to buy any for them. And our officers of Colmogro and Dwina, and of other our castles and townes shall not looke ouer their wares, nor take any custome thereof: neither shall those English merchants sir William Garrard and his company be iudged by any of them. And when the English merchants shall send from our kingdome their owne people into their owne countrey by land ouer other kingdomes whatsoeuer they be, they may without ware send their owne people at their pleasure. And when any matter of law doth fall out in their trade of merchandise, then they shall be iudged by our chancellers and law shalbe done with equitie betwixt our people and them: and when they cannot be iudged by law, they then shal be tried by lots, and whose lot is first taken out, he shall haue the right. [Sidenote: Triall by lots.] And if it happen any of those merchants to haue any matter of law in any other part of our dominions for trade of merchants, then our captaines, iudges, and chiefe officers shall heare the matter, and administer iustice with equity and trueth, and where law can take no place, to be tried by lots, and his lot that is first taken out to haue the right, and for their matters of law no custome to be payed.

[Sidenote: The riuer of Ob traffikable.] Furthermore, we for our sisters sake Elizabeth haue granted, that none beside sir William Garrard and his company, out of what kingdome soeuer it be, England or other, shall come in trade of merchandise nor otherwise to Colmogro, nor to the riuer Ob, nor within Wardhouse, nor to Petzora, nor Cola, nor Mezen, nor to the abbey of Petchingo, nor to the island of Shallawy, nor to any mouth of the riuer of Dwina, nor to any part of the North countrey of our coast. And if any merchant, out of what countrey soeuer it be, doe come with ship or shippes, busses, or any other kinde of vessell to any of our harbours, within all our North parts, we will that then the people and goods, ship or ships, shalbe confiscate, and forfeited to vs the Emperour and great Duke.

Giuen in our kingdome and house of Mosco, the yeere from the beginning of the world 7076, in the moneth of September, and in the 34 yeere of our reigne, and in our conquest of Cazan 16, and in our conquest of Astracan 15.

Perused and allowed by vs:
  Anthonie Ienkinson.
  William Rowly.
  Thomas Hawtry.
  Thomas Sowtham.
  Rafe Rutter, our translatour
    hereof of the
    Russe tongue.

* * * * *

A letter of M. Henrie Lane to M. Richard Hakluit, concerning the first ambassage to our most gracious Queene Elizabeth from the Russian Emperour anno 1567, and other notable matters incident to those places and times.

Worshipfull sir, because I finde you haue the successe and proceedings of Osep Napea the first ambassadour of the Russian Emperour to the Maiesties of King Philip and Queene Marie, at what time and at his returne I was remaining in Russia, and do not finde that the perfect knowledge of the first ambassage from thence to this our Souereigne Ladie Queene Elizabeth is come to your hands, betweene whose Highnesse and the ambassadours I was interpretour, I thinke good to expresse it. In August Anno 1567 arriued at London with their retinue two especiall authorised messengers, named Stephen Twerdico, and Theodore Pogorella, with letters and presents to her Maiesty, at that time being at Otelands, where diuers of the chiefe merchants of the Russian company did associate them, and I there doing my duetie and office of interpretour, her Maiestie gaue them audience. First they rehearsed the long stile and Maiesty of their Master, with his most friendly and hearty commendations to her Highnesse, and then they testified the singuler great ioy and pleasure that he conceiued to heare of her most princely estate, dignitie and health: and lastly, they deliuered their letters and presents. The presents sent vnto her Maiesty were Sables, both in paires for tippets, and two timbars, to wit, two times fortie, with Luserns and other rich furres. [Sidenote: The vse of furres wholesome, delicate, graue and comely.] For at that time that princely ancient ornament of furres was yet in vse. And great pitie but that it might be renewed, especiall in Court, and among Magistrates, not onely for the restoring of an olde worshipfull Art and Companie, but also because they be for our climate wholesome, delicate, graue and comely: expressing dignitie, comforting age, and of longer continuance, and better with small cost to be preserued, then these new silks, shagges, and ragges, wherein a great part of the wealth of the land is hastily consumed.

These ambassadours were appointed lodging and enterteinement by the Moscouie company at their house then in Seething Lane, and were sundrie times after permitted to be in presence. And in May 1568 tooke their leaue at Greenwich, where they vnderstood and had the Queenes Maiesties minde, letters and reward. [Sidenote: The trade to S. Nicholas offensiue to diuers princes and states Eastward.] At the latter part of her talke, her Highnesse considering that our trade to Saint Nicholas since the beginning had bene offensiue to diuers princes, states, and merchants Eastward vsed these speeches or the like: Who is or shall be more touched by detractours, with flying tales and vntrue reports, then Princes and Rulers, to the breach of loue and vnitie? your Master and I in things that passe by word and writing, I doubt not will keepe and performe promises. If he heare the contrary of me, let him suspend his iudgement, and not be light of credit, and so will I. These words they termed her Maiesties golden speech: and kneeling downe, kissed her hand, and departed.

The letters that these two messengers brought, were deliuered to me by my Lord Treasurour, being then Secretarie, to be translated, the copies whereof I had, but now cannot finde. The copie of the Queenes Maiesties letter I send inclosed herewith vnto your worship. I also haue sent you a copy of a letter written from the king of Polonia to the Queenes Maiestie, with other letters from some of our nation and factours, declaring the displeasure for our trafficke to the Russes from Anno 1558 to the yere 1566, especially by the way of the Narue: in which yere of 1566, hauing generall procuration and commission from the Company, I was in the Low countrey at Antwerpe and Amsterdam, and sometimes in company with Polacks, Danskers, and Easterlings: and by, reason I had bene a lidger in Russia, I could the better reply and proue, that their owne nations and the Italians were most guiltie of the accusations written by the king of Poland.

This king Sigismundus [Footnote: Sigismund II, the last of the Jagellon race, added Livonia to his kingdom. He reigned from 1548 to 1572. It was after his death that the King of Poland became an elective instead of an heritary sovereign.] (whose ambassadours very sumptuous I haue seene at Mosco) was reported to be too milde in suffering the Moscouites. [Sidenote: Smolensko won by the Russe.] Before our trafficke they ouerranne his great dukedome of Lituania, and tooke Smolensco, carrying the people captiues to Mosco. [Sidenote: Polotzko taken.] And in the yere 1563, as appeareth by Thomas Alcocks letter, they suffered the Russe likewise in that Duchy to take a principall city called Polotzko, with the lord and people thereof. Likewise the said Sigismundus and the king of Sweden did not looke to the protection of Liuonia, but lost all, except Rie and Reuel, and the Russe made the Narue his port to trafficke, not onely to vs, but to Lubec and others, generall. And still from those parts the Moscouites were furnished out of Dutchland by enterlopers with all arts and artificers, and had few or none by vs. The Italians also furnished them with engines of warre, and taught them warrelike stratagemes, and the arte of fortification. In the dayes of Sigismund the Russe would tant the Polacks, that they loued their ease at home with their wiues, and to drinke, and were not at commandement of their king. This Sigismund had to wife the daughter of Ferdinando, Charles the fifts brother, and he died without issue. [Sidenote: Polotzko recouered by Stephanus Batore.] Since, which time their late elected king Stephanus Batore [Footnote: Stephen Bathore, the second Elected-King, established the Cossacks as a militia. He died in 1586.] kept the Russe in better order, and recouered Polotzko againe in the yere 1579. Thus with my hearty farewell I take my leaue of your worship.

Your assured friend Henrie Lane.

* * * * *

A Letter of the most excellent Maiestie of Queene Elizabeth, sent by
  Stephen Twerdico and Pheodata Pogorella, messengers of the Emperour of
  Russia, vnto their Master the 9th of May 1568.

Imperatori Moscouitarum, &c.

ELIZABETHA &c. Literas vestrŠ, Maiestatis superiori anno 1567, decimo die mensis Aprilis datas, vestri mercatores Stephanus Twerdico, et Pheodata Pogorella, qui has nostras perferunt, nobis tradidere. Quos vestros mercatores in omni suo apud nos et nostros obeundo negotio, ita tractari, et libenti voluntate, et expresso nostro mandato curauimus, vt non solum vestrŠ Maiestatis pro illis postulationi, sed eorundem etiam hominum expectationi plenR satisfactum esse confidamus. Id quod e͜ fecimus studiosi͏̈s, quod plane perspectum, probÚque cognitum habeamus, nostros omnes, qui bona cum gratia nostra, nostrar͏mque literarum commendatione, istuc, sub vestro imperio negotiaturi veniunt, pari, cum vestrŠ Maiestatis fauore, tum vestrorum subditorum humanitate, vbiuis acceptos esse. QuŠ nostra vtrobique, et muttuŠ inter nos amicitiŠ et gratŠ inter nostros beneuolentiŠ officia, vt crebra et perpetua existant, nos admodum postulamus. Quem animi nostri sensnm fusius hi vestri, et opportunius suo sermone coram declarabunt: Quibus non dubitamus, quin vestra Maiestas amplam fidem sit tributura. Deus &c. Grenouici nono die Maij 1567.

* * * * *

The ambassage of the right worshipfulll Master Thomas Randolfe, Esquire, to the Emperour of Russia, in the yeere 1568, briefly written by himselfe.

[Sidenote: In this voyage went Thomas Bannister, and Geofrey Ducket, for their voyage into Persia.] The 22 day of Iune, in the yere of our Lord 1568, I went aboord the Harry, lying in the road at Harwich with my company, being to the number of fortie persons or thereabout: of which the one halfe were gentlemen, desirous to see the world.

Within one dayes sailing, we were out of the sight of land, and following our course directly North, till we came to the North Cape, we sailed for the space of twelue dayes with a prosperous winde, without tempest or outrage of sea: hauing compassed the North Cape we directed our course flat Southeast, hauing vpon our right hand Norway, Wardhouse, Lapland, all out of sight till we came to Cape Gallant: and so sailing betweene two bayes, the two and thirtieth day after our departure from Harwich, we cast ancre at Saint Nicholas road. In all the time of our voyage, more then the great number of Whales ingendering together, which we might plainly beholde, and the Sperma CetŠ, which we might see swimming vpon the sea, there was no great thing to be woondered at. Sometimes we had calmes, wherein our Mariners fished, and tooke good store of diuers sorts. [Sidenote: The abbey of S. Nicholas of 20 monks.] At S. Nicholas we landed the 23 of Iuly, where there standeth an abbey of Monks (to the number of twentie) built all of wood: the apparell of the Monks is superstitious, in blacke hoods, as ours haue bene. Their Church is faire, but full of painted images, tapers, and candles. Their owne houses are low, and small roomes. They lie apart, they eat together, and are much giuen to drunkennesse, vnlearned, write they can, preach they doe neuer, ceremonious in their Church, and long in their prayers.

At my first arriuall I was presented from their Prior with two great rie loaues, fish both salt and fresh of diuers sorts, both sea fish and fresh water, one sheepe aliue, blacke, with a white face, to be the more gratefull vnto me, and so with many solemne words inuiting me to see their house, they tooke their leaue.

[Sidenote: The English house at S. Nicholas.] Towne or habitation at S. Nicholas there is none more then about foure houses neere the abbey, and another built by the English Company for their owne vse.

This part of the countrey is most part wood, sauing here and there pasture and arable ground, many riuers and diuers Islands vnhabited, as the most part of the countrey is, for the coldnesse in Winter.

S. Nicholas standeth Northeast: the eleuation of the pole 64 degrees. [Sidenote: The riuer of Dwina.] The riuer that runneth there into the sea is called Dwina, very large, but shallow. This riuer taketh his beginning about 700 miles within the countrey, and vpon the riuer standeth Colmogro, and many prety villages, well situated for pasture, arable land, wood, and water. The riuer pleasant betweene hie hils of either side inwardly. inhabited, and in a maner a wildernesse of hie firre trees, and other wood.

[Sidenote: Colmogro.] At Colmgoro being 100 versts, which we account for three quarters of a mile euery verst, we taried three weeks, not being suffered to depart before the Emperour had word of our comming, who sent to meet vs a gentleman of his house, to conuey vs, and to see vs furnished of victuals, and all things needfull, vpon his owne charge.

The allowance of meat and drinke was for euery day two rubbles, besides the charge of boats by water, and foure score post horses by land, with aboue 100 carts to cary my wines, and other cariage.

Colmogro is a great towne builded all of wood, not walled, but scattered house from house. The people are rude in maners, and in apparell homely, sauing vpon their festiuall, and marriage dayes.

The people of this town finding commodity by the English mens traffike with them are much at their commandement, giuen much to drunkenesse, and all other kind of abominable vices.

[Sidenote: An English house with lands at Colmogro.] In this towne the English men haue lands of their owne, giuen them by the Emperour, and faire houses, with offices for their commodity, very many.

Of other townes vntill I come to Vologda, I write not, because they are much like to this, and the inhabitants not differing from them.

I was fiue whole weeks vpon the riuer of Dwina till I came to Vologda, being drawen with men against the streame, for other passage there is none.

Vologda standeth vpon the riuer of Vologda, which commeth into Dwina. The towne is great and long, built all of wood, as all their townes are.

In this towne the Emperour hath built a castle inuironed with a wall of stone, and bricke, the walles faire and hie, round about. Here (as in all other their townes) are many Churches; some built of bricke, the rest of wood, many Monks and Nunnes in it: a towne also of great traffike, and many rich merchants there dwelling.

From hence we passed by land towards Mosco in poste, being 500 versts great, which are equall with our miles. In their townes we baited or lay, being post townes.

[Sidenote: The description of the inland of Moscouie.] The countrey is very faire, plaine and pleasant, well inhabited, corne, pasture, medowes enough, riuers, and woods, faire and goodly.

At Yeraslaue we passed the riuer of Volga, more than a mile ouer. This riuer taketh his beginning at Beal Ozera, and descendeth into Mare Caspium, portable thorow of very great vessels with flat bottomes, which farre passe any that our countrey vseth.

To saile by this riuer into Mare Caspium the English company caused a barke to be built of 27 tunns, which there was neuer seene before: This barke built and ready rigged to the sea with her whole furniture cost not the company aboue one hundreth marks there.

[Footnote: His arriual at Mosco.] To Mosco we came about the end of September, receiued by no man, not so much as our owne countreymen suffered to meet vs, which bred suspition in me of some other course intended, then we had hitheto found.

[Footnote: A special house at Mosco, built for Ambassadours.] We were brought to a house built of purpose by the Emperour for Ambassadours, faire and large, after the fashion of that countrey.

Two gentlemen were appointed to attend vpon me, the one to see vs furnished of victuals, and that we lacked nothing of the Emperors allowance: the other to see that we should not goe out of the house, nor suffer any man to come vnto vs, in which they left nothing vndone that belonged to their charge. But specially he that looked to our persons so straightly handled vs; that we had no small cause to doubt that some euill had bene intended vnto vs. No supplication, sute, or request could take place for our liberty, nor yet to come to his presence.

Hauing passed ouer 17 weeks in this sort, the Emperour sendeth word that we should be ready against Tuesday the 20 of Februarie, at eight a clocke in the morning.

[Sidenote: Two Pristaues.] The houre being come that I should go to the Court, the two gentlemen Pristaues (as they call them) came vnto me apparelled more princely then before I had euer seene them. They presse vs to depart, and mounted vpon their owne horses, and the Ambassador vpon such a one as he had borrowed, his men marching on foot, to their great griefe.

The Ambassadour (being my selfe) was conueyed into an office where one of the chancellors doeth vse to sit, being there accompanied with the two foresayd gentlemen: I taried two long houres before I was sent for to the Emperor. In the end message being brought that the Emperour was set, I was conueyed by my gentlemen vp a paire of staires thorow a large roome, where sate by my estimation 300 persons, all in rich attire, taken out of the Emperors wardrobe for that day, vpon three ranks of benches, set round about the place, rather to present a maiestie, then that they were either of quality or honor.

[Sidenote: His admission to the Emperors presence.] At the first entry into the chamber I with my cap gaue them the reuerence, such as I iudged, their stately sitting, graue countenances and sumptuous apparell required, and seeing that it was not answered againe of any of them I couered my head, and so passing to a chamber where the Emperor was, there receiued me at the doore from my two gentlemen or gouernors, two of the Emperors counsellors, and shewed me to the Emperor, and brought me to the middle of the chamber, where I was willed to stand still, and to say that which I had to say. I by my Interpretor opened my message as I receiued it from the Queene my Mistresse, from whom I came, at whose name the Emperor stood vp, and demanded diuers questions of her health and state: whereunto answere being made, he gaue me his hand in token of my welcome, and caused me to sit downe, and further asked me diuers questions.

[Sidenote: The Queenes present.] This done, I deliuered her Maiesties present, which was a notable great Cup of siluer curiously wrought, with verses grauen in it, expressing the histories workmanly set out in the same.

[Sidenote: The Emperors speech to the Ambassadour.] All being sayd and done (as appeared) to his contentment, he licenced me and my whole company to depart, who were all in his presence, and were saluted by him with a nod of his head, and sayd vnto me: I dine not this day openly for great affaires I haue, but I will send thee my dinner, and giue leaue to thee and thine to go at liberty, and augment our allowance to thee, in token of our loue and fauor to our sister the Queene of England.

I with reuerence tooke my leaue, being conueyed by two other of greater calling then those that brought me to the Emperors sight, who deliuered me to the two first gentlemen, who conducted me to the office where I first was, where came vnto me one called the Long duke, with whom I conferred a while, and so returned to my lodging.

Within one houre after in comes to my lodging a duke richly apparelled, accompanied with fiftie persons, ech of them carying a siluer dish with meat, and couered with siluer. The duke first deliuered twenty loaues of bread of the Emperors owne eating, hauing tasted the same, and deliuered eury dish into my hands, and tasted of euery kinde of drinke that he brought.

This being done, the duke and his company sate downe with me, and tooke part of the Emperors meat, and filled themselues well of all sorts, and went not away from me vnrewarded.

Within few nights after the Emperour had will to speake secretly with me, and sent for me in the night by the Long duke: the place was farre off, and the night colde; and I hauing changed my apparell into such as the Russes do weare, found great incommoditie thereby.

[Sidenote: A second conference with the Emperor.] Hauing talked with him aboue three houres, towards the morning I was dismissed, and so came home to my lodging, where I remained aboue six weeks after, before I heard againe from the Emperour, who went the next day to Slouoda, the house of his solace. After the end of which sixe weeks, which was about the beginning of April, the Emperour returned from Slouoda aforesayd, and sent for me againe to make repaire vnto him. And being come, I dealt effectually with him in the behalfe of our English merchants, and found him so graciously inclined towards them, that I obtained at his hands my whole demands for large priuileges in generall, together with all the rest my particular requests. [Sidenote: Andrew Sauin Ambassadour to the Queene.] And then he commended to my conduct into England, a noble man of his, called Andrew Sauin, as his Ambassadour, for the better confirmation of his priuileges granted, and other negotiations with her Maiesty. And thus being dispatched with full contentment, the sayd Ambassadour and my selfe departed, and imbarked at S. Nicholas about the end of Iuly, and arriued safely at London in the moneth of September following.

* * * * *

A copie of the priuiledges granted by the right high and mightie Prince, the Emperour of Russia, &c. vnto the right worshipfull fellowship of English merchants, for the discouerie of new trades: and hither sent by Thomas Randolfe esquire, her Maiesties Ambassadour to the sayd Emperour, and by Andrew Sauin his Ambassadour in the yere of our Lord God, 1569.

One God euerlasting and without and before the beginning, the Father, the Sonne, and the holy Ghost, the blessed Trinitie, our onely God, maker and preseruer of all things, replenisher of all things euery where, who by thy goodnesse doest cause all men to loue the giuer of wisedome our onely

Mediatour, and leader of vs all vnto blessed knowledge by the onely Sonne his word, our Lord Iesus Christ, holy and euerlasting Spirit, and now in these our dayes teachest vs to keepe Christianitie, and sufferest vs to enioy our kingdome to the happy commodity of our land, and wealth of our people, in despight of our enemies, and to our fame with our friends.

We Iohn Vasiliwich by the grace of God, great lord, Emperour, and great duke of all Russia, Volodemer, Moscouia, Nouogrod, Emperour of Cazan, Tuersky, Vgorsky, Permisky, Vadsky, Bulgaria, and many others, lord and great duke of the Low countreys of Nouogrod, Chernigosky, Resansky, Polotsky, Rastow, Veraslaue, Bealosera, Owdorsky, Condinsky, and all Siberland, great commander of all the North parts, lord of Leifland, and many other Northward, Southward, and Westward.

Whereas our sister Elizabeth by the grace of God Queene of England, France and Ireland, defender of the faith, hath written vnto vs her letters for her merchants, who hath made sute that we should grant our goodnesse to the merchants which are of one company, and giue them free leaue to come to traffike in our kingdome to Colmogro, and to the countrey of Dwina, and to our great citie of Moscouia, and to all the cities in our dominions, and thorow our countrey to Boghar, to Persia, Casbin, and Chardy, and to all other countreys.

1 We Iohn Vasiliwich Emperour and great duke of all Russia, (for our sister Elizabeths sake, Queene, of England) haue giuen and granted to the English merchants, the Gouernors, Cousuls, Assistants and fellowship, sir Wil. Garrard Knight, Rowland Haiward Alderman, Ioh. Thamworth Esquire, Iohn Riuers Alderman, Henry Beecher Alderman, Consuls: Sir Wil. Chester Knight, Edward Iackman Alderman, Lionel Ducket Alderman, Edward Gilbert, Laurence Huse, Francis Walsingham, Clement Throgmorton Iohn Quarles, Nicholas Wheeler, Thomas Banister, Iohn Harrison, Francis Burnham, Anthony Gamage, Iohn Somers, Richard Wilkinson, Ioh. Sparke, Richard Barne, Robert Woolman, Thomas Browne, Thomas Smith, Thomas Allen, Thomas More, William Bully, Richard Yong, Thomas Atkinson, Assistants: Iohn Mersh Esquire, Geofrey Ducket, Francis Robinson, Matthew Field, and all the rest of their company and fellowship, and to their successours and deputies, to come with ships and other vessels into our countery at Colmogorod, and Dwina, and to all the North parts now being ours, or that hereafter shall at any time be in our possession, by sea, riuer or land, euen to our great Citie of Mosco, in all the townes of our Countrey, to Cazan and Astracan, to Nouogorod the great, to Plesko and Leifland, Vriagorod, to Narue, and all other townes of Leifland. 2 And to passe through our land to Boghar, Persia, Casbin, Charday, and other Countreyes: And wheresoeuer they come there to be

and abide freely, and to barter and bargaine freely all wares of sale, without custome of all people, and Marchants strangers whatsoeuer.

And if so be they bring any fine wares out of Englande, or any other Countrey from Boghar, Persia, Casbin, or from any other place, and those their wares that come by the way of Narue, or any other part into our Dominion, to bring the same wares into our treasure, and our Treasurers to view the same wares, and to take into our Treasurie of the same such as shalbe needful for vs. And all such wares as we shal not need, our Chancellour to redeliuer the same: And after the view of our Chancellours, to barter it freely to whom they will, not selling any of their wares needful for vs, before our Chancellour haue seene the same. And all other grosse and heauy wares that shall be needful to our vse not being brought to Mosco, to declare and tell our Chancellour of the same wares: And to giue a note thereof by name, and how much they leaue there, not brought to Mosco; and then if we neede not the said wares, the English Marchants, their seruants and Factors, to conuey their wares the neerest way to Vstiug the great, and so to Colmogorod, or elsewhere at their pleasure, there to barter and sell the same. But those wares that shalbe needfull for our Treasurie, they shall not hide from vs in any case.

And when our Chancellours shall send our aduenture, with the said Marchants or their Factors, they to take our aduentures with them, and to sell, and to barter for such wares as shalbe meete for our Treasurie, and to returne it into our Treasurie.

And when we shall sende any aduenture into England then our Chancellour to giue them a yeeres warning, that their ships may be prouided thereafter, that by taking in of our wares, they leaue not their owne behind them.

And to take our aduenture yeerely when they goe into Persia.

Neither shall the English marchants receiue or colour any of our peoples goods, nor barter nor sell it in any wise: likewise our people not to barter for the sayd English merchants or occupy for them.

3 And when they shall come into our Empire of Casan and Astracan, and other places of our Dominions, then our Captaines of Casan and Astracan, and our authorised people, quietly to let them passe, not taking any toll or custome of their wares, nor once to make search thereof.

And when we shal send no adueture with them, yet to suffer them freely to passe, not viewing their wares, nor taking any kinde of custome. And whatsoeuer English marchant will bargaine with our Marchants or Factors ware for ware to barter the same at their pleasure.

And whatsoeuer their Marchant or Factors will sell their wares at their house at Mosco, which house I granted them at S. Maxims at the Mosco, they to sell the ware to our people, either strangers as they may best vtter it, keeping within their house, arshines, measures, and waights vnder seales.

4 We haue granted them the saide house at S. Maxims in the halfe free, and without standing rent, as heretofore we did grant it the said English Marchants, sir Wil. Garrard, and the Company, maintayning in the said house one housekeeper a Russe, and two Russe seruants, or some of their owne countrey men, and none other Russes besides the aforesayde. And the said housekeepers that shall liue at their house with the English marchants neither to buy nor sel any wares for them, but that the said marchants themselues or their factors, shall buy, sell, and barter their owne wares: and our Moscouie marchants not to take the said Englishmens wares to sell them in our townes, nor to buy any wares for them, neither the English marchant to colour any Russe wares at any towne.

5 And whatsoeuer English marchant will sell his wares at Colmogorod, Dwyna, Vologda, Yeraslaue, Castran, Nouogorod the lower, Casan, Astracan, Nouogrod the great, Vopsko, the Narue, Vriagorod, or at any other townes, they to sel their wares there at their pleasure: And of all wares aswell of other countreis as of Russia, no officer or other to take any custome, neither in any place to stay them in any wise, neither take any kinde of toll of them for their wares whatsoeuer.

6 And whatsoeuer marchant shall bargaine or buy any wares of English marchants: The said Russe not to returne those wares vpon the marchants hands againe, but to giue ready money for the said wares, otherwise they to craue the Iustice to giue right, and to execute the lawe vpon the same with all expedition. And when the English marchants or factors shal trauaile from Moscouie after the dispatch of their wares and businesse, then to shew themselues vnto our Chancellours, whatsoeuer wares of theirs shall goe from Mosco, they not to shew the same wares to any our officers, nor pay no custome nor toll in any place.

7 If it so happen the English marchants haue any wracke, and the shippes be brought to any port of our Dominions, we to command the said goods to be enquired and sought out, and to be giuen to the English marchants, being here abiding at that time in our Countrey, the factors, seruants, or deputies, of the Company aforesayd, to whom we haue granted this our gratious letter.

And if there happen none of the English merchants, factors, seruants, or deputies to be in our Countreis at such time, then we wil all the said goods to be sought out and bestowed in some conuenient place, and when any of the Company aforewritten, bringing these our letters, shall come for their goods, we to command their goods to be restored vnto them.

8 Likewise wee haue graunted leaue to the English merchants, their Gouernours, Consuls, and assistants, namely, sir William Garrard knight, Rowland Howard, and to the Companie, to builde houses at Vologda, Colmogro, and the seaside, at Iuangorod, at Cherell, and in all other places our Dominions, as shall be needeful for their trade. And they to keepe at the said house one housekeeper, a Russe, and two or three men to keepe their wares at the said houses, making sale thereof to whom they will, they, their Factors or deputies: the said housekeeper not to buy or sell for them.

9 Also we haue giuen and graunted to the English Marchants, their house which they haue by your goodnesse at S. Maximes in the Zenopski, and other their houses in the towne of Zenopski, made for the better assurance of their goods, and all such as they shall set vp hereafter shal be of the Opressini [Marginal note: Or chosen side.], and will make them knowen to all them of Opressini.

10 And whereas by our goodnes we haue graunted them a Ropehouse at Vologda, being farre from the English Merchants house, now we haue giuen them to build a house for that vse by the said English house, and haue giuen and graunted them (of our goodnesse) ground, one hundreth and fourescore fadome long, and fiftie fadomes in breadth, according to their owne request.

11 Also we haue of our goodnesse giuen and graunted to the English Merchants, leaue to buy them a house at Wichida, and there to search our mines of yron. And where they shal happily find it, there to set vp houses for the making of the same yron: and to make the same, of our goodnesse haue graunted them woods; fiue or sixe miles compasse about the sayd houses, to the making of the sayd yron, and not to exceede these bounds, and limits: And where they shall cut the sayde wood, not to set vp any village or farme there, bringing the artificers for making of their yron, out of their owne Countrey, and to learne our people that arte, and so freely occupying the said yron in these our Dominions, transporting also of the same home into Englande, allowing for euery pound one dingo, or halfe penie.

12 And if any of the said yron shalbe needfull for our workes, then we to take of the said yron to our worke, vpon agreement of price, paying money out of our Treasurie for the same: And when the said English Merchants or Factors shal send their owne people out of our Realme into their Countrey, ouer land through any Countrey whatsoeuer, freely to send the same with our words.

13. Also we of our goodness haue graunted, that if any man misuse the said English, the Factors or seruants, or the saide English Merchants; their Factors or seruants abuse any other at Moscouie, or any other out townes whatsoeuer within our Dominions in trade of Marchandise or otherwise, then they to haue vpright iustice in all such matters of our counsaile the Opressini without all let or delay: But if our Iustice may not agree the parties, then lots to be made, and to whose lotte it shall fall, to him the right to be giuen, and that only our counsaile at Moscouie, and none of our Captaines, or authorised people, or officers in any other our townes, giue iudgement vpon the said English Merchants for any thing.

14 Also, if any stranger shall haue matter of controuersie with any English Merchant, Factor or seruant, abiding within these our Realmes, or contrariwise any English Merchant, Factor or seruant, against any other stranger, in all those causes our Counsaile of the Opressini, to giue them Iustice, and to make an agreement and end betweene the parties, without all delay: And none to deale therein, saue our Counsaile of the Opressini.

15 And if any man haue action against any English Merchant being absent, that then in his absence it shalbe lawfull for any other Englishman at his assignation to answere his cause.

16 If any Englishman happen to be wounded or beaten to death, or any Russe or stranger slaine or beaten. 17 Or any stollen goods to be found in the said English houses, then our Counsellors to cause the guiltie persons to be sought out, and to doe right and Iustice in the cause, and the partie that is guiltie, if he deserue punishment, to be corrected accordingly after his offence: That the said English Merchants, factors and seruant, sustaine thereby no hinderance or damage.

18 And whatsoeuer English Marchant, Factor, seruant, or deputie, shalbe guilty of any fault, deseruing our displeasure, then our Counsellors to cause the guiltie partie to goe vnder suerties, and their goods to be sealed and kept, vntill our pleasure be further knowen, and our Counsaile to examine their offence, and so to report it vnto vs, that we may command what shall be done therein, and none other to be arrested or haue their goods sealed, which are not guiltie of that offence, nor to stay or apprehend them in any of our Dominions for the same.

19 If any English Marchant, Factor or seruant shall offend, it shalbe lawfull for their Agent to doe iustice vpon the said partie, or to send him home into England at his pleasure.

20 If any English Marchant, Factor or seruant, haue lent or hereafter shall lende money to any of our people, or credite them with wares, and so depart into any forreigne Countrey, or die before the debt be due to be

payde, then our people and Marchants to paye the sayde debt, to whom soeuer shall be appointed to the sayd roome or charge, and the saide English Marchant, factor, or seruant, to bring his bill of debt to our Counsell, to shewe them what is due, and what money is owing them for any wares: and thus to doe truly, not adding any whit to the debt, and our Counsel to command the debt to be discharged vnto the English Marchant, factor, or seruant, without delay.

21 And whatsoeuer English Marchant shall be arrested for debt, then our Counsell to command the partie vnder arrest to be deliuered to the Agent: and if he haue no suertie, to binde the Agent with him, for the better force of the bond.

And if any Englishman be endebted, we will the Creditor not to cast him in prison, or to deliuer him to the Sergeant, lest the officer lose him, but to take ware in pawne of the debt.

22 Also of our goodnes, we haue granted the English Marchants to send our Commission to all our Townes, Captaines, and authorised men, to defende and garde the said Marchants from all theeues, robbers, and euill disposed persons.

23 If in comming or going to and fro our dominions, the Marchants, the factors, or seruants be spoyled on the sea, our Counsell shall send our letters, and will them to be sought out, and where they shall finde the goods, cause it to be restored againe, and the offender to be punished, according to our commandement.

24 Also of our goodnes, we haue granted the saide Merchants to take vp Brokers, Packers, Wayers, and such like labourers, as shall be needefull for them, paying for their hier as the labourers and they shall agree.

25 We likewise of our goodnes, haue licensed the English Marchants in our Townes of Mosco, Nouogorod the great, and Plesko, that the Coiners of the said Townes shall melt Dollers, and coine money for them, without custome, allowing for coales, and other necessaries, with the workemanship.

26 Also of our goodnes, we haue granted to the sayd English Merchants, to take poste horse at needfull times, leauing with our officers a note how many they take, and not else, in no case hindering or diminishing our treasurie.

27 Also for our sister Queene Elizabeths sake, we of our goodnes haue granted to the merchants within written, this our letter, and to their successors, that no Englishman, nor any other stranger, come without the Queenes leaue to Colmogorode, the riuer of Vob, Vasiagy, Pechora, Cola,

Mezena, Pechingo, Zeleuetskyes Island, the riuer of Shame, nor to no other hauen of Dwina, nor to any part of the northside of Dwina, by hetherward of Wardhouse, to any hauen, with shippe, Busse, or any other vessell, nor to occupie in any kind of waies, but only the said English Companie, and their successors, to whom we of our goodnes haue granted this priuiledge.

28 Also that no English Merchant, without the Queenes leaue, shall come With any wares, to the Narue, or Vriogorod.

29 And whatsoeuer English Merchant, stranger, or other, of whatsoeuer countrey he be, shall come with any shippe; Busse, or any other vessel, to any of the said hauens, of the north side, to any part of Dwina, by North the Narue, or Vriogorod, without the Queenes leaue or knowledge, not being of the company aboue written, we to apprehende and take the same vessell from those strangers and Merchants, the one halfe to vs the Emperour, and great Duke, and the other halfe to the company of English Merchants.

30 Also of our goodnes we haue granted the said company of English merchants, that no English merchants or strangers shall passe through our dominions, to Boghar, Persia, Casbin, Charday, or other Countreys, saue onely the company of English merchants and our owne messengers.

31 Also whatsoeuer Englishman, comming out of England or any other Countrey, into our dominions, without the Queenes leaue, and knowledge, not being of the sayd company, written within those our letters, mind, and purpose, to abide in our realme, contrary to the Queenes will and pleasure, or any way abuse himselfe, the Agent shall freely send him home, to the Queene his Soueraigne: which if the Agent of himselfe be vnable to do, let him pray for ayd of the captaines and officers of our townes there being, and so send him to prison, and will the sayd captaines not to hinder the sayd Agent from sending home such euill persons into England.

32 And if any man within our countrey runne away to any other towne or place, the English merchants and factours, to haue free libertie to apprehend him, and take their goods from him againe.

33 And as for our priuilege giuen to Thomas Glouer, Ralfe Rutter, Christopher Bennet, Iohn Chappell, and their adherents, we haue commanded the same priuileges to be taken from them.

34 Also we of our goodnesse haue granted the sayd company of English merchants, their successours, seruants and deputies, that doe or shall remaine at Mosco, or elsewhere within our dominions freely to keepe their owne law: and in any wise none of ours to force them to our law or faith against their will.

Moreouer, besides and with the company of English merchants, we permit all strangers, to trade to our towne of Narue, Iuanogorod, and other our townes of Liefland, as they haue done beforetime. Giuen from the beginning of the world 7077, in the moneth of Iune 20, Indiction 12, the yere of our lordship and reign 35, and of our Empire of Rusland 23. Cazan 17, Astracan 15.

* * * * *

Other speciall grants by his Maiesties priuate letters at the sute of M. Randolfe Ambassadour.

Releasement out of prison of Fitzherbert, that was accused for writing of letters against the Emperour.

Liberty giuen to Thomas Greene that was accused and troubled vpon suspition of his dealing with the Ambassadour, and licence giuen to him to trafficke as he was accustomed.

Andrew Atherton and his sureties released at the Narue and his seruant at the Mosco, that were in trouble for sending the merchants letters into England.

A letter granted to Thomas Southam to the Councell, for iustice against them that stole the pearles.

His Maiesties fauor promised to the Artificers, and liuings to be appointed them as they can best deserue.

A letter to the merchants that went into Persia, to passe freely without impeachment in his dominions, as also letters of fauour to the great Shaugh of Persia.

A grant vnto the company that at what time soeuer they send to the discouery of Cataya, they shalbe licenced to repaire vnto this countrey, and haue such conducts and guides, mariners, vessels, men and victuals as they shall stand in need of.

It is also promised by Knez Alfanas, and Peter Gregoriwich in the Emperours name, that if Benet Butler or any English man complaine, deface, hinder in way of traffike or otherwise go about to discredit the worshipfull company, and their doings, that therein they shall not be heard, and the doers to be punished, as in such cases they shalbe iudged to haue deserued.

Certaine persons granted to be sent home into England that serued the company, and were practisers against them in that countrey.

* * * * *

A Commission giuen by vs Thomas Randolfe Ambassadour for the Queenes
Maiestie in Russia, and Thomas Bannister, &c. vnto Iames Bassendine, Iames Woodcocke and Richard Browne, the which Bassendine, Woodcocke, and
Browne we appoint ioyntly together, and aiders, the one of them to the other, in a voyage of discouery to be made (by the grace of God) by them, for searching of the sea, and border of the coast, from the riuer Pechora, to the Eastwards, as hereafter foloweth Anno 1588. The first of August.

In primis, when your barke with all furniture is ready, you shall at the beginning of the yere (assoone as you possibly may) make your repaire to the Easterne part of the riuer Pechora, where is an Island called Dolgoieue, and from thence you shall passe to the Eastwards alongst by the Sea coast of Hugorie, or the maine land of Pechora, and sailing alongst by the same coast, you shall passe within seuen leagues of the Island Vaigats, which is in the straight, almost halfe way from the coast of Heugorie, vnto the cast of Noua Zembla, which Island Vaigats and Noua Zembla you shall finde noted in your plat [Footnote: map], therefore you shall not need to discouer it: but proceed on alongst the coast of Hugory, towards the riuer Obba.

[Sidenote: Cara Reca. Naramsi Reca.] There is a Bay [Footnote: Gulf of Kara.] betweene the sayd Vaigats, and the riuer Obba, that doth bite to the Southwards, into the land of Hugory, in which Bay are two small riuers, the one called Cara Reca [Footnote: River Kara.], the other Naramsy [Footnote: Probably the River Juribei.], as in the paper of notes which are giuen to you herewith may appeare: in the which Bay you shall not need to spend any time for searching of it, but to direct your course to the riuer Ob (if otherwise you be not constrained to keepe alongst the shore) and when you come to the riuer Ob you shall not enter into it, but passe ouer vnto the Easterne part of the mouth of the sayd riuer.

And when you are at the Easterne part of Obba Reca, you shall from thence passe to the Eastwards, alongst by the border of the sayd coast, describing the same in such perfect order as you can best do it. You shall not leaue the sayd coast or border of the land, but pass alongst by it, at least in sight of the same, vntil you haue sailed by it so farre to the Eastwards and the time of the yeere so farre spent, that you doe thinke it time for you to returne with your barke to Winter, which trauell may well be 300 or 400 leagues to the Eastwards of the Ob, if the Sea doe reach so farre as our hope is it doth: but and if you finde not the said coast and sea to trend so farre to the Eastwards, yet you shall not leaue the coast at any time, but proceed alongst by it, as it doth lie, leauing no part of it vnsearched, or seene, vnlesse it be some bay, or riuer, that you doe certeinly know by the report of the people, that you shall finde in those borders, or els some certeine tokens whereby you of your selues may iudge it to be so. For our hope is that the said border of land and sea doth in short space after you passe the Ob, incline East, and so the Southwards. And therefore we would haue no part of the land of your starreboord side, as you proceed in your discouery, to be left vndiscouered.

But and if the said Border of land do not incline so to the Eastwards as we presuppose it, but that it doe proue to incline and trend to the Northwards, and so ioyne with Noua Zembla, making the sea from Vaigats to the Eastwards but a bay: yet we will that you do keepe alongst by the said coast, and so bring vs certaine report of that forme and maner of the same bay.

And if it doe so proue to be a bay, and that you haue passed round about the same, and so by the trending of the land come backe vnto that part of Noua Zembla that is against Vaigats whereas you may from that see the said Island Vaigats, if the time of the yeere will permit you, you shall from thence passe alongst by the said border and coast of Noua Zembla to the Westwards, and so to search whether that part of Noua Zembla doe ioyne with the land that Sir Hugh Willoughbie discouered in anno 53, [Footnote: There is, of course, no such land.] and is in 72 degrees, and from that part of Noua Zembla 120 leagues to the Westwards, as your plat doeth shew it vnto you: and if you doe finde that land to ioyne with Noua Zembla, when you come to it, you shall proceed further along the same coast, if the time of the yere will permit it, and, that you doe think there will be sufficient time for you to returne backe with your barke to Winter either at Pechora or in Russia, at your discretion: for we refer the same to your good iudgements, trusting that you will lose no time, that may further your knowledge in this voyage.

Note you, it was the 20 of August, 56 yer the Serchthrift began to returne backe from her discouerie, to Winter in Russia, and then she came from the Island Vaigats, being forcibly driuen from thence with an Easterly winde and yce, and so she came into the riuer Dwina, and arriued at Colmogro the 11 of September, 56. If the yce had not bene so much that yere as it was in the Streights, on both sides of the Island Vaigats, they in the said pinnesse would that yere haue discouered the parts that you are now sent to seek: which thing (if it had pleased God) might haue bene done then: but God hath reserued it for some other. Which discouerie, if it may be made by you, it shall not only proue profitable vnto you, but it will also purchase perpetuall fame and renowme both to you and our country. And thus not doubting of your willing desires, and forwardnesse towards the same, we pray God to blesse you with a lucky beginning, fortunate successe, and happily to end the same. Amen.

Necessarie notes to be obserued, and followed in your discouerie, as hereafter followeth.

When your barke with all furniture and necessaries shall be in readinesse for you to depart to the sea (if it be that you take your barke at S. Nicholas, or any part of Dwina Reca) you shall from thence, euen as timely in the spring as the yce will permit you, saile, and make all expedition that may be, vnto the mouth of the riuer Pechora (as your commission doth leade you) and as you passe by the coast all alongst (notwithstanding the plat that sheweth you the description of the said coast, from Dwina vnto Vaigats) yet you shall seeke by all the meanes that you can, to amend the same plat, vsing as many obseruations, as you possibly can do: and these notes following are to be obserued by you principally.

1 First, that you do obserue the latitude as often, and in as many places as you may possibly do it, noting diligently the place where you do so obserue the same.

2 Also that you doe diligently set with your compasse, how the land doth lie from point to point, all alongst as you goe, and to vse your iudgements how farre there may be betweene ech of them.

3 Item, that you do alwayes vse to draw the proportion and biting of the land, aswell the lying out of the points, and headlands, vnto the which you shall giue some apt names (at your discretion) as also the forme of the Bayes, and to make some marke in drawing the forme, and border of the same, where the high cliffes are, and where low land is, whether sandy hilles, or whatsoeuer: omit not to note any thing that may be sensible and apparant to you, which may serue to any purpose.

4 In passing along by any coast, that you keepe your lead going often times, and sound at the least once euery glasse, and oftener if you thinke good as occasion doth serue, and note diligently the depth with the maner of the ground, and at euery time, how farre the same sounding may be from the next shore to it: and how the next point or headland doth beare from you. And in the sea after you set off from your port, you shall orderly at the end of euery foure glasses sound, and if you finde ground, note the depth and what ground, but if you can finde no ground, you shall also note in what depth you could find no ground.

5 Also that you do diligently obserue the flowing, and ebbing in euery place, and how the tides do set, which way the flood doth come, and how much water it doth high in euery place, and what force the same tide hath to driue a ship in an houre, as neere as you can iudge it.

6 Also that you doe seeke to obserue with the instrument which I deliuer you herewith, according as I taught you at Rose Island, the true platformes,

and distances, in as many places as conueniently you may, for it serueth very aptly your purpose.

7 Also that you take with you paper and ynke, and keepe a continuall iournall or remembrance day by day, of all such things as shall fall out worth the knowledge, not forgetting or omitting to write it, and note it, that it may be shewed and read at your returne.

8 These orders if you shall diligently obserue, it will be easie for you to make a plat and perfect description of your discouery, and so shall your notes be sufficient to answere that which is looked for at your hands. But withall you may not forget to note as many things as you can learne and vnderstand by the report of any people whatsoeuer they be, so that it appertaine any way to our desires. And thus the Lord God prosper your voyage, Amen. [Footnote: Though dated 1588, this journey took place in 1578. Nothing is really known of the result of the expedition; but it has been supposed that the English vessel, which was wrecked at the mouth of the Ob about 1580, and whose crew was massacred by Samoyeds (*Purchas*, iii. p. 546; *Hamel*, p. 238), was the one bearing Bassendine and his companions.]

* * * * *

Certaine letters in verse, written by Master George Turberuile [Footnote: Born at Whitchurch about 1530; educated at New College, Oxford; supposed to have died about 1600. "Occasional felecity of diction, a display of classical allusion, and imagery taken from the customs and amusements of the age ate not wanting; but the warmth, the energy, and the enthusiasm of poetry are sought for in vain." (*Drake*, Shakespeare and his Times, p. 456).] out of Moscouia, which went as Secretarie thither with Master Tho. Randolph, her Maiesties Ambassadour to the Emperour 1568, to certeine friends of his in London, describing the maners of the Countrey and people.

To his especiall friend Master Edward Dancie. [Footnote: Probably the grandson of Sir Thomas Moore, and son of his second daughter, Elizabeth Dancy.]

My Dancie deare, when I recount within my brest,
My London friends, and wonted mates, and thee aboue the rest:
I feele a thousand fits of deepe and deadly woe,
To thinke that I from land to sea, from blisse to bale did go.
I left my natiue soile, full like a retchlesse man,
And vnacquainted of the coast, among the Russes ran:
A people passing rude, to vices vile inclinde,
Folke fit to be of Bacchus traine, so quaffing is the kinde.

Drinke is their whole desire, the pot is all their pride,
The sobrest head doth once a day stand needfull of a guide.
If he to banket bid his friends, he will not shrinke
On them at dinner to bestow a douzen kindes of drinke:
Such licour as they haue, and as the countrey giues,
But chiefly two, one called Kuas, whereby the Mousiket[1] liues.
Small ware and waterlike, but somewhat tart in taste,
The rest is Mead of honie made, wherewith their lips they baste.
And if he goe vnto his neighbour as a guest,
He cares for litle meate, if so his drinke be of the best.
No wonder though they vse such vile and beastly trade,
Sith with the hatchet and the hand, their chiefest gods be made.
Their Idoles haue their hearts, on God they neuer call,
Vnlesse it be (Nichola Bough)[2] that hangs against the wall.
The house that hath no god, or painted Saint within,
Is not to be resorted to, that roofe is full of sinne.
Besides their priuate gods, in open places stand
Their crosses vnto which they crooche, and blesse themselues with hand.
Deuoutly downe they ducke, with forehead to the ground,
Was neuer more deceit in ragges, and greasie garments found:
Almost the meanest man in all the countrey rides,
The woman eke, against our vse, her trotting horse bestrides.
In sundry colours they both men and women goe,
In buskins all, that money haue on buskins to bestoe.
Each woman hanging hath a ring within her eare,
Which all of ancient vse, and some of very pride doe weare.
Their gate is very braue, their countenance wise and sadde.
And yet they follow fleshy lustes, their trade of liuing badde.
It is no shame at all accompted to defile
Anothers bedde, they, make no care their follies to concile,
Is not the meanest man in all the land but hee,
To buy her painted colours doeth allow his wife a fee,
Wherewith she deckes her selfe, and dies her tawnie skinne,
She pranks and paints her smoakie face, both brow, lip, cheeke, and chinne.
Yea those that honest are, if any such there bee
Within the land, doe vse the like: a man may plainely see.
Vpon some womens cheekes the painting how it lies,
In plaister sort, for that too thicke her face the harlot dies.
But such as skilfull are, and cunning Dames indeede,
By dayly practise doe it well, yea sure they doe exceede.
They lay their colours so, as he that is full wise,
May easly be deceiu'd therein, if he doe trust his eyes.
I not a little muse, what madnesse makes them paint

Their faces, waying how they keepe the stooue by meere constraint.
For seldome when, vnlesse on Church or marriage day
A man shall see the Dames abroade, that are of best aray.
The Russie meanes to reape the profit of her pride,
And so he mewes her to be sure, she lye by no mans side.
Thus much, friend Dancie, I did meane to write to thee,
To let thee weete in Russia land, what men and women bee.
Hereafter I perhaps of other things will write
To thee and other of my friends, which I shall see with sight:
And other stuffe besides, which true report shall tell,
Meane while I end my louing lines, and bid thee now farewell.

[Footnote 1: Moudjick, a servant.]
[Footnote 2: St. Nicholas.]

To Spencer.

If I should now forget, or not remember thee,
Thou Spencer might'st a foule rebuke, and shame impute to mee,
For I to open shew did loue thee passing well,
And thou wert he at parture, whom I loathde to bid farewell.
And as I went thy friend, so I continue still,
No better proofe thou canst then this desire of true good will
I doe remember well when needes I should away,
And that the Poste would licence vs, no longer time to stay:
Thou wrongst me by the fist, and holding fast my hand,
Didst craue of me to send thee newes, and how I liked the land.
It is a sandie soile, no very fruitful vaine,
More waste and wooddie grounds there are, then closes fit for graine.
Yet graine there growing is, which they vntimely take,
And cut or eare the corne be ripe, they mowe it on a stacke:
And laying sheafe by sheafe, their haruest so they dry,
They make the greater haste, for feare the frost the corne destroy.
For in the winter time, so glarie is the ground,
As neither grasse, nor other graine, in pastures may be found.
In coms the cattell then, the sheepe, the colt, the cowe,

Fast by his bed the Mowsike then[1] a lodging doth allowe,
Whom he with fodder feeds, and holds as deere as life:
And thus they weare the winter with the Mowsike and his wife.
Seuen months the Winter dures, the glare it is so great,
As it is May before he turne his ground to sow his wheate.
The bodies eke that die vnburied lie they then,
Laid vp in coffins made of firre, as well the poorest men,
As those of greater state: the cause is lightly found,

For that in Winter time, they cannot come to breake the ground.
And wood so plenteous is, quite throughout all the land,
As rich, and poore, at time of death assurd of coffins stand.
Perhaps, thou musest much, how this may stand with reason,
That bodies dead can vncorrupt abide so long a season.
Take this for certaine trothe, as soone as heate is gone,
The force of cold the body binds as hard as any stone,
Without offence at all to any liuing thing:
And so they lye in perfect state, till next returne of Spring.
Their beasts be like to ours, as farre as I can see
For shape, and shewe, but somewhat lesse of bulke, and bone they be.
Of watrish taste, the flesh not firme, like English beefe,
And yet it seru's them very well, and is a good releefe:
Their sheep are very small, sharpe singled, handfull long;
Great store of fowle on sea and land, the moorish reedes among.
The greatnes of the store doeth make the prices lesse,
Besides in all the land they know not how good meate to dresse.
They vse neither broach nor spit, but when the stoue they heate,
They put their victuals in a pan, and so they bake their meate.
No pewter to be had, no dishes but of wood,
No use of trenchers, cups cut out of birche are very good.
They vse but wooden spoones, which hanging in a case
Eache Mowsike at his girdle ties, and thinkes it no disgrace.
With whitles two or three, the better man the moe,
The chiefest Russies in the land, with spoone and kniues doe goe.
Their houses are not huge of building, but they say,
They plant them in the loftiest ground, to shift the snow away,
Which in the Winter time, eache where full thicke doth lie:
Which makes them haue the more desire, to set their houses hie.
No stone work is in vse, their roofes of rafters bee,
One linked in another fast, their wals are all of tree.
Of masts both long, and large; with mosse put in betweene,
To keepe the force of weather out, I neuer earst haue seene
A grosse deuise so good, and on the roofe they lay
The burthen barke, to rid the raine, and sudden showres away.
In euery roome a stoue, to serue the Winter turne,
Of wood they haue sufficient store, as much as they can burne.
They haue no English glasse, of slices of a rocke.
Hight Sluda they their windows make, that English glasse doth mocke.
They cut it very thinne, and sow it with a thred
In pretie order like to panes, to serue their present need.
No other glasse, good faith doth giue a better light:
And sure the rocke is nothing rich, the cost is very slight.

The chiefest place is that, where hangs the god by it,
The owner of the house himselfe doth neuer sit,
Unlesse his better come, to whom he yealds the seat:
The stranger bending to the god, the ground with brow most beat
And in that very place which they most sacred deeme,
The stranger lies: a token that his guest he doth esteeme.
Where he is wont to haue a beares skinne for his bed,
And must, in stead of pillow, clap his saddle to his head.
In Russia other shift there is not to be had,
For where the bedding is not good, the boalsters are but bad
I mused very much, what made them so to lie,
Sith in their countrey Downe is rife, and feathers out of crie:
Vnlesse it be because the countrey is so hard,
They feare by nicenesse of a bed their bodies would be mard,
I wisht thee oft with vs, saue that I stood in feare
Thou wouldst haue loathed to haue layd thy limmes vpon a beare,
As I and Stafford did, that was my mate in bed:
And yet (we thanke the God of heauen) we both right well haue sped.
Loe thus I make an ende: none other newes to thee,
But that the countrey is too colde, the people beastly bee.
I write not all I know, I touch but here and there,
For if I should, my penne would pinch, and eke offend I feare.
Who so shall read this verse, coniecture of the rest,
And thinke by reason of our trade, that I do thinke the best.
But if no traffique were, then could I boldly pen
The hardnesse of the soile, and eke the maners of the men.
They say the Lions paw giues iudgement of the beast:
And so may you deeme of the great, by reading of the least.

[Footnote: *Suggested emendation*: Them.]

To Parker. [Footnote: Matthew Parker, Archbishop of Canterbury. See an excellent account of him and his writings in Allibone's Dictionary.]

My Parker, paper, pen, and inke were made to write,
And idle heads, that little do, haue leisure to indite:
Wherefore, respecting these, and thine assured loue,
If I would write no newes to thee, them might'st my pen reproue.
And sithence fortune thus hath shou'd my shippe on shore:
And made me seeke another Realme vnseene of me before:
The maners of the men I purpose to declare.
And other priuate points besides, which strange and geazon are.
The Russie men are round of bodies, fully fac'd,
The greatest part with bellies bigge that ouerhang the waste,
Flat headed for the most, with faces nothing faire,

But browne, by reason of the stone, and closenesse of the aire:
It is their common vse to shaue or els to sheare
Their heads, for none in all the land long lolling locks doth weare,
Vnlsse perhaps he haue his souereigne prince displeas'd,
For then he neuer cuts his haire, vntil he be appeas'd,
A certaine signe to know who in displeasure be,
For euery man that viewes his head, will say, Loe this is he.
And during all the time he lets his locks to grow,
Dares no man for his life to him a face of friendship show.
Their garments be not gay, nor handsome to the eye,
A cap aloft their heads they haue, that standeth very hie,
Which Colpack they do terme. They wears no ruffes at all;
The best haue collers set with pearle, which they Rubasca call.
Their shirts in Russie long, they worke them downe before,
And on the sleeues with coloured Silks, two inches good and more.
Aloft their shirts they weare a garment iacket wise
Hight Onoriadka, and about his burlie waste, he tyes
His portkies, which in stead of better breeches be:
Of linnen cloth that garment is, no codpiece is to see.
A paire of yarnen stocks to keepe the colde away,
Within his boots the Russie weares, the heeles they vnderlay
With clouting clamps of steele, sharpe pointed at the toes,
And ouer all a Shuba furd, and thus the Russe goes.
Well butned is the Shube, according to his state,
Some Silke, of Siluer other some: but those of poorest rate
Do weare no Shubs at all, but grosser gownes to sight,
That reacheth downe beneath the calfe, and that Armacha hight:
These are the Russies robes. The richest vse to ride
From place to place, his seruant runnes, and followes by his side.
The Cassacke beares his felt, to force away the raine:
Their bridles are not very braue, their saddles are but plaine.
No bits but snaffles all, of birch their saddles be,
Much fashioned like the Scottish seates, broad flakes to keepe the knee
From sweating of the horse, the pannels larger farre
And broader be then ours, they vse short stirrups for the warre:
For when the Russie is pursued by cruel foe,
He rides away, and suddenly betakes him to his boe,
And bends me but about in saddle as be sits,
And therewithall amids his race his following foe he hits.
Their bowes are very short, like Turkie bowes outright,
Of sinowes made with birchen barke, in cunning maner dight.
Small arrowes, cruell heads, that fell and forked bee,
Which being shot from out those bowes, a cruel way will flee.

They seldome vse to shoo their horse, vnlesse they ride
In post vpon the frozen flouds, then cause they shall not slide,
He sets a slender calke, and so he rides his way.
The horses of the countrey go good fourescore versts a day,
And all without the spurre, once pricke them and they skippe,
But goe not forward on their way, the Russie hath his whippe
To rappe him on the ribbes, for though all booted bee,
Yet shall you not a paire of spurres in all the countrey see.
The common game is chesse, almost the simplest will
Both giue a checke and eke a mate, by practise comes their skill.
Againe they dice as fast, the poorest rogues of all
Will sit them downe in open field, and there to gaming fall
Their dice are very small, in fashion like to those
Which we doe vse, he takes them vp, and ouer thumbe he throwes
Not shaking them a whit, they cast suspiciously,
And yet I deeme them voyd of art that dicing most apply.
At play when Siluer lacks, goes saddle, horse and all,
And eche thing els worth Siluer walkes, although the price be small.
Because thou louest to play friend Parker other while,
I wish thee there the weary day with dicing to beguile.
But thou weart better farre at home, I wist it well,
And wouldest be loath among such lowts so long a time to dwell.
Then iudge of vs thy friends, what kinde of life, we had,
That neere the frozen pole to waste our weary dayes were glad.
In such a sauage soile, weere lawes do beare no sway,
But all is at the king his will, to saue or else to slay.
And that sans cause, God wot, if so his minde be such.
But what meane I with Kings to deale? we ought no Saints to touch.
Conceiue the rest your selfe, and deeme what liues they lead,
Where lust is Lawe, and Subiects liue continually in dread.
And where the best estates haue none assurance good
Of lands, of liues, nor nothing falles vnto the next of blood.
But all of custome doeth vnto the prince redowne,
And all the whole reuenue comes vnto the King his crowne.
Good faith I see thee muse at what I tell thee now,
But true it is, no choice, but all at princes pleasure bow.
So Tarquine ruled Rome as thou remembrest well,
And what his fortune was at last, I know thy selfe canst tell.
Where will in Common weale doth beare the onely sway,
And lust is Lawe, the prince and Realme must needs in time decay.
The strangenesse of the place is such for sundry things I see,
As if I woulde I cannot write ech priuate point to thee.
The colde is rare, the people rude, the prince so full of pride,

The Realme so stored with Monks and nunnes, and priests on euery side:
The maners are so Turkie like, the men so full of guile,
The women wanton, Temples stuft with idols that defile
The Seats that sacred ought to be, the customes are so quaint,
As if I would describe the whole, I feare my pen would faint.
In summe, I say I neuer saw a prince that so did raigne,
Nor people so beset with Saints, yet all but vile and vaine.
Wilde Irish are as ciuill as the Russies in their kinde,
Hard choice which is the best of both, ech bloody, rude and blinde.
If thou bee wise, as wise thou art, and wilt be ruld by me,
Liue still at home, and couet not those barbarous coasts to see.
No good befalles a man that seeks, and findes no better place,
No ciuill customes to be learned, where God bestowes no grace.
And truely ill they do deserue to be belou'd of God,
That neither loue nor stand in awe of his assured rod:
Which though be long, yet plagues at last the vile and beastly sort.
Of sinnill wights, that all in vice do place their chiefest sport.

A dieu friend Parker, if thou list, to know the Russes well,
To Sigismundus booke repaire, who all the trueth can tell:
For he long earst in message went vnto that sauage King.
Sent by the Pole, and true report in ech respect did bring,
To him I recommend my selfe; to ease my penne of paine,
And now at last do wish thee well, and bid farewell againe.

* * * * *

The fourth voyage into Persia, made by M. Arthur Edwards Agent, Iohn Sparke, Laurence Chapman, Christopher Faucet, and Richard Pingle, in the yeere 1568. declared in this letter written from Casbin in Persia by the foresaide Laurence Chapman to a worshipfull merchant of the companie of Russia in London. Anno Domini 1569. Aprill 28.

[Sidenote: Their arriuall at Bilbil the 14. of August 1568.] Worshipfull sir, my duetie alwayes remembred, and your prosperous health, and good successe in all your affaires wished, to the glory of God, and your owne hearts desire, &c. May it please you to vnderstand that your Agent M. Arthur Edwards and we departed from Yeraslaue in Iuly 1568. and the 14. of August arriued at our port called Bilbil, with your ship the Grace of God, and the goods in her in good safetie, God bee thanked for it, finding there neither the people so ready to ayd vs for the bringing of her in, and vnlading of the goods, nor yet so obedient to the Shaughs priuilege, as the worshipfull company haue bene informed. Our goods brought vpon land, we were compelled to open and sel as they would set the price, or otherwise it would haue bene worse for vs. [Sidenote: Prince Erasbec.] Being so satisfied to their contentment, we were speedily aided with camels by the prince Erasbec Sultan his appointment, to carry our goods to Shamaki, to which place we attained the first of September, finding it so throughly furnished with maner of commodities by occasion of our late comming, and by such as came before vs, that no man would aske to buy any one piece of karsie of vs, and lying then the space of one whole moneth before your Agent Arthur Edwards would disperse vs abroade with the goods, such as came out of Russia afterwardes, had brought their goods to that and other places, and spoyled those sayles wee might haue made, being sent abroad in time conuenient, being no little hinderance to the worshipfull, as also great griefe vnto vs to see. To conclude, through our dayly calling vpon him, he bent himselfe for Casbin, taking with him the greatest summe of the goods, and two of the worshipfuls seruants, to witte, Iohn Sparke and my selfe, to helpe and procure the better sale for the same: [Sidenote: Christopher Faucet and Richard Pingle.] and leauing at Shamaki Christopher Faucet and Richard Pingle with three hundred and fiftie pieces of karsies in their handes, supposed to be solde there or in Arrash before hee should be able to make his return from Casbin, which, so farre foorth as I can vnderstand, lie for the greatest part vnsolde. And being vpon our way, at a certaine towne called Ardouil, we chanced to barter nine pieces of karsies with those merchants for fourescore and foure batemans of cynamom, selling the karsies at one hundred and fiftie shawghs the piece.

And being at that present not farre from Teueris, called the principal place in this countrey for vttering of cloth or karsies, by much intreatie I perswaded your Agent to send thither to prooue what might be done, and receiuing from him foure and fiftie pieces of karsies, as also his commission for the sale of the same, I proceeded on that voyage my selfe, and one Tolmach in company with me, finding in that place great store of broad cloth and karsies brought thither, some part by the Turkes who be resident there, some by the Armenians, who fetch them at Aleppo, and some by the townesmen, who trauell vnto Venice and there buy them, so that no man offered me one penie more then a hundred and fourtie shawghs for a karsie: and hauing special commission and charge from your Agent not to stay there aboue the space of seuen dayes after my arriuall there, but to repaire to Casbin with all speed, and furthermore, hauing regard to keepe vp the price of the worshipfuls commodities, according to their desire, I found meanes to barter them away for spices, such as were there to be had, neither in goodnesse nor yet in price to my content: [Sidenote: Warre against the Portingals at Ormuz.] neuerthelesse, considering the colde sales which were there, as well for your karsies, as also the hot newes, that Ormuz way was shut vp by occasion that the Indians do warre against them, which is true in deed: and againe the desire that the worshipfull hath to haue such commodities bought, I thought it necessary to buy them, the prices and weight whereof appeareth at large by my accompt sent to the worshipfull, and is, as I thinke, the whole summe of spices bought at this time.

[Sidenote: The gouernour of Grozin his Merchant.] It chanced me in that place to meet with the gouernours merchant of Grozin, who was not a litle desirous to bargen with me for a hundred pieces of karsies for his master called Leuontie, and offering me so good bands for the paiment of the money or silke to the merchants contentment vpon the deliuery of them, as in any place within all this countrey is to be had: and offering me besides his owne letter in the behalfe of his master, that no custome should be demanded for the same, and the obtaining also at his masters hand as large a priuilege for the worshipful to trauel into all parts of his dominion, as the Shaugh had giuen them, and hearing good report made of him by the Armenians also, and that he was a Christian, I was much more the willing to bargen with him, and sold him a hundred pieces for a hundred and threescore shawghs a piece, to be paid to the merchant in Grozin either in money or silke to his contentment, within three dayes after the deliuerie of the karsies there, hauing a band of him made by the Metropolitanes owne hand, for the performance of the same, which is as sure as any here is to be deuised: and vpon the same I sent my Tolmach from me backe to Shamaki, with such goods as I bought at Teueris, and to the end hee might cause the worshipfuls seruants there to see this bargen accomplished. [Sidenote: The generall inconsistencie in the merchants and dealers of those parts.] At whose arriuall there, as I do perceiue, the Captaine would not accomplish his bargen to take them, but saith, hee hath no need of them; such is the constancie of all men in the countrey, with whomsoeuer you shal bargen. If the ware be bought, and they doe mislike it afterwards, they will bring it againe, and compel you to deliuer the money for it againe, regarding the Shawghs letters, which manifesteth the contrary, as a straw in the winde: by meanes whereof, the worshipfull may know whether all be true that hath bene written of this countrey people or not.

I am informed by all the brokers in Teueris, that the way once open to Ormuz, from whence commeth no such store of spices as the worshipfull doeth looke for, that here will bee put a way in Teueris, some for money, and other some for barter, to the number of three hundred or foure hundred pieces of karsies, being in coulers and goodnesse to the examples here sent you, the rest of the karsies to make them vp a thousand, and broad clothes to the summe of a hundred, bee as many as will be put away yeerely in this countrey, so farre as yet I can perceiue.

[Sidenote: The trade between the Venetians and the Armenians not easily to be broken.] To breake the trade betwixt the Venetians and the whole company of the Armenians it is not possible, vnlesse the worshipful will finde some meanes to receiue of them yerely to the number of 100. catters or mules lading, and deliuer them for the same one third part money, the rest cloth and karsies fitted in coulers meete for this countrey: the examples, as abouesaid, are sent vnto you.

At Amadia sixe dayes iourney from Teueris, grow abundance of galles, which are brought vp yerely by the Venetians, and be solde there for two bistes the Teueris bateman, which as your Agent here saith, maketh sixe pound English weight, but I doubt it wil not so be proued. Neuerthelesse it is supposed much good will bee done by buying of them: which might at this present haue partly bene proued; it so be that some could do but halfe that which hath bene written.

Touching drugges, I finde many as well at Teueris, as also in Casbin, but the goodnesse nothing like to such as be brought into England out of other places: and the price is so high that smal gaine will be had in buying of them: albeit, if I had bene furnished with money, as I might haue bene, if some would, I would haue bought some, to the ende the goodnesse of them might haue bene seene in England. At my comming to Casbin I found no maner of sales of any commoditie made, but all lying there whole, and newes giuen out (as your Agent saith) that the Shaugh would buy all such commodities as he had, and giue him silke and spices for the same: but by report the Shaugh neuer tooke cloth into his treasurie all the dayes of his life, and will not now begin: his whole trade is in raw silke, which he selleth alwayes for money to the Armenians and Turkes, and such other as vse to buy it: thus hoping of that which is not like to be had, hee hath driuen off the time, not sending to any other places: by means whereof the worshipfuls goods lie vnsold to this day to their great hinderance, which I for my part am not a litle sory to see.

[Sidenote: Babylon 15 days iourney from Casbin.] Babylon is from hence fifteene dayes tourney, whereas by true report be great store of Dates, and sold for a bisse the batman, the commoditie fit for England, and the place so neere vnto vs might easily haue bene knowen, if hee, whose deeds and sayings differ much, had bene willing to the same. Casan also is but seuen dayes iourney from hence, and a place by report, where most store of spices be at all times to be had, ouer and aboue any place in this countrey: it could not be granted by him to be seen and proued at this time: if this be losse to the worshipfull, referre it to the want of one which can do that which he speaketh in words.

To trauell in this countrey is not onely miserable and vncomfortable for lacke of townes and villages to harbour in when night commeth, and to refresh men with wholesome victuals in time of need, but also such scarsitie of water, that sometime in three dayes iourney together, is not to be found any drop fit for man or beast to drinke, besides the great danger we stand in for robbing by these infidels, who doe account it remission of sinnes to wash their hands in the blood of one of vs. Better it is therefore in mine opinion to continue a beggar in England during life, then to remaine a rich Merchant seuen yeeres in this Countrey, as some shall well find at their comming hither.

[Sidenote: His voyage to Gilan.] By commandement of the Agent also I went to Gilan, as well to see what harbor was there for your ship, as also to vnderstand what commoditie is there best sold, and for what quantitie. I found the way from hence so dangerous and troublesome, that with my pen I am not able to note it vnto you: no man traueleth from hence thither, but such poore people as need constraineth to buy Rice for their reliefe to liue vpon, and they lay not aboue twentie batmans vpon a catter, and it lieth no lower then the skirts of the saddle, and he escapeth very hardly that commeth there with the same.

The towne of Laighon, which was the chiefest place in all that land, haue I seen, and Langro and Rosar also, which be now ouerrun by the Shaugh and his power, and be so spoiled, and the people so robbed, that not one of them is able to buy one karsie. The best commoditie there to bee bought, is raw silke, and is sold in the Summer time for 38. shaughs the Laighon batman, which is litle aboue 40. li. waight, and for ready money: also there is to bee had what store of Alom you will, and sold there for one bisse the Teueris batman.

[Sidenote: The malice of the Turkish merchants.] In these partes be many Turkie merchants resident, which giue an outward shew, as though they were glad of our comming hither, but secretly they be our mortall enemies, searching by all meanes to hinder our sales, because we should the sooner giue ouer our trade thither, which in processe of time I hope will growe to better perfection. They wish vs to go to Hallape with the rest of our commodities vnsold, where they say we shall haue good intertainment in spight of the great number of Venetians which be there resident, and the custome but two in the hundred, and our karsies to be sold presently, had we neuer so many, for twelue duckets, which maketh of this money 165. shaughs: but by such as know the place, market and custome, it is reported to vs credibly to the contrary, and that such karsies as ours be, are not sold for aboue 8. duckets there: the custome thirtie in the hundred and more, that no place in the world so well furnished with good cloth and karsies, and of so braue colour as that place is, supposing it to bee craftily purposed of them, to bring vs into trouble, which God defend vs from.

[Sidenote: The price of spices.] The price of spices be these, at this present enhansed by reason the way is shut to Ormus, which when God shall send open, I purpose (God willing) to see, and at my returne to aduertise the worshipfull what benefit is there to be had in all points, so neere as I can learne: Pepper 25. shaughs the Teueris batman: Cloues 50. shaughs, Long pepper 25. shaughs, Maces large 50. shaughs, Ginger 24. shaughs, ready money all, or els looke not vpon them. And the best sort of rawe silke is sold for 60. shaughs the Teueris batman. Thus for want of further matter to inlarge, I ende for this time, beseeching God to preserue you in continuall health.

By your obedient seruant,

Lawrence Chapman.

* * * * *

Notes concerning this fourth voyage into Persia, begun in the moneth of Iuly 1568. gathered by M. Richard Willes from the mouth of Master Arthur
Edwards which was Agent in the same.

When he came first to the Sophies presence, at his court in Casbin, bringing his interpreter with him, and standing farre off, the Sophie (sitting in a seat roiall with a great number of his noble men about him) bad him come neere, and that thrise, vntill he came so neere him that he might haue touched him with his hand. Then the first demand that he asked him was, from what countrey he came: he answered, that he came from England. Then asked hee of his noble men, who knew any such countrey? But when Edwards saw that none of them had any intelligence of that name, he named Inghilterra, as the Italians call England. [Sidenote: Londro, London.] Then one of the noble men said Londro, meaning thereby London, which name is better knowen in far countries out of Christendom, then is the name of England. When Edwards heard him name Londro, he said that that was the name of the chiefe citie of England, as was Teueris of the chiefe city of Persia. He asked him many things more, as of the realme of England, maruelling that it should be an Island of so great riches and power, as Edwards declared vnto him: of the riches and abundance of our merchandize he further vnderstood by our traffike in Moscouia and other countreis. He demanded also many thinges of the Queenes maiestie, and of the customes and lawes of the realme: saying oftentimes in his owne language, Bara colla, (that is to say) Well sayd. He asked also many things of King Philip, and of his wars against the Turke at Malta. Then he demanded of him what was the chiefe cause of his resort into his realme. And being certified that it was for the trade of merchandize he asked what kind of merchandize he could bring thither. Such (sayd hee) as the Venetian merchants do, which dwelling in our country in the city of Londro send to Venice, and from thence into Turkie by Halepo and Tripoli in Syria, from whence, as by the second and third hands, with great charges of many customs and other things thereunto pertaining, they are at the length brought into your countrey and cities of Persia. What merchandize are those? sayd the Sophie. Edwards answered, that they were great abundance of fine karsies, of broad clothes of all sorts and colours, as skariets, violets, and other of the finest cloth of all the world. [Sidenote: The Venetians traffike in England.] Also, that the Venetians brought out of England not onely such clothes ready made, but furthermore great plenty of fine wooll to mingle with their wools, of which they could not otherwise make fine cloth: affirming that there went out of England yeerly that waies, aboue two hundredth thousand karsies, and as many broad clothes, beside fine wooll and other merchandize, beside also the great abundance of like clothes, the which were caried into Spaine, Barbarie, and diuers other countries. The Sophie then asked him by what means such merchandize might be brought into Persia. Right wel sir (said he) by the way of Moscouia, with more safetie and in much shorter time then the Venetians can bring them: first from England to Venice, and from thence into Persia by the way of Turkie. And therefore if it shall please your maiestie to grant vs free passage into all your dominions, with such priuiledges as may appertaine to the safegard of our liues, goods and merchandize, we will furnish your countries with all such merchandize and other commodities, in shorter time, and better cheape then you may haue the same at the Turks hands. This talke and much more was between the Sophie and Edwards for the space of two houres: all which things liked him so well, that shortly after he granted to the sayd Arthur Edwards other priuiledges for the trade of merchandize into Persia, all written in Azure and gold letters, and deliuered vnto the lord keeper of the Sophie his great seale. The lord keeper was named Coche Califay, who sayd that when the Shaugh (that is the king or prince) did sit to seale any letters, that last priuiledge should be sealed and deliuered to Laurence Chapman. In this priuiledge is one principall article for seruants or merchants: That if the Agent do perceiue that vpon their naughtie doings, they would become Bursormen, that then the Agent wheresoeuer he shall find any such seruant or seruants, to take them and put them in prison, and no person to keepe them or maintaine them. This article was granted in respect of a custome among the Persians, being Mahumetans, whose maner is friendly to receiue and wel entertaine, both with gifts and liuing, all such Christians, as forsaking their religion, wil become of the religion of the Persians. Insomuch that before this priuiledge was granted, there was great occasion of naughty seruants to deceiue and rob their masters, that vnder the colour of professing that religion, they might liue among them in such safetie, that you might haue no lawe agaynst them, either to punish them or to recouer your goods at their hands, or elsewhere. For before the Sophie (whom they say to be a maruelous wise and gracious prince) seemed to fauour our nation, and to grant them such priuiledges, the people abused them very much, and so hated them, that they would not touch them, but reuiled them, calling them Cafars and Gawars, which is, infidels or misbeleeuers. But after they saw how greatly the prince fauoured them, they had them afterward in great reuerence, and would kisse their hands and vse them very friendly. For before they tooke it for no wrong to rob them, defraud them, beare false witnesse against them, and such merchandizes as they had bought or sold, make them take it againe, and change it as often as them listed. And if any stranger by chance had killed one of them, they would haue the life, of two for one slaine, and for the debts of any stranger would take the goods of any other of the same nation, with many other such like abuses, in maner vnknowen to the prince, before the complaints of our men made vnto him for reformation of such abuses: which were the cause that no merchant strangers of contrary religion durst come into his dominions with their commodities, which might be greatly to the profite of him and his subiects.

The Articles of the second priuiledge deliuered to Laurence Chapman, which are to be annexed vnto the former priuiledge.

10 Item, that the merchants haue free libertie, as in their first priuiledge, to goe: vnto Gilan, and all other places of his dominions, now or hereafter when occasion shall be giuen.

11 Item, if by misfortune any of their ships should breake, or fall vpon any part of his dominions on the sea coast, his subiects to helpe with all speed to saue the goods and to be deliuered to any of the sayd merchants that liueth: or otherwise to be kept in safetie vntil any of them come to demaund them.

12 Item, if any of the said merchants depart this life in any citie or towne, or on the high way, his gouernours there to see their goods safely kept, and to be deliuered to any other of them that shall demand them.

13 Item, the said merchants to take such camel-men as they themselues wil, being countrey people, and that no Kissell Bash do let or hinder them. And the said owners of the camels to bee bound to answere them such goods as they shal receiue at their hands, and the camel-men to stand to the losses of their camels or horses.

14 Item more, that the sayd Cariers do demaund no more of them, then their agreement was to pay them.

15 Item more, if they be at a price with any Cariers, and haue giuen earnest, the camel-men to see they keepe their promise.

16 Item, if any of the said merchants be in feare to trauel to giue them one or more to go with them and see them in safetie with their goods, to the place they will goe vnto.

17 Item, in all places, to say, in all cities, townes or villages on the high way, his subiects to giue them honest roume, and victuals for their money.

18 Item, the sayd merchants may in any place, where they shall thinke best, build or buy any house or houses to their owne vses. And no person to molest or trouble them, and to stand in any Carauan where they will, or shal thinke good.

The commodities which the merchants may haue by this trade into Persia are thought to bee great, and may in time perhaps be greater then the Portugals trade into the East Indies, forasmuch as by the way of Persia into England, the returne may be made euery yeere once: whereas the Portugals make the returne from Calecut but once in two yeers, by a long and dangerous voiage all by sea: for where as the citie and Island of Ormus, lying in the gulfe of Persia, is the most famous Mart towne of all East India, whither all the merchandises of India are brought, the same may in shorter time and more safelie be brought by land and riuers through Persia, euen vnto the Caspian sea, and from thence by the countreis of Russia or Moscouia by riuers, euen vnto the citie of Yeraslaue, and from thence by land 180. miles to Vologda, and from thence againe all by water euen vnto England.

The merchandises which he had out of Persia for the returne of wares are silke of all sortes of colours, both raw and wrought. Also all maner of spices and drugs, pearles, and precious stones, likewise carpets of diuers sortes, with diuers other rich merchandises. It was told me of them that came last from Persia, that here is more silke brought into some one city of Persia, then is of cloth brought into the city of London. Also that one village of Armenia named Gilgat doeth carie yeerely fiue hundred, and sometime a thousand mules laden with silke to Halepo in Soria of Turkie, being 4. dayes iourney from Tripoli, where the Venetians haue their continuall abiding, and send from thence silks which they returne for English karsies and other clothes into all partes of Christendome.

The maner how the Christians become Busormen, and forsake their religion.

I haue here noted before that if any Christian wil become a Busornan, that is, one that hath forsaken his faith, and be a Mahometan of their religion, they giue him many gifts and sometimes also a liuing. The maner is, that when the deuill is entred into his heart to forsake his faith, he resorteth to the Soltan or gouenour of the towne, to whom hee maketh protestation of his diuelish purpose. The gouernour appointeth him a horse, and one to ride before him on another horse, bearing a sword in his hand, and the Busorman bearing an arrow in his hand, and rideth in the citie, cursing his father and mother: and if euer after he returne to his owne religion, he is guiltie of death, as is signified by the sword borne before him. A yong man, a seruant of one of our merchants, because he would not abide the correction of his master for his faults, was minded to forsake his faith. But (as God would) he fell suddenly sicke and died, before he gaue himself to the deuill. If he had become a Busorman, he had greatly troubled the merchants: for if he then would haue said that halfe their goods had bene his, they would haue giuen credite vnto him. For the auoiding of which inconuenience, it was granted in the priuiledges, that no Busorman, &c. as there appeareth.

In Persia in diuers places oxen and kine beare the tents and houshold stuffe of the poore men of the countrey, which haue neither camels nor horses.

Of the tree which beareth Bombasin cotton, or Gossampine.

In Persia is great abundance of Bombasin cotton, and very fine: this groweth on a certaine litle tree or brier, not past the height of a mans waste or litle more: the tree hath a slender stalke like vnto a brier, or to a carnation gillifloure, with very many branches, bearing on euery branch a fruit or rather a cod, growing in round forme, containing in it the cotton: and when this bud or cod commeth to the bignes of a walnut, it openeth and sheweth foorth the cotton, which groweth still in bignes vntill it be like a fleece of wooll as big as a mans fist, and beginneth, to be loose, and then they gather it as it were the ripe fruite. The seeds of these trees are as big as peason, and are blacke, and somewhat flat, and not round; they sowe them in plowed ground, where they grow in the fields in great abundance in many countries in Persia, and diuers other regions.

The writing of the Persians.

Arthur Edwards shewed me a letter of the Sophie, written in their letters backward, subsigned with the hands both of the Sophy and his Secretarie. The Sophies subscription was onely one word (his name I suppose was Shaugh) written in golden letters vpon red paper. The whole letter was also written on the same piece of red paper, being long and narow, about the length of a foote, and not past three inches broad. The priuate signet of the Sophie was a round printed marke about the bignes of a roial, onely printed vpon the same paper without any waxe or other seale, the letters seem so mishapen and disordered, that a man would thinke it were somewhat scribled in maner at aduentures. Yet they say that almost euery letter with his pricke or circumflexe signifieth a whole word. Insomuch that in a piece of paper as big as a mans hand their writing doeth containe as much as doeth ours almost in a sheet of paper.

* * * * *

The fift voiage into Persia made by M. Thomas Banister, and master Geofrey Ducket, Agents for the Moscouie companie, began from England in the yeere 1568, and continuing to the yeere 1574 following. Written by P. I. from the mouth of M. Lionel Plumtree.

Vpon the 3. day of Iuly 1568, they embarked themselues at Yeraslaue, being accompanied with Lionel Plumtree, and some 12. English men more, in a Barke called the Thomas Bonauenture of the burden of 70. tunnes, taking also along with them of Russes to the number of 40. for their vse and imploiments. [Sidenote: The English Barke assaulted neere Astracan by the Nagaian Tartars.] It fell out in the way, before they came to Astracan by 40. miles, that the Nagaian Tartars, being a kind of thieuish and cruel people, made an assault vpon them with 18. boates of theirs, each of them being armed, some with swords, some with speares, and some others with bowes and arrowes, and the whole number of them they discouered to be about 300. men. They for their parts, although they could haue wished a quiet voyage and iourney without blowes and violence, yet not willing to be spoiled with such Barbarians as they were, began to defend themselues against their assault, by meanes whereof a very terrible and fierce fight folowed and continued hot and sharpe for two houres, wherein our men so wel plaied their parts with their caliuers, that they forced the Tartars to flee with the losse of 120 of them, as they were afterwards enformed by a Russe prisoner, which escaped from the Nagaians, and came to them to Astracan, at which towne they arriued the 20. of August.

[Sidenote: Astracan besieged by 70000 Turks and Tartars.] In this towne of Astracan they were somewhat hindered of their iourney, and staied the space of sixe weekes by reason of a great army of 70000. Turkes and Tartars which came thither vpon the instigation of the great Turke, hoping either to haue surprised it suddenly or by continuance of siege to win the same. But in the end by reason that the winter approched, as also, because they had receiued newes of a great expedition, which the Emperour of Russia was in prouiding for the defence of the said place, they were constrained to raise their siege, and to leaue the town as they found it.

Vpon their departure our men had opportunitie to proceed on their voyage, and vsing the occasion, they left Astracan, and came to Bilbil towards the end of October: from whence they went to Shauaran, where (as they lodged in their tentes) they were greatly molested with strange troopes of sholcaues or foxes, which were so busie with them that they tooke their meate and victuals out of their lodgings, and deuoured to the bare bones in one night a mighty wilde Bore that was sent vnto them for a present from the gouenour of the countrey.

Hauing staied here some three or foure daies in prouiding of cariages and other necessaries for their iourney, they departed thence and came to Shamaky, which is foure dayes iourney from the aforesayd Shauaran. In this towne of Shamaky their whole company spent out the Winter, and from thence in April folowing they tooke their iourney towards Ardouil a place of great account and much esteemed, by reason of the sepulchres of the Emperours of Persia, which for the most part lie there buried, and so is growen to bee a place of their superstitious deuotion. In this towne of Ardouil they soiourned the space of 5. or 6. moneths, finding some traffiques and sales, but to no purpose, the towne being more inhabited and frequented with gentlemen and noblemen then merchants.

The difference of religion bred great broiles in this towne whiles they remained there: for the brother sought the destruction of the brother, and the neerest kinsmen rose vp one against another, insomuch that one of their company Lionel Plumtree hath seene in one day sometimes 14 slaine in a garboile. And he being further desirous to see their maner of fight, or rather somewhat more curious to behold, then mistrustful of their blowes, was like to haue borne a share in their bloodie tragedie, being twise wounded with their shot and arrowes, although not to the death.

At this towne the Shah Thomas sent a messenger for our men to come to his presence at Casbin, to whom Thomas Banister failed not to goe, although master Ducket lay very sicke at Ardouil, and in such case that they almost despaired of his recouerie. Hee being come to the Shaugh was receiued and entertained of him with great fauour and speciall countenance, and had the most part of all his requests granted him, this onely excepted, that whereas he entreated a priuiledge or sufferance to transport and cary through his dominions certaine horses into India, the Shaugh seemed both to yeeld thereunto, and yet did not altogether denie it, but referred it to some further time. As for the point of traffique, he could not make that motion or request that was not so soone granted as it was preferred: and the Shaugh himselfe bought there of him many karsies, and made him as good paiment as any man could wish, and oftentimes would send his mony for the wares before the wares were deliuered, that he might be the surer of this honourable intended dealing.

One thing somewhat strange I thought good in this place to remember, that whereas hee purposed to send a great summe of money to Mecca in Arabia, for an offering to Mahomet their prophet, hee would not send any money or coyne of his owne, but sent to the English merchants to exchange his coyne for theirs, according to the value of it, yeelding this reason for the same, that the money of the merchants was gotten by good meanes, and with good consciences, and was therefore woorthie to be made for an oblation to their holy prophet, but his owne money was rather gotten by fraud, oppression and vnhonest meanes, and therefore was not fit to serue for so holie a vse.

After sixe moneths spent in Casbin the sayde Thomas Banister departed towards the great citie of Taruis, where being arriued, he found M. Ducket well recouered of his sicknesse, whom he had left ill at Ardouil.

At this Citie the foresayd Master Ducket made sales of the English commodities, remaining there to that purpose the space of two yeeres and a halfe. And besides other kindes of merchandises of that countrey, he bought great stores of gals which grow in great abundance at a place within one dayes iourney of the aforesayd Taruis.

After this Thomas Banister departed from Tauris, and went to Shamaky to giue order for the transporting of those commodities which were bought for England. And hauing dispatched them away, he went there hence to Arrash, a towne foure dayes iourney with camels from Shamaky for the buying of rawe silke. [Sidenote: The death of Thomas Banister and Laurence Chapman.] But there by reason of the vnwholesomnesse of the aire, and corruption of the waters in the hole time of the yeere, he with Lawrence Chapman and some other English men vnhappily died: which being knowen of M. Ducket, he immediately came from Taruis to Arrash, to take possession of the goods, for otherwise by the custome of the countrey, if there had bene no merchant or other friend of his to enter vpon that which he left, all had fallen into the Shaughs hands, which goods notwithstanding could not bee recouered from the officers, which had seized and sealed vp the same, vntill M. Ducket had bene in person with the Shaugh, and had procured his order for the deliuerie thereof.

[Sidenote: Humfrey Greensell burnt at Ormus.] Lionel Plumtree, in the meane time that M. Ducket was at Casbin in sute for goods, vpon the perswasion of certaine Bogharians, made prouision for a iourney to Cathaia, with cariages and commodities, and hauing all things ready, departed secretly with a Carauan: but being gone forwards on his way sixe dayes iourny, some fifty horsemen by the procurement of Humfrey Greensell (who afterwards being at Ormus in the East Indies, was there cruelly burnt in the Inquisition by the Portingals) were sent after him in poste from Sultan Erasbec, the Shaughs lieutenant, to fetch him backe againe, not suffering him to passe on so perillous and dangerous a iourney for feare of diuers inconueinces that might follow.

After this M. Ducket returned from Casbin to Shamaky againe, and immediately made preparation for a iourney to Cassan, being about foure dayes iourney from Shamaky, and caried with him foure mules laden with mony.

In the way of his trauel he passed through Persepolis, sometime the roiall seate of the Emperors of Persia, but now ruined and defaced, whereof remaine to be seene at this day two gates onely that are distant one from the other the space of 12 miles, and some few pinnacles in the mountains and conueiances for fresh water.

The foresaid Cassan is a towne that consisteth altogether of merchandise, and the best trade of all the land is there, being greatly frequented by the merchants of India.

Here our men bought great store of al maner of wrought silkes, and some spices, and good store of Turkie stones.

The towne is much to be commended for the ciuil and good gouernment that is there vsed. An idle person is not suffred to liue amongst them.

The child that is but fine yeeres old is set to some labour. No ill rule, disorder or riote by gaming or otherwise, is there permitted. Playing at Dice or Cards is by the law present death.

At this Cashan they remained about the space of tenne weekes, and then came down againe to Shamaky, and after some time spent in diuers places of the countrey for buying of rawe silke and other commodities, they came at last to Shauaran againe, where their ship was in harbour and then they shipt all their goods and embarked themselues also, setting sayle the eight day of May, in the yeere 1573. intending to fetch Astracan. By reason of the varietie of the windes and dangerous flats of the Caspian sea, they beat it vp and downe some 20. dayes. And the 28. day riding at anker vpon the flats, certaine Russe Cassaks, which are outlawes or banished men, hauing intelligence of their being there, and of the great wealth that they had with them, came to them with diuers boates vnder the colour of friendship, and entered their ship, but immediately they tooke their hatchets and slew diuers of the Russes that were of the ship vpon the hatches: Whereupon master Ducket, Lionell Plumtree, William Smith, the master, a man of singular valure, and Amos Riall being vnder the Spardecke did so well behaue themselues, that they skowred the hatches, and slew 14 of the Cassaks gunners, and hurt and wounded about 30 more; being of them al in number 150. at the least, armed with caliuers and other weapons fit for so villanous a purpose.

[Sidenote: The English ship taken by the Cassaks.] M. Ducket notwithstanding and the rest aforesaid receiued diuers wounds from the enemie, and were so hurt, and withall so oppressed with the multitude and force of them, that they were at last constrained to make an agreement with the Cassaks by rendring the ship into their hands, hauing receiued first their othes sworne by their crucifixes, not to do any further harme to their persons.

Thus the shippe being taken, and all the English grieuously hurt, the Cassaks immediately discharged the ship of them, putting them all into the ship boate with two or three Persian targets full of horse flesh and swines flesh, without further victuals or reliefe: they being in that case, made the best hast they could to get to Astracan: and being come to the towne, master Ducket made great sute to the captaine to haue men and boates set out for the rescuing and recouering of the ship if it were possible: who immediately sent out his sonne with fortie boates and fiue hundred men to pursue the Pirats, and by good hap came to the place where they rid at anker with the ship, but by reason of their foolishnes in striking vp their drums before they were come neere them, the Cassaks discouering the boates, cut their gables and put out to sea, whereupon the boates not being able to folow them, returned againe to Astracan. After which, 60 boates more were sent out to pursue them againe the second time: and that second army came to a place where they found many of these Cassaks and slew them, and found out the places where they had hid certaine parcels of their goods in the earth in the chests of the ship: all which they recouered againe for the English merchants, to the value of 5000 li. of 30 or 40 thousand pound, but all the rest the Cassaks in the ship had caried away.

In the same place they found further diuers of the Cassaks which the Englishmen had slaine, buried in the earth, and wrapt some in fortie or fiftie yards of Sattin and Taffataes, and some in Turkie carpets cut and spoiled by those villanous Pirats, of whom afterwards as many as could be taken, by the Persians who entirely loued the English merchants, were put to most cruell torments in all places according to their deserts.

But our men being thus spoyled of their goods, and wounded in their bodies, remained about two moneths at Astracan for their better recouerie: and hauing gotten some reasonable strength, they then prouided boates and went vp the riuer of Volga to Cazan, with such goods as they had recouered from the Cassaks. [Sidenote: Ice in the beginning of October.] From Cazan they went towards Yeraslaue, but in the way the ice intercepted them about the beginning of October, where suddenly in the night they were taken with a cruell and vehement frost, and therewithall the waters so congeled, that their boates were crushed and cut in sunder with the ice, whereby they sustained both a further danger of life and losse of goods: but as much as they could preserue with much adoe, they conueyed ouer land in sleds to Vologda, and from thence sent much of it to Saint Nicholas to be laden in the ships for England.

But Master Ducket, Lionel Plumtree and Amos Riall went with some parcels to the Mosko, and there sold certaine quantities of it to the Emperour, who pitying the mightie losse that they had sustained by his owne rebellious people and subiects, bought himselfe as much as hee liked, and payed present money for the same. [Sidenote: 1574.] So that Winter being spent out in Mosko, and such wares prouided by them as serued for England, they departed to Saint Nicholas, and there embarked in the moneth of August: and hauing endured a very terrible passage in nine weekes and three dayes, with some hardnesse of victuals, contrary and furious windes, and other sea accidents, they arriued at London in the moneth of October, one thousand fiue hundred seuentie and foure, and so make an ende of an vnfortunate voyage: which if it had pleased God to prosper, that all things had come home as safely as they were carefully prouided, and painfully laboured for, it had proued the richest voiage and most profitable returne of commoditie, that had euer bene vndertaken by English merchants, who, notwithstanding all misfortunes, lost nothing of their principall aduenture, but onely the interest and gaine that might haue risen by the vse of their stocke in the meane time.

* * * * *

Further obseruations concerning the state of Persia, taken in the foresayd fift voyage into those partes, and written by M. Geffery Ducket, one of the Agents emploied in the same.

Shamaky is the fairest towne in all Media, and the chiefest commoditie of that countrey is rawe silke, and the greatest plentie thereof is at a towne three dayes iourney from Shamaky called Arash: [Sidenote: Grosin or Georgia.] and within 3. dayes iourney of Arash is a countrey named Grosin, whose inhabitants are Christians, and are thought to be they which are otherwise called Georgians: there is also much silke to be sold. The chief towne of that countrey is called Zegham, from whence is caried yeerely into Persia, an incredible quantitie of Hasell nuts, all of one sort and goodnesse, and as good and thin shaled as are our Filberds. Of these are caried yeerely the quantitie of 4000. Camels laden.

Of the name of the Sophy of Persia, and why he is called the Shaugh, and of other customes.

The king of Persia (whom here, we call the great Sophy) is not there so called, but is called the Shaugh. It were there dangerous to cal him by the name of Sophy, because that Sophy in the Persian tongue, is a begger, and it were as much as to call him. The great begger. He lieth at a towne called Casbin, which is situate in a goodly fertile valley of 3. or 4. daies iourney in length. The towne is but euil builded, and for the most part all of bricke, not hardened with fire, but only dried at the sunne, as is the most part of the building of all Persia. The king hath not come out of the compasse of his owne house in 33. or 34. yeeres, whereof the cause is not knowen, but as they say, it is vpon a superstition of certaine prophesies to which they are greatly addicted: he is now about 80. yeeres of age, and very lusty. And to keepe him the more lusty, he hath 4. wiues alwayes, and about 300. concubines, and once in the yeere he hath all the faire maidens and wiues that may be found a great way about brought vnto him, whom he diligently peruseth, feeling them in all parts, taking such as he liketh, and putting away some of them which he hath kept before, and with them that he putteth away, he gratifieth some such as hath done him the best seruice. And if hee chance to take any mans wife, her husband is very glad thereof, and in recompense of her, oftentimes he giueth the husband one of his old store, whom he thankfully receiueth.

[Sidenote: How strangers are used.] If any stranger being a Christian shall come before him, he must put on a new paire of shooes made in that countrey, and from the place where be entreth, there is digged as it were a causey all the way, vntil he come to the place where he shal talke with the king who standeth alwayes aboue in a gallerie, when he talketh with any strangers: and when the stranger is departed, then is the causey cast downe, and the ground made euen againe.

Of the religion of the Persians.

Their religion is all one with the Turkes, sauing that they differ who was the right successor of Mahumet. The Turkes say that it was one Homer and his sonne Vsman. But the Persians say that it was one Mortus Ali, which they would prooue in this maner. They say there was a counsell called to decide the matter who should be the successor: and after they had called vpon Mahumet to reueale vnto them his will and pleasure therein, there came among them a little Lizard, who declared that it was Mahumets pleasure that Mortus Ali should be his successor. [Sidenote: A goodly and well grounded religion.] This Mortus Ali was a valiant man and slew Homer the Turkes prophet. He had a sword that hee fought withall, with the which hee conquered all his enemies, and killed as many as he stroke. When Mortus Ali died, there came a holy prophet, who gaue them warning that shortly there would come a white Camell, vpon the which he charged them to lay the body and sword of Mortus Ali, and to suffer the Camel to cary it whither he would. The which being performed, the said white camell caried the sword and body of Mortus Ali taken vp into heauen, for whose return they haue long looked in Persia. And for this cause the king alwayes keepeth a horse ready sadled for him, and also of late kept for him one of his owne daughters to be his wife, but she died in the yere of our Lord, 1573. And they say furthermore, that if he come not shortly, they shalbe of our beliefe: much like the Iewes, looking for their Messias to come and reigne among them like a worldly king for euer, and deliuer them from the captiuitie which they are now in among the Christians, Turkes, and Gentiles.

The Shaugh or king of Persia is nothing in strength and power comparable vnto the Turke: for although he hath a great Dominion, yet is it nothing to be compared with the Turks: neither hath he any great Ordinance or gunnes, or harquebusses. Notwithstanding his eldest sonne Ismael about 25. yeeres past, fought a great battell with the Turke, and slew of his armie about an hundred thousand men: who after his returne was by his father cast into prison, and there continueth vntil this day: for his father the Shaugh had him in suspicion that he would haue put him downe, and haue taken the regiment vnto himselfe.

[Sidenote: Their opinion of Christ.] Their opinion of Christ is, that he was an holy man and a great Prophet, but not like vnto Mahumet: saying, that Mahumet was the last prophet by whom all things were finished, and was therefore the greatest. To prooue that Christ was not Gods sonne, they say that God had neuer wife, and therefore could haue no sonne or children. They go on pilgrimage from the furthest part of Persia vnto Mecha in Arabia, and by the way they visite also the sepulchre of Christ at Ierusalem, which they now call Couch Kaly.

The most part of spices which commeth into Persia is brought from the Island of Ormus, situate in the gulfe of Persia called Sinus Persicus, betweene the maine land of Persia and Arabia, &c. The Portingals touch at Ormus both in their voyage to East India and homeward againe, and from thence bring all such spices as are occupied in Persia and the regions thereabout: for of pepper, they bring very small quantitie, and that at a very deare price.

The Turkes oftentimes bring pepper from Mecha in Arabia, which they sell as good cheape as that which is brought from Ormus. Silkes are brought from no place, but are wrought all in their owne countrey. Ormus is within two miles of the maine land of Persia, and the Portingals fetch their fresh water there, for the which they pay tribute to the Shaugh or king of Persia.

[Sidenote: Their money.] Within Persia they haue neither gold nor siluer mines, yet haue they coined money both of gold and siluer, and also other small moneys of copper. There is brought into Persia an incredible summe of Dutch dollars, which for the most part are there imploied in raw silke.

[Sidenote: Their bookes and learning.] They haue few bookes and lesse learning, and are for the most part very brutish in al kind of good sciences, sauing in some kind of silke works, and in such things as pertaine to the furniture of horses, in the which they are passing good.

[Sidenote: Such was the law of the Macedonians for treason.] Their lawes are as in their religion, wicked and detestable. And if any man offend the prince, he punisheth it extremely, not onely in the person that offendeth, but also in his children, and in as many as are of his kin. Theft and murther are often punished, yet none otherwise then pleaseth him that is ruler in the place where the offence is committed, and as the partie offending is able to make friends, or with money to redeeme his offence.

[Sidenote: Dissention for religion.] There is oftentimes great mutinie among the people in great Townes which of Mortus Ali his sonnes was greatest: insomuch that sometimes in the towne two or three thousand people are together by the eares for the same, as I haue seene in the towne of Shamaky and Ardouil, and also in the great City of Tiueris, where I haue seene a man comming from fighting, in a brauerie bringing in his hand foure or fiue mens heads, carying them by the haire of the head: for although they shaue their heads most commonly twise a weeke, yet leaue they a tuft of haire vpon their heads about 2. foote long. I haue enquired why they leaue the tuft of haire vpon their heads. They answered that thereby they may easiler be carried vp into heauen when they are dead.

[Sidenote: Their priests and preaching. Their Lent.] For their religion they haue certairie priests who are apparelled like vnto other men. They vse euery morning and afternoone to go vp to the tops of their churches, and tell there a great tale of Mahumet and Mortus Ali: and other preaching haue they none. Their Lent is after Christmas, not in abstinence from flesh onely, but from all meats and drinks, vntill the day be off the side, but then they eate somtimes the whole night. And although it be against their religion to drinke wine, yet at night they will take great excesses thereof and be drunken. Their Lent beginneth at the new Moone, and they do not enter into it vntill they haue seene the same: neither yet doeth their Lent end, vntill they haue seen the next new Moone, although the same (through close weather) should not be seen in long time.

[Sidenote: Their saints and holy men. Pilgrimage.] They haue among them certaine holy men whom they call Setes, counted holy for that they or any of their ancestors haue been on pilgrimage at Mecha in Arabia, for whosoeuer goeth thither on pilgrimage to visite the sepulchre of Mahumet, both he and all his posteritie are euer after called Setes, and counted for holy men, and haue no lesse opinion of themselues. And if a man contrary one of these, he will say that he is a Saint, and therefore ought to be beleeued, and that hee cannot lie, although he lie neuer so shamefully. Thus a man may be too holy, and no pride is greater then spirituall pride of a mind puffed vp with his own opinion of holinesse. These Setes do vse to shaue their heads all ouer, sauing on the sides a litle aboue the temples, the which they leaue vnshauen, and vse to braid the same as women do their haire, and to weare it as long as it will grow.

[Sidenote: Their praier and worshipping of God and Mahumet.] Euery morning they vse to worship God, Mahumet, and Mortus Ali, and in praying turne themselues toward the South, because Mecha lieth that way from them. When they be in trauell on the way, many of them will (as soone as the Sunne riseth) light from their horses, turning themselues to the South, and will lay their gownes before them, with their swords and beads, and so standing vpright worship to the South: and many times in their prayers kneele downe, and kisse their beads, or somwhat els that lieth before them.

[Sidenote: Washing and outward clenlinesse.] The men or women doe neuer goe to make water, but they vse to take with them a pot with a spout, and after they haue made water, they flash some water vpon their priuy parts, and thus doe the women as well as the men: and this is a matter of great religion among them, and in making of water the men do cowre downe as well as the women.

[Sidenote: Their swearing.] When they earnestly affirme a matter, they will sweare by God, Mahumet, or Mortus Ali, and sometimes by all at ones: as thus in their owne language, saying, Olla, Mahumet, Ali. But if he will sweare by the Shaughs head, in saying Shaugham basshe, you may then beleeue him if you will.

[Sidenote: The king's magnificence.] The Shaugh keepeth a great magnificence in his court: and although sometimes in a moneth or six weekes none of his nobilitie or counsaile can see him, yet goe they daily to the court, and tary there a certaine time vntil they haue knowen his pleasure whether hee will commaund them any thing or not. [Sidenote: Pursuiuants.] Hee is watched euery night with a thousand of his men, which are called his Curshes, who are they that hee vseth to send into the Countreis about his greatest affaires. When he sendeth any of them (if it be to the greatest of any of his nobilitie) he will obey them, although the messenger should beat any of them to death.

[Sidenote: The kings company with his wiues and concubines.] The Shaugh occupieth himselfe alwayes two dayes in the weeke in his Bathstoue, and when he is disposed to goe thither, he taketh with him fiue or sixe of his concubines, more or lesse, and one day they consume in washing, rubbing, and bathing him, and the other day in paring his nailes, and other matters. The greatest part of his life hee spendeth amongst his wiues and concubines. Hee hath now reigned about fiftie and foure yeeres, and is therefore counted a very holy man, as they euer esteeme their kings, if they haue reigned fiftie yeeres or more: for they measure the fauour of God by a mans prosperitie, or his displeasure by a mans misfortune or aduersitie. The great Turk hath this Shaugh in great reuerence, because he hath reigned king so long time.

[Sidenote: The succession of the kingdom.] I haue sayd before that hee hath foure wiues, and as many: concubines as him listeth: and if he chance to haue any children by any of his concubines, and be minded that any of those children shall inherite after him, then when one of his wiues dieth, the concubine whom hee so fauoureth, hee maketh one of his wiues, and the childe whom he so loueth best, he ordaineth to bee king after him.

[Sidenote: Circumcision.] What I heard of the maner of their mariages, for offending of honest consciences and chaste ears, I may not commit to writing: their fasting I haue declared before. They vse circumcision vnto children of seuen yeeres of age, as do the Turkes.

[Sidenote: Their houses, and maner of eating.] Their houses (as I haue sayd) are for the most part made of bricke, not burned but only dried in the Sunne: In their houses they haue but litle furniture of houshold stuffe, except it be their carpets and some copper worke: for all their kettles and dishes wherein they eate, are of copper. They eate on the ground, sitting on carpets crosse legged as do Tailors. There is no man so simple but he sitteth on a carpet better or worse, and the whole house or roume wherein he sitteth is wholy couered with carpets. Their houses are all with flat roofes couered with earth: and in the Sommer time they lie vpon them all night.

[Sidenote: Bondmen and bondwomen.] They haue many bond seruants both men and women. Bondmen and bondwomen, is one of the best kind of merchandise that any man may bring. When they buy any maydes or yong women, they yse to fede them in all partes, as with vs men doe horses: when one hath bought a yong woman, if he like her, be will keepe her for his owne vse as long as him listeth, and then selleth her to an other, who doth the like with her. So that one woman is sometimes sold in the space of foure or fiue yeeres, twelue, or twentie times. If a man keepe a bondwoman for his owne vse, and if hee find her to be false to him, and giue her body to any other, he may kill her if he will.

[Sidenote: Women bought and sold, and let to hire.] When a merchant or traueller commeth to any towne where he entendeth to tary any time, he hireth a woman, or sometimes 2. or 3. during his abode there. And when he commeth to an other towne, he doeth the like in the same also: for there they vse to put out their women to hire, as wee do here hackney horses.

[Sidenote: Abundance of oile issuing out of the ground.] There is a very great riuer which runneth through the plaine of Iauat, which falleth into the Caspian sea, by a towne called Bachu, neere vnto which towne is a strange thing to behold. For there issueth out of the ground a marueilous quantitie of oile, which oile they fetch from the uttermost bounds of all Persia: it serueth all the countrey to burn in their houses.

This oyle is blacke, and is called Nefte: [Footnote: These springs are still in existence.] they vse to cary it throughout all the Countrey vpon kine and asses, of which you shall oftentimes meet with foure or fiue hundred in a company. [Sidenote: Oleum Petroleum.] There is also by the said towne of Bachu another kind of oyle which is white and very precious: and is supposed to be the same that here is called Petroleum. There is also not far from Shamaky, a thing like vnto tarre, and issueth out of the ground, [Footnote: These springs are still in existence.] whereof we haue made the proofe, that in our ships it serueth well in the stead of tarre.

[Sidenote: Two sorts of kine.] In Persia are kine of two sorts: the one like vnto ours in these partes: the other are marueilous euill fauoured, with great bones and very leane, and but litle haire vpon them: their milke is walowish sweete: they are like vnto them which are spoken of in the Scripture, which in the dreame of Pharao signified the seuen deare yeeres: for a leaner or more euill fauoured beast can no man see.

[Sidenote: Foxes in great plenty.] In the countrey of Shiruan (sometime called Media) if you chance to lie in the fields neere vnto any village, as the twilight beginneth, you shall haue about you two or three hundred foxes, which make a marueilous wawling or howling: and if you looke not well to your victuals, it shal scape them hardly but they will haue part with you.

The Caspian sea doeth neither ebbe nor flowe, except sometimes by rages of wind it swelleth vp very high: the water is very salt. Howbeit, the quantitie of water that falleth out of the great riuer of Volga maketh the water fresh at the least twentie leagues into the sea. The Caspian sea is marueilous full of fish, but no kind of monstrous fish, as farre as I could vnderstand, yet hath it sundry sortes of fishes which are not in these parts of the world.

The mutton there is good, and the sheepe great, hauing very great rumpes with much fat vpon them.

Rice and mutton Is their chiefe victual.

* * * * *

The copy of a letter sent to the Emperour of Moscouie, by Christopher Hodsdon and William Burrough, Anno 1570.

MOst mightie Empefour, &c. Whereas Sir William Garrard and his felowship the company of English merchants, this last Winter sent hither to the Narue three ships laden with merchandise, which was left here, and with it Christopher Hodsdon one of the sayd felowship, and their chiefe doer in this place, who when hee came first hither, and vntil such time as hee had dispatched those ships from hence, was in hope of goods to lade twelue or thirteene sails of good ships, against this shipping, wherefore he wrote vnto the sayd Sir William Garrard and his companie to send hither this spring the sayd number of thirteene ships. And because that in their comming hither wee found the Freebooters on the sea, and supposing this yeere that they, would be very strong, he therefore gaue the said sir William and his companie aduise to furnish the sayd number of ships so strongly, as they should bee able to withstand the force of the Freebooters: whereupon they haue according to his aduice sent this yeere thirteene good ships together well furnished with men and munition, and all other necessaries for the warres, of which 13. ships William Burrough one of the said felowship is captaine generall, vnto whom there was giuen in charge, that if hee met with any the Danske Freebooters, or whatsoeuer robbers and theeues that are enimies to to your highnesse, he should doe his best to apprehend and take them. [Sidenote: Fiue ships of Freebooters taken.] It so hapned that the tenth day of this moneth the sayd William with his fleete, met with sixe ships of the Freebooters neere vnto an Island called Tuttee, which is about 50. versts from Narue vnto which Freebooters he with his fleete gaue chase, and took of them the Admirall, wherein were left but three men, the rest were fled to shore in their boats amongst the woods vpon Tuttee, on which he set fire and burned her. He also tooke foure more of those ships which are now here, and one ship escaped him: out of, which foure ships some of the men fled in their boates and so escaped, others were slaine in fight, and some of them when they saw they could not escape, cast themselues willingly into the Sea and were drowned. So that in these fiue ships were left but 83. men.

The said Wil. Borough when he came hither to Narue, finding here Chistopber Hodsdon aforenamed, both the said Christopher and William together, in the name of sir William Garrard and the rest of their whole companie and felowship, did present vnto your highnesse of those Freebooters taken by our ships 82. men, which we deliuered here vnto Knez Voiuoda, the 13. of this moneth. One man of those Freebooters we haue kept by vs, whose name is Haunce Snarke a captaine. And the cause why we haue done it is this: When wee should haue deliuered him with the rest of his felowes vnto the Voiuodaes officers, there were of our Englishmen more then 50. which fell on their knees vnto vs, requesting that he might be reserued in the ship, and caried back into England: and the cause why they so earnestly intreated for him, is, that some of those our Englishmen had bene taken with Freebooters, and by his meanes had their liues saued with great fauour besides, which they found at his hands. Wherefore if it please your highnesse to permit it, we will cary him home with vs into England, wherin we request your maiesties fauour: notwithstanding what you command of him shalbe obserued.

Wee haue also sent our seruant to your highnesse with such bestellings and writings as wee found in those shippes: whereby your Maiestie may see by whom, and in what order they were set out, and what they pretended, which writings wee haue commended vnto Knez Yoriue your Maiesties Voiuoda at Plesco, by our seruant. And haue requested his futherance for the safe deliuerie of them to your maiesties hands: which writings when you haue perused we desire that they may be returned vnto vs by this our seruant, as speedily as may bee: for these ships which we now haue here will be soone dispatched from hence, for that we haue not goods to lade aboue the halfe of them. And the cause is, we haue this winter (by your maiesties order) bene kept from traffiquing to the companies great losse. But hoping your maiestie will hereafter haue consideration thereof, and that we may haue free libertie to trafique in all partes of your maiesties Countries, according to the priuledge giuen vnto vs, we pray for your maiesties health, with prosperous successe to the pleasure of God. From Narue the 15 of Iuly, Anno 1570.

Your Maiesties most humble and obedient,

Christopher Hodsdon. William Borough.

* * * * *

A letter of Richard Vscombe to M. Henrie Lane, touching the burning of the
 Citie of Mosco by the Crimme Tartar, written in Rose Island the 5. day of August, 1571.

Master Lane I haue me commended vnto you. The 27. of Iuly I arriued here with the Magdalene, and the same day and houre did the Swalow and Harry arriue here also. At our comming I found Master Proctor here, by whom we vnderstand very heauie newes. [Sidenote: the citie of Mosco burnt by the Crimme. Englishmen smothered at the burning of Mosco.] The Mosco is burnt euerie sticke by the Crimme the 24, day of May last, and an innumerable number of people: and in the English house was smothered Thomas Southam, Tofild, Wauerly, Greenes wife and children, two children of Rafe, and more to the number of 25. persons were stifeled in our Beere seller: and yet in the same seller was Rafe, his wife, Iohn Browne, and Iohn Clarke preserued, which was wonderfull. [Sidenote: M. Glouer and M. Rowley preserued.] And there went into that seller master Glouer and master Rowley also: but because the heate was so great, they came foorth againe with much perill, so that a boy at their heeles was taken with the fire, yet they escaped blindfold into another seller, and there, as Gods will was, they were preserued. The Emperour fled out of the field, and many of his people were caried away by the Crimme Tartar: to wit, all the yong people, the old they would not meddle with, but let them alone, and so with exceeding much spoile and infinite prisoners, they returned home againe. What with the Crimme on the one side, and his crueltie on the other, he hath but few people left. Commend me to mistresse Lane your wife, and to M. Locke, and to all friends.

Yours to command, Richard Vscombe.

* * * * *

A note of the proceeding of M. Anthonie Ienkinson, Ambassadour from the Queens most excellent Maiestie, to the Emperour of Russia, from the time of his ariuall there, being the 26. of Iuly 1571, vntill his departure from thence the 23. of Iuly 1572.

The said 26. day I arriued with the two good ships called the Swalow and the Harry in safetie, at the Baie of S. Nicholas in Russia aforesayd, and landed at Rose Island, from whence immediately I sent away my interpreter Daniel Siluester in post towards the Court, being then at the Mosco, whereby his maiestie might as well bee aduertised of my arriual in his Dominions, as also to knowe his highnesse pleasure for my further accesse. And remaining at the sayd Island two or three dayes, to haue conference with your Agent about your affaires, I did well perceiue by the words of the sayd Agent and others your seruants, that I was entred into great perill and danger of my life: for they reported to mee that they heard said at the Mosco, that the princes displeasure was such against me, that if euer I came into his country againe. I should loose my head, with other words of discouragement. Whereat I was not a little dismaid, not knowing whether it were best for me to proceed forwards, or to returne home againe with the ships for the safeguard of my life. But calling to mind mine innocencie and good meaning, and knowing my selfe not to haue offended his Maiestie any maner of wayes either in word or deed, or by making former promises not performed, heretofore by mine enemies falsely surmised: and being desirous to come to the triall thereof, whereby to iustifie my true dealings, and to reprooue my sayd enemies, as well here as there, who haue not ceased of late by untrue reports to impute the cause of the sayd Emperours displeasure towards you to proceed of my dealings, and promises made to him at my last being with him (although by his letters to the Queenes Maiestie, and by his owne words to me the contrary doeth appeare) I determined with my selfe rather to put my life into his hands, and by the prouidence of God to prosecute the charge committed unto me, then to returne home in vaine, discouraged with the words of such, who had rather that I had taried at home, then to be sent ouer with such credite, whereby I might sift put their euil doings, the onely cause of your losse.

Wherefore, leauing the said ships the nine and twentieth day of the month, I departed from the seaside, and the first of August arriued at Colmogro, where I remaided attending the returne of my said messenger with order from his Maiestie.

But all the Countrey being sore visited by the hand of God with the plague, passage in euery place was shut up, that none might passe in paine of death: My Messenger being eight hundreth miles upon his way, was stayed, and kept at a towne called Shasco, and might not bee suffered to goe any further, neither yet to returne backe againe, or sende vnto me: by meanes whereof in the space of foure moneths, I could neither heare nor know what was become of him, in which time my said messenger found meanes to aduertise the Gouernour of the Citie of Vologda, as well of his stay, as of the cause of his comming thither, who sent him word that it was not possible to passe any neerer the Prince without further order from his Maiestie, who was gone to the warres against the Swethens, and that he would aduertise his highnesse so soone as he might conueniently. And so my said messenger was forced to remaine there still without answere. During which time of his stay through the great death (as aforesaid) I found meanes to send another messenger, with a guide by an vnknowen way through wildernesse a thousand miles about, thinking that way he should passe without let: but it prooued contrary, for likewise hee being passed a great part of his iourney, fell into the handes of a watch, and escaped very hardly, that hee and his guide with their horses had not bene burnt, according to the lawe prouided for such as would seeke to passe by indirect wayes, and many haue felt the smart thereof which had not wherewith to buy out the paine: neither could that messenger returne backe vnto me.

And thus was I kept without answere or order from his Maiestie, and remained at the saide Colmogro, vntil the 18. of Ianuary following, neither hauing a gentleman to safegard me, nor lodging appointed me, nor allowance of victuals according to the Countrey fashion for Ambassadours, which argued his grieuous displeasure towards our nation. And the people of the Countrey perceiuing the same, vsed towards mee and my company some discourtesies: but about the 28. day aforesaid, the plague ceased, and the passages being opened, there came order from his Maiestie that I should haue poste horses, and bee suffered to depart from Colmogro to goe to a Citie called Peraslaue neere to the Court, his Maiestie being newly returned from the said warres. And I arriued at the said Peraslaue the 3. of February, where I remained vnder the charge of a gentleman, hauing then a house appointed me and allowance of victuals, but so straightly kept, that none of our nation or other might come or sende vnto me, nor I to them.

And the 14. of March folowing, I was sent for to the Court, and being within three miles of the same, a poste was sent to the Gentleman which had charge of me, to returne backe againe with me to the said Peraslaue, and to remaine there vntil his Maiesties further pleasure, wherewith I was much dismayed, and marueiled what that sudden change ment, and the rather, because it was a troublesome time, and his Maiestie much disquieted through the ill success of his affaires, (as I did vnderstand.) And the twentieth of the same, I was sent for again to the Court, and the 23. I came before his Maiestie, who caused mee to kisse his hand and gaue gratious audience vnto my Oration, gratefully receiuing and accepting the Queenes Maiesties princely letters, and her present, in the presence of all this nobilitie. After I had finished my Oration, too long here to rehearse, and deliuered her highnesse letters, and present (as aforesaid) the Emperour sitting in royall estate stood up and said, How doth Queene Elizabeth my sister? is she in health? to whom I answered, God doth bless her Maiestie with health, and peace, and doeth wish the like vnto thee Lord, her louing brother. Then his Maiestie sitting downe againe, commanded all his nobilitie and others to depart, and auoyde the chamber, sauing the chiefe Secretarie, and one of the Counsell, and willing me to approach neere vnto him with my Interpretor, said vnto me these words.

Anthony, the last time thou wast with vs heere, wee did commit vnto thee our trustie and secret Message, to be declared vnto the Queenes Maiesties herselfe thy Mistresse at thy comming home, and did expect thy comming vnto vs againe at the time we appointed, with a full answere of the same from her highnesse. And in the meane time there came vnto us at seuerall times three messengers, the one called Manly, the other George Middleton, and Edward Goodman, by the way of the Narue about the Merchants affaires: to whom wee sent our messengers to know whether thou Anthony, were returned home in safetie, and when thou shouldest returne vnto vs againe: but those messengers could tell vs nothing, and did miscall, and abuse with euil words, both our messenger and thee, wherewith wee were much offended. And vnderstanding that the said Goodman had letters about him we caused him to be searched, with whom were found many letters, wherein was written much against our Princely estate, and that in our Empire were many vnlawfull things done, whereat we were much grieued, and would suffer none of those rude messengers to haue accesse vnto vs: and shortly after wee were infourmed that one Thomas Randolfe was come into our Dominions by the way of Dwina, Ambassadour from the Queene, and we sent a Gentleman to meete and conduct him to our Citie of Mosco, at which time wee looked that thou shouldest haue returned vnto vs againe. And the said Thomas being arriued at our said Citie, wee sent vnto him diuers times, that hee should come and conferre with our Counsell: whereby we might vnderstand the cause of his comming, looking for answere of those our princely affaires committed vnto thee. But hee refused to come to our said Counsell: wherefore, and for that our saide Citie was visited with plague, the saide Thomas was the longer kept from our presence. Which being ceased, foorthwith wee gaue him accesse and audience, but all his talke with vs was about Merchants affaires, and nothing touching ours. Wee knowe that Merchants matters are to bee heard, for that they are the stay of our Princely treasures: But first Princes affaires are to be established, and then Merchants. After this the said Thomas Randolfe was with vs at our Citie of Vologda, and wee dealt with him about our Princely affaires, whereby amitie betwixt the Queenes Maiestie and vs might bee established for euer, and matters were agreed and concluded betwixt your Ambassadour and vs, and thereupon wee sent our Ambassadour into England with him to ende the same: but our Ambassadour returned vnto vs againe, without finishing our said affaires, contrary to our expectation, and the Agreement betwixt vs, and your said Ambassadour.

This when his Maiestie had made a long discourse, I humbly beseeched his highnesse to heare me graciously, and to giue me leaue to speake without offence, and to beleeue those wordes to be true which I should speake. Which he graunted, and these were my words.

Most noble and famous Prince, the message which thy highnesse did sende by me vnto the Queene her most excellent Maiestie touching thy Princely and secret affaires, immediately, and so soone as I came home, I did declare both secretly and truely vnto the Queenes Maiestie her selfe, word for word, as thou Lord diddest commaund mee. Which her highnesse did willingly heare and accept, and being mindefull thereof, and willing to answere the same, the next shipping after, her Maiestie did sende vnto thee, Lord, her highnesse Ambassadour Thomas Randolfe, whose approoued wisedome and fidetitie was vnto her Maiestie well knowen, and therefore thought meete to bee sent to so worthy a Prince, who had Commission not onely to treate with thy Maiestie of Merchants affaires, but also of those thy Princely and secret affaires committed vnto me. And the cause (most gracious Prince) that I was not sent againe, was, for that I was imployed in seruice vpon the Seas against the Queenes Maiesties enemies and was not returned home at such time as Master Thomas Randolfe departed with the Shippes, to come into thy Maiesties Countrey, otherwise I had bene sent. And whereas thy Maiestie saith, that Thomas Randolfe would not treate with thy Counsell of the matters of his Legation, hee did (Lord) therein according to his Commission: which was: First to deale with thy Maiestie thy selfe, which order is commonly vsed among all Princes, when they send their Ambassadours about matters of great waight. And whereas the saide Thomas is charged that hee agreed and concluded vpon matters at the same time, and promised the same should be perfourmed by the Queene her

Maiestie: Whereupon (Lord) than diddest send thy Ambassadour with him into England, for answere thereof: It may please thy Maiestie to vnderstand, that as the saide Thomas Randolfe doeth confesse, that in deede hee had talke with thy Highnesse, and Counsell diuers times about princely affaires: euen so hee denieth that euer hee did agree, conclude, or make any promise in any condition or order, as is alleaged, otherwise then it should please the Queene her Maiestie to like of at his returne home, which hee did iustifie to thy Highnes Ambassador his face in England. Wherefore, most mighty Prince, it doth well appeare, that either thy Ambassador did vntruly enforme thy Maiestie or els thy princely minde, and the true meaning of the Queenes highnes her Ambassador, for want of a good Interpreter, was not well vnderstood: and how thankefully the Queene her Maiestie did receiue thy highnes commendations, and letters sent by thy Maiesties Ambassador, and how gratiously shee gaue him audience sundry times, vsing him with such honour in all points for thy sake, Lord, her louing brother, as the like was neuer shewed to any Ambassador in our Realme, and how honourably with full answere in all things, her Maiestie dismissed him, when hee had finished all thy princely affaires (as it seemed) to his owne contentation, it may well appeare by a true certificate lately sent with her highnes letter vnto thee Lord, by her messenger Robert Beast, and her Maiestie did suppose that thy Ambassador would haue made report accordingly, and that by him thy highnes would haue bene satisfied in all things: otherwise she would haue sent her Maiesties Ambassador with him vnto thee Lord againe. [Sidenote: Andrea Sauin Ambassadour from the Emperour.] But now her highnes perceiuing that thy Maiestie is not fully satisfied in thy Princely affaires, neither by Thomas Randolfe, her highnes Ambassador, nor by thine owne Ambassador Andrea Sauin, nor yet by her Maiesties letter sent by the said Andrea: and also vnderstanding thy great griefe and displeasure towards Sir William Garrard, and his company, merchants tracking in thy Maiesties dominions, hath thought good to send mee at this present vnto thee Lord Emperor, and great duke; as wel with her highnes ful mind, touching thy princely affaires, as also to know the iust cause of thy Maiesties said displeasure towards the said company of merchants; and hath commanded me to answere to all things in their behalfe, and according to their true meanings. For her highnes doth suppose thy Maiesties indignation to proceede rather vpon the euill, and vntrue reports of thy late Ambassador in England, and of such wicked persons of our nation resident here in thy highnes dominions, rebels to her Maiestie, and their Countrey, then of any iust deserts of the said merchants, who neuer willingly deserued thy highnesse displeasure, but rather fauour in all their doings and meanings. And since the first time of their traffiking in thy Maiesties dominions, which is now nineteene yeres, the said merchants haue bene, and are alwayes ready and willing truely to serue thy highnesse of all things meete for thy Treasurie, in time of peace and of warre in despite of all thy enemies: although the Princes of the East Seas were agreed to stoppe the sound, and the way to the Narue, and haue brought, and do bring from time to time such commoditie to thee, Lord, as her Maiestie doeth not suffer to be transported foorth of her Realme to no other prince of the world. And what great losses the said sir William Garrard, with his company hath sustained of late yeeres in this trade, as well by shipwracke, as by false seruants it is manifestly knowen: and what seruice the said companies Ships did vnto thy Maiestie against thy enemies, two yeeres past in going to the Narue, when they fought with the King of Poles shippes Freebooters, and burnt the same and slew the people, and as many as were taken aliue deliuered vnto thy Capaine at the Narue, I trust thy highnesse doth not forget. Wherefore most mighty prince, the premises considered, the Queene her most excellent Maiestie thy louing sister, doeth request thy highnes to restore the said sir William Garrard with his company into thy princely fauour againe, with their priuiledges for free traffique with thy accustomed goodnes and iustice, to be ministred vnto them throughout all thy Maiesties dominions, as aforetime: and that the same may be signified by thy Princely letters, directed to thy officers in all places, and thy highnesse commaundement or restraint to the contrary notwithstanding. And further that it will please thy Maiestie, not to giue credite to false reports, and vntrue suggestions of such as are enemies, and such as neither would haue mutuall amitie to continue betwixt your Maiesties, nor yet entercourse betwixt your countries. And such rebels of our nation, as Ralfe Rutter, and others which lye lurking here in thy highnes dominions, seeking to sowe dissentions betwixt your Maiesties by false surmises, spending away their masters goods riotously, and will not come home to giue vp their accompts, aduancing them selues to be merchants, and able to serue the highnes of all things fit for thy treasure, whereas indeed they by of no credite, nor able of themselues to do thy Maiestie any seruice at all: the Queenes highnes request is, that it would please thy Maiestie to commaund that such persons may be deliuered vnto me to be caried home, least by their remayning here, and hauing practises and friendship with such as be not thy highnesse friendes, their euil doing might be a cause hereafter to withdraw thy goodnes from sir William Garrard and his company, who haue true meaning in all their doings, and are ready to serue thy highnesse at all times, vsing many other words to the aduancement of your credits, and the disgracing of your enemies, and so I ended for that time.

Then sayd his Maiestie, We haue heard you, and will consider of all things further when wee haue read the Queene our sisters letters: to whom I answered, that I supposed his Maiestie should by those letters vnderstand her highnesse full minde to his contentation, and what wanted in writing I had credite to accomplish in word. Wherewith his maiestie seemed to be wel pleased, and commaunded me to sit downe. And after pawsing a while, his maiestie said these words vnto me, It is now a time which we spend in fasting, and praying, being the weeke before Easter, and for that we will shortly depart from hence, towards our borders of Nouogrod, wee can not giue you answere, nor your dispatch here, but you shall goe from hence, and tary vs vpon the way, where wee will shortly come, and then you shall knowe our pleasure, and haue your dispatch. And so I was dismissed to my lodging, and the same day I had a dinner ready drest sent me from his Maiestie, with great store of drinkes, of diuers sorts, and the next day following, being the foure and twentieth of March aforesayde, the chiefe Secretary to his Maiesty, sent vnto mee a Gentleman, to signifie vnto mee, that the Emperours Maiesties pleasure was, I should immediately depart towards a Citie, called Otwer, three hundred miles from the aforesaid Sloboda, and there to tary his highnes comming vnto a place called Staryts, threescore miles from the sayd Otwer.

Then I sent my Interpretor to the chiefe Secretary, requesting him to further, and shew his fauour vnto our saide merchants in their sutes, which they should haue occasion to moue in my absence: who sent me word againe, that they should be wel assured of his friendship, and furtherance in all their sutes. And forthwith post horses were sent me, with a Gentleman to conduct me. And so departing from the said Sloboda, I arriued at the said Otwer, the 28. of March aforesaid, where I remained til the eight of May folowing. Then I was sent for to come vnto his Maiestie, to the sayd Staryts, where I arriued the tenth of the same, and the twelfth of the same I was appointed to come to the chiefe Secretary, who at our meeting said vnto me these words.

Our Lord Emperor, and great Duke, hath not onely perused the Queene her highnes letters sent by you, and thereby doeth perceiue her minde, as well touching their princely affaires, as also her earnest request in the merchants behalfe, but also hath well pondered your words. And therefore his Maiesties pleasure is, that you let me vnderstand what sutes you haue to moue in the merchants behalfe, or otherwise, for that tomorrowe you shall haue accesse againe vnto his highnes, and shall haue full answere in all things, with your dispatch away.

Then after long conference had with him of diuers matters I gaue him in writing certaine briefe articles of requests, which I had drawen out ready, as foloweth:

1 First the Queenes Maiestie her request is, that it would please the Emperors highnesse to let me know the iust cause of his great displeasure fallen vpon Sir William Garrard, and his company, who neuer deserued the same to their knowledge.

2 Also that it would please his highnes not to giue credite vnto false and vntrue reports, by such as seeke to sowe dissension, and breake friendship betwixt the Queenes highnesse, and his Maiestie.

3 Also that it would please his Maiestie to receiue the said sir William Garrard, with his company into his fauour againe, and to restore them to their former priuiledges and liberties, for free traffike in, and through, and out of al his Maiesties dominions, in as ample maner as aforetime, according to his princely letters of priuiledge, and accustomed goodnes.

4 Also it would please his highnes to graunt, that the said company of merchants may haue iustice of all his subiects, as well for money owing vnto them, as other their griefes and iniuries, throughout al his dominions suffred since the time of his displeasure, during which time, the merchants were forced by seuere iustice to answer to al mens demands, but theirs could not be heard.

5 Also that his Maiestie would vnderstand, that much debts are owing to the said merchants by diuers of his Nobilitie, whereof part are in durance, and some executed, and the said merchants know not howe to be paide, and answered the same, except his highnes pitie their case, and commaund some order to be taken therein.

6 Also, it would please his highnes to commaund that the saide merchants may be payde all such summe or summes of money as are owing, and due vnto them by his Maiestie, for wares, as well English as Shamaki, taken into his highnes treasury by his officers in sundry places, the long forbearing whereof hath bene, and is great hinderance to the said company of merchants.

7 Also it would please his Maiestie to vnderstand, that at this present time there are in Persia of English Merchants, Thomas Banister, and Geffrey Ducket, with their company, and goods, ready to come into his Maiesties countrey of Astracan, and would haue come the last yeere, but that the ship, with our merchants and mariners appointed to goe for them, were stayed at Astracan by his highnes Captaine there, to the great hinderance of the said merchants. Wherefore it may now please his Maiestie to direct his princely letters vnto his Captaines, and rulers, both at Astracan and Cazan, not onely to suffer our people, as well merchants as mariners, quietly and freely to passe and repasse with their shippes, barkes, or other vessels downe the riuer Volga, and ouer the Mare Caspium, to fetch the sayd English merchants, with their company and goods, out of the sayd Persia, into his Maiesties dominions, but also that it would please his highnes streightly to command, that when the sayd Thomas Banister, and Geffrey Ducket, with their charge, shal arriue at the sayd Astracan, his Maiesties Captaine there, and in all other places vpon the riuer Volga, shall so ayde and assist the sayd

merchants, as they may be safely conducted out of the danger of the Crimmes, and other their enemies.

8 Also it may please his highnes to vnderstand, that lately our merchants comming from Shamaki haue bene ill vsed by his Maiesties Customers, both at Astracan and Cazan, at both which places they were forced to pay custome for their wares, although they solde no part thereof, but brought the same into his highnesse treasury at Sloboda: and the sayd Customers did not only exact, and take much more custome than was due by his Maiesties lawes, but also for want of present money, tooke wares much exceeding their exacted custome, and doe keepe the same as a pawne. It may therefore please his highnes to direct his princely letters to the said Customers, to signifie vnto them his great goodnes againe restored vnto the said English merchants, as also to command them to send the said merchants their said goods so detained, vp to the Mosco, they paying such custome for the same as shall be by his Maiestie appointed.

9 Also that it would please his highnesse to grant, that sir William Garrard with his companie may establish their trade for merchandise at Colmogro in Dwina, and that such wares as shal be brought out of our Countrey fit for his treasurie might be looked vpon, and receiued by his officers there: and that his Maiesties people traffiking with our merchants may bring downe their commodities to the saide Colmogro, by meanes whereof the saide English merchants auoyding great troubles and charges, in transporting their goods so farre, and into so many places of his dominions, may sell the same better cheape, to the benefite of his Maiesties subiects.

10 Also if it seemed good to his highnes, that the whole trade likewise from Persia, Boghar, and all other those Countreys beyond the Mare Caspium, might be established at Astracan, the ancient marte towne in times past, which would be both for the great honour and profite of his Maiesty, and subiects, as I am well able to prooue, if it will please his highnesse to appoint any of his counsell to talke with me therein.

11 Also forasmuch as it pleased his Maiestie, immediatly after the burning of the mosco, to command that the said English merchants should giue in a note into his Treasury, for their losses sustained by the said fire, which was done by William Rowly, then chiefe Agent for sir William Garrard and his company, and the particulars in the same note consumed with the said fire did amount to the summe of 10000. rubbles and aboue: It may please his highnes of his accustomed goodnes and great clemencie to consider of the same, and to giue the said company so much as shal seeme good vnto his Maiestie, towards their said losses.

12 Also it will please his highnesse to vnderstand that the Queenes most excellent Maiestie, at the earnest sute and request of Andrea Sauin his

Maiesties Ambassadour, did not onely pardon and forgiue Thomas Glouer his great and grieuous offences towards her highnesse committed, onely for his Maiesties sake, but also commanded sir William Garrard with his company, to deale fauourably with the said Glouer in his accompts, to whom he was indebted greatly, and being their seruant, detained their goods in his hands a long time: whereupon the said sir William Garrard with his company counted with the said Glouer, and ended all things euen to his saide contentation, and was found to bee debter to the said company 4000. rubbles and aboue, and bound himselfe both by his solemne othe, and his hand-writing, to pay the same immediately after his returne into Russia with the said Andrea Sauin, vnto Nicholas Proctor chiefe Agent there, for the said company of merchants. But although it is now two yeeres past, since the said agreement, and that the said Nicholas hath diuers and sundry times requested the said money of the said Thomas, yet will he not pay the same debt, but maketh delay from time to time, alleadging that his Maiestie oweth him a great summe of money, without the payment whereof he cannot be able to pay the said merchants his due debt long forborne, to their great hinderance. In consideration of the premisses. It may please his highnesse to giue order that the said Glouer may be payd, and that he may discharge his debt to the said company of merchants, and the rather for that hee found such mercie and fauour in England, onely for his Maiesties sake.

13 Also forasmuch as Ralfe Rutter a rebell to the Queenes Maiestie, and an enemie to his Countrey, and to sir William Garrard and his company, hath of long time remained here, liuing of the spoyles and goods of the said merchants, which he wrongfully detained in his handes, riotously spending the same, during the time that he was their seruant, and would not come home when he was sent for, and also for that the Queenes Maiestie doth vnderstand, that the saide Ralfe, with other his adherents, doe seeke by all false meanes to sowe dissension, and breake amitie betwixt their Maiesties, and to ouerthrowe the trade of the said merchants: Her highnes request is, that the said Ralfe with his complices may be deliuered vnto me, to be caried home, and none other of her Maiesties subiects, not being of the socitie of the said sir William Garrard and his company, to be suffered to traffike within his highnes dominions, but to be deliuered to their Agent to bee sent home: for that the said merchants with great charges and losses, both by shipwracke, and riotous seruants, did first finde out this trade, and haue continued the same these 19. yeeres, to their great hinderance.

14 Also whereas diuers masters and artificers of our Nation are here in his Maiesties seruice, and do finde themselues grieued that they cannot haue licence to depart home into their natiue Countrey at their will and pleasure: the Queenes Maiesties request is according to her highnes writing in that

behalfe, that not onely it will please his Maiestie to permit and suffer such artificers here resident in the seruice of his highnes to haue free libertie to depart and go home with me, if they request the same, but also all other the like which shall come hereafter to serue his Maiesty, to haue free libertie to depart likewise, without any let or stay.

15 Also it may please his Maiesty to vnderstand that during the time of my long being at Colmogro, attending his highnesse pleasure for my farther accesse, I with my company haue not onely bene ill vsed and intreated there, and likewise the merchants there, by one Besson Myssereuy his Maiesties chiefe officer, who hath dishonoured me, and smitten my people, and oweth the saide merchants much money, and will not pay them: but also the saide Besson hath spoken wordes of dishonour against the Queenes Maiestie. Wherefore it may please his highnesse to send downe with me to Colmogro, a Gentleman, as well chiefly to search foorth his euil behauiour towards her Maiestie, as towards me her highnesse Ambassador, and to punish him accordingly: and also that it would please his Maiestie to sende downe his letter of iustice by vertue whereof the said Besson may be forced to pay all such money as he oweth to the sayd merchants, without delay.

16 Also that it would please his highnesse to understand, that sir William Garrard with his company vnderstanding of the great dearth in his Maiesties dominions, by licence of the Queens Maiestie (not otherwise permitted) hath sent certaine ships laden with corne into his highnesse Countrey of Dwyna, rather for the reliefe of his Maiesties subiects then for any gaine: yet the good will of the said merchants lightly regarded, they were forbidden to sel the said corne, to their great discouragement hereafter to send any more. Wherefore it may please his highnesse, to tender the good will of the said merchants, as well in sending the saide corne, as in all other things, ready to serue his Maiestie, and to direct his letters to his officers of Dwina, to suffer the saide merchants with their company, to sell the said corne by measure great or small at their pleasure, without paying custome.

These articles being deliuered to the chiefe Secretary, as aforesayde, and our talke ended for that time. I departed to my lodging, accompanied with certaine Gentlemen. The next day being the 13. of May aforesaid. I had warning earely in the morning, to prepare my selfe to be at the Court, betwixt the houres of 10. and 11. of the clocke, where I should haue accesse unto the presence of the Prince, as well to receiue answere of all things, as to bee dismissed to goe home. At which houres I was sent for to the Court, and brought into the Chamber of presence, where his Maiestie did sit apparelled most sumptuously, with a riche Crowne vpon his head, garnisned with many precious stones, his eldest sonne sitting by him and many of his Nobilitie about him: and after my duetie done, his highnesse commanded me to approach very neere vnto him, and sayde vnto me these words.

Anthony: the Queen our louing sister her letters wee haue caused to be translated, and doe well vnderstand the same, and of, all things as well therein contained, as by worde of mouth by you to vs declared wee haue well considered, and doe perceiue that our secret message vnto you committed, was done truely according to our minde (although wee were aduertised to the contrary) and nowe wee are by you fully satisfied. [Sidenote: The causes of the Emperors displeasure.] And when wee did sende our Ambassadour into England, about those our great and waightie affaires to conclude the same with the Queene our sister, our Ambassadour coulde ende nothing for want of such assurance as was requisite in princely affaires, according to the maner of all Countreys, but was dismissed vnto vs againe, with letters of small effect, touching the same, and no Ambassadour sent with him from the Queene: which caused vs to thinke that our princely affaires were set aside, and little regarded, wherewith we were at that time much grieued: for the which cause, and for the euil behauiour of your merchants, resident in our dominions (who haue diuers wayes transgressed and broken our laws, liuing wilfully in all their doings) we did lay our heauie displeasure vpon them, and did take away from them their priuiledge, commaunding that the same throughout all our dominions should be voyd, and of none effect: and thereupon did write to the Queene our sister touching our griefes. And nowe her highnesse hath sent vnto vs againe, you her Ambassadour, with her louing letters and full minde, which we doe thankefully receiue, and are thereby fully satisfied. And for that our princely, and secret affaires were not finished to our contentation at our time appointed according to our expectation, we doe now leaue of all these matters, and set them aside for the time, because our minde is nowe otherwise changed, but hereafter when occasion shall mooue vs to the like, wee will then talke of those matters againe. And for that it hath pleased the Queene, our louing sister to send vnto vs at this present, and doeth desire to continue in friendship with vs for euer (which we doe gratefully accept, and willingly agree to the same) wee of our goodnesse for her highnesse sake, will not onely from hencefoorth put away, and forget all our displeasure towards the same Sir William Garrard and his company (as though they had neuer offended vs) but also will restore them to their priuiledges, and liberties, in, and throughout all our dominions, and will signifie the same by our letter, in all Townes and Cities, where the said merchants do traffique, as we will showe them fauor as aforetime, if they do not deserue the contrary. And if the Queene our sister had not sent thee Anthony vnto vs at this present, God knoweth what we should haue done to the said merchants, or whether would haue called back our indignation.

Then I humbly beseeched his Maiestie, to let me know the particular offences committed by the said merchants, and the offendors names, to the intent I might make report thereof vnto the Queenes Maiestie, my mistres, accordingly, that the said offendors might receiue iust punishment for their deserts: but he said, I should not know them, because he had cleerely remitted al offences: and further, that it was not princely to forgiue, and after to accuse the parties, whereby her Maiesties displeasure might fall vpon them at home. Notwithstanding I did after vnderstand some part thereof, by other means.

Then his Maiestie proceeding in talke said: As touching the articles of request, concerning the merchants affaires which you did yesterday deliuer vnto our Secretary, we haue not onely read the same our selfe, but also haue appointed our said Secretary to declare vnto you our minde, and answere to the same. And for that we are now vpon our iourney towards our borders, and will depart from hence shortly, we will dismisse you to the Queene our louing sister, your mistres, with our letters & full mind by word of mouth, touching all your requests, & will send a gentleman one of our houshold with you to safe conduct you to your ships: and of our goodnes will giue you victuals, boates, men, and post horses, so many as you shall neede. And therewith his Maiestie standing vp, and putting off his cappe, said vnto me these words, Doe our hearty commendations vnto our louing sister, Queene Elizabeth, vnto whom we wish long life, with happie successe: and therewith his highnes extended his hand to me to kisse, and commanded his sunne, sitting by him, to send the like commendations, which he did, whose hand likewise I kissed. And then his Maiestie caused me to sit downe, and commaunded wine and drinkes of diuers sorts to be brought, whereof he gaue me to drinke with his owne hand, and so after I departed.

Then the next day, being the 14. of May aforesaid, I was sent for to come to the chief Secretary, & one other of the counsel with him, who at our meeting said vnto me these words; We a appointed by the Emperor his maiesty, to giue you answere from his Highness, touching your requests deliuered in writing, which his Maiestie himselfe hath perused & answered as followeth.

1 To the first request it is answered, that all his Maiesties griefes and displeasure (now put away from the merchants) did grow, because the Queenes Maiestie did not accomplish and ende with his Ambassador, his secrete and waighty affaires, according to his expectation, and the promise made by Thomas Randolph, at his being here: and also of the ill behauiour of your merchants resident here in our Countrey, as his Maiestie did himselfe yesterday declare vnto you.

2 To the second, his Maiesty willeth you to vnderstand that he hath not, nor will not hereafter be moued to breake friendship with the Queenes Maiesty, without good and iust cause.

3 To the third, you are answered by the Emperors Maiestie himselfe, that his great goodnes and fauour againe vnto the merchants shall be restored, and the same to be knowen by his gratious letters of priuilege now againe granted.

4 To the fourth, his Maiesty hath commanded, that your merchants here resident shall exhibite, and put in writing vnto me his Maiesties Secretarie, all their griefes and complaints, as well for debts, as other iniuries offred them since the time of his Highnes displeasure, and they shall haue iustice truly ministred throughout all his Maiesties Dominions without delay.

5 To the fifth, his maiesty doth not know of any debts due vnto the merchants, by any of his Noblemen, as is alleaged: and whether it be true or no, he knoweth not: the trueth whereof must be tried out, and thereupon answere to be giuen: and hereafter his maiestie would not haue the merchants to trust his people with too much.

6 To the sixth, it is answered, that his maiesty hath commanded search to be made what money is owing to the marchants, for wares receiued into his treasury, as in the article: (the most of the bookes of accompt being burnt in the Musco) and such as is due, and found meete to be paid, shall be paid forthwith to the marchants, their factors or seruants, which shall come for the same. And for paiment of the rest, his maiesties further pleasure shall be signified hereafter.

7 To the 7 his Maiesties answers is, that letters shall be written forthwith to his captaines of Astracan, and Cazan, and other his officers, vpon the riuer Volga, to whom it appertaineth, not onely to suffer your people, both marchants, and mariners, to passe with their ships, or barkes, from Astracan, ouer the Mare Caspium, to fetche Thomas Banister and Geofry Ducket, with their company, and goods out of Persia, but also when they shall arriue within his Maiesties dominions, to aide and assist them, and see them safely conducted vp the riuer Volga, from danger of enemies.

8 To the eight, his maiestie hath commanded letters to be written to the customers, both of Astracan and Cazan, to make restitution to the English merchants of their goods so deteined by them for custome, and to take custome for the same, according to his maiesties letters of priuilege.

9 10 To the ninth and tenth articles, his Maiestie will consider of those matters, and hereafter will signifie his princely pleasure therein.

11 To the eleuenth, as touching an inuentorie giuen into the, treasury what goods the merchants had burnt in the Mosco, in their houses there, his Maiesties pleasure was to vnderstand the same, to the intent he might know the losses of all strangers at that present, but not to make restitution, for that it was Gods doing, and not the Emperours.

12 To the twelfth, concerning Thomas Glouer, his Maiestie was enformed by his Ambassador of the Queenes great mercy and clemencie towards the said Thomas, for his sake, which his Highnes receiued in good part, but what agreement or dealings was betwixt the said sir William Garrard and his company, and the said Glouer, or what he doth owe vnto the said merchants, his Maiestie doth not know. And as for the money which the said Thomas saith is owing vnto him by the Emperour, his Maiesties pleasure is, that so much as shall be found due, and growing vpon wares deliuered vnto the treasurie, out of the time of his Maiesties displeasure, shall be paid forthwith to the said Thomas, and the rest is forfeited vnto his Maiestie, and taken for a fine, as appertaining to Rutter and Bennet, accompted traitors vnto his Highnes, during the time of his displeasure.

13 To the thirteenth article, concerning Rutter to deliuered vnto you, to be caried home, the answere was, that as his Maiestie will not detaine any English man in his countrey, that is willing to go home, according to the Queenes request: euen so will he not force any to depart, that is willing to tary with him. Yet his Highnes, to satisfie the Queenes Maiesties request, is contented at this present to send the said Ralfe Rutter home with you, and hath commanded that a letter shall be written vnto his chiefe officer at the Mosco, to send the said Rutter away with speed, that he may be with you at Vologda, by the fine of May, without faile: and touching the rest of your request in the said article, his Maiesties pleasure shall be signified in the letters of priuilege, granted to the said merchants.

14 To the fourteenth, touching artificers, his Maiestie will accomplish all the Queenes Highnes request in that behalfe, and now at this present doth licence such and so many to depart to their natiue countrey as are willing to goe.

15 To the 15, touching Besson Messeriuey, the Emperors maiestie is much offended with him, and will send down a gentleman with you to inquire of his ill behauior, as wel for speaking of vndecent words against the Queens maiestie as you haue alleaged, as also against you, and the merchants for his outrages mentioned in the article, and the said Besson being found guilty, to be imprisoned and punished by seuere iustice accordingly, and after to put in sureties to answere the Emperors high displeasure, or els to be brought vp like a prisoner by the said gentleman to answere his offences before his Maiestie. And his highnes doth request that the Queenes highnes would

doe the like vpon Middleton and Manlie her messengers sent thither two yeeres past, and of all others for their ill behauiour towards his maiestie, as may appeare by letters sent by Daniel Siluester from his highnes, least by the bad demeanor of such lewd persons, the amity and friendship betwixt their maiesties might be diminished.

16 To the 16 and last article, touching the corne brought into the Emperors dominions by the merchants, his maiestie doth greatly commend them for so wel doing, and hath commanded to giue you a letter forthwith in their behalf, directed to his officers of Duina, to suffer the said merchants to selle their corne, by measure great or small at their pleasure without custome.

Thus I receiued a full answere from his Maiestie by his chiefe Secretarie and one other of his counsel, to the 16 articles afore rehearsed, by me exhibited in writing touching your affaires, with his letter also sent by me to the Queenes maiesty. Which being done, I requested that the new letters of priuilege granted by his highnes vnto you might be forthwith dispatched to the intent I might carie the same with me. Also I requested that such money due to you, which it had pleased his maiesty to command to be payd, might be deliuered to me in your behalfe.

Touching the letters of priuilege, the Secretary answered me, it is not possible you can haue them with you, for they must be first written and shewed vnto the Emperor, and then three to be written of one tenour according to your request, which cannot bee done with speede, for that his maiesties pleasure is, you shall depart this night before him, who remooueth himselfe to morrow toward Nouogrod: but without faile the sayd letters shall be dispatched vpon the way, and sent after you with speede to Colmogro. And as touching the money which you require, it cannot be paid here because we haue not the bookes of accounts, for want whereof we know not what to paie: wherefore the best is that you send one of the merchants after the Emperor to Nouogrod, and let him repaire vnto me there, and without faile I will paie all such money as shall be appointed by his maiestie to be paid after the bookes seene.

But forasmuch as there was none of your seruants with me at that present (although I had earnestly written vnto your Agent Nicholas Proctor by Richard Pringle one of your owne seruants, one moneth before my comming to Starites, where I had my dispatch, that he should not faile to come himselfe, or send one of your seruants to mee hither, to follow all such sutes as I should commence in your behalfs, which he neglected to doe to your great hinderance) I requested the said Secretarie that I might leaue Daniel my interpreter with him, aswell for the receipt of money, as for the speedy dispatch of the letters of priuiledge, but it would not be granted in any wise that I should leaue any of mine owne companie behind me, and thereupon I did take my leaue with full dispatch, and departed to my lodging, and foorthwith there came vnto me a gentleman who had charge as wel to conduct me and prouide boates, men, post horses and victuals all the way to the sea side, being a thousand and three hundred miles, as also to doe iustice of the sayd Bessen, as aforesaid. And he said vnto me, the Emperours pleasure is, that you shall presently depart from hence, and I am appointed to goe with you. And that night I departed from the said Starites, being the fourteenth of May aforesayd. And passing a great part of my iourney, I arriued at the citie of Vologda the last of the sayd May, where I remained fiue daies as well expecting a messenger to bring vnto me the new letters of priuiledge, as the comming of Rutter, whom the Emperours Maiestie himselfe commanded before my face should bee sent vnto me without faile, and I did see the letters written to the chiefe officers at the Mosco for the same. Neuerthe lesse the said Rutter did not come, neither could I heare of him after, nor know the sudden cause of his stay contrary to the princes owne word and meaning, as I suppose. But I could not help the matter being farre from the prince, neither could I tell how to haue redresse, because by absence I could not complaine. Notwithstanding I vsed my indeuour, and sent a messenger Iohn Norton one of your seruants from Vologda to Nouogrod, where the court then lay, expressely with letters, as well to aduertise his maiestie that the sayd Rutter was not sent vnto me according to his highnes commandement and order, as also about the dispatch of the said letters of priuiledge and receit of your money, with straight charge that he should in any wise returne vnto me againe before the departing of the ships. And the first day of Iune I departed from the said Vologda by water towards Colmogro, where I arriued the 21 of Iune aforesaid, and remained there vntil the 23 of Iuly, looking for the said Iohn Norton to haue returned vnto me in al that time, which had respite fully enough in that space both to go to the court to dispatch his busines, and to haue returned againe vnto me, but he came not, for it was otherwise determined before his going, as I did after vnderstand, and can more at large by worde of mouth declare vnto your worships the occasion thereof.

Neuerthelesse, I am well assured before this time your Agent hath receiued into his hands the sayd letters of priuiledges, and shall haue dispatch with expedition in all things touching your affaires, according to his maiesties grant by me obtained, and as he hath written to the Queenes maiestie at this present, wishing that as now by my going the Emperour hath withdrawen his grieuous displeasure from you, and restored you againe into his fauour, so your Agent and others your seruants there resident may behaue, and endeuour themselues to keepe and augment the same, whose euill doings haue bene the onely occasion of his indignation now remitted.

* * * * *

The names of such countries as I Anthony Ienkinson haue trauelled vnto, from the second of October 1546, at which time I made my first voyage out of England, vntill the yeere of our Lord 1572, when I returned last out of Russia.

First, I passed into Flanders, and trauelled through all the base countries, and from thence through Germanie, passing ouer the Alpes I trauelled into Italy, and from thence made my iourney through the Piemont into France, throughout all which realme I haue throughly iournied.

I haue also trauelled through the kingdomes of Spaine and Portingal, I haue sailed through the Leuant seas euery way, and haue bene in all the chiefe Islands within the same sea, as Rhodes, Malta, Sicilia, Cyprus, Candie, and diuers others.

I haue bene in many partes of Grecia, Morea, Archaia, and where the olde citie of Corinth stoode.

I haue trauelled through a great part of Turkie, Syria, and diuers others countries in Asia minor.

I haue passed ouer the mountaines of Libanus to Damasco, and trauelled through Samaria, Galile, Philistine or Palestine, vnto Ierusalem, and so through all the Holy land.

I haue bene in diuers places of Affrica, as Algiers, Cola, Hona, Tripolis, the gollet within the gulfe of Tunis.

I haue sailed farre Northward within the Mare glaciale, where we haue had continuall day, and sight of the Sunne ten weekes together, and that nauigation was in Norway, Lapland, Samogitia, and other very strange places.

I haue trauelled through all the ample dominions of the Emperour of Russia and Moscouia, which extende from the North sea, and the confines of Norway, and Lapland euen to the Mare Caspium.

I haue bene in diuers countries neere about the Caspian sea, Gentiles, and Mahometans, as Cazan, Cremia, Rezan, Cheremisi, Mordouiti, Vachin, Nagaia, with diuers others of strange customes and religions.

I haue sailed ouer the Caspian sea, and discouered all the regions thereabout adiacent, as Chircassi, Comul, Shascal, Shiruim, with many others.

I haue trauelled 40 daies iourney beyond the said sea, towards the Oriental India, and Cathaia, through diuers deserts and wildernesses, and passed through 5 kingdomes of the Tartars, and all the land of Turkeman and Zagatay, and so to the great citie of Boghar in Bactria; not without great perils and dangers sundry times.

After all this, in An. 1562, I passed againe ouer the Caspian sea another way, and landed in Armenia, at a citie called Derbent, built by Alexander the great, and from thence trauelled through Media, Parthia, Hircania, into Persia to the court of the great Sophie called Shaw Tamasso, vnto whom I deliuered letters from the Queenes Maiestie, and remained in his court 8 moneths, and returning homeward, passed through diuers other countries. Finally I made two voyages more after that out of England into Russia, the one in the yeere 1566, and the other in the yeere 1571. And thus being weary and growing old, I am content to take my rest in mine owne house, chiefly comforting my selfe, in that my seruice hath been honourably accepted and rewarded of her maiestie and the rest by whom I haue bene imploied.

* * * * *

A letter of Iames Alday to the Worshipfull M. Michael Lock, Agent in London for the Moscouie company, touching a trade to be established in Lappia, written 1575.

I haue in remembrance (worshipful Sir) the talke we had when I was with you, as touching the trade in Lappia: [Sidenote: He maruelleth the company do not conferre with him of Lappia.] And certeinly I haue something marueiled that in all this time the right wor. your societie haue not giuen order that some little conference (by you, or with some other) might haue bin had with me touching those parts, considering they know (as I thinke) that I remained there one whole yere and more, by which meanes reason would that I should haue learned something. But the cause why they haue not desired to conferre with me (as I iudge) resteth onely in one of these 4 cases, that is to say, either they thinke themselues so throughly certified of that trade, as more neede not be spoken thereof, or that they haue no lust more to deale that waies, or that they hold mee so vntrusty to them that they dare not open their minds, for feare or doubt, I should beare more affection to others then to them, and so discouer their secrets: or els they think me of so simple vnderstanding, that I am not worthy to be spoken with in these matters. To which 4 cases I answere as followeth: [Sidenote: 5 English men wintered in Lappia.] First, if they think themselues so throughly certified as more need not to be spoken: certeinly I something maruel by whom it should be: for in the winter past there lay but 5 English persons there, viz. Christopher Colt, Roger Leche, Adam Tunstal cooper, one lad, and I: for Henry Cocknedge was the whole winter at Mosco. [Sidenote: Christopher Colt a simple merchant.] And of these persons, as touching Colt, I think him (if I may without offence speake my conscience) the most simple person that was there, (as touching the vnderstanding of a marchant) although indeed he tooke vpon him very much to his owne harme and others I doubt, for he vsed himselfe not like a marchant, neither shewed diligence like a worthy seruant or factor, but lay still in a den al the whole winter, hauing wares lying vpon his hand, which he would not imploy to any vse: although sundry waies there were that he might haue put his wares in ready money with gaine, and no great aduenture, which money would haue bin more acceptable to the poore Lappes and fishermen at the spring, than any kind of wares: [Sidenote: Good trade in winter in Lappia.] but his fond head did as he that had the talent in the Gospel, and yet he had counsel to the contrary which he disdained, so that men perceiuing his captious head, left not only to counsell him, but also some, in as much as they might, kept him from knowledge of the trade that might be in that country, the winter time, which is better peraduenture then most men think of. Wherefore if Colt haue written or said any thing touching those countries, it is doubtful whether it toucheth the effect or not, considering he lay still all the winter without trial of any matter. [Sidenote: Henry Cocknedge, honest but ignorant.] And for Henry Cocknedge assuredly speaking so much as I do perfectly know, I must needs say that he is a very honest young man, and right careful of his business, and in that respect worthy to be praised. But yet he being absent in the winter other then by hearesay he could not learne, so that his instructions may be something doubtful. [Sidenote: Roger Leche expert of Lappia.] And like as of the lad nothing can be learned, so am I sure that Tunstal the Cooper hath not yet beene spoken with, so that those of parts certeine knowledge cannot as yet be learned, except by Roger Leche, of whom I confesse knowledge may be had, for indeed there is no English man liuing that hath like knowledge in those countries as he hath, nor that is able to do so much with the people as he may: he in the winter trauailed one waies and other nere 300 miles: he of a litle made somthing, and learned not only the maners, conditions and customs of the people, but also he learned of al kind of commodities in those regions how they may be bought at the most aduantage, that gaine may be made of them: So that I confesse, if he hath giuen intelligence to the right Wor. company, then haue they no neede to speake with me or any other for to learne of those countries (except it be to heare mine opinion) which in truth I wil alwaies open unto them. But the effect of the beneficial secrets of that countrey is to be inquired of him, & in mine opinion worthy to be learned, except, as in the second case, they list no more to deale that waies. [Sidenote: If the companie do not enter into the trade of Lappia, others will preuent them.] To which I answere, that if they deal not that waies, & that with speede they seeke not to preuent others that mean to deale there, although not English men, let them then not thinke long to haue any profitable trade in Russia: for the greater part of that benefit wil be wiped from them, or 5 yeere to an end, as I will shew good reason, if I be demanded the question. [Sidenote: The trade of Vedagoba.] Therefore if they will maintaine the Russia trade with aduantage, then ought they to looke to this in time, so may they keepe the Russia trade as it is, and likewise make a trade in Lappia more profitable then that, and therefore this is to bee considered, rather then to prohibite Englishmen from the trade of Vedagoba. For if they looke not to this, and that in time, they may be likened (if it might be without offence spoken) to two dogs that striue for the bone whiles the third run away with it: and yet mean I not otherwise, but in such order, as not Englishmen only, but also Hollanders, Brabanders, & others may be iustly and vtterly put from the trade in Lappia, and the company to keepe the whole trades to themselues without interruption of any, to their great benefit, which I wish from the bottome of my heart, as euer I wished wealth to mine owne person: And thereby hold me excused in the third case I write of. [Sidenote: He can say somewhat though not much.] And for the fourth as touching my iudgment, as I confesse it is not very deepe, so I thanke God I am not vtterly without vnderstanding (although I be poore) and therefore peraduenture holden out of reputation, yet God doth distribute his gifts as it pleaseth him. I haue seen wise men poore in my time, & foolish men rich, and some men haue more knowledge then they can vtter by speech, which, fault was once obiected against me by a learned man of this realme: but surely how weak soeuer my vtterance is, my meaning is faithful and true, and I wish in my heart to your laudable company al the gaine that may be, or els I pray God to confound me as a false dissembler. [Sidenote: 1183 barrels of oyle bough by others. Colt sold 27 barrels to a Hollander.] It greeueth me to see how of late they haue bin brought to great charges, beating the bush, as the old terme is, & other men taking the birds: this last yere hauing in Lappia 2 ships, as I am partly informed, they both brought not much aboue 300 barrels of traine oile, yet am I sure there was bought besides them of the Russes, Corels, & Lappes, 1183 barrels, besides 27 barrels Colt sold to Iacob the Hollander, at two barrels for one Northerne dozen. And yet there is a greater inconuenience springing, which if it take a little deeper roote it will be (I feare) too hard to be pulled up, which for loue & good will (God is my witnes) I write of, wishing as to my deare friends that they should looke to it in time, if they meane to keepe the trade of Russia or Lappia. And thus loue hath compelled me to write this aduertisement, which I wish to be accepted in as good part, as I with good will haue written it.

* * * * *

The request of an honest merchant to a friend of his, to be aduised and directed in the course of killing the Whale, as followeth. An. 1575.

I pray you pleasure me in getting me perfect information of the matter hereunder specified.

For the prouision and furniture for a shippe of 200 tunnes, to catch the Whale fish in Russia, passing from England. How many men to furnish the ship.

How many fishermen skilful to catch the Whale, & how many other officers and Coopers.

How many boats, and what fashion, and how many men in each boate.

What wages of such skilful men and other officers, as we shall neede out of Biskay.

How many harping irons, speares, cordes, axes, hatchets, kniues, and other implements for the fishing, and what sort and greatnes of them.

How many kettles, the greatnesse and maner of them, and what mettall, and whether they bee set on triuets or on furnaces for boiling of the traine oyle, and others.

What quantitie of caske, and what sort of caske, and what number of hoopes and twigges, and how much thereof to be staued for the traine.

What quantitie of victuals, and what kinde of victuals for the men in all the ship for 4 moneths time.

For the common mariners and officers to gouerne the ship, we shall not need any out of Biskaie, but onely men skilful in the catching of the Whale, and ordering of the oile, and one Cooper skilful to set vp the staued caske.

Also what other matters are requisite to be knowen, and done for the said voyage to catch the Whale, not here noted nor remembred.

These requests were thus answered, which may serue as directions for all such as shall intend the same voyage, or the like for the Whale.

A proportion for the setting forth of a ship of 200 tunne, for the killing of the Whale.

There must be 55 men who departing for Wardhouse in the moneth of April, must bee furnished with 4 kintals and a halfe of bread for euery man.

250 hogsheds to put the bread in.

150 hogsheds of Cidar.

6 kintals of oile.

8 kintals of bacon.

6 hogsheds of beefe.

100 quarters of salt.

150 pound of candles.

8 quarters of beanes and pease.

Saltfish & herring, a quantitie conuenient.

4 tunnes of wines.

Half a quarter of mustard seed, and a querne.

A grindstone.

800 empty shaken hogsheds.

350 bundles of hoopes, and 6 quintalines.

800 paire of heds for the hogsheds.

10 Estachas called roxes for harping irons.

10 pieces of Arporieras.

3 pieces of Baibens for the Iauelines small.

2 tackles to turne the Whales.

A halser of 27 fadom long to turne the Whales.

15 great Iauelines.

18 small Iauelins.

50 harping irons.

9 machicos to cut the Whale withal.

2 doozen of machetos to minch the Whale.

2 great hookes to turne the Whale.

3 paire of Can hookes.

6 hookes for staues.

3 dozen of staues for the harping irons.

6 pullies to turne the Whale with.

10 great baskets.

10 lampes of iron to carie light.

5 kettles of 150 li. the piece, and 6 ladles.

1000 of nailes for the pinnases.

560 of nailes of Carabelie for the houses, and the Wharfe.

18 axes and hatchets to cleaue wood.

12 pieces of lines, and 6 dozen of hookes.

2 beetles of Rosemarie.

4 dozen of oares for the pinnases.

6 lanternes.

500 of Tesia.

Item, gunpouder & matches for harquebushes as shalbe needfull.

Item, there must be carried from hence 5 pinnases, fiue men to strike with harping irons, two cutters of Whale, 5 coopers, & a purser or two.

A note of certaine other necessarie things belonging to the Whalefishing, receiued of master W. Burrough.

A sufficient number of pullies for tackle for the Whale.

A dozen of great baskets.

4 furnaces to melt the Whale in.

6 ladles of copper.

A thousand of nailes to mend the pinnases.

500 great nailes of spikes to make their house.

3 paire of bootes great and strong, for them that shall cut the Whale.

8 calue skins to make aprons or barbecans.

* * * * *

The deposition of M. William Burrough to certaine Interrogatories ministred
 vnto him concerning the Narue, Kegor, &c. to what king or prince they doe
 appertaine and are subiect, made the 23 of Iune, 1576.

These articles seeme to haue bene ministred vpon the quarel between Alderman Bond the elder, and the Moscouie company, for his trade to the Narue without their consent.

[Sidenote: The first Interrogatorie.] First, whether the villages or townes vulgarely called the Narue, Kegor, Pechingo and Cola, and the portes of the same townes, as well at the time of the grant of the letters of priuilege by the Emperour to our merchants, as also in the yeeres of our Lord, 1566, 1567, 1568, 1569, 1570, 1571, 1572, 1573, 1574, and 1575 respectiuely were (as presently they be) of the iurisdicition, and subiect to the mightie prince the Emperour of Russia: and whether the saide Emperour of Russia, by all the time aforesaide, was chiefe lord and gouernour respectiuely of the said places, and so vulgarly knowen, had, and reputed: and whether the said townes and places, and either of them be situated towards the North and Northeast or Northwest, and between the North and the East point: and be the same places whereunto by force of the said priuilege, it is forbidden to any other subiect to haue traffike, sauing to the societie aforesaid.

[Sidenote: The deponents answer.] To this Interrogatorie the deponent saith, that it is true that the villages, townes and places vulgarly called the Narue, Kegor, Peshingo and Cola, and the portes thereof, at the time of the grant of the said priuilege (as he iudgeth) were reputed respectiuely to be vnder the iurisdiction, and subiect to the Emperour of Russia, and so from the time of the said grant, vnto the yeere, 1566, and that in the yeeres of our Lord, 1566, 67, 68, 69, 70, 71, 72, 73, 74, and 1575. respectiuely they were (as presently they be) of the iurisdiction, and subiect vnto the mighty prince the Emperour of Russia, and the same Emperour of Russia, by all the time aforesaide, was chiefe gouernour respectiuely of the said places, and so vulgarly knowen, had and reputed. And that all the said places are situated from London Northwards, between the East and the North, and within the grant of the letters patents, and priuileges of the said companie of merchants for the discouery of new trades, and the same places whereunto by force of the said letters patents, it is forbidden to any other subiect to haue traffike sauing to the societie aforesaid.

Notwithstanding the Deponent saith, that he hath heard it credibly reported by diuers, that the king of Denmarke of late yeeres, or euery yeere once, hath had one of his subiects or more by him selfe, or with his guide a Lappian, that hath at the places Cola, Kegor, and diuers other places in Lappia, taken of the Lappies certain tribute or head pence, which the said Lappie haue willingly giuen to winne fauour of the saide prince, and to liue quietly by his subiects, the people of Finmarke which border vpon their countrey whereof, Wardhouse is the strongest hold, and bordereth neere vnto them. Hee hath also hearde that in the time of peace betweene the saide Emperour of Russia, and the kings of Sweden, there was yeerely for the king of Sweden one or more that came into Lappia vnto diuers places, in maner as the king of Denmarkes seruant vseth to doe, and did demaund of them some tribute or duetie which they willingly paide: but since the late warres betweene the saide Emperour and king of Sweden, hee hath not heard of any thing that hath bene paide by them to the king of Sweden:

such is the simplicitie of this people the Lappies, that they would rather giue tribute to all those that border vpon their countrey, then by denying it haue their ill willes.

But the trueth is, as this Deponent saith, that the saide mightie prince the Emperour of Russia is the chiefe lord and gouernour of the saide countrey of Lappia, his lawes and orders are obserued by them, hee takes toll and custome &c. of them. They are infidels, but if any of them become Christians it is after the Russe law. If there happen any controuersie betweene those people, such as cannot be ended amongst themselues, or by the Emperours deputies in that countrey, they repaire to the Mosko as their highest Court, and there haue it ended. [Sidenote: Pechingo abbey.] Betweene the place specified Kegor, and the confines of Finmarke aforesaide in Lappia, is the monasterie Pechingo, which are monkes, and vse the Russe lawe, the chiefe or head of that abbey is alwayes appointed by the cleargie in Mosko.

Also in the yeere of our Lord 1557, the said Deponent was at the place Kegor, in the moneth of Iune, the 29 day being S. Peters day, at which time was a great assembly of people at a mart there, the Russes, Kerils and Lappians on the one side subiects to the said mighty prince the Emperour of Russia, and the Norwegians or Norses and people of Finmarke subiects to the King of Denmarke on the other part, they did barter and exchange fish for other commodities. The deputie for the Russe had the chief gouernment of the said Mart, and tooke toll of those people that were subiect to his master, and the captaine of Wardhouse had then the gouernment of the people subiect to his master the king of Denmark. He saith also, that betweene the abbey Pechingo, and the abbey of S. Nicholas in Russia, vpon the border of the said coast of Lappia, he hath bene vpon the shore at diuers places, where fresh riuers fall into the Sea, where are commonly taken fresh salmon, all which places he doth know for certaine, that they were farmed out to the subiects of the said Emperour, and he the said Emperour receiued yeerely the rent for them. And further he saith that it hath bene forther credibly reported vnto him, that there is not any such riuer or creek of fresh water which falleth out of the said countrey of Lappia into the sea, between the said abbey Pechingo, and the bay of S. Nicholas, but they are all and euery of them farmed out, and the Emperour receiueth the rent for them.

[Sidenote: The second Interrogatorie.] Item, whether as well before, as also within the memorie of men, till the time of the graunt of the said letters patents any of the English merchants (sauing the merchants of the said societie) subiects of this realme of England, haue commonly exercised or frequented businesse or trade in the said villages or townes called the

Narue, Kegor, Pechingo, and Cola, or in any of them, or in any ports or territories of the said Emperour of Russia.

[Sidenote: The deponents answer.] To this Interrogatorie the Deponent answereth, that the subiects of this realme before the graunt of the said letters patent did not commonly exercise, neither frequent or trade to any of the said places called the Narue, Kegor, Pechingo or Cola, or to any of them.

* * * * *

Certaine reasons to disswade the vse of a trade to the Narue aforesaide, by way through Sweden.

The merchandise of the Narue are gross wares, viz. flaxe, hempe, waxe, tallow and hides.

The traffique at that place standeth vpon the agreement and liking of the Emperour of Russia, with the king of Sweden: for all these merchandises that are brought thither come from Plescoue, Nouogrod, and other parts of the Emperours dominions.

For transporting those merchandises from Narue to Stockholm, or what other place shall be thought conuenient in Sweden, it must be in vessels of those countries, which wilbe of smal force to resist Freebooters, or any other that shall make quarrel or offer violence against them.

When the goods are brought into Sweden, they must be discharged, and new laden into smaller vessels, to cary the same by riuer or lake a part of the way, and againe to be vnladen and transported by land to Newles.

So as the ordinary charges for transporting of goods from Narue to Newles by way as aforesaid, besides the spoile by so often lading and vnlading, cariage by land, and the dangers of the seas, pirats, &c. will be such as when it shalbe so brought to Newles it wil be as deare to the merchants in that place as it shall be worth to be sold in London, wherefore the trade that wayes cannot be profitable to our nation.

Moreouer, when the goods shall be in Newles, it may bee thought doubtfull to bring it thence quietly without disliking or forcible resistance of the king of Denmarke, forasmuch as he maketh quarrell, and alleageth damage vnto him in his tolles of the Sound by our trade to S. Nicholas, how much more will he now doe by this way, and with how much greater aduantage may he performe it? The danger that may grow in our trade to Russia, by way of S. Nicholas, through the displeasure that the Emperour may conceiue by our trade with the Sweden to Narue is also to be considered.

* * * * *

A remembrance of aduise giuen to the merchants, touching a voyage for Cola abouesaid. 1578.

Whereas you require my counsell after what order the voyage for Cola is to be set forth, I answere that I know no better way then hath bene heretofore vsed, which is after this maner. First of all we haue hired the ship by the great, giuing so much for the wearing of the tackle and the hull of the shippe, as the ship may be in bignesse: and if shee bee about the burden of a hundred tunnes, we pay fourescore pound, and so after that rate: and thereunto we doe vicual the ship our selues, and doe ship all our men our selues, shipping no more men, nor giuing them more wages then we should doe if they went of a merchants voyage, for it hath bene a great helpe to our voiage hitherto, to haue our men to fish with one boate, & costing vs no more charges then it should do, if our men should lie and doe nothing sauing the charges of salt, & of lines, which is treble paid for againe. For this last yere past our men killed with one boat betwixt 9. or 10. thousand fish, which yeelded to vs in money with the oile that came of it, about 15. or 16. score pounds, which is a great helpe to a voyage. And besides all this, our ship did take in so much pile and other commodities as we bestowed 100. whole clothes in. But because, as I doe suppose, it is not the vse of London to take ships to fraight after that order before prescribed, neither I think that the mariners wil take such paines as our men will: Therefore my counsell is, if you thinke good, to freight some ship of Hul or Newcastle, for I am sure that you may haue them there better cheap to freight, then here at London. Besides al this, one may haue such men as will take paines for their merchants. [Sidenote: Hull the best market of England for sale of fish.] And furthermore when it shal please God that the ship shal returne to come to discharge at Hull, which will be the most for your profit for the sales of all such like commoditie as comes from that place, as for fish, oyle, and Salmon chiefly, hee that will seeke a better market for the sales then at Hull, he must seeke it out of England, for the like is not in England. This is the best way that I can deuise, and most for your profite, and if you will, I will also set you downe all the commodities that are necessarie for such a voyage, and which way also that the Hollanders may within two or three yeeres be forced to leaue off the trade of Cola which may easily be done. For if my abilitie were to my will, I would vse the matter so that they should either leaue off the trade, or els cary light ships with them home againe.

* * * * *

A dedicatorie Epistle vnto the Queenes most excellent Maiestie, written by Master William Burrough late Comptroller of Her Highnesse nauie, and annexed vnto his exact and notable mappe of Russia, briefly containing (amongst other matters) his great trauailes, obseruations, and experiments both by sea and land, especially in those Northeastern parts.

To the most high and renowmed Princesse ELIZABETH by the grace of God
  Queene of England, France and Ireland, &c.

My minde earnestly bent to the knowledge of nauigation and, Hydrographie from my youth (most excellent my dread Soueraigne) hath eftsoones beene moued by diligent studie to search out the chiefest points to them belonging: and not therewith sufficed hath also sought by experience in diuers discoueries and other voyages and trauailes to practise the same. I was in the first voyage for discouerie of the partes of Russia, which begun in anno 1553. (being then sixteene yeeres of age) also in the yeere 1556. in the voyage when the coastes of Samoed and Noua Zemble, with the straightes of Vaigatz were found out: and in the yeere 1557, when the coast of Lappia, and the bay of S. Nicholas were more perfectly discouered. Since which time, by my continuall practise in the voyages made yeerely to S. Nicholas in Russia, or to the Narue, and to some other countreys also by Sea: as likewise in passing from S. Nicholas to Mosco, and from Mosco to Narue, and from thence backe againe to S. Nicholas by land, in the yeeres 1574. and 1575. (being then Agent in those countries for the companie of English merchants for discoueries of new trades) setting downe alwayes with great care and diligence, true obseruations and notes of al those countreys, Islands, coasts of the sea, and other things requisite to the arts of Nauigation and Hydrographie; and with like diligence gathering exact notes and descriptions of the wayes, riuers, cities, townes, &c. as I passed by Land: I finde my selfe sufficiently furnished to giue report vnto your Maiesty, and to make description of those North parts of the world in forme and maner of euery leagues distance that I haue passed and seene in al those my trauels. The places herein described, which I haue not seene and tried my selfe, I haue set downe by the best authorities that I could finde, and therein may erre with the learned Gerardus Mercator, Abraham Ortelius, and the rest: but for the maine part which is from Rochel in France hither to London, and from hence Eastward to Narue by sea, and from thence to Mosco and to S. Nicholas by land: also from hence Northwards and Northeastwards by Sea to Saint Nicholas, and to the straight of Vaigatz (first crauing humbly your highnesse pardon) I dare boldly affirme (and that I trust without suspect of arrogancie, since truely I may say it) I haue here set it open to the view, with such exactnesse and trueth, and so placed euery thing aright in true latitude and longitude, (accompting the longitudes from the Meridian of London, which I place in 21 degrees) as till this time no man hath done the like: neither is any man able by learning onely, except he trauaileth as I haue done. For as it may be truely saide of Nauigation and Hydrographie, that no man can be cunning in the one which wanteth conuenient knowledge in the other: and as neither of them can be had without the helpes of Astronomie and Cosmographie, much lesse without these two grounds of all artes, Arithmetike and Geometrie: so none of the best learned in those sciences Mathematicall, without conuenient practise at the sea can make iust proofe of the profite in them: so necessarily dependeth art and reason vpon practise and experience. Albeit there are diuers both learned and vnlearned, litle or nothing experienced, which in talke of nauigation will enter deeply and speake much of and against errours vsed therein, when they cannot reforme them. Such also haue written thereof, pretending singular great knowledge therein, and would so be accompted of, though in very deede not worthy the name of good and sufficient pilots. To whom I thinke it shall not be amisse in defence of rules builded vpon reason, and in practise allowed, thus much to say for answere. It is so, that there are rules vsed in nauigation which are not perfectly true: among which the streight lines in sea-cardes, representing the 32. points of the compasse or windes are hot holden to be the least, but noted of such talkers for principall, to condemne the occupiers thereof for ignorant: yet hath the famous and learned Gerardus Mercator vsed them in his uniuersal mappe. But such as condemne them for false, and speake most against their vse cannot giue other that should serue for nauigation to better purpose and effect. Experience (one of the keyes of knowledge) hath taught mee to say it. Wherein with my abilitie, together with some part of my studie, I am rather moued (in this my plot) to make some triall vnto your maiestie: for that I perceiue that such attempts of newe discoueries (whereunto this noble Island is most aptly situated) are by your royall maintenance so willingly furthered: beseeching your highnesse so to accept of these my trauailes, as a pledge of my well willing to my countrey, and of my loyall seruice to your maiestie, whose healthfull happie life and reigne God continue which is Almightie. Amen.

Your Maiesties most humble subiect

William Burrough.

* * * * *

The Queenes Maiesties letters to Shaugh Thamas the great Sophi of Persia, sent by Arthur Edwards, William Turnbull, Matthew Tailbois, and Peter Gerard appointed Agents for the Moscouie companie, in their sixt voyage to Persia, begun in the yeere 1579.

To the most noble and inuincible Emperour of Persia, King of Shiruan, Gilan, Grosin, Corassan, and great Gouernour of the Indies.

Elizabeth by the grace of God Queene of England, France and Ireland, defender of the faith &c. To the most noble and inuincible Emperour of Persia, King of Shiruan, Gilan, Grosin, Corassan, and great gouernour euen vnto the Indies, sendeth greeting. Most noble and inuincible Prince, it is now tenne yeeres since, [Footnote: 1568.] or thereabouts, wherein (after the honourable ambassade of the noble man Anthony Ienkenson our well beloued subiect, to your most noble and inuincible father performed) we laboured to bring to passe by Thomas Bannister and Gefferey Ducket merchants our subiects, that throughout all the kingdomes subiect to his empire, free power might be giuen to Will. Garrard, Thomas Ofley, William Chester, knights, Rowland Haiward, Lionel Ducket, William Allen, Thomas Bannister, Gefferey Ducket, Lawrence Chapman, Merchants, and vnto their societie, to enter into his lands and countreys at al times when they would and could, there to exercise and vse their trade of merchandise, and from thence likewise after exchange or sale made of those wares, which they should bring with them with his like good leaue and fauour, to carie from thence those things wherwith his dominions do abound and with vs be scant. Which our petition the most noble prince your father took so thankfully and in such good part, that he not onely graunted franke and commodious leaue, as was desired: but the same he would to bee vnto them most free and beneficiall, and to haue continuance for many yeeres and times. The benefite of the which his wonderfull liberality, our subiects did enioy with such humanitie and freedome as there could be no greater, till the time that by reason of wars more and more increasing in those parts, by the which our subiects were to make their iourney into Persia, they were debarred and shut from that voyage and traffique. The which traffique the said societie being eftsoones desirous to renew to the weale and commoditie of both our dominions they haue now sent into Persia their factors and Agents Arthur Edwards, William Turnbull, Matthew Tailbois, Peter Gerrard merchants, with their associats, whom we beseech your inuincible maiesty to entertaine with that fauour wherewith your father did imbrace Tho. Bannister & Geffrey Ducket, and to enfranchise their whole societie with that freedome, that neither they through any their misdemeanours towards your subiects, may thereof seeme vnworthy (as we hope they will not) neither we our selues otherwise enioy them, then with the perpetuall remembrance of your good affection towards vs, and with the like fauourable inclination of our part towards you. The matter itself and tract of time shall sufficiently proue the foresaid maner of traffike vnprofitable to neither of vs. For so hath one God the chiefe gouernour of all things disposed of our affaires on earth, that ech one should need other. And as for our people and subiects of the English nation, in verie deed your maiesty shal find them made and fashioned so pliant to the perfourmance of all dueties of humanity, that it can neuer repent you to haue graunted them this franke traffic, nor shame vs to haue obteined it for them at your hands. That therefore it may please your maiesty to yeeld vnto them this at our request, most earnestly we beseech you. And we (as it wel beseemeth a prince) if euer hereafter we may, wil show our selfe not to bee vnmindful of so great a benefit. We wish your maiesty wel and prosperously to fare. Giuen at our palace of Westminster the 10. day of Iune, in the yere of our Lord 1579. and of our reigne the 21.

* * * * *

Aduertisements and reports of the 6. voyage into the parts of Persia and Media, for the companie of English merchants for the discouerie of new trades, in the yeeres 1579. 1580. and 1581. gathered out of sundrie letters written by Christopher Burrough, seruant to the saide companie, and sent to his vncle Master William Burrough.

First it is to be vnderstood, that the ships for the voiage to S. Nicholas in Russia, in which the factors and merchandise for the Persian voiage were transported, departed from Grauesend the 19. of Iune, 1579. which arriued at S. Nicholas in Russia the 22. of Iuly, where the factors and merchants landed, and the merchandise were discharged and laden into doshnikes, that is, barkes of the countrey, to be caried from thence vp by riuer vnto Vologda. And the 25. day of the said Iulie, the doshnikes departed from Rose Island by S. Nicholas vp the riuer Dwina, Peremene, that is to say, in poste, by continual sailing, rowing, setting with poles, or drawing of men, which came to Colmogro the 27. day, and departed the 29. of Iulie vp the said riuer Dwyna, and came to Vstyoug (which is at the head of the riuer Dwina, and mouth of Sughano) the 9. of August, where they stayed but a small time, prouiding some victuals, and shifting certaine of their cassacks or barkmen, and so departed thence the same day vp the riuer Sughano, and came to Totma (which is counted somewhat more then halfe the way from Vstioug) the 15. day, where they shifted some of their cassaks, and departed thence the same day, and came to the citie Vologda the 19. of August, where they landed their goods, and staied at that place till the 30. of the same. [Sidenote: Yeraslaue.] Hauing prouided at Vologda, Telegas, or wagons, whereupon they laded their goods, they departed thence with the same by land towards Yeraslaue the said 30. of August at eight of the clocke in the morning, and came to the East side of the riuer Volga ouer against Yeraslaue, with 25. Telegas laden with the said goods the seuenth of September at fiue of the clocke afternoone. Then the three stroogs or barks prouided to transport the saide goods to Astracan (where they should meete the ship that should carie the same from thence into Persia) came ouer from Yeraslaue vnto the same side of the riuer Volga, and there tooke in the said goods. And hauing prepared the said barks ready with all necessary furniture they departed with them from Yeraslaue downe the riuer of Volga on the 14. day of September at nine of the clocke in the morning, and they arriued at Niznouogrod the 17. day at three of the clocke aftenoone, where they shewed the Emperors letters to passe free without paying any custome, and taried there about three houres to prouide necessaries, and then departing, arriued at Cazan (or neere the same towne) on the 22. of September at fiue of the clocke afternoone, where (through contrary windes, and for prouiding new cassaks in the places of some that there went from them) they remained till the 26. day, at what time they departed thence about two of the clocke after noone, and arriued at Tetushagorod, which is on the Crim side of Volga, and in latitude 55. degrees 22. minutes, the 28. day at ten in the forenoone, where they ankered, and remained about 3. houres, and departing thence came to Oueak, which is on the Crim side (on the Westerne side of Volga) the fift of October about fiue of the clocke in the morning. [Sidenote: Great store of Licoris.] This is accounted halfe the way between Cazan and Astracan: and heere there groweth great store of Licoris: the soile is very fruitfull; they found there apple trees, and cherrie trees. The latitude of Oueak is 51. degrees 30. minutes. At this place had bene a very faire stone castle called by the name Oueak, and adioining to the same was a towne called by the Russes, Sodom: this towne and part of the castle (by report of the Russes) was swalowed into the earth by the iustice of God, for the wickednesse of the people that inhabited the same. There remaineth at this day to be seen a part of the ruines of the castle, and certaine tombs, wherein as it seemeth haue bin laid noble personages: for vpon a tombe stone might be perceiued the forme of a horse and a man sitting on it with a bow in his hand, and arrowes girt to his side: there was a piece of a scutchion also vpon one of the stones, which had characters grauen on it, whereof some part had beene consumed with the weather, and the rest left vnperfect: by the forme of them that remained, we iudged them to be characters of Armenia: and other characters were grauen also vpon another tombe stone. [Sidenote: Perauolok.] Nowe they departed from Oueak the said fift of October at fiue of the clocke after noone, and came to Perauolok the 10. day about eleuen or twelue of the clocke that night, making, no abode at that place, but passed alongst by it. This worde Perauolok in the Russe tongue doeth signifie a narrow straight or necke of land betweene two waters, and it is so called by them, because from the riuer Volga, at that place, to the riuer Don or Tanais, is counted thirty versts, or as much as a man may well trauell on foote in one day. And seuen versts beneath, vpon an Island called Tsaritsna the Emperour of Russe hath fiftie gunners all the summer time to keepe watch, called by the Tartar name Carawool. Between this place and Astracan are fiue other Carawools or watches.

1 The first is named Kameni Carawool, and is distant from Perauolok 120 versts.

2 The second named Stupino Carowool, distant from the first 50 versts.

3 The third called Polooy Carowool, is 120 versts distant from the second.

4 The fourth named Keezeyur Carawool, is 50 versts distant from the third.

5 The fift named Ichkebre, is 30 versts distant from the fourth, and from Ichkebre to Astracan is 30 versts.

[Sidenote: Astracan.] The 16 of October they arriued at Astracan, with their three stroogs in saftie about nine of the clock in the morning, where they found the ship prouided for the Persia voyage in good order and readinesse. [Sidenote: Peter Garrard.] The 17 day the foure principal factors of the company, Arthur Edwards, William Turnbull, Matthew Talbois, and Peter Garrard, were inuited to dine with the chiefe diake or secretary of Astracan (Vasili Pheodorouich Shelepin) who declared vnto them the troubles that were in Media and Persia: and how the Turke with helpe of the Crims had conquered, and did possesse the greatest part of Media: also he laid before them that Winter was at hand, and if they should put out with their ship to the sea, they should bee constrained to take what hazards might happen them by wintring in the parts of Media, or els where, for backe againe to that place there was no hope for them to returne: whereupon the said factors determined to stay there all Winter to learne farther of the state of those countreis.

[Sidenote: Ice at Astracan for foure moneths.] The 19 of Nouember the winde being Northerly, there was a great frost, and much ice in the riuer: the next day being the 20 of Nouember the ice stood in the riuer, and so continued vntill Easter day.

The 22 December departed this life Iohn Moore the gunner of the ship.

[Sidenote: Anno 1580.] Thursday the 7 of Ianuary betweene 8. and 9. of the clocke at night there appeared a crosse proceeding from the moone, with two galles at the South and North end thereof.

The 6. of Ianuary being Twelfe day (which they call Chreshenia) the Russes of Astracan brake a hole in the ice vpon the riuer Volga, and hallowed the water with great solemnity according to the maner of their countrey, at which time all the souldiers of the towne shot off their smal pieces vpon the ice, and likewise to gratifie the captaine of the castel being a Duke, whose name is Pheodor Michalouich Troiocouria, who stood hard by the ship, beholding them as they were on the riuer, was shot off all the ordinance of our ship being 15. pieces, viz. 2. faulcons, 2. faulconers, 4. fowlers, 4. fowlers chambers, and 3. other small pieces made for the stroogs to shoote hailestones, and afterwards the great ordinance of the castle was shot off.

On the 31. of Ianuary there happened a great eclipse of the moone, which began about 12 of the clock at night, and continued before she was cleare an houre and a halfe by estimation, which ended the first of February about halfe an houre past one in the morning: she was wholly darkned by the space of halfe an houre.

The 26. of February the towne of Nagay Tartars, called the Yourt, which is within 3. quarters of a mile of the castle of Astracan, by casualty was set on fire about 10. of the clock at night, and continued burning til midnight, whereby one halfe of it was burnt, and much cattell destroyed. The Nagayes that inhabite that towne, are the Emperour of Russia his vassals: It is supposed there are of them inhabiting that place of men, women, and children, the number of seuen thousand. That night the Allarum was made in the castle and towne of Astracan. The captaine thereof had all his souldiers in very good order and readinesse, being of them in number two thousand gunners and cassaks, that is to say, a thousand gunners which are accounted meere souldiers, and are not put to any other seruice then the vse of their pieces, watch, &c. as souldiers which alwaies keepe the castle, and the cassaks also vsing their pieces, do keepe the towne, and are commonly set to all kind of labours.

The 7. of March 1580. the Nagayes and Crims came before Astracan to the number of one thousand foure hundred horsemen, which incamped round about, but the nearest of them were two Russe versts and a halfe off from the castle and town: some of them lay on the Crims side of Volga, and some on the Nagay side, but none of them came vpon the Island that Astracan standeth on. [Sidenote: Astracan situate vpon an Island.] It was said that two of the prince of the Crims his sonnes were amongst them. They sent a messenger on the eight day to the captain of Astracan, to signifie that they would come and visit him: who answered, he was ready to receiue them: and taking a great shot or bullet in his hand, willed the messenger to tel them that they should not want of that geare, so long as it would last. The ninth day newes was brought that the Crims determined to assault the towne or castle, and were making of fagots of reede, to bring with them for that purpose. The tenth day two Russes that were captiues, and two of the Tartars bondmen ranne away from the Nagayes, and came into Astracan. The same day word was brought to the Duke of two Nagayes which were seene at Gostine house, supposed to be spies, but were gone againe from thence before they were suspected. This Gostine house is a place a little without the towne where the Tisiks (or Persian merchants) do vsually remaine with their merchandize. The 11. day the said Nagayes, and one more with them, came againe to that house earely in the morning, where they were taken by the Russes, and brought to the captaine of the castle, and being examined, confessed that their coming was onely to seeke two of their bondmen that were runne from them: whereupon their bondmen were deliuered to them: which fauour the said captaine comonly sheweth if they be not Russies, and they were set at libertie. The 13. day they brake vp their camps, and marched to the Northwards into the countrey of Nagay.

[Sidenote: The variation of the compass in Astracan was 13. deg. 40. minutes.] The 16. of April the variation of the compasse obserued in Astracan was 13. deg. 40. min. from North to West. This spring there came newes to Astracan that the queene of Persia (the king being blind) had bene with a great army against the Turks that were left to possesse Media, and had giuen them a great ouerthrow: yet notwithstanding Derbent, and the greatest part of Media were still possessed and kept by the Turks. The factors of the company consulting vpon their affayres, determined to leaue at Astracan the one halfe of their goods with Arthur Edwards, and with the other halfe the other three factors would proceed in the ship on their proposed voyage to the coast of Media, to see what might be done there: where, if they could not find safe traffike, they determined to proceed to the coast of Gilan, which is a prouince nere the Caspian sea bordering, vpon Persia: and thereupon appointed the said goods to be laden aboord the ship, and tooke into her also some merchandize of Tisiks or Persian.

The 29. of April Amos Rial, and Anthony Marsh, the companies' seruants were sent from Astracan by the said factors, vp the riuer Volga to Yeraslaue, with letters of aduise to be sent for England, and had order for staying the goods in Russia that should come that yeere out of England for mainteining the trade purposed for Persia, vntill further triall were made what might be done in those parts.

[Sidenote: May.] The first day of May in the morning, hauing the shippe in readinesse to depart, the factors inuited the duke Pheodor Micalouich Proicoorow, and the principall secretary Vasili Pheodorouich Shelepin, with other of the chiefes about the duke to a banket aboord the ship, where they were interteined to their good liking, and at their departure was shot off all the ordinance of the ship, and about nine of the clocke at night the same day they weyed anker, and departed, with their ship from Astracan, and being but little winde, towed her with the boat about three versts, and then ankered, hauing with them a pauos or lighter to helpe them at the flats. The second day at foure of the clocke in the morning they weyed and plyed downe the riuer Volga toward the Caspian sea. [Sidenote: Vchoog.] The seuenth of May in the morning they passed by a tree that standeth on the left hand of the riuer as they went downe, which is called Mahomet Agatch, or Mahomets tree, and about three versts further, that is to say, to the Southwards of the said tree is a place called Vchoog, that is too say, the Russe weare: (but Ochoog is the name of a weare in the Tartar tongue) where are certain cotages, and the Emperour hath lying at that place certaine gunners to gard his fishermen that keepe the weare. This Vchoog is counted from Astracan 60. versts: they proceeded downe the said riuer without staying at the Vchoog. [Sidenote: Shoald water.] The ninth and tenth dayes they met with shoald water, and were forced to lighten their ship by the pauos: the 11. day they sent backe to the Vchoog for an other pauos: This day by mischance the shippe was bilged on the grapnell of the pauos, whereby the company had sustained great losses, if the chiefest part of their goods had not bene layde into the pauos: for notwithstanding their pumping with 3. pumps, heauing out water with buckets, and all the best shifts they could make, the shippe was halfe full of water ere the leake could be found and stopt The 12. day the pauos came to them from the Vchoog, whereby they lighted the shippe of all the goods. [Sidenote: Flats.] The 13. day in the morning there came to them a small boat, sent by the captaine of Astracan, to learne whether the shippe were at sea cleare of the flats. The 15. day by great industry and trauell they got their ship cleere off the shoals and flats, wherewith they had beene troubled from the ninth day vntill then: they were forced to passe their shippe in three foot water or lesse. [Sidenote: Chetera Bougori.] The 16. day they came to the Chetera Bougori, or Island of Foure Hillocks, which are counted forty versts from Vchoog, and are the furthest land towards the sea. [Sidenote: The Caspian Sea.] The 17. day they bare off into the sea, and being about twelue versts from the Foure hillocks, riding in fiue foot and a halfe water about eleuen of the clocke in the forenoone, they tooke their goods out of the pauoses into the shippe, and filled their shippe with all things necessary. [Sidenote: 45. degrees 20. minutes. The first obseruation in the Caspian Sea.] The 18. day in the morning about seuen of the clock, the pauoses being discharged departed away towards Astracan, the winde then at Southeast, they rode still with the shippe, and obseruing the eleuation of the pole at that place, found it to be 45. degrees 20. minutes. The 19. day, the wind Southeast, they rode still. The 20. day the winde at Northwest they set saile about one of the clocke in the morning, and stered thence South by West, and Southsouthwest about 3. leagues, and then ankered in 6. foot and a halfe water, about nine of the clocke before noone, at which time it fell calme: the eleuation of the pole at that place 45. degrees 13. minuts. The 21. hauing the winde at Northwest, they set saile, and stered thence South by West, and South vntil eleuen of the clocke, and had then nine foote water: and at noone they obserued the latitude, and found it to be 44. degrees 47. minuts: then had they three fathoms and a halfe water, being cleare of the flats. It is counted from the Foure hillocks to the sea about fiftie versts. [Sidenote: Brackish water farre within the sea.] From the said noonetide vntil foure of the clocke they sayled South by East fiue leagues and a halfe: then had they fiue fathoms and a halfe and brackish water: from that till twelue at night they sayled South by East halfe a league, East tenne leagues: then had they eleuen fathome, and the water salter. From that till the 22. day three of the clocke in the morning they sayled three and fifty leagues, then had they sixtene fathome water: [Sidenote: 43. degrees 15. minuts.] from thence they sayled vntil noone South and by West seuen leagues and a halfe, the latitude then obserued 43. degrees 15. minuts, the depth then eight and twentie fathoms, and shallow ground: from that vntill eight of the clocke at night, they sayled South by East fiue leagues and a halfe, then had they three and fortie fathoms shallow ground. From thence till the 23, foure a clocke in the morning, they sayled Southsouthwest three leagues and a halfe: then could they get no ground in two and fiftie fathoms deepe. From thence vntil noone they sayled South nine leagues, then the latitude obserued was 42. degrees 20. minuts. [Sidenote: 41. degrees 32. minuts.] From that till the 24. day at noone they sayled South by West seuenteen leagues and a halfe, then the latitude obserued was 41. degrees 32 minuts. From noone till seuen of the clocke at night, they sailed Southsouthwest foure leagues, then had they perfect sight of high land or hilles, which were almost couered with snow, and the mids of them were West from the ship, being then about twelue leagues from the nearest land: they sounded but could finde no ground in two hundred fathoms. [Sidenote: 40. degrees 54. minuts.] From thence they sayled Southwest vntil midnight: about three leagues from thence till the 25. day foure of the clocke in the morning, they sayled West three leagues, being then litle winde, and neere the land, they tooke in their sayles, and lay hulling: at noone the latitude obserued, was 40. degrees 54. minuts: they sounded but could get no ground in two hundred fathoms. At four of the clocke in the afternoone, the winde Northwest, they set their sailes, and from thence till the 26. day at noone they sailed East southeast foure leagues. From thence they sailed till eight of the clocke at night Southwest three leagues, the winde then at North. From thence they sailed vntill the 27. day two of the clocke in the morning, Westsouthwest eight leagues, the winde blowing at North very much. From the sayd two til foure of the clocke they sailed South by West one league: then being day light, they saw the land plaine, which was not past three leagues from them, being very high ragged land. [Sidenote: Bilbill.] There were certaine rocks that lay farre off into the sea, about fiue leagues from the same land, (which are called Barmake Tash) they sayled betweene those rocks, and the land, and about fiue of the clocke they passed by the port Bilbill, where they should haue put in but could not: and bearing longst the shoare about two of the clocke afternoone, they came to Bildih in the countrey of Media or Sheruan, against which place they ankered in 9. foot water. Presently after they were at anker, there came aboord of them a boat, wherein were seuen or eight persons, two Turks, the rest Persians, the Turkes vassals, which bade them welcome, and seemed to be glad of their arriuall, who told the factors that the Turke had conquered all Media, or the countrey Sheruan, and how that the Turks Basha remained in Derbent with a garrison of Turkes, and that Shamaky was wholly spoyled, and had few or no inhabitants left in it. [Sidenote: Bachu port.] The factours then being desirous to come to the speech of the Basha, sent one of the Tisikes (or merchants that, went ouer with them from Astracan, passingers) and one of the companies seruants Robert Golding, with those souldiours, to the captaine of Bachu, which place standeth hard by the sea, to certifie him of their arriuall, and what commodities they had brought, and to desire friendshippe to haue quiet and safe traffike for the same. Bachu is from Bildih, the place where they road, about a dayes iourney, on foote easily to be trauelled, which may be sixe leagues, the next way ouer land; it is a walled towne, and strongly fortified. When the sayd messenger came to the captaine of Bachu, the said captaine gaue him very friendly entertainment, and after he vnderstood what they were that were come in the shippe, and what they had brought, he seemed to reioyce much thereat: who gaue the said Golding liccence to depart backe the next day, being the eight and twentieth day: and promised that he would himselfe come to the shippe the next day following: with which answere the said Golding returned and came to the ship the sayd eight and twentieth day about nine of the clocke at night. The nine and twentieth day in the morning the factours caused a tent to be set vp at shoare neare the shippe, against the comming of the sayd captaine: who came thither about three of the clock after noone, and brought about thirtie souldiers, that attended on him in shirts of male, and some of them had gauntlets of siluer, others of steele, and very faire. The factors met him at their tent, and after very friendly salutations passed betweene them, they gaue him for a present a garment of cloth of veluet, and another of scarlet, who accepted the offer gratefully. After they had talked together by their interpretors, as well of the state of the voyage and cause of their coming thither, as also learned of the sayde captaine the state of that countrey, the factours made request vnto him, that he would helpe them to the speech of the Basha, who answered that their demand was reasonable, and that he would willingly shew them therein what pleasure he could, and sayd, because the way to Derbent, where the Basha remayned, was dangerous, he would send thither and certifie him of their arriuall, and what commodities they had brought, and such commodities as they would desire to exchange or barter the same for he would procure the said Basha to prouide for them: and therefore willed the factors to consult together, and certifie him what they most desired, and what quantity they would haue prouided: so whilest the factors were consulting together thereupon the captaine talked with a Tisike merchant that came ouer in the ship with them from Astracan, which Tisike, among other matters in talke, certified the captaine, that the night before, the factors and their company were determined to haue returned backe againe to Astracan, and that they were about to wey their ankers, which indeed was true, [Sidenote: Thomas Hudson of Limehouse, maister of the English barke.] but the maister of the barke Thomas Hudson of Limehouse perswaded them that the wind was not good for them to depart, &c. When the factors came againe to talke with the captaine, they desired to goe to the Basha, and that he would safely conduct them thither: he granted their requests willingly, desiring them to goe with him to a village hard by, and there to abide with him that night, and the next day they should go to Bachu, and from thence to proceede on their iourney to Derbent. They were vnwilling to go that night with him, because their prouision for the way was not in readinesse, but requested that they might stay til the morning. [Sidenote: M. Christopher Burrough.] Thereupon the captaine sayd it was reported vnto him, that they ment the night before to haue gone away: and if it should so happen, he were in great danger of losing his head: for which cause he requested to haue some one for a pledge: wherefore M. Garrard one of the factors offered himselfe to go, who, because he could not speake the Russe tongue tooke with him Christopher Burrough, and a Russe interpretour: that night they road from the seaside, to a village about ten miles off, where at supper time the captaine had much talke with M. Garrard of our countrey, demanding where about it did lie, what countreys were neare vnto it, and with whom we had traffike, for by the Russe name of our countrey he could not coniecture who we should be: but when by the situation he perceiued we were Englishmen, he demanded if our prince were a mayden Queene: which when he was certified of, then (quoth he) your land is called Enghilterra, is it not? answere was made, it was so: whereof he was very glad, when he knew the certainety. He made very much of them, placing M. Garrard next to himselfe, and Christopher Burrough, with the Russie interpretour for the Turkie tongue hard by. There was a Gillan merchant with him at that present, of whom he seemed to make great account: him he placed next to himselfe on the other side, and his gentlemen sate round about him talking together. Their sitting is vpon the heeles, or crosse legged.

Supper being brought in, he requested them to eate. After their potage (which was made of rice) was done, and likewise their boyled meat, there came in platters of rice sodden thicke, and hony mingled with all: after all which, came a sheepe roasted whole, which was brought in a tray, and set before the captaine: he called one of his seruitors, who cut it in pieces, and laying thereof vpon diuers platters, set the same before the captaine: then the captaine gaue to M. Garrard and his company one platter, and to his gentlemen another, and to them which could not well reach he cast meat from the platters which were before him. Diuers questions he had with M. Garrard and Christopher Burrough at supper time, about their diet, inquiring whether they eat fish or flesh voluntarily or by order. Their drinke in those partes is nothing but water. After supper (walking in the garden) the captaine demanded of M. Garrard, whether the vse was in England to lie in the house or in the garden, and which he had best liking of: he answered, where it pleased him, but their vse was to lie in houses: whereupon the captaine caused beds to be sent into the house for them, and caused his kinsman to attend on them in the night, if they chanced to want anything: he hinselfe with his gentlemen and souldiers lying in the garden.

In the morning very early he sent horse for the rest of the company which should go to Derbent, sending by them that went tenne sheepe for the shippe. In that village there was a stoue, into which the captaine went in the morning, requesting M. Garrard to go also to the same to wash himselfe, which he did. Shortly after their comming out of the Stoue, whilest they were at breakfast, M. Turnbull, M. Tailboyes, and Thomas Hudson the M. of the shippe, came thither, and when they had all broken their fasts, they went to Bachu: but Christopher Burrough returned to the ship, for that he had hurt his leg, and could not well endure that trauell. And from Bachu they proceeded towards Derbent, as it was by the captaine promised, being accompanied on their way for their safe conduct, with a gentleman, and certaine souldiers, which had the captaine of Bachu his letters to the Basha of Derbent, very friendly written in their behalfe. [Sidenote: The receiuing of the English into Derbent.] In their iourney to Derbent they forsooke the ordinarie wayes, being very dangerous, and trauelled thorow woods till they came almost to the towne of Derbent: and then the gentleman road before with the captaines letters to the Basha, to certifie him of the English merchants comming, who receiuing the letters and vnderstanding the matter, was very glad of the newes, and sent forth to receiue them certaine souldiours gunners, who met them about two miles out of the towne, saluting them with great reuerence, and afterwardes road before them: then againe met them other souldiours, somewhat neerer the castle, which likewise hauing done their salutations road before them, and then came foorth noble men, captaines, and gentlemen, to receiue them into the castle and towne. As they entered the castle, there was a shot of twentie pieces of great ordinance, and the Basha sent M. Turnbull a very faire horse with furniture to mount on, esteemed to be worth an hundred markes, and so they were conueyed to his presence: who after he had talked with them, sent for a coate of cloth of golde, and caused it to be put on M. Turnbulles backe and then willed them all to depart, and take their ease, for that they were wearie of their iourney, and on the morrow he would talke further with them. The next day when the factors came againe to the presence of the Basha according to his appointment, they requested him that he would grant them his priuilege, whereby they might traffike safely in any part and place of his countrey, offering him, that if it pleased his Maiestie to haue any of the commodities that they had brought, and to write his mind thereof to the captaine of Bachu, it should be deliuered him accordingly. The Bashaes answer was, that he would willingly giue them his priuilege: yet for that he regarded their safetie, hauing come so farre, and knowing the state of his countrey to be troublesome, he would haue them to bring their commodity thither, and there to make sale of it, promising he would prouide such commodities as they needed, and that he would be a defence vnto them, so that, they should not be iniured by any: wherupon the factors sent Thomas Hudson backe for the ship to bring her to Derbent, and the Basha sent a gentleman with him to the captaine of Bachu, to certifie him what was determined, which message being done, the captaine of Bachu, and the Bashaes messenger, accompanied with a doozen souldiours, went from Bachu with Thomas Hudson, and came to the ship at Bildih the 11 day of Iune. [Sidenote: The latitude of Bildih 40. deg. 25. min. The variation of the compas 10. deg. 40. min.] After the captaine and his men had beene aboord and seene the ship, they all departed presently, but the gentleman, messenger from the Basha, with three other Turks, remained aboord, and continued in the ship till she came to Derbent: the latitude of Bildih by diuers obseruations is 40. degrees 25 minuts: the variation of the compasse 10. degrees 40 minuts from North to West. After the returne of Thomas Hudson backe to Bildih, they were constrayned to remaine there with the shippe through contrary windes vntill the 16. day of Iune foure of the clocke in the morning, at which time they weyed anker, set saile and departed thence towards Derbent, and arriued at anker against Derbent East and by South from the sayd castle in foure fathome and a halfe water, the 22. day of Iune at ten of the clocke in the morning: then they tooke vp their ordinance, which before they had stowed in hold for easing the shippe in her rowling. In the afternoone the Basha came downe to the waterside against the shippe, and hauing the said ordinance placed, and charged, it was all shotte off to gratifie him: and presently after his departure backe, he permitted the factors to come aboord the shippe. The 29. day their goodes were vnladen and carried to the Bashaes garden, where he made choyce of such things as he liked, taking for custome of euery fiue and twenty karsies, or whatsoeuer, one, or after the rate of foure for the hundred. The factors after his choyce made, determined to send a part of the rest of the goods to Bachu, for the speedier making sale thereof, for which cause they obteyned the Bashaes letter to the captaine of Bachu, written very fauourably in their behoofe: and thereupon was laden and sent in a small boat of that countrey in merchandize, to the value (very neere) of one thousand pound sterling: videlicet, one hundred pieces of karsies, seuen broad clothes, two barrels of cochenelio, two barrels of tinne, foure barrels of shaffe. There went with the same of the companies seruants William Wincle, Robert Golding, and

Richard Relfe, with two Russies, whereof one was an interpretor, besides foure barkemen. They departed from Dertent with the saide barke the 19. of Iuly, and arriued at Bildih the 25. day: their passage and carriage of their goods to Bachu was chargeable, although their sales when they came thither were small: they had great friendship shewed them of the captaine of Bachu, as well for the Bashaes letter, as also for the factors sakes, who had dealt friendly with him, as before is declared. Robert Golding desirous to vnderstand what might be done at Shamaky, which is a dayes iourney from Bachu, went thither, from whence returning, he was set on by theeues, and was shot into the knee with an arrow, who had very hardly escaped with his life and goods, but that by good hap he killed one of the theeues horses with his caliuer, and shot a Turke thorow both cheeks with a dag. [Sidenote: Zere Island.] On the sixt day of August the factors being aduertised at Derbent that their ship was so rotten and weake, that it was doubtfull she would not cary them backe to Astracan, did thereupon agree and bargen at that place with an Armenian, whose name was Iacob, for a barke called a Busse, being of burden about 35. tunnes which came that yere from Astracan, and was at that instant riding at an island called Zere, about three or foure leagues beyond or to the Eastwardes of Bildih, which barke for their more safety, they ment to haue with them in their return to Astracan, and thereupon wrote vnto Wincoll and the rest at Bachu, that they should receiue the same Busse, and lade in her their goods at Bildih to be returned to Derbent, and to discharge their first boate, which was obserued by them accordingly. [Sidenote: The English suffer shipwracke.] When all their goods were laden aboord the sayd Busse at Bildih, and being ready to haue departed thence for Derbent, there arose a great storme with the winde out of the sea, by force whereof the cables and halsers were broken, and their vessell put a shoare, and broken to pieces against the rockes: euery of them that were in her saued their liues, and part of the goods. But there was a Carobia or cheste, wherein were dollars, and golde, which they had receiued for the commodities, of the company, which they sold at Bachu, which at the taking out of the Busse, fell by the Barkes side into the water amongst the rockes, and so was lost. The packes of cloth which they could not well take out of the Busse were also lost, other things that were more profitable they saued.

The 18. of August, the Factors receiued from the Basha 500. Batmans of raw silke, parcell of the bargaine made with him, who bade them come the next day for the rest of the bargaine.

The 19. day the Factors went to the Basha according to his appointment, but that day they could not speake with him, but it was deliuered them as from him, that they should looke and consider whether any thing were due vnto him or not, which grieued the Factors: and thereupon M. Turnebull answered, that their heads and all that they had were at the Bashaes pleasure: But then it was answered there was no such matter in it: but that they should cast vp their reckonings, to see how it stood betweene them. The 20. day they cast vp their reckonings. The 21. they went to haue spoken with the Basha, but were denied audience.

[Sidenote: Arthur Edwards died at Astracan.] The 22. day they heard newes by a Busse that came from Astracan, that Arthur Edwards (whom the Factors left at Astracan with the moietie of the goods) was dead, who departed this life [Footnote: Left blank in Original.] of …

[Sidenote: September.] The 23. day the Factors receiued more from the Bacha 500. Batmans of silke. The 4. of September newes was brought to Derbent, that Golding comming from Shamaky was set on by theeues (Turkes) and had hurt one of them.

The 5. Tobias Atkins the gunners boy died of the fluxe, who was buried the 6. day 2. miles to the Southward of the Castle of Derbent, where the Armenian Christians do vsually bury their dead. About the 20 of September newes came to Derbent, that the Busse which they had bought of Iacob the Armenian as before, was cast away at Bildih, but they receiued no certaine newes in writing from any of our people.

The 26. of September was laden aboord the ship 40. bales of silke. From the 26. til the 2. of October, they tooke into the ship, bread, water, and other necessary prouision for their sea store: the said 2. day of October, the Factors were commanded vpon the suddaine to auoide their house, and get them with their prouision out of the towne: Whereupon they were constrained to remoue and carry their things to the sea side against the ship, and remained there all the night. The cause of this sudden auoyding them out of the towne (as afterwards they perceiued) was for that the Basha had receiued newes of a supplie with treasure that the Turke had sent, which was then neare at hand comming toward him.

The 3. day of October all things were brought from the shoare aboord the ship: and that day the Factors went to the Basha to take their leaue of him, vnto whom they recommended those the Companies seruants, &c. which they had sent to Bachu, making accompt to leaue them behinde in the Countrey: who caused their names to be written, and promised they should want nothing, nor be iniured of any. After this leaue taken, the Factors went aboord purposing presently to haue set saile and departed towards Astracan, the winde seruing well for that purpose at South Southeast: [Sidenote: The Armenian village.] And as they were readie to set saile, there came against the ship a man, who weued: whereupon the boate was sent a shoare to him, who was an Armenian sent from William Wincoll, with his writing tables, wherein the said Wincoll had written briefly, the mishap of the losse of the Busse, and that they were comming from Bildih towardes Derbent, they, and such things as they saued with a small boate, forced to put a shoare in a place by the sea side called the Armenian village: Where upon the Factors caused the shippe to stay, hoping that with the Southerly winde that then blew, they would come from the place they were at to the ship, but if they could not come with that winde, they ment to saile with the shippe, with the next wind that would serue them, against the place where they were, and take them in, if they could: which stay and losse of those Southerly windes, was a cause of great troubles, that they afterwardes sustained through yce, &c. entering the Volga as shalbe declared.

The 4. day the winde South Southeast, the shippe rode still: This day Christopher Burrow was sent to shore to Derbent to prouide some necessaries for the voyage, and with him a Tisike or two, which should goe in the shippe passengers to Astracan. [Sidenote: The Turke his treasure sent to Derbent.] And being on shoare he saw there the comming in of the Turkes treasure, being accompanied with 200. souldiers, and one hundreth pioners, besides Captaines and Gentlemen: the Basha with his captaines and souldiers very gallantly apparelled and furnished went out from Derbent about three or foure miles, to meete the said treasure, and receiued the same with great ioy and triumph. Treasure was the chiefe thing they needed, for not long before the souldiers were readie to breake into the Court against the Basha for their pay: there was a great mutinie amongst them, because hee had long differed and not payed them their due. The treasure came in seuen wagons, and with it were brought tenne pieces of brasse.

In the parts of Media where they were, there was no commoditie to be bought of any value, but raw silke, neither was that to be had but at the Bashaes hands: who shortly after their comming thither taxed the Countrey for that commoditie. His dealing with our Merchants as it was not with equitie in all points according to his bargaine, so it was not extreme ill. Of the commodities they carried hee tooke the chiefest part, for which he gaue but a small price in respect of the value it was there worth, and because he had prouided such quantitie of commoditie for them, which otherwise they could not haue had, the Countrey being so troublesome, and trauaile by land so dangerous, he vsed them at his pleasure.

The newes that was reported vnto them at Astracan touching the warres betweene the Turkes and Persians differed litle from the truth: for the Turkes armie with the aide of the Crims, (being in number by the information of two Spaniards that serued in those wars, about 200000) inuaded and conquered the Countrey of Media in Anno 1577. [Sidenote: Osman Basha.] When the great Turke vnderstood of the conquest, he appointed Osman Basha (the said Basha, and now Captaine of Derbent) gouernour of the whole Countrey, who settled himselfe in Shamaky the chiefe Citie of Media, and principall place of traffike, vnto whom was sent from the great Turke, in signification of the gratefull acceptation of his seruice and the great conquest, a sword of great value.

After the said Basha had brought the Countrey in order to his liking, and placed garrisons where he thought conuenient, the armie was dissolued and sent backe; when the Persians vnderstood that the Turkes armie was dissolued and returned, they gathered a power together, and with the Queene of their Countrey as chiefe, they entred the Countrey of Media, and ouerranne the same with fire and sword, destroying whatsoeuer they found, as well people, cattell, as whatsoeuer els, that might be commodious to the Turkes. And after they had so ouerrunne the Countrey, they came to Shamaky, where the said Basha Lieutenant generall of the great Turke was settled, and besieged it: whereupon the Basha seeing hee could not long indure to withstande them, fled thence to Derbent where he now remaineth.

[Sidenote: Derbent built by Alexander the great.] Derbent is a strong Castle which was built by Alexander the great, the situation whereof is such that the Persians being without ordinance, are not able to winne it but by famine. When the Turkes were fled from Shamaky, the Persians entred the same and spoyled it, leauing therein neither liuing creature nor any commoditie, and so returned backe into Persia, and setled themselues about Teueris, where there grewe some question among them for the kingdome. Afterwards the Persians hauing intelligence of an armie from the Turke comming into Media, gathered themselues together in a great armie and encountring the said Turkes, set vpon them on the sudden, and vanquished them, putting them all to the sword. This ouerthrow of the Turkes grieued the Basha of Derbent, and made him to haue the more care for his own safetie. Moreouer, newes was brought vnto him that the Kisel Bashaes, (that is to say the nobles and Gentlemen of Persia) were minded to set vpon him, and that neere vnto Bachu there lay an army ready to besiege it. Whereupon the Basha oftentimes would ride about the Castle of Derbent viewing the same, and the springs that did come to it, and where he saw any cause of reformation it was amended.

[Sidenote: The latitude of Derbent 41. deg. 52. min. The variation of the compasse.] The latitude of Derbent (by diuers obseruations exactly there made) is 41. deg 52. min. The variation of the Compasse at that place about 11. degrees from North to West. From Derbent to Bildih by land 46. leagues. From Shamaky to Bachu about 10. leagues which may be 30. miles. From Bachu to Bildih fiue or sixe leagues by land, but by water about 12. leagues. From the Castle Derbent Eastwards, there reach two stone wals to the border of the Caspian sea, which is distant one English mile. Those walls are 9. foote thicke, and 28. or 30. foote high, and the space betweene them is 160. Geometricall paces, that is 800. foot. There are yet to be perceiued of the ruine of those wals, which do now extend, into the sea about halfe a mile: also from the castle Westward into the land, they did perceiue the ruines of a stone wall to extend, which wal, as it is reported, did passe from thence to Pontus Euxinus, and was built by Alexander the great when the Castle Derbent was made.

The 5 of October about noone the winde Northnortheast they wayed ancre, and set saile from Derbent, being alongst the coast to the Southwards to seeke their men: but as they had sailed about foure leagues the winde scanted Easterly, so that they were forced to ancre in three fathom water.

The 6 day they wayed ancre, and bare further off into the sea, where they ancred in seuen fathom water, the ship being very leake, and so rotten abaft the maine mast, that a man with his nailes might scrape thorow her side.

The 7 day about 7 of the clocke in the morning, they set saile, the winde Southwest. They considered the time of the yere was far spent, the ship weake, leake and rotten, and therefore determining not to tarry any longer for Wincoll and his fellowes, but to leaue them behinde, bent themselues directly towards Astracan: and sailing Northnortheast vntill midnight about 16 leagues, the winde then came to the Northnorthwest, and blew much, a very storme, which caused them to take in their sailes, sauing the fore corse, with which they were forced to steere before the sea, South by West, and Southsouthwest. And on the 8 day about two of the clocke in the morning their great boat sunke at the ships sterne, which they were forced to cut from the ship to their great griefe and discomfort: for in her they hoped to saue their liues if the ship should haue miscaried. [Sidenote: Nezauoo.] About 10 of the clocke before noone they had sight of the land about 5 leagues to the South of Derbent, and bare longst the coast to the Southeastwards vnto Nezauoo, where they came at ancre in three fathoms, and black oze, good ancre holde, whereof they were glad, as also that the winde was shifted to the Northwest, and but a meane gale. Wincoll and the rest of his fellowes being in the Armenian village, which is about 18 versts to the Westwards of Nezauoo, the place where against they rode at ancre, saw the ship as she passed by that place, and sent a man in the night following alongst the coast after her, who came against the ship where she rode, and with a firebrand in the top of a tree made signes, which was perceiued by them in the shippe, whereupon they hoisted out their skiffe, and sent her ashore to learne what was meant by the fire: which returned a letter from Wincoll, wherein he wrote that they were with such goods as they had at the Armenian village, and prayed that there they might with the same goods be taken into the ships. The 9 day it was litle winde, they wayed and bare a little farther off into the sea towards the said village, and ancred. The 10 day they sent their skiffe to the Armenian village to fetch those men and the goods they had, with order that if the winde serued, that they could not returne to fetch the ship, they of the ship promised to come for them, against the said village. This day it was calme.

The 11 day the winde Northwest they rode still. The 12 day the winde Southeast they wayed ancre, and bare against and nere to the Armenian village where they ancred, and then the skiffe came aboord and tolde them that our people at shore were like to be spoiled of the Tartars, were it not that the gunners defended them: then was the skiffe sent backe againe to charge them at any hand they should hasten aboord the ship whatsoeuer it cost them. Whereupon, all the company came aboord the same day sauing Richard Relfe and two Russes, but as soone as the skiffe was returned aboord the ship, the winde blew at Southeast, and the sea was growen, so as they were forced to take in their skiffe into the ship, and rode stil till the 13 day, [Sidenote: Two Spaniards deliuered by our Englishmen.] and then being faire weather, early in the morning the skiffe was hoisted out of the ship, and sent to shore to fetch the said Relfe and the two Russes, which were ready at the shore side, and with them two Spaniards that were taken captiues at the Goletta in Barbary, which serued the Turke as souldiers. Those Spaniards (of Christian charity) they brought also aboord the ship to redeeme them from their captiuity, which were brought ouer into England, and set free and at liberty here in London, in September 1581. The winde this day at Northnortheast, faire weather. The 14 day they sent the skiffe to shore, and filled fresh water. The 15 day they rode still, being litle winde and fog. The 16 day the winde Eastsoutheast, they wayed ancre and set saile, bearing Northwards towards Astracan, and the same night they ancred in ten fathoms water, about fiue miles from the shore of the Shalkaules countrey, which place is eight leagues Northnorthwest from Derbent. The 17 day the winde at North very stormy, they rode still all that day and night. The 18 the winde all Southeast about one of the clocke afternoone, they wayed ancre, and sailed thence till foure of the clocke Northnortheast sixe leagues, then they might see the land Northwest about tenne leagues from the winde Southeast: from thence they sailed til midnight Northnortheast twelue leagues. From thence till the 19 day seuen a clocke in the morning they sailed Northnortheast eight leagues: the winde then Eastsoutheast, a faire gale, they sounded and had 17 fathoms, and sand, being (as the Master iudged) about the head of Shetley: from thence till 12 of the clocke at noone they sailed North 5 leagues, the winde then at East a faire gale, they sounded and had 5 fathoms. From thence till eight of the clocke at night, they sailed North 7 leagues, the winde then at Northeast with small raine, they tooke in their sailes, and ancred in 3 fathoms water and soft oze, where they rode still all night, and the 20 day and night the winde Northeast, as before with small raine.

The 21 day the winde Northwest, they likewise rode still. The 22 day about 3 of the clocke in the afternoone, they wayed ancre, the winde Westnorthwest, and sailed from thence till sixe of the clocke at night North 4 leagues, then they ancred in 2 fathoms and a halfe soft oze, the winde at West a small breath.

The 23 day about 7 of the clocke in the morning, they wayed ancre, and set saile, being litle winde Easterly, and sailed till 2 of the clocke after noone Northwest in with the shore about sixe leagues, and then ancred in 6 foot water, hauing perfect sight of the low land (sand hilles) being about 3 miles from the nerest land. This place of the land that they were against, they perceiued to be to the Westwards of the 4 Islands (called in the Russe tongue Chetera Bougori) and they found it afterwards by due proofe, to be about 50 versts, or 30 English miles to the Southwest, or Southwest by South, from the sayd Chetera Bougori.

The 24 day the winde at East, and by South, a Sea winde called Gillauar, caused them to ride still. The 25 day they thought good to send in their skiffe Robert Golding, and certaine Russes, to row him alongst Northwards by the shore, to seeke the foure Islands, and so to passe vnto the Vchooge, and there to land the sayd Robert Golding to proceed to Astracan, to deliuer Amos Riall a letter, wherein he was required to prouide Pauoses to meet the shippe at the sayd Islands, and the skiffe with the Russes were appointed to returne from the Vchooge with victuals to the shippe, which skiffe departed from the shippe about nine of the clocke in the forenoone. The 26, 27, 28, and 29 dayes, the windes Easterly and Northeast, they rode still with their ship. The 30 day the winde Southeast, they wayed, and set saile to the Northeastwards: but the ship fell so on the side to the shorewards, that they were forced eftsoones to take in their saile, and ancre againe, from whence they neuer remoued her. [Sidenote: A strange accident of prouision for their reliefe.] That day they shared their bread: but in their want God sent them two couies of partridges, that came from the shore, and lighted in and about their ships, whereby they were comforted, and one that lay sicke, of whose life was small hope, recouered his health.

[Sidenote: Nouember.] The 4 of Nouember the skiffe returned to the ship with some victuals, and certified that the foure Islands were about 60 versts from them to the Northeastwards. When Robert Golding came to Astracan, and deliuered there the Factors letters to Amos Rial, the duke, captaine of that place, was done to vnderstand of the ships arriuall, and of the state they were in, and their request for Pauoses, who was very glad to heare of their safe returne, and appointed to be sent with all speed two

Pauoses and a Stroog, with gunners to gard and defend them. With the which Stroog and Pauoses, Amos Riall went downe to the Chetera Bougori, or 4. Islands aforesayd, where he stayed with those barks, according to the Factors appointment. The 5 day they purposed to send from the ship their skiffe with the carpenter, and 4 Russes to row him to the 4 Bougories, to request Amos Riall to come from thence with the Pauoses to the shippe with all possible speed. The skiffe with those men departed from the ship in the morning, and within one houre they met with a small boat with Russes rowing towards the ship, which came from the Ouchooge with a wilde swine and other victuals, to sell: with the same boat the skiffe returned backe to the ship after the Russes had receiued and were satisfied for the victuals they brought: the same day they returned with their boat backe toward the Ouchooge, and with them in the same boat was sent the Carpenter of the shippe to the Chetera Bougori, which were in their way, to declare vnto Amos Riall the message before appointed him. From the 5 vntill the 9 day the ship rode still with contrary winds Easterly. The same 9 day came to the shippe certaine Russes in a small boat, which brought with them some victuals sent by Amos Riall, and declared that he with the Pauoses and Stroog had remained at the Chetera Bougori fiue dayes, expecting the comming thither of the ship. The 10 day being doubtfull of the Pauoses comming, they sent Thomas Hudson Master of the ship in the skiffe (and with her went the foresayd skiffe boat) towards the Chetera Bougori to the Pauoses to bring word whether they would come to the ship or not, the wind then at Northeast with fogge. The 11 day the winde Northerly with fogge, the ship rode still. The 12 day Amos Riall, Christopher Fawcet, and a new gunner came to the ship, and with them the M. Thomas Hudson returned; but the Stroog with the gunners remained at the Chetera Bougori; and from thence (when it begun to freese) returned to Astracan. Amos Riall declared that he sent the carpenter backe from the Chetera Bougori in a small boat on the 10 day, and marueiled that he was not come to the shippe (but in the fogge the day before as afterwards they learned) missed the shippe, and ouershot her, and afterwards returning backe, he found the ship at ancre, and nothing in her but the Russes that were left to keepe her, and then he departed thence, and went to the Vchooge, and there stayed. Presently vpon the comming of the Pauoses to the ship they vsed as much speed as might be, to get the goods out of the shippe into them, and after the goods were laden in, they tooke in also of the shippes ordinance, furniture and prouiston, as much as they could.

[Sidenote: Ice the 13 of Nouember in the mouth of the riuer of Volga.] The 13 day in the morning Amos Riall was sent away in a small boat towards Astracan, to prouide victuals and cariages to relieue and helpe them, who could passe no further then the foure Islands, but was there ouertaken with yce, and forced to leaue his boat, and from thence passed poste to

Astracan, finding at the Vchooge the Carpenter returned from his ill iourney, very ill handled, with the extremitie of the colde. The same day they departed also in those lighters with the goods towards the Chetera Kougori, leauing the ship at once, and in her two Russes, which with three more that went in the Pauoses, to prouide victuals for themselues and the rest, and therewith promised to returne backe to the ship with all speed, had offered to undertake for twenty rubbles in money to cary the ship into some harborow, where she might safely winter, or els to keepe her where she rode all winter which was promised to be giuen them if they did it: and the same day when with those lighters they had gotten sight of the foure Islands being about eight versts Southwest from them, the winde then at Northeast, did freese the sea so as they could not row, guide, stirre or remoue the saide lighters, but as the wind and yce did force them. [Sidenote: The 16 day.] And so they continued driuing with the yce, Southeast into the sea by the space of forty houres, and then being the sixteenth day the yce stood. Whiles they droue with the yce, the dangers which they incurred were great: for oftentimes when the yce with the force of winde did breake, pieces of it were tossed and driuen one vpon another. with great force, terrible to beholde, and the same happened at sometimes so neere vnto the lighters, that they expected it would haue ouerwhelmed them to their vtter destruction: but God who had presented them from many perils before, did also saue and deliuer them then.

Within three or foure dayes after the first standing of the yce, when it was firme and strong, they tooke out all their goods, being fourty and eight bales or packes of raw silke, &c. layde it on the yce, and couered the same with such prouisions as they had. [Sidenote: Trauaile upon the yce.] Then for want of victuals, &c they agreed to leaue all the goods there vpon the yce, and to go to the shore: and thereupon brake vp their Chests and Carobias, wherewith, and with such other things as they could get, they made sleddes for euery of them to draw vpon the yce, whereon they layed their clothes to keepe them warme, and such victuals as they had, and such other things as they might conueniently cary, and so they departed from the sayd goods and Pauoses very earely about one of the clocke in the morning, and trauailing on the yce, directed their way North, as neere as they could iudge, and the same day about two of the clocke in the afternoone, [Sidenote: Chetera Babbas.] they had sight of the Chetera Babbas (foure hillocks of Islands so called) vnto the same they directed themselues, and there remained that night.

The goods and Pauoses which they left on the yce they iudged to be from those Chetera Babbas about 20 versts.

And the next morning departed thence Eastwards, and came to the Chetera Bougories (or foure Islands before spoken of) before noone (the distance betweene those places is about 15 versts) where they remained all that night, departing thence towards Astracan: the next morning very early they lost their way through the perswasion of the Russes which were with them, taking too much towards the left hand (contrary to the opinion of M. Hudson) whereby wandering upon the yce foure dayes, not knowing whether they were entred into the Crimme Tartars land or not, at length it fortuned they met with a way that had bene trauailed, which crost backwards towards the sea: that way they tooke, and following the same, within two dayes trauaile it brought them to a place called Crasnoyare (that is to say in the English tongue) Red cliffe, which diuers of the company knew.

[Sidenote: The English ship cut in pieces with yce] There they remained that night, hauing nothing to eat but one loafe of bread, which they happened to finde with the two Russes that were left in the ship to keepe her all the Winter (as is aforesaid) whom they chanced to meet going towards Astracan, about fiue miles before they came to the sayd Crasnoyare, who certified them that the ship was cut in pieces with the yce, and that they had hard scaping with their liues.

In the morning they departed early from Crasnoyare towards the Ouchooge and about nine of the clocke before noone, being within 10 versts of the Vchooge, they met Amos Riall, with the carpenter, which he found at Ouchooge, and a gunner newly come out of England, and also 65 horses with so many Cassaks to guide them, and 50 gunners for gard, which brought prouision of vituals, &c. and were sent by the Duke to fetch the goods to Astracan. The meeting of that company was much ioy vnto them.

[Sidenote: December] The Factors sent backe with Amos Riall and the sayd company to fetch the goods, Thomas Hudson the Master, Tobias Paris his Mate, and so they the sayd Factors and their company marched on to the Vchooge, where they refreshed themselues that day, and the night following. And from thence proceeded on towards Astracan, where they arriued the last day of Nouember. These that went for the goods after their departure from the Factors trauelled the same day vntil they came within 10 versts of the Chetera Babbas, where they rested that night. The next morning by the breake of day they departed thence, and before noone were at the Chetera Babas, where they stayed all night; but presently departed thence Thomas Hudson with the Carpenter and gunner to seeke where the goods lay: who found the same, and the next day they returned backe to their company at the Chetera Babbas, and declared vnto them in what sort they had found the sayd goods.

The 3 day early in the morning they departed all from the 4 Babbas towards the said goods, and the same day did lade all the goods they could find vpon the said sleds, and with all conuenient speed returned backe towards Astracan. And when they came to the Chetera Bougori, where they rested the night, in the morning very early before the breake of day, they were assaulted by a great company of the Nagays Tartars horsemen, which came showting and hallowing with a great noise, but our people were so inuironed with the sleds, that they durst not enter vpon them, but ranne by, and shot their arrows amongst them, and hurt but one man in the head, who was a Russe, and so departed presently. Yet when it was day, they shewed themselues a good distance off from our men, being a very great troop of them, but did not assault them any more. [Sidenote: Their returne to Astracan.] The same day our men with those cariages, departed from thence towards Astracan, where they arriued in safety the 4 December, about 3 of the clocke in the afternoone, where our people greatly reioyced of their great good happe to haue escaped so many hard euents, troubles and miseries, as they did in that voyage, and had great cause therefore to praise the Almighty, who had so mercifully preserued and deliuered them. They remained the winter at Astracan, where they found great fauour and friendship of the duke, captaine, and other chiefe officers of that place: but that Winter there happened no great matter worth the noting.

[Sidenote: The breaking vp of the yce.] [Sidenote: Morgan Hubblethorne dier sent into Persia.] In the spring of the yeere 1581, about the mids of March, the yce was broken vp, and cleare gone before Astracan, and the ninth of Aprill, hauing all the goods that were returned from the parts of Media, laden into a Stroog, the Factors, William Turnebull, Matthew Tailboyes, Giles Crow, Christopher Burrough, Michael Lane, Laurence Prouse gunner, Randolfe Foxe, Tho. Hudson, Tobias Parris, Morgan Hubblethorne, the dier, Rich, the Surgean, Rob. Golding, Ioh. Smith, Edw. Reding carpenter, and William Perrin gunner hauing also 40 Russes, whereof 36 were Cassacks to row, the rest merchants passengers, departed from Astracan with the sayd Stroog and goods vp the Volga towards Yeraslaue. They left behinde them at Astracan, with the English goods and merchandise there remaining, Amos Riall, W. Wincoll, and Richard Relfe, and appointed them to sell and barter the same, or so much thereof as they could to the Tisiks, if there came any thither that spring, and to others as they might, and the rest with such as they should take in exchange to returne vp to Yeraslaue that Summer, when the Emperors carriage should passe vp the Volga. The 21 day they came with their Stroog to the Perauolok, but made no stay at that place: for they had beene much troubled with yce in their comming from Astracan. [Sidenote: May.] The 3 of May about noone they came to Oueak, and from thence proceeding vp the riuer, on the 17 day William Turnebull departed from the Stroog in a small boat, and went before towards Tetusha to prouide victuals, and send downe to the Stroog, from which place they were then about 230 versts.

The 23 day they met a boat with victuals, which William Turnebull sent from Tetusha, and the same day they arriued with their Stroog at Tetusha, where they stayed all night, and the next morning betimes departed thence, but W. Turnebull was gone in the small boat before to Cazan, to prouide necessaries from thence, and to make way for their dispatch. The 26 day they arriued with their Stroog at Cazan, where they remained till the fourth of Iune: the Factors sent Giles Crow from Cazan to the Mosco, with their letters the 30 of May. The 4 day of Iune they departed from Cazan with their Stroog, and arriued at Yeraslaue the 22 day about 5 of the clocke in the morning.

The 23. day they prouided Telegos, to carry the goods to Vologda. The 24. day hauing the goods laden vpon Telegos, they departed with the same towards Vologda, and remained there fiue versts from Yeraslaue.

The 29 day they came to Vologda, with all their goods in safety, and good order. The same 29. William Turnbull and Peter Garrard departed from Vologda post by water towards Colmogro, the third of Iuly, hauing their goods laden in a small doshnik, they departed with the same from Vologda towards Rose Island by S. Nicholas; where they arriued in safety the 16 of Iuly, and found there the Agents of Russia, and in the rode the ships sent out from England, almost laden ready to depart.

The 25 day departed for England (out of the rode of S. Nicholas) the ship Elizabeth.

The 26 day departed thence the Thomas Allen and Mary Susan, and in the Thomas Allen went William Turnbul, Matthew Tailboys, Thomas Hudson, and others. The goods returned of the Persia voyage were laden into the ship, William and Iohn, whereof was Master, William Bigat, and in her with the same goods came Peter Garrard and Tobias Parris.

The 11 of August, the same ship being laden and despatched departed from the rode of S. Nicholas, and with her in company another of the companies fraighted ships, called the Tomasin, whereof was M. Christopher Hall. In their returne homewards they had some foule weather, and were separated at the sea, the William and Iohn put into Newcastle the 24 of September: from whence the sayd Peter Garrard and Tobias Parris came to London by land, and brought newes of the arriual of the ship.

The 25 of September both the sayd ships arriued at the port of London in safety, and ankered before Limehouse and Wapping, where they were discharged, 1581.

* * * * *

Obseruations of the latitudes and meridian altitudes of diuers places in Russia, from the North to the South: Anno 1581.

Michael Archangel.
    Meridian altitude obserued at Michael the Archangel, 42. degrees, 30. minuts.
    The true latitude, 64. degrees, 54. minuts.

The English house in Colmogro.
    The English house in Colmogro, in latitude, 64. d. 25. m.
    The meridian altitude there obserued, the 29. of Iuly, 42. d. 15. m.

Recola.
    Meridian altitude the 30 of Iuly, 41. d. 40. m.
    Declination 16. d. 6. m.
    64. d. 20. m.

Yeegris.
    Meridian 4 of August, 41. d. 50. m.
    Declination Northerly, 14. d. 49. m.
    62. d. 59. m.

Towlma.
    Meridian altitude, the 15 of August, 40. d. 45. m.
    Declination Northerly, 11. d. 2. m.
    60. d. 17. m.

Vologda.
    Meridian altitude, the 20 of August, 40. d.
    Declination Northerly, 9. d. 17. m.
    59. d. 17. m.

Vologda.
    Meridian altitude, 21 of August, 39. d. 36. m.
    Declination, 8. d. 56. m.
    59. d. 20. m.

Yeraslaue.
    Latitude, by gesse, 57. d. 50. m.

Swyoskagorod.
    Meridian altitude, 21. September, 31. d.
    Declination, 2. d. 56. m.
    56. d. 4. m.

Ouslona Monastery.
    Meridian altitude, 23. September, 30. d. 26. m.

Declination, 2. d. 56. m.
55. d. 51. m.

Tetuskagorod.
Meridian altitude, 28. September, 28. d. 28. m.
Declination, 5. d. 35. m.
55. d. 22. m.

Oueek.
Meridian altitude, 5. October, 30. d. 12. m.
Declination, 8. d. 18. m.
51. d. 30. m.

Astracan:
Astracan meridian altitude, 22. October, 29. d. 36. m.
Declination, 14. d. 16. m.
46. d. 10. m.

Astracan:
Meridian altitude, 1 of Nouember, 26. d. 35. m.
Declination, 17. d. 16. m.
46. d. 9. m.

* * * * *

Certaine directions giuen by M. Richard Hackluit of the Middle Temple, to M. Morgan Hubblethorne, Dier, sent into Persia, 1579.

1. For that England hath the best cloth and wool in the world, and for that the clothes of the realme haue no good vent, if good dying be not added: therfore it is much to be wished that the dying of forren countreyes were seene, to the end that the arte of dying may be brought into the Realme in greatest excellency: for thereof will follow honour to the Realme, and great and ample vent of our clothes: and of the vent of clothes, will follow the setting of our poore on worke, in all degrees of labour in clothing and dying: for which cause most principally you are sent ouer at the charge of the city: and therfore for the satisfying the lords, and of the expectation of the merchants and of your company, it behooues you to haue care to returne home with more knowledge then you caried out.

2. The great dearth of clothes is a great let in the ample vent of clothes, and the price of a cloth, for a fifth, sixth and seuenth part riseth by the colour and dying: and therefore to deuise to die as good colours with the one halfe of the present price were to the great commodity of the Realme, by sauing of great treasure in time to come. And therefore you must haue great care to haue knowledge of the materials of all the countreys that you shall passe

thorow, that they may be vsed in dying, be they hearbs, weeds, barks, gummes, earths, or what els soeuer.

3 In Persia you shall finde carpets of course thrummed wooll, the best of the world, and excellently coloured: those cities and townes you must repaire to, and you must vse meanes to learne all the order of the dying of those thrummes, which are so died as neither raine, wine, nor yet vineger can staine: and if you may attaine to that cunning, you shall not need to feare dying of cloth: For if the colour holde in yarne and thrumme, it will holde much better in cloth.

4 For that in Persia they haue great colouring of silks, it behooues you to learne that also, for that cloth dying and silke dying haue a certaine affinity, and your merchants mind to bring much raw silke into the Realme, and therefore it is more requisit you learne the same.

5 In Persia there are that staine linnen cloth: it is not amisse you learne it if you can: it hath bene an olde trade in England, whereof some excellent clothes yet remaine: but the arte is now lost, and not to be found in the Realme.

6 They haue a cunning in Persia to make in buskins of Spanish leather flowers of many kindes, in most liuely colours, and these the Courtiers do weare there: to learne which arte were no harme.

7 If any Dier of China, or of the East parts of the world, be to be found in Persia, acquaint yourselfe with him, and learne what you may of him.

8 You shall finde Anile there, if you can procure the herbe that it is made of, either by seed or by plant, to cary into England, you may doe well to endeuour to enrich your countrey with the same: but withall learne you the making of the Anile, and if you can get the herbe, you may send the same dry into England, for possibly it groweth here already.

9 Returne home with you all the materials and substances that they die withall in Russia, and also in Persia, that your company may see all.

10 In some litle pot in your lodging, I wish you to make daily trials in your arte, as you shall from time to time learne ought among them.

11 Set downe in writing whatsoeuer you shall learne from day to day, lest you should forget, or lest God should call you to his mercy: and by ech returne I wish you to send in writing whatsoeuer you haue learned, or at the least keepe the same safe in your coffer, that come death or life your countrey may ioyne the thing that you goe for, and not lose the charge, and trauell bestowed in this case.

12 Learne you there to fixe and make sure the colour to be giuen by logge wood: so shall we not need to buy woad so deare, to the enriching of our enemies.

13 Enquire of the price of leckar, and all other things belonging to dying.

14 In any wise set downe in writing a true note from whence euery of them doe come, and where, and in what countrey ech of them doth grow, I meane where the naturall place of ech of them is, as how neere to such a city, or to such a sea, or to such a portable riuer in Russia, Persia, or elsewhere.

15 If before you returne you could procure a singular good workeman in the arte of Turkish carpet making, you should bring the arte into this Realme, and also thereby increase worke to your company.

* * * * *

Commission giuen by sir Rowland Hayward knight, and George Barrie, Aldermen and gouernours of the company of English Merchants, for discouery of new trades, vnto Arthur Pet, and Charles Iackman, for a voyage by them to be made, for discouery of Cathay, 1580. in forme following.

In the name of God Almightie, and euerlasting. Amen. This writing for commission Tripartite, made the twentieth day of May Anno Dom. 1580. and in the 22. yeere of the reigne of our Souereigne Lady Elizabeth by the grace of God, Queene of England, France and Ireland, defender of the faith, &c. Betweene sir Rowland Hayward knight, and George Barne, Aldermen of the Citie of London and Gouernours of the company of English Merchants, for discouery of new trades, for the behoofe, and in the name of the said company, on the first partie, and Arthur Pet of Ratcliffe, in the Countie Middlesex, Captaine, Master, and chiefe ruler of the good barke, called the George of London, of the burthen of 40. tunnes, or thereabouts, on the second partie, and Charles Iackman of the Popler, in the said Countie of Middlesex, Captaine, Master and ruler of the good barke, called the William of London, of the burthen of 20. tunnes, or thereabouts, (which barkes are now riding at anker in the riuer of Thames against Limehouse) on the third partie: witnesseth, that the said Gouernours, and company haue hired the saide Arthur Pet, to serue in the said barke, called the George, with nine men and a boy: [Sidenote: Burroughs streits.] And likewise the said Charles Iackman, to serue in the said barke, called the William, with fiue men and a boy, for a voyage by them to be made by Gods grace, for search and discoueries of a passage by sea from hence by Boroughs streights, and the Island Vaigats, Eastwards to the countreis or dominions of the mightie Prince, the Emperour of Cathay, and in the same vnto the Cities of Cambalu and Quinsay, or to either of them.

The which passage (vpon authoritie of writers, and great reason) is conceiued to bee from the Vaigats Eastwards, according to the description in plat of spirall lines, made by master William Burrough, whereof either of the saide Arthur Pet, and Charles Iackman, haue one deliuered vnto them, and also one other sailing carde, and a blanke plat for either of them. But if it should not be in all points, according to that description, yet we hope that the continent or firme land of Asia doth not stretch it selfe so farre Northwards, but that there may be found a sea passeable by it, betweene the latitude of 70. and 80. degrees. And therefore we haue appointed you with these two barkes to make triall of the same: wishing you both to ioyne in friendship together, as most deere friends and brothers, to all purposes and effects, to the furtherance and orderly performing of the same voyage. And likewise order your companies, that they of the one barke may haue such loue and care, to helpe and succour them of the other, as most deere friends and brothers would doe: so as it may appeare, that though they be two barkes, and two companies, (which is so appointed for your greater comfort and assurance) yet that you are wholy of one minde, and bend your selues to the vttermost of your powers, to performe the thing that you are both employed for.

Doe you obserue good order in your dayly seruice, and pray vnto God, so shall you prosper the better.

We would haue you to meete often together, to talke, conferre, consult, and agree how, and by what meanes, you may best performe this purposed voyage, according to our intents. And at such meeting we thinke it requisite, that you call vnto you your mates, and also Nicholas Chanceler, (whom wee doe appoint as merchant, to keepe accompt of the merchandise you shall buy or sell, barter or change) to the ende that whatsoeuer God should dispose of either of you, yet they may haue some instructions and knowledge howe to deale in your place, or places. And of all your assemblies and consultations together, and the substance of matter you shal at euery time agree vpon we would haue you to note them in the paper bookes that wee giue you for that purpose, vnto each barke one. We do appoint Arthur Pet in the George, as Admiral, to weare the flagge in the maine top, and Charles Iackman in the William, as Viceadmirall. For good orders to be taken for your good and orderly keeping of company together, which we wish may be such, as you should neuer lose sight the one of the other, except by both your consents, to discouer about an Island, or in some riuer, when and where you may certainly appoint to meete together againe, we referre the same to your discretions.

And now for your good direction, in this voyage, we would haue you with the next good winde and weather, that God shall send thereunto meete and conuenient, after the 22. day of this present moneth of May, saile from this riuer of Thames, to the coast of Finmarke, to the North Cape there, or to the Wardhouse, and from thence direct your course to haue sight of Willoughbies land, and from it passe alongst to the Noua Zembla, keeping the same landes alwayes in your sight on your larboordsides (if conueniently you may) to the ende you may discouer, whether the same Willoughbies land be continent and firme land with Noua Zembla, or not: notwithstanding we would not haue you to entangle your selues in any Bay, or otherwise, so that it might hinder your speedy proceeding to the Island Vaigats.

[Sidenote: The land of Samoeda.] And when you come to Vaigats, we would haue you to get sight of the maine land of Samoeda, which is ouer against the South part of the same Island, and from thence with Gods permission, to passe Eastwards alongst the same coast, keeping it alwayes in your sight (if conueniently you may) vntill you come to the mouth of the riuer Ob, and when you come vnto it, passe ouer the said riuers mouth vnto the border land, on the Eastside of the same (without any stay to bee made for searching inwardly in the same riuer) and being in sight of the same Easterly land, doe you in Gods name proceed alongst by it, from thence Eastwards, keeping the same alwayes on your starboord side in sight, if you may, and follow the tract of it, whether it incline Southerly or Northerly (as at times it may do both) vntill you come to, the Countrey of Cathay, or the dominion of that mightie Emperour.

And if God prosper your voyage with such good successe, that you may attaine to the same, doe you seeke by all meanes you can to arriue to the Cities Cambalu, and Quinsay, or to the one of them. But if it happen that you cannot conueniently come to either of those places, or shalbe driuen to remaine and winter in some other port or place of his dominion, do you seeke by all meanes possible to winne fauour and liking of the people, by gifts and friendly demeanes towards them, and not to offer violence, or do wrong to any people or nation whatsoeuer, but therein to be innocent as doues, yet wilie as serpents, to auoid mischiefe, and defend you from hurt. [Sidenote: The Queenes letters.] And when you shall haue gotten friendship through your discreete ordering of your selues, towards the people, doe you learne of them what you can of their Prince, and shewe them one of the Queenes Maiesties, letters, which she sendeth with you (by either of you one, made of one substance and effect, for ech of you particularly) written in Latine, whereunto her Maiestie hath subscribed, and caused her signet seale to be set, the effect of the same letters you haue also written in English, for your own vnderstanding thereof.

The same her Maiesties letters you shall procure to deliuer vnto the same mightie Prince, or Gouernour, with some present to be giuen, such as you shall thinke meete and conuenient, vsing your selues in all points according to the effect of the same letters, and procure againe from the same Prince, his letters accordingly.

And if God so prosper your voyage, that you may this Summer passe the Streights, and compasse about the Northernmost land of Asia, vnto the country of Cathay, or dominion of that mightie Prince, and wintering in it, may obtaine from him his letters of priuiledge against the next yeeres spring, you may then after your first setting foorth, search and discouer somewhat further then you had discouered before your wintering, so farre as you shall thinke conuenient with regard had, and alwayes prouided, that you may returne home hither, to giue vs aduise of your proceedings the same Summer, or before the sharpenes or extremitie of winter ouertake you.

And if it happen you cannot this summer attaine to the border of Cathay, and yet find the land beyond the Ob, to stretch it selfe Easterly, with the sea adioyning vnto it nauigable, doe you then proceed on your discouery (as before said) alongst the same continent, so farre as you can this summer, hauing care in the trauel to finde out some conuenient harborow and place, where you may winter: and when you thinke it conuenient, put your selfe to wintering, where if you happen to finde people, you shall deale with them, as we haue before aduised you to do with the people of Cathay, &c. And if you can learne that they haue a prince or chiefe gouernour, do you procure to deliuer vnto the same Prince or gouernour one of the Queenes Maiesties letters, as before said, and seeke to obtaine againe his letters accordingly. If you so happen to winter and obtaine letters of priuiledge, finding the countrey and people, with the commodities to bee such, that by vsing trade thither with the people, and for the commodities, it may be beneficial vnto vs (as we hope you may) the same wil be some good liking vnto vs: notwithstanding we would haue you the next summer (by the grace of God) at your first setting out of your wintering harborough, proceed alongest that tract of land to Cathay, if you see likelihood to passe it (for that is the Countrey that we chiefly desire to discouer) and seeing you are fully victualed for two yeres and vpwards, which you may very wel make to serue you for two yeres and a halfe, though you finde no other help, you may therefore be the bolder to aduenture in proceeding vpon your discouery: which if you do, we doubt not, but you shall atchieue the Countrey of Cathay, and deliuer to the prince there, one of her Maiesties letters, bringing from thence the same princes letters answerable: and so in the yeere of our lord 1582. returne home with good newes, and glad tidings, not onely vnto vs the aduenturers in this voyage, but also to our whole Countrey and nation, which God graunt you do, Amen.

But if it happen that the land of Asia, from beyond the riuer Ob, extend it selfe Northwards to 80. degrees, or neerer the poole, whereby you find it to leade you into that extremitie, that small or no hope may be looked for, to saile that way to Cathay, doe you notwithstanding followe the tract of the same land, as farre as you can discouer this Summer, hauing care to finde out by the way a conuenient place for you to Winter in, the which (if you may discouer the same lande of Asia this Summer to extend it selfe to 80. degrees of latitude, and vpwards or to 85. degrees) we wish then that the same your wintering place may be in the riuer of Ob, or as neere the same riuer as you can, and finding in such wintering place, people, be they Samoeds, Yowgorians, or Molgomzes, &c. doe you gently entreat with them as aforesaide, [Sidenote: The Queenes letters.] and if you can learne that they haue a prince or chiefe gouernour amongst them, doe you deliuer him one of her Maiesties letters, and procure thereof an answere accordingly: do you procure to barter and exchange with the people, of the merchandise and commodities that you shall cary with you, for such commodities as you shall finde them to haue, &c.

[Sidenote: The Citie of Siberia.] If you so happen to winter, we would haue you the next Summer to discouer into the riuer Ob, so farre as conueniently you may: And if you shall finde the same riuer (which is reported to be wide or broad) to be also nauigable and pleasant for you, to trauell farre into, happely you may come to the citie Siberia, or to some other towne or place habited vpon or neere the border of it, and thereby haue liking to winter out the second winter: vse you therein your discretions.

[Sidenote: Willoughbies land.] But if you finde the said riuer Ob to be sholde, or not such as you may conueniently trauell in with your barkes, do you then the next summer return backe through Buroughs streights: And from that part of Noua Zembla, adioyning to the same streights, doe you come alongst the tract of that coast Westwards, keeping it on the starbord side, and the same alwayes in sight, if conueniently you may, vntil you come to Willoughbies land, if outwards bound you shall not happen to discouer and trie whether the said Willoughbies land ioyne continent with the same Noua Zembla, or not. But if you shall then proue them to be one firme and continent, you may from Noua Zembla direct your course vnto the said Willoughbies land, as you shall thinke good, and as you may most conueniently: and from Willoughbies land you shall proceed Westwards alongst the tract of it, (though it incline Northerly) euen so farre as you may or can trauell, hauing regard that in conuenient time you may returne home hither to London for wintering.

And for your orderly passing in this voyage, and making obseruations in the same, we referre you to the instructions giuen by M. William Burrough, whereof one copie is annexed vnto the first part of this Indenture, vnder our seale, for you Arthur Pet, another copie of it is annexed to the second part of this Indenture, vnder our seale also, for you Charles Iackman, and a third copy thereof is annexed vnto the third part of this Indenture, remaining with vs the saide companie, sealed and subscribed by you the said Arthur Pet and Charles Iackman.

And to the obseruing of all things contained in this Commission (so neere as God will permit me grace thereunto) I the said Arthur Pet doe couenant by these presents to performe them, and euery part and parcell thereof. And I the said Charles Iackman doe for my part likewise couenant by these presents to performe the same, and euery part thereof, so neere as God will giue me grace thereunto.

And in witnes thereof these Indentures were sealed and deliuered accordingly, the day and yeere first aboue written. Thus the Lorde God Almightie sende you a prosperous voyage, with happie successe and safe returne, Amen.

* * * * *

Instructions and notes very necessary and needfull to be obserued in the purposed voyage for discouery of Cathay Eastwards, by Arthur Pet, and Charles Iackman: giuen by M. William Burrough. 1580.

When you come to Orfordnesse, if the winde doe serue you to goe a seabord the sands, doe you set off from thence, and note the time diligently of your being against the said Nesse, turning then your glasse, whereby you intende to keepe your continuall watch, and apoint such course as you shal thinke good, according as the wind serueth you: And from that time forwards continually (if your ship be lose, vnder saile, a hull or trie) do you at the end of euery 4 glasses at the least (except calme) sound with your dipsin lead, and note diligently what depth you finde, and also the ground. But if it happen by swiftnes of the shippes way, or otherwise, that you cannot get ground, yet note what depth you did proue, and could finde no ground (this note is to be obserued all your voyage, as well outwards as homewards.). But when you come vpon any coast, or doe finde any sholde banke in the sea, you are then to vse your leade oftener, as you shal thinke it requisite, noting diligently the order of your depth, and the deeping and sholding. And so likewise doe you note the depth into harboroughs, riuers, &c.

[Sidenote: How to note downe in his Iornall of the voyage, his dead reckoning, and other obseruations.] And in keeping your dead reckoning, it is very necessary that you doe note at the ende of euery foure glasses, what way the shippe hath made (by your best proofes to be vsed) and howe her way hath bene through the water, considering withall for the sagge [Footnote: i.e., Current.] of the sea, to leewards, accordingly as you shall finde it growen: and also to note the depth, and what things worth the noting happened in that time, with also the winde vpon what point you finde it then, and of what force or strength it is, and what sailes you beare.

But if you should omit to note those things at the end of euery foure glasses, I would not haue you to let it slip any longer time, then to note it diligently at the end of euery watch, or eight glasses at the farthest.

Doe you diligently obserue the latitude as often, and in as many places as you may possible, and also the variation of the Compasse (especially when you may bee at shoare vpon any land) noting the same obseruations truely, and the place and places where, and the time and times when you do the same.

[Sidenote: For noting the shape and view of the land at first discouery, &c.] When you come to haue sight of any coast or land whatsoeuer, doe you presently set the same with your sailing Compasse, howe it beares off you, noting your iudgement how farre you thinke it from you, drawing also the forme of it in your booke, howe it appeares vnto you, noting diligently how the highest or notablest part thereof beareth off you, and the extreames also in sight of the same land at both ends, distinguishing them by letters, A. B. C. &c. Afterwards when you haue sailed 1. 2. 3. or 4. glasses (at the most) noting diligently what way your barke hath made, and vpon what point of the Compasse, do you againe set that first land seene, or the parts thereof, that you first obserued, if you can well perceiue or discerne them, and likewise such other notable points or signes, vpon the land that you may then see, and could not perceiue at the first time, distinguishing it also by letters from the other, and drawing in your booke the shape of the same land, as it appeareth vnto you, and so the third time; &c.

And also in passing alongst by any and euery coast, doe you drawe the maner of biting in of euery Bay, and entrance of euery harborow or riuers mouth, with the lying out of euery point, or headland, (vnto the which you may giue apt names at your pleasure) and make some marke in drawing the forme and border of the same, where the high cliffs are, and where lowe land is, whether sande, hils, or woods, or whatsoeuer, not omitting to note any thing that may be sensible and apparant to you, which may serue to any good purpose. If you carefully with great heede and diligence, note the obseruations in your booke, as aforesaid, and afterwards make demonstration thereof in your plat, you shall thereby perceiue howe farre the land you first sawe, or the parts thereof obserued, was then from you, and consequently of all the rest: and also how farre the one part was from the other, and vpon what course or point of the Compasse the one lieth from the other.

[Sidenote: For obseruing of tides and curants.] And when you come vpon any coast where you find floods and ebs, doe you diligently note the time of the highest and lowest water in euery place, and the slake or still water of full sea, and lowe water, and also which way the flood doeth runne, how the tides doe set, how much water it hieth, and what force the tide hath to driue a ship in one houre, or in the whole tide, as neere as you can iudge it, and what difference in time you finde betwene the running of the flood, and the ebbe. And if you finde vpon any coast the currant to runne alwayes one way, doe you also note the same duely, how it setteth in euery place, and obserue what force it hath to driue a ship in one houre, &c.

[Sidenote: To take the plateformes of places within compasse of view vpon land.] Item, as often, and when as you may conueniently come vpon any land, to make obseruation for the latitude and variation, &c. doe you also (if you may) with your instrument, for trying of distances, obserue the platforme [Footnote: i.e., survey the place.] of the place, and of as many things (worth the noting) as you may then conueniently see from time to time. These orders if you diligently obserue, you may thereby perfectly set downe in the plats, that I haue giuen you your whole trauell, and description of your discouery, which is a thing that will be chiefly expected at your hands. But withall you may not forget to note as much as you can learne, vnderstand or perceiue of the maner of the soile, or fruitfulnesse of euery place and countrey you shall come in, and of the maner, shape, attire and disposition of the people, and of the commodities they haue, and what they most couet and desire of the commodities you see, and to offer them all courtesie and friendship you may or can, to winne their loue and fauour towardes you, not doing or offering them any wrong or hurt. And though you should be offered wrong at their handes, yet not to reuenge the same lightly, but by all meanes possible seeke to winne them, yet alwayes dealing wisely and with such circumspection that you keepe your selues out of their dangers.

Thus I beseech God almightie to blesse you, and prosper your voyage with good and happie successe, and send you safely to returne home againe, to the great ioy and reioycing of the aduenturers with you, and all your friends and our whole countrey, Amen.

* * * * *

Certaine briefe aduises giuen by Master Dee, to Arthur Pet, and Charles Iackman, to bee obserued in their Northeasterne discouerie, Anno 1580.

If we reckon from Wardhouse to Colgoieue Island 400. miles for almost 20. degrees difference onely of longitude very neere East and West, and about the latitude of 70. degrees and two thirde parts: From Colgoieue to Vaigats 200. miles for 10. degrees difference onely in longitude, at 70. degrees of latitude also: From Vaigats to the promontorie Tabin 60. degrees difference of longitude (the whole course, or shortest distance being East and West) in the latitude likewise of 70. degrees, maketh 1200. miles: then is summa totalis from Wardhouse to Tabin 600. leagues, or 1800. English miles. Therefore allowing in a discouery voiage for one day with another but 50. English miles; it is euident that from Wardhouse to Tabin, the course may bee sailed easily in sixe and thirtie dayes; but by Gods helpe it may be finished in much shorter time, both by helpe of winde prosperous, and light continuall for the time requisit thereunto.

[Sidenote: M. Dee gaue them a Chart of his owne making, which here refers them vnto.] When you are past Tabin, or come to the longitude of 142. degrees, as your chart sheweth, or two, three, foure, or fiue degrees further Easterly, it is probable you shall finde the land on your right hand runne much Southerly and Eastward, [Footnote: Had he said forty degrees, he would have made a remarkable guess.] in which course you are like either to fall into the mouth of the famous riuer Oechardes, [Footnote: The Oechardes is probably the Hoang Ho, and Cambalu may then be Pekin.] or some other, which yet I coniecture to passe by the renowmed Citie of Cambalu, and the mouth to be in latitude about 50. or 52. degrees, and within 300. or 400. miles of Cambalu it selfe, being in the latitude of 45. degrees Southerly of the saide riuers mouth, or els that you shal trend about the very Northerne and most Easterly point of all Asia, passing by the prouince Ania, and then to the latitude of 46. degrees, keeping still the land in view on your right hand (as neere as you may with safetie) you may enter into Quinsay [Footnote: Query, Canton?] hauen, being the chiefe citie in the Northern China, as I terme it for distinctions sake, from the other better knowen.

And in or about either or both of these two warme places, you may to great good purpose bee occupied the whole winter, after your arriuall in those quarters, as sometime by sea, sometime in notable fresh riuers, sometime in discreet view and noting downe the situation of the Cities within land, &c. and euer assaying to come by some charts or maps of the countrey, made and printed in Cathay or China, and by some of their bookes likewise for language, &c. You may also haue opportunitie to saile ouer to to Iapan Island, where you shall finde Christian men Iesuits of many countreys of Christendome some, and perhaps some Englishmen, at whose handes you may haue great instruction and aduise for your affaires in hand.

* * * * *

Notes in writing, besides more priuie by mouth, that were giuen by M. Richard Hakluyt of Eiton in the Countie of Hereford, Esquire, Anno 1580: to M. Arthur Pet, and to M. Charles Iackman, sent by the Merchants of the Moscouie companie for the discouery of the Northeast straight, not altogether vnfit for some other enterprise of discouery, hereafter to be taken in hand.

What respect of Islands is to be had and why.

Whereas the Portingals haue in their course to their Indies in the Southeast certaine ports and fortifications to thrust into by the way, to diuers great purposes: so you are to see what Islands, and what ports you had neede to haue by the way in your course to the Northeast. For which cause I wish you to enter into consideration of the matter, and to note all the Islands, and to set them downe in plat, to two ends: that is to say, That we may deuise to take the benefit by them, And also foresee how by them the Sauages or ciuill Princes may in any sort annoy vs in our purposed trade that way.

And for that the people to the which we purpose in this voyage to go, be no Christians, it were good that the masse of our commodities were always in our owne disposition, and not at the will of others. Therefore it were good that we did seeke out some small Island in the Scithian sea, where we might plant, fortefie, and staple safely, from whence (as time should serue) wee might feed those heathen nations with our commodities without cloying them, or without venturing our whole masse in the bowels of their countrey.

And to which Island (if neede were, and if wee should thinke so good) wee might allure the Northeast nauie, the nauie of Cambalu to resort with their commodities to vs there planted, and stapling there.

And if such an Island might be found so standing as might shorten our course, and so standing, as that the nauie of Cambalu, or other those parties might conueniently saile vnto without their dislike in respect of distance, then would it fal out well. For so, besides lesse danger and more safetie, our ships might there vnlade and lade againe, and returne the selfe same summer to the ports of England or of Norway.

And if such an Island may be for the stapling of our commodities, to the which they of Cambalu would not saile, yet we might hauing ships there, imploy them in passing betweene Cambalu and that stapling place.

Respect of hauens and harborowes.

And if no such Islands may bee found in the Scithian sea toward the firme of Asia, then are you to search out the ports that be about Noua Zembla, all along the tract of that land, to the end you may winter there the first yeere, if you be let by contrary winds, and to the end that if we may in short time come vnto Cambalu, and vnlade and set saile againe for returne without venturing there at Cambalu, that you may on your way come as farre in returne as a port about Noua Zembla: that the summer following, you may the sooner be in England for the more speedy vent of your East commodities, and for the speedier discharge of your Mariners: if you cannot goe forward and backe in one selfe same Summer.

And touching the tract of the land of Noua Zembla, toward the East out of the circle Arcticke in the mote temperate Zone, you are to haue regard: for if you finde the soyle planted with people, it is like that in time an ample vent of our warme woollen clothes may be found. [Sidenote: A good consideration.] And if there be no people at all there to be found, then you shall specially note what plentie of whales, and of other fish is to he found there, to the ende we may turne out newe found land fishing or Island fishing, or our whalefishing that way, for the ayde and comfort of our newe trades to the Northeast to the coasts of Asia.

Respect of fish and certaine other things.

And if the aire may be found vpon that tract temperate, and the soile yeelding wood, water, land and grasse, and the seas fish, then we may plant on that maine the offals of our people, as the Portingals do in Brasill, and so they may in our fishing in our passage, and diuers wayes yeelde commoditie to England by harbouring and victualling vs.

And it may be, that the inland there may yeeld masts, pitch, tarre, hempe, and all things for the Nauie, as plentifully as Eastland doth.

The Islands to be noted with their commodities and wants.

To note the Islands, whether they be hie land or low land, mountaine, or flat, grauelly, clay, chalkie, or of what sorte, woody or not woody, with springs and riuers or not, and what wilde beastes they haue in the same.

And whether there seeme to be in the same apt matter to build withall, as stone free or rough, and stone to make lime withall, and wood or coale to burne the same withall.

To note the goodnesse or badnesse of the hauens and harborowes in the Islands.

If a straight be found, what is to be done, and what great importance it may be of.

And if there be a straight in the passage into the Scithian seas, the same is specially and with great regard to be noted, especially if the same straight be narrow and to be kept. I say it is to be noted as a thing that doeth much import: for what prince soeuer shall be Lorde of the same; and shall possesse the same, as the king of Denmarke doeth possesse the straight of Denmarke, he onely shall haue the trade out of these regions into the Northeast parts of the world for himselfe, and for his priuate profit, or for his subiects onely, or to enioy wonderfull benefit of the toll of the same, like as the king of Denmarke doth enioy of his straights by suffring the merchants of other Princes to passe that way. If any such straight be found, the eleuation, the high or lowe land, the hauens neere, the length of the straights, and all other such circumstances are to be set downe for many purposes: and al the Mariners in the voyage are to be sworne to keepe close all such things, that other Princes preuent vs not of the same, after our returns vpon the disclosing of the Mariners, if any such thing should hap.

Which way the Sauage may bee made able to purchase our cloth and other their wants.

If you find any Island or maine land populous, and that the same people hath need of cloth, then are you to deuise what commodities they haue to purchase the same withall.

If they be poore, then are you to consider of the soile, and how by any possibilitie the same may be made to inrich them, that hereafter they may haue something to purchase the cloth withall.

If you enter into any maine by portable riuer, and shall find any great woods, you are to note what kind of timber they be of, that we may know whether they are for pitch, tarre, mastes, dealeboord, clapboord, or for building of ships or houses, for so, if the people haue no vse of them, they may be brought perhaps to vse.

Not to venture the losse of any one man.

You must haue great care to preserue your people, since your number is so small, and not to venture any one man in any wise.

To bring home besides merchandize certaine trifles.

Bring home with you (if you may) from Cambalu or other ciuil place, one or other yong man, although you leaue one for him.

Also the fruites of the Countreys if they will not of themselues dure, drie them and so preserue them.

And bring with you the kernels of peares and apples, and the stones of such stonefruits as you shall find there.

Also the seeds of all strange herbs and flowers, for such seeds of fruits and herbs comming from another part of the world, and so far off, will delight the fansie of many for the strangenesse, and for that the same may grow, and continue the delight long time.

If you arriue at Cambalu or Quinsay, to bring thence the mappe of that countrey, for so shall you haue the perfect description, which is to great purpose.

To bring thence some old printed booke, to see whether they haue had print there before it was deuised in Europe as some write.

To note their force by sea and by land.

If you arriue in Cambalu or Quinsay, to take a speciall view of their Nauie, and to note the force, greatnesse, maner of building of them, the sailes, the tackles, the ankers, the furniture of them, with ordinance, armour, and munition.

Also, to note the force of the wals and bulwarks of their cities, their ordonance, and whether they haue any caliuers, and what powder and shot.

To note what armour they haue.

What swords.

What pikes, halberds and bils.

What horses of force, and what light horses they haue.

And so throughout to note the force of the Countrey both by sea and by land.

Things to be marked to make coniectures by.

To take speciall note of their buildings, and of the ornaments of their houses within.

Take a speciall note of their apparell and furniture, and of the substance that the same is made of, of which a Merchant may make a gesse as well of their commoditie, as also of their wants.

To note their Shoppes and Warehouses, and with what commodities they abound, the price also.

To see their Shambles, and to view all such things as are brought into the Markets, for so you shall soone see the commodities, and the maner of the people of the inland, and so giue a gesse of many things.

To note their fields of graine, and their trees of fruite, and how they abound or not abound in one and other, and what plenty or scarsitie of fish they haue.

Things to be caried with you, whereof more or lesse is to bee caried for a shew of our commodities to be made.

Karsies of all orient colours, specially of stamell, broadcloth of orient colours also.

Frizadoes, Motlies, Bristow friezes, Spanish blankets, Baies of al colours, specially with Stamel, Worsteds, Carels, Saies, Woadmols, Flanels, Rash, &c.

Felts of diuers colours.

Taffeta hats.

Deepe caps for Mariners coloured in Stamel, whereof if ample bent may be found, it would turne to an infinite commoditie of the common poore people by knitting.

Quilted caps of Leuant taffeta of diuers colours, for the night.

Knit stocks of silke of orient colours.

Knit stocks of Iersie yarne of orient colours, whereof if ample vent might folow the poore multitude should be set in worke.

Stocks of karsie of diuers colours for men and for women.

Garters of silke of seuerall kinds, and of colours diuers.

Girdles of Buffe and all other leather, with gilt and vngilt buckles, specially waste girdles, waste girdles of veluet.

Gloues of all sorts knit, and of leather.

Gloues perfumed.

Points of all sorts of silke, threed, and leather, of all maner of colours.

Shooes of Spanish leather of diuers colours, of diuers length, cut and vncut.

Shooes of other leather.

Veluet shooes and pantophles.

These shooes and pantophles to be sent this time, rather for a shew then for any other cause.

Purses knit, and of leather.

Nightcaps knit, and other.

A garnish of pewter for a shew of a vent of that English commoditie, bottles, flagons, spoones, &c. of that mettall.

Glasses of English making.

Venice glasses.

Looking glasses for women, great and faire.

Small dials, a few for proofe, although there they will not hold the order they do here.

Spectacles of the common sort.

Others of Christall trimmed with siluer, and other wise.

Hower glasses.

Combes of Iuorie.

Combes of boxe.

Combes of horne.

Linnen of diuers sorts.

Handkerchiefs with silke of seuerall colours wrought.

Glazen eyes to ride with against dust.

Kniues in sheaths both single and double, of good edge.

Needles great and small of euery kind.

Buttons greater and smaller, with moulds of leather and not of wood, and such as be durable of double silke, and that of sundry colours.

Boxes with weights for gold, and of euery kind of the coine of gold, good and bad, to shew that the people here vse weight and measure, which is a certaine shew of wisedom, and of certaine gouernment setled here.

All the seuerall siluer coynes of our English monies, to be caried with you, to be shewed to the gouernours at Cambalu, which is a thing that shall in silence speake to wise men more then you imagine.

Locks and keyes, hinges, bolts, haspes, &c. great and small of excellent workemanship, whereof if vent may be, hereafter we shall set our subiects in worke, which you must haue in great regard. For in finding ample vent of any thing that is to be wrought in this realme, is more woorth to our people besides the gaine of the merchant, then Christchurch, Bridewell, the Sauoy, and all the Hospitals of England.

For banketting on shipboord persons of credite.

First, the sweetest perfumes to set vnder hatches to make the place sweet against their comming aboord, if you arriue at Cambalu, Quinsey, or in any such great citie, and not among Sauages.

Marmelade.

Figs barrelled.

Sucket

Raisins of the sunne.

Comfets of diuers kinds made of purpose by him that is most excellent, that shal not dissolue.

Prunes damaske.

Dried Peares.

Smalnuts.

Walnuts.

Almonds.

Oliues to make them taste their wine.

The apple Iohn that dureth two yeres to make shew of our fruits.

Hullocke.

Sacke.

Vials of good sweet waters, and casting bottels of glasses to besprinkle the ghests withall, after their comming aboord.

Suger to vse with their wine if they will.

The sweet oyle of Zante, and excellent French vineger, and a fine kind of Bisket stieped in the same do make a banketting dish, and a little Sugar cast in it cooleth and comforteth, and refresheth the spirits of man.

Cynamon water/Imperiall water: is to be had with you to make a shew of by taste, and also to comfort your sicke in the voyage.

With these and such like, you may banket where you arriue the greater and best persons.

Or with the gift of these Marmelades in small boxes, or small vials of sweet waters you may gratifie by way of gift, or you may make a merchandize of them.

The Mappe of England and of London.

Take with you the mappe of England set out in faire colours, one of the biggest sort I meane, to make shew of your countrey from whence you come.

And also the large Mappe of London to make shew of your Citie. And let the riuer be drawen full of Ships of all sorts, to make the more shew of your great trade and traffike in trade of merchandize.

Ortelius booke of Mappes.

If you take Ortelius booke of Mappes with you to marke all these Regions, it were not amisse: and if need were to present the same to the great Can, for it would be to a Prince of marueilous account.

The booke of the attire of all Nations.

Such a booke caried with you and bestowed in gift would be much esteemed, as I perswade my selfe.

Bookes.

If any man will lend you the new Herball and such Bookes as make shew of herbes, plants, trees, fishes, foules and beasts of these regions, it may much delight the great Can, and the nobilitie, and also their merchants to haue the view of them: for all things in these partes so much differing from the things of those regions, since they may not be here to see them, by meane of the distance, yet to see those things in a shadow, by this meane will delight them.

The booke of Rates.

Take with you the booke of Rates, to the end you may pricke all those commodities there specified, that you shall chance to find in Cambalu, in Quinsey, or in any part of the East, where you shall chance to be.

Parchment.

Rowles of Parchment, for that we may vent much without hurt to the Realme, and it lieth in small roume.

Glew.

To carie Glew, for that we haue plenty and want vent.

Red Oker for Painters.

To seeke vent because we haue great mines of it, and haue no vent.

Sope of both kindes.

To try what vent it may haue, for that we make of both kinds, and may perhaps make more.

Saffron.

To try what vent you may haue of Saffron, because this realme yeelds the best of the world, and for the tillage and other labours may set the poore greatly in worke to their reliefe.

AquauitŠ.

By new deuises wonderful quantities may be made here, and therefore to seeke the vent.

Blacke Conies skins.

To try the vent at Cambalu, for that it lieth towards the North, and for that we abound with the commoditie, and may spare it.

Threed of all colours.

The vent may set our people in worke.

Copper Spurres and Hawkes bels.

To see the vent for it may set our people in worke.

A note and Caueat for the Merchant.

That before you offer your commodities to sale, you indeuour to learne what commodities the countrey there hath. For if you bring thither veluet, taffeta, spice, or any such commoditie that you your selfe desire to lade your selfe home with, you must not sell yours deare, least hereafter you purchase theirs not so cheape as you would.

Seeds for sale.

Carie with you for that purpose all sorts of garden seeds, as wel of sweete strawing herbs, and of flowers, as also of pot herbes and all sorts for roots, &c.

Lead of the first melting.

Lead of the second melting of the slags.

To make triall of the vent of Lead of all kinds.

English iron, and wier of iron and copper.

To try the sale of the same.

Brimstone.

To try the vent of the same, because we abound with it made in the Realme.

Antimonie a Minerall.

To see whether they haue any ample vse there for it, for that we may lade whole nauies of it, and haue no vse of it vnlesse it be for some small portion in founding of bels, or a litle that the Alcumists vse: of this you may haue two sortes at the Apothecaries.

Tinder boxes with Steele, Flint & Matches and Tinder, the Matches to be made of Iuniper to auoid the offence of Brimstone.

To trie and make the better sale of Brimstone by shewing the vse.

Candles of Waxe to light.

A painted Bellowes.

For that perhaps they haue not the vse of them.

A pot of cast iron.

To try the sale, for that it is a naturall commoditie of this Realme.

All maner of edge tools.

To be sold there or to the lesse ciuil people by the way where you shall touch.

What I would haue you there to remember.

To note specially what excellent dying they vse in these regions, and therefore to note their garments and ornaments of houses: and to see their Die houses and the Materials & Simples that they vse about the same, and to bring musters and shewes of the colours and of the materials, for that it may serue this clothing realme to great purpose.

To take with you for your owne vse.

All maner of engines to take fish and foule.

To take with you those things that be in perfection of goodnesse.

For as the goodnesse now at the first may make your commodities in credite in time to come: so false and Sophisticate commodities shall draw you and all your commodities into contempt and ill opinion.

* * * * *

A letter of Gerardus Mercator, written to M. Richard Hakluyt of Oxford, touching the intended discouery of the Northeast passage, An. 1580.

LiterŠ tuŠ (vir humanissime) 19. Iunij dem¨m mihi redditŠ fuerunt: vehementer dolui visis illis tantam, non modo temporis, sed mult. magis tempestiuŠ instructionis iacturam factam esse. Optassem Arthurum Pet de quibusdam non leuibus ante suum discessum prŠmonitum fuisse.

Expeditissima sanè per Orientem in Cathaium est nauigatio: et sŠpè miratus sum, eam foeliciter inchoatam, desertam fuisse, velis in occidentem translatis, postquam plus quÓm dimidium itineris vestri iam notum haberent. [Sidenote: Ingens sinus post Insulam Vaigats et Nouam Zemblam.] Nam post Insulam Vaigats et Noua Zembla continuˬ ingens sequitur Sinus, quem ab ortu Tabin immane promontorium complectitur. In hunc medium maxima illabuntur flumina, quŠ vniuersam Regionem Sericam perluentia vtque existimo in intima continentis vsque magnis nauigijs peruia, facillimam rationem exhibent quaslibet merces ex Cataio, Mangi, Mien, cŠterÝseque circumfusis regnis contrahendi, atque in Angliam deportandi. CŠter¨m c¨m non temerè cam nauigationem intermissam crederem, opinabar ab Imperatore Russorum et MoscouiŠ obstaculum aliquod interiectum fuisse. Quod si verˬ cum illius gratia vlterior illac nauigatio detur, suaderem profecto non prim¨m Tabin promontorium quŠrere, atque explorare, sed Sinum hunc atque flumina, in ijsque portum aliquem commodissimum, stationÚmque Anglicis Mercatoribus deligere, ex quo deinceps maiore opportunitate, minorib˙sque periculis Tabin promontorium, et totius Cathai circumnauigatio indagari posset. [Sidenote: Tabin promontorium ingens.] Esse autem ingens in Septentrionem excurrens promontorium Tabin, non ex Plinio tant¨m, ver¨m et alijs scriptoribus, et tabulis aliquot (licèt rudius depictis) certum habeo. Polum etiam Magnetis haud longè vltra Tabin situm esse, certis Magnetis obseruationibus didici: circa quem et Tabin plurimos esse scopulos, difficilÚmque et periculosam nauigationibus existimo: difficiliorem tamen ad Cathaium accessum fore opinor, ea pua nunc vÝa in Occidentem tentatur. Propinquior enim fiet hŠc nauigatio polo Magnetis quÓm altera, ad quem propi¨s accedere non puto tutum esse. [Sidenote: Quo propius ad polum acceditur, eˬ directorium Nauiticum magis a Septentrione deuiat.] Quia verˬ Magnes alium quam Mundi polum habet, quo ex omni parte, respicit: quo propi¨s ad eum acceditur, eˬ directorium illud Nauticum magnetis virtute imbutum, magis Ó Septentrione deuiat, nunc in Occidentem, nunc in Orientem, prout quis vel orientalior, vel occidentalior est illo Meridiano qui per vtrumque polum Magnetis, et Mundi ducitur, Mirabilis est hŠc varietas, et quŠ nauigantem plurim¨m fallere potest, nisi hanc Magnetis inconstantiam nˬrit, et ad poli, eleuationem per instrumenta subinde respiciat. In hac re si non sit instructus D. Arthurus, aut ea sit dexteritate, vt deprehenso errore eum inuenire et castigare possit timeo ne deuias faciat ambages, tempus ilium fallat, et semiperacto negotio, Ó gelu prŠoccupetur: Aiunt enim Sinum illum forti¨s quotannis congelari. Quod si contingat: hoc quod consultius mihi visum fuit, proximum illi erit refugium, vt in eo sinu, ijsque fluminibus quŠ dixi, portum quŠrat et per Legatum aliquem, cum magno Cham nomine SerenissimŠ ReginŠ, notitiam, amicitißmque contrahat: quam opinor Maximo orbis Imperatori gratam, imo gratissimam fore propter remotissima commercia. [Sidenote: Bautisus et Oechardus maxima flumina in hunc Sinum illabuntur.] Opinor ab ostijs Bautisi et Oechardi fluminum maximorum, vsque ad Cambalu Regiam summam Chami, non vltra 300. milliaria Germanica esse, et iter sumendum per Ezinam vrbem regni Tangut, quŠ 100. tant¨m milliarijs Germanicis ab ostijs distare videtur, et paret Magno Cham.

[Sidenote: Postulata Mercatoris de quibus certior fieri cupit.] Valde optarem cognoscere, quÓm altŔ communiter exurgat Šstus maris in eo MoscouiŠ portu quem vestri pro statione habent, et in alijs vers¨s orientem locis vsque ad Tabin. Item, an mare in hoc districtu semper in vnam partem, videlicet Orientem, aut Occidentem fluat, an verˬ pro ratione Šstuum fluat et refluat, in medio inquam canali, hoc est, an ibi, sex horis in occasum, et iterum sex in ortum fluat, an verˬ semper hi eandem partem: aliŠ enim speculationes non parum vtiles hinc dependent. Idem optarem Ó D. Frobiscero in occidentem obseruari. Quod ad sinum Merosro, et Canadam, ac Nouam Franciam attinet, ea in meis tabulis desumpta sum ex quadam Tabula marina, quŠ Ó quodam sacerdote ex earum ditionum Naucleri peritissimi Galli descriptione excerpta fuit, et illustrissimo Principi Georgio ab Austria episcopo Leodiensi oblata. Non dubito, quin quantum ad littorum situm attinet et poli eleuationem, ad veritatem ea quÓm proximŔ accedant. Habebat enim ea tabula prŠter scalam graduum latitudinis per medium sui extensam, aliam prŠterea praticularem NouŠ FranciŠ littoribus adiunctam, qua deprauatŠ latitudines, occasione, erroris Magnetis ibi commissŠ, castigarentur. Iacobi Cnoyen Buscoducensis itinerarium per omnem Asiam, Affricam, et Septentrionem, olim mihi Amicus AntuerpiŠ ab alio mutuˬ acceptum communicauit, eo vsus sum, et reddidi: post multos annos eundem ab amico repetij et reminisci ille non potuit Ó quo accepisset. Gulielmi Tripolitani et Ioannis de plano Carpini scripta non vidi, tant¨m excerpta ex illis quŠdam in alijs scriptis libris inueni. AbilfadŠ Epitome gaudeo verti, vtinam citˬ habeamus.

HŠc (mi Domine) tuis reponenda putaui: si quid est aliud quod Ó me desideres, libentissimŔ tibi communicabo: hoc vicissim amanter Ó tua humanitate petens, vt quŠ ex vtriusque nauigationis cursu obseruata nancisci poteris, mihi communices, penes me pro tuo arbitrio manebunt omnia, et quŠcunque inde collegero, fideliter ad te perscribam, si forte ad pulcherrimum, vtilissim¨mque orbi Christiano hoc nauigationis institutum aliquid opis et consilij adferre possint. Bene vale, vir doctissime. Duisburgi in Cliuia. 28. Iulij 1580.

[Sidenote: Dulce mare inter Nouam Zemblam et Tabin suspicatur.]
Redeunte
Arthuro, quŠso discas ab illo quŠ optaui, et num aticubi in suo itinere,

dulce mare, aut parum salsum inuenerit: suspicor enim mare inter Noua Zembla, et Tabin dulce esse.

T.H. paratissimus quantus quantus sum,

Gerardus Mercator.

The same in English.

Sir I receiued your letters the 19. of Iune: it grieued me much that vpon the sight of them the time being spent, I could not giue any conuenient instructions: I wish Arthur Pet had bene informed before his departure of some special points. The voyage to Cathaio by the East, is doutlesse very easie and short, and I haue oftentimes marueiled, that being so happily begun, it hath bene left of, and the course changed into the West, after that more then halfe of your voiage was discouered. For beyond the Island of Vaigats and Noua Zeembla, there foloweth presently a great Baie, which on the left side is inclosed with the mightie promontorie Tabin. [Sidenote: A great gulfe is beyond Vaigats, whereinto mighty riuers descend.] Into the mids hereof there fall great riuers, which passing through the whole countrey of Serica, and being as I thinke nauigable with great vessels into the heart of the continent, may be an easie means whereby to traffique for all maner of merchandize, and transport them out of Cathaio, Mangi, Mien, and other kingdoms thereabouts into England. But considering with my selfe that that nauigation was not intermitted, but vpon great occasion, I thought that the Emperor of Russia and Moscouie had hindered the proceeding thereof. [Sidenote: The best course to be taken in discoueries.] If so be that with his grace and fauour a furthur nauigation may be made, I would counsell them certainly not first to seeke out the promontorie Tabin, but to search this baie and riuers aforesayd, and in them to picke and chuse out some conuenient port and harborough for the English merchants, from whence afterward with more opportunitie and lesse perill, the promontorie Tabin and all the coast of Cathaio may bee discouered. And that there is such a huge promontorie called Tabin, I am certainly perswaded not onely out of Plinie, but also other writers, and some Maps (though somewhat rudely drawen:) and that the Pole of the Loadstone is not farre beyond Tabin, I haue learned by the certaine obseruations of the Loadstone: about which pole and Tabin I thinke there are very many rockes, and very hard and dangerous sailing: and yet a more hard and difficile passage I think it to bee this way which is now attempted by the West, for it is neerer to the pole of the Loadstone, to the which I thinke it not safe to approach. And because the Loadstone hath another pole then that of the world, to the which from all parts it hath a respect, the neerer you come vnto it, the more the needle of the Compasse doeth varie from the North, sometimes to the West, and sometimes to the East, according as a man is to the Eastward or to the Westward of that Meridian, that passeth by both the poles of the Magnes and the World.

This is a strange alteration and very apt to deceiue the Sailer, vnlesse hee know the vnconstancie and variation of the Compasse, and take the eleuation of the pole sometimes with his instruments. If master Arthur be not well prouided in this behalfe, or of such dexteritie, that perceiuing the errour he be not able to correct the same, I feare lest in wandering vp and downe he lose his time, and be ouertaken with the ice in the midst of the enterprise. For that gulfe, as they say, is frozen euery yere very hard. Which if it be so, the best counsel I could giue for their best safetie, were to seeke some harborough in that baie, and those riuers whereof I haue spoken, and by some Ambassador to make friendship and acquaintance with the great Can, in name of the Queenes maiestie, which I beleeue will be gratefull to the mightiest Emperour in the world, yea most excellent for the length of the traffique, and great distance of the places. [Sidenote: The mouthes of Bautisus and Oechardus 300. leagues from Cambalu.] I thinke from the mouthes of the mighty riuers Bautisus and Oechardus to Cambalu the chiefest seat of the prince the Can, there are not past 300. Germaine miles, and to passe by Ezina a citie of the kingdom of Tangut, which seemeth to be but 100. Germaine miles from the mouthes of the sayd riuers, and is subiect to the great Can.

I would gladly know how high the sea doeth flowe commonly in the port of Moscouia where your men do harborow, and in other Easterly places vnto Tabin. [Sidenote: Vpon the obseruations of the tides depend great speculations.] And also whether the sea in this streight do flow alwaies one way to the East or to the West, or whether it do ebbe and flow according to the matter of the tides in the middle of the chanel, that is to say, whether it flow there sixe houres into the West, and as many backe againe to the East, for hereupon depend other speculations of importance. I would wish M. Frobisher to obserue the same Westwards. Concerning the gulfe of Merosro and Canada, and new France which are in my mappes, they were taken out of a certaine sea card drawn by a certaine priest out of the description of a Frenchman, a Pilot very skilfull in those partes, and presented to the worthy Prince George of Austria, bishop of Liege: for the trending of the coast, and the eleuation of the pole, I doubt not but they are very neere the trueth: For the Charte had beside a scale of degrees of latitude passing through the middest of it, another particularly annexed to the coast of New France, wherewith the errour of the latitudes committed by reason of the variation of the compasse might be corrected. The historie of the voyage of Iacobus Cnoyen Buschoducensis throughout al Asia, Affrica, and the North, was lent me in time past by a friend of mine at Antwerpe. After I had vsed it, I restored it againe: after many yeeres I required it againe of my friend, but hee had forgotten of whom hee had borrowed it. The writings of Gulielmus Tripolitanus, and Ioannes de Plano Carpini I neuer saw: onely I found certaine pieces of them in other written hand bookes. I am glad the Epitomie of Abilfada is translated, I would we might haue it shortly.

Thus much Sir I thought good to answere your letters: if there bee anything els that you would require of me, I will most willingly communicate it with you, crauing this likewise of your curtesie, that whatsoeuer obseruations of both these voyages shall come to your hands, you would impart them to me, they shall all remaine with mee according to your discretion and pleasure, and whatsoeuer I gather of them, I will faithfully signifie vnto you by letter if happily they may yeeld any helpe or light vnto this most excellent enterprise of nauigation, and most profitable to our Christian common wealth. Fare, you well most learned friend. At Duisburg in Cliueland, 28. of Iulie, the yeere, 1580.

At Arthur his returne I pray you learne of him the things I haue requested, and whether any where in his voiage, he found the sea fresh, or not very salt: for I suppose the Sea betweene Noua Zembla and Tabin to be fresh.

Yours wholly to my power to be commanded.

Gerardus Mercator.

* * * * *

The discouerie made by M. Arthur Pet and M. Charles Iackman, of the Northeast parts, beyond the Island of Vaigatz, with two Barkes: the one called the George, the other the William, in the yeere 1580. Written by Hugh Smith.

[Sidenote: May.] Upon Monday the 30. of May, we departed from Harwich in the afternoone, the winde being at South, and to the Eastward. The ebbe being spent, we could not double the pole, and therefore were constrained to put in againe vntill next day in the morning, being the last of May: which day wee wayed our ankers about 3. a clocke in the morning, the wind being West southwest. The same day we passed Orfordnesse at an East Sunne, and Stamford at a West Sunne, and Yarmouth at a West northwest sunne, and so to Winterton, where we did anker al night: it was then calme, and the flood was come.

[Sidenote: Iune.] The next day being the first of Iune, we set saile at 3. a clocke in the morning, and set our course North, the wind at the Southwest, and at Southsouthwest.

The 10. day about one of the clocke in the afternoone, wee put into Norway to a place where one of the headlands of the sound is called Bottel:

the other headland is called Moile. [Sidenote: Kene an Island of Norway.] There is also an Island called Kene. Here I did find the pole to be eleuated 62. deg. it doeth flowe there South, and it hieth 7. or 8. foote, not aboue.

The 11. day in the morning the winde came to the South and to the Southeast: the same daye at sixe in the afternoone we set saile, and bare along the coast: it was very foule weather with raine and fogge.

[Sidenote: The North cape doubled.] The 22. day the wind being at West, we did hall the coast East northeast, and East. The same day at 6. in the morning we did double the north cape. About 3. in the afternoone wee past Skites bearenesse, and hald along the coast East, and East southeast, and all the same night wee halled Southeast, and Southeast by East.

[Sidenote: Wardhouse.] The 23. day about 3. in the morning we came to Wardhouse, the wind at the Northwest The cause of our comming in was to seeke the William, whose companie we lost the 6. day of this moneth, and to send letters into England. About one of the clock in the after noone the William also came into Wardhouse to vs in good safetie, and all her company in good health.

The 24. the wind came to the East Northeast. This day the William was hald a ground, because she was somewhat leake, and to mend her steerage. This night about 12. of the clocke she did hale a flote againe.

The 25. day the wind was at East northeast.

The 26. day the Toby of Harwich departed from Wardhouse for London, Thomas
Greene being master, to whom we deliuered our letters.

The 27. day the wind was at South southeast, and the 28. also.

The 29. day about 6. in the afternoone, the wind came to the West northwest for the space of one houre, and presently to the East againe, and so was variable all the same night.

The 30. about sixe in the morning, the winde came to East southeast, and continued so all the same day.

[Sidenote: Iuly.] The first of Iuly about 5. in the afternoone, the wind was at Northnorthwest: and about 7. of the clocke we set saile from Wardhouse East and by South.

The second day about 5. in the morning, the wind was East, and East Southeast, and we did lie to the shorewards. And about 10. in the morning the wind came to South southeast, and we laid it to the Eastward: sometime we lay East by South, some time East southeast, and sometimes East by North. [Sidenote: Willoughbies land.] About 5. in the afternoone we bare with the William, who was willing to goe with Kegor, because we thought her to be out of trie, and sailed very ill, where we might mend her steerage: whereupon Master Pet not willing to go into harborough said to Master Iackman, that if he thought himselfe not able to keepe the sea, he should doe as he thought best, and that he in the meanetime would beare with Willoughbies land, for that it was a parcel of our direction, and would meete him at Veroue Ostroue, or Vaigats, and so we set our course East northeast, the winde being at Southeast.

[Sidenote: 50. leagues from Kegor.] The 3 day the winde at Southeast we found the pole to be eleuated 70. degrees 46. minuts. The same night at 12. of the clocke we sounded, but had no ground, in 120. fathoms, being fifty leagues from the one side by our reckoning East northeast from Kegor.

The 4. day all the morning was calme. This day we found the pole to be eleuated 71. degrees 38. minutes. This day at 9. in the afternoone the wind at Northeast with a gentle gale, we hald along Southeast by East.

The 5. day the wind at Northwest, we hald East and East by South: this day we saw land, but we could not make it, the wind being Northerly, so that we could not come neere to it.

The 6. day about 2. in the afternoone, the wind at North northwest, we halde East southeast with a faire and gentle gale: this day we met with ice. About 6. in the arternoone it became calme: we with saile and oares laide it to the Northeast part, hoping that way to cleare vs of it: for that way we did see the head part of it, as we thought. Which done, about 12. of the clocke at night we gate cleere of it. We did think it to be ice of the bay of Saint Nicholas, but it was not as we found afterwards.

[Sidenote: A site of perfect land.] The seuenth day we met with more yce at the East part of the other yce: we halde along a weather the yce to finde some ende thereof by east northeast. This day there appeared more land North from vs being perfect land: the ice was betweene vs and it, so that we could not come neerer to it.

The same morning at sixe of the clocke wee put into the ice to finde some way through it, wee continued in it all the same day and all the night following, the winde by the North and Northwest. Wee were constrained to goe many pointes of our compasse, but we went most an Easterly course.

The eight day the winde at North northwest, we continued our course, and at fiue in the morning we sounded, and had 90. fadoms red oze. This day at foure in the afternoone we sounded againe, and had 84. fadoms oze, as before. At sixe in the after noone we cleared our selues of the ice, and hald along Southeast by South: we sounded againe at 10. a clocke at night, and had 43. fathom sandy oze.

The 9. day at 2. in the morning, we sounded againe, and had 45. fadoms, then there appeared a shadow of land to vs East Northeast, and so we ran with it the space of 2. houres, and then perceiuing it was but fogge, we hald along Southeast.

[Sidenote: 70. deg. 3. min.] This day at 2 in the afternoone we sounded and had fiftie fadams blacke oze. Our latitude was 70. degrees three minutes. At 10. a clocke at night we sounded againe and had fiftie fadoms black oze.

The tenth day the wind being at North northwest, we haled East and by North, which course we set, because at ten of the clocke afore noone wee did see land, and then wee sounded hauing 35. fadoms blacke oze. All this day there was a great fogge, so that wee durst not beare with the land to make it, and so we kept an outwardly course. [Sidenote: An Island.] This day at 6. in the afternoone we espied land, wherewith we halled, and then it grew calme: we sounded and had 120. fadoms blacke oze: and then we sent our boat a land to sound and proue the land. The same night we came with our ship within an Island, where we rode all the same night. The same night wee went into a bay to ride neere the land for wood and water.

[Sidenote: The maine land.] The 11. day the wind came to the East southeast: this day about a league from vs to the Eastwards, we saw a very faire sound or riuer that past very farre into the countrey with 2. or 3. branches with an Island in the midst.

The 12. of Iuly the wind was East Southeast. [Sidenote: Barebay.] This day about 11. a clocke in the morning, there came a great white beare down to the water side, and tooke the water of his owne accord, we chased him with our boate, but for all that we could doe, he gote to land and escaped from vs, where we named the bay Barebay. This day at 7. in the after noone we set saile, for we had good hope that the winde would come Westerly, and with saile and oares we gate the sea. All the night it was calme with fogge.

The 13. day in the morning the wind was very variable with fog, and as it cleared vp wee met with great store of ice, which at the first shewed like land. This ice did vs much trouble, and the more because of the fog, which continued vntill the 14. day 12. of the clocke.

The 14. day in the morning we were so inibayed with ice, yet we were constrained to come out as we went in, which was by great good fortune, or rather by the goodnesse of God, otherwise it had bene impossible, and at 12. of the clock we were cleere of it, the wind being at South and South by West. [Sidenote: 70. deg. 26. min.] The same day we found the pole to be eleuated 70. degrees 26. minutes: [Sidenote: The supposed maine of Noua Zembla.] we lay along the coast Northwest, thinking it to be an Island, but finding no end in rowing so long, we supposed it to be the maine of Noua

Xembla. [Footnote: They were really in the Gulf of Petchora.] About 2. in the afternoone we laide it to the Southward to double the ice, which wee could not doe vpon that boorde, so that we cast about againe and lay West along vnder the ice. About seuen in the afternoone we gote about the greatest part thereof. About 11. a clock at night we brought the ice Southeast of us, and thus we were ridde of this trouble at this time.

The 15. day about 3. in the morning, the winde was at South southwest: wee cast about and lay to the Eastwards: the winde did Wester, so that wee lay South southwest with a flawne sheete, and so we ranne all the same day. About 8. in the after noone we sounded, and had 23. fadoms small grey sand. This night at twelue of the clocke we sounded againe, and had 29. fadoms sand, as afore.

The 16. day vnto 3. in the morning we hald along East Southeast, where we found 18. fadoms red sand, then we hald along Northeast. [Sidenote: Many ouerfals.] In these soundings wee had many ouerfals. This day at 10. of the clocke we met with more ice, which was very great, so that we coulde not tell which way to get cleere of it. Then the winde came to the South Southeast, so that we lay to the Northwards. We thought that way to cleere our selues of it, but that way we had more ice. About 6. in the afternoone, the wind came to the East. Then we lay to the Southwards that wee had 30 fadoms black oze. This day we found the pole to bee eleuated 69. deg. 40. minutes, and this night at 12. a clocke we had 41. fadoms red sand.

The 17. day at 3. in the morning, we had 12. fadoms. At 9. we had 8. and 7. all this day we ran South and South by West, at the depth aforesaid, red sand, being but shallow water. At eight in the afternoone, the winde with a showre and thunder came to the Southwest, and then we ranne East Northeast. [Sidenote: The bay of Pechora.] At 12. at night it came to the South and by East, and all this was in the bay of Pechora.

The 18. day at 7. in the morning we bare with the headland of the bay, where wee founde two Islands. There are also ouerfals of water or tides. We went betweene the maine and the Island, next to the head, where we had about 2. fadoms and a halfe. We found the pole eleuated 69. deg. 13. minutes. [Sidenote: They had sight of Vaigatz.] This day we had sight of Vaigatz: the land of the maine of Pechora did trend Southeast, we hald East southeast, and had 10. fadoms oze all the same day vntill 4. in the after noone, then being calme, we ankered in 10. fadoms all the same night.

The 19. day at two in the morning we set saile, and ran South and South southwest all the same day at 8. 7. and 6. fadoms, this was off the South part of Vaigatz, this part of the land lieth North and South. This day at 4. in the afternoone we found shallow water sometime 4. fadoms, sometime 3. and 2. and a halfe, and one fadome and a halfe: there we ankered and sent our boate away to sound, and all to leeward we had 4 foote and 3. foote, and 2. foot, there was not water for the boate betweene Vaigatz and the other side: finding no more water, there was no other way but to goe backe as we came in, hauing the wind Northwest, so at twelue at night we set saile.

The 20. day we plied to the Northwards, and got deepe water againe 6. and 7. fadoms.

The 21. day the winde by the Northwest, we hald along the coast North and
North northwest, we had 8. and 9. and 10. fadoms.

The 22. day the winde came to the Southwest, we bare along the coast of Vaygatz, as we found it to lie North and by West, and North northwest, and North. [Sidenote: An Island hauing store of wood and water.] The winde blewe very much with great fogge, we lacking Water and wood bare within an Island where wee founde great store of wood and water, there were three or foure goodly sounds. Vnder two points there was a crosse set vp, and a man buried at the foote of it. Vpon the said crosse Master Pet did graue his name with the date of our Lorde, and likewise vpon a stone at the foote of the crosse, and so did I also, to the end that if the William did chaunce to come thither, they might haue knowledge that wee had bene there. At eight in the afternoone the winde came to the North northwest, we set saile and turned out of the Bay. The same night the winde came to the West, so that wee lay North along the land.

[Sidenote: 6. faire islands.] The 23. day at fiue in the morning, the wind came to the Southwest, a Sea boord we sawe a great number of faire Islands, to the number of sixe: a sea boord of these Islands, there are many great ouerfals, as great streames or tides: we halde Northeast and East northeast as the land did trend. At eight aforenoone the winde came to the Southeast with very much wind, raine and fogge, and very great store of ice a sea boorde: so we lay to the Southwest to attaine to one of the Islands to harbour vs if the weather did so extremely continue and to take in our boate, thinking it meete so to doe, and not to towe her in such weather. About twelue of the clocke it became very calme vpon the sudden, and came vp to the West Northwest, and Northwest by West, and then we tooke in our boate, and this done, there came downe so much winde, as we were not able to steere afore it, with corse and bonnets of each, we hald South with the land, for so the land did trend. This day all the afternoone we sailed vnder a great land of ice, we sailed betweene the land and it, being not able to crosse it. About twelue at night we found the ice to stretch into the land, that we could not get cleare to the Eastward, so we laide it to the shore, and there we founde it cleare hard aboord the shore, and we found also a very faire Island which makes a very good harbour, and within are 12. fadoms.

[Sidenote: An Island to the East of Vaigatz 4. or 5. leagues] This Island is to the Eastwards of Vaigatz 4 or 5. leagues. This land of the maine doth trend Southeast, and Southeast by East. It is a very faire coast, and euen and plaine, and not full of mountaines nor rocks: you haue but shallow water of 6. or 7. fadoms, about a league from the shore, all this morning we hailed East southeast This day we found the pole to be eleuated 69. degrees 14. minutes. About 12 a clocke we were constrained to put into the ice to seeke some way to get to the Northwards of it, hoping to haue some cleare passage that way, but there was nothing but whole ice. About nine in the afternoone we had sight of the William, and when wee sawe her, there was a great land of ice betweene her and vs, so that we could not come one to the other, but as we came neere to her, we sounded our trumpet and shot off two muskets, and she put out her flag vpon her foretopmaste in token that she did see vs: all this time wee did shorten our sailes, and went with our foresaile and mainetopsaile, seeking the best way through the broken ice, she making away the best that she could to follow vs, we put out our flagge to answere her again with the like: thus we continued all the aftemoone till about 12. a clocke at night, and then we moored our ship to a piece of ice to tarie for the William.

[Sidenote: The Willaim and the George meete againe.] The 25. day about fiue in the morning, the William came to vs, being both glad of our meeting. The William had her sterne post broken, that the rudder did hang clean besides the sterne, so that she could in no wise port her helme, with all hands she did lighten her sterne and trimme her head, and when we had brought her forward all that we could, wee brought a cable vnder her sterne, and with our capstaine did wind vp her sterne, and so we made it as wel as the place would giue vs leaue, and in the ende wee brought her to steere againe. Wee acknowledge this our meeting to be a great benefits of God for our mutuall comfort and so gaue his Maiestie thanks for it. All the night after we tooke our rest being made fast vpon a piece of ice: the wind was at the West Northwest, but we were so inclosed with ice that we coulde not tell which way to passe. Windes wee haue had at will, but ice and fogge too much against our willes, if it had pleased the Lod God otherwise.

The 26. day the wind was at West Northwest: we set saile to the Northwardes, to seeke if we could finde any way cleare to passe to the Eastward, but the further we went that way, the more and thicker was the ice, so that we coulde goe no further. So about foure in the afternoon we were constrained to moare vpon another piece of ice. I thinke we sailed in all a league this day, here we had 15. fadoms oze, and this oze is all the chanell ouer. All the same day after foure of the clocke, and all the night we tarried there, being without all good hope, but rather in despaire. This day Master Iugman did see land East Northeast from vs, as he did thinke, whether it were land or no, I cannot tell well, but it was very like land: but the fogges haue many times deceiued vs. [Footnote: And did so again in this instance.]

The 27. day the winde was at Northwest. This day at nine in the morning we set saile to seeke the shore. Further into the ice we could not goe, and at seuen in the afternoone we moared to a piece of ice, and the William with vs, here we had 14. fathoms oze. At three in the aftemoone we warpt from one ice to another. At nine in the afternoone we moared againe to a piece of ice vntill the next day. All this night it did snow with much wind, being at West Northwest, and at Northwest, and by West.

The 28. day the winde came to the Southwest, and Southsouthwest: this day was a very faire day. [Sidenote: Their returne.] At one in the afternoone master Pet and master Iackman did conferre together what was best to be done considering that the windes were good for vs, and we not able to passe for ice, they did agree to seeke to the land againe, and so to Vaygatz, and there to conferre further. At 3. in the afternoone we did warpe from one piece of ice to another to get from them if it were possible: here were pieces of ice so great, that we could not see beyond them out of the toppe. Thus we warped vnlil 9. in the afternoone, and then we moared both our shippes to a great and high piece of ice, vntil the next morning.

[Sidenote: The currant runneth with the winde.] The nine and twenty day the winde came to the Southwest, wee set saile at fiue in the morning to plie into the shore if it were possible, we made many turnes among the ice to small purpose, for with the winde doeth the currant runne. This day by misfortune a piece of ice stroke of our greepe afore at two afternoone, yet for all this we turned to doe our best. The William being incumbred with ice, and perceiuing that shee did litle good, tooke in all her sailes, and made her selfe fast to a piece of ice, and about foure in the afternoone she set saile to followe vs. We were afraide that shee had taken some hurt, but she was well. At seuen afore noone we tooke in all our sailes to tarie for the William, and made our shippe fast to a piece of ice: the William before she came to vs tooke in all her sailes, and moared to another piece of ice, and thus we continued vntill the next morning.

The 30. day the winde at Southeast, and by South, and at 9. in the morning we set saile, and sooner would haue done if the William had bene by vs, but we did tary for her to know whether all was well with her: But as soone as we made saile, she did the like. All this day we did our best to seeke our way as the ice would giue vs leaue, sometime we lay South, sometime West, and sometime East, and thus we continued vntill eight at night, and then being calme, wee made our ship fast to a picce of ice, and went to supper. In the meane time the wind with a faire gentle gale came vp to the East, and East and by South, but there came downe a showre of raine with it, which continued the space of one houre: Which being done, it became calme againe, so that wee could doe no good all that night, but tooke our rest vntill the next day.

The 31. the winde being at Southwest, we set saile to turne to windeward at three a clock in the morning. In this turning we did litle good, for the currant would not giue vs leaue. For as the winde is, so is the currant. We did our best vntill ten of the clock, and then perceiuing that we did no good, and being inclosed with ice, wee made our ships fast to a piece of ice: All this day the William lay still, and did as much good as we that did labour all the forenoone. Thus we took our rest all the same day.

In the afternoone we set saile, the winde being at South and by East, we lay to the Westwards, as Southwest and Southwest and by South, and sometime to the Westward as wee might. Thus we continued vntil 9. at night, and then we could go no further for ice: so we with the William were constrained to make our ship fast to a piece of ice al the same night This day we found the pole eleuated 69. degrees 20. minutes, and here we had 17. fathoms oze.

[Sidenote: August.]The first day of August was verie calme in the morning, the winde beeing at West Northwest. About twelue the winde came to the West, and continued so all the same night with great fogge.

The second day the winde was at Southwest all day with rayne and fogge. All this day wee were inclosed with ice, so that we were forced to lye still. Here we had one and twentie fathoms oze. At sixe in the afternoone the winde was at West with very much foule weather, and so continued all the same night.

The third day the winde was at West, and West by North, and West Northwest, this day we lay still inclosed with yce, the weather being darke with fogge: thus abiding the Lords leasure, we continued with patience. And sounding we found 21. fathoms.

The fourth day we lay still inclosed with ice, the winde being at West Northwest, this ice did euery day increase vpon vs, yet putting our trust in God, we hoped to be deliuered out of it in good time.

The fift day all the morning it rained with very much wind, being at South Southeast: about 3. in the afternoone we set sayle, and presently it became calme for the space of one houre, then the wind came to the North Northeast. and here we had 33. fathoms: thus we made way among the yce Southwest, and Southsouthwest, and West, as we might finde our way for the space of 3. houres: [Sidenote: A whole land of yce.] then we met with a whole land of yce, so that we could go no further: here we moared our ship to tarie for a further opening. Here we found 45. fathoms oze, and all the night was very darke with fogge.

The sixt day hauing no opening of the yce wee lay still, the winde being at West, and West by South: here we had sixty three fathoms oze: all the same night the winde was at the West Northwest.

The 7. day the winde was at West, and West and by North all day. And all this day we lay still being inclosed with yce, that we could not stirre, labouring onely to defend the yce as it came vpon vs. Here we had 68. fathoms oze.

The 8. day was very faire and calme but foggy. This day towards night there was litle winde by the South Southwest: then the yce began a litle to open, and here we had 70. fathoms oze: all the night was foggy.

The 9. day the winde was at Northwest, and by West all the afternoone we lay still because of the yce, which did still inclose vs. [Sidenote: 70. degr. 4. min.] This day we found the pole eleuated seuenty degrees, 4. minutes, we had 63. fathoms oze: this night was a very fayre night, but it freezed: in the morning we had much adoe to goe through the same: [Sidenote: Frost.] and we were in doubt that if it should haue freezed so much the night following, we should hardly haue passed out of it. This night there was one star that appeared to vs. [Marginal note: The appearing of the starres, signe of Winter.]

The tenth day the winde was at East Northeast with very small gale. Wee with saile and oares made way through the yce: about fiue in the morning we set saile: sometime we laye Southwest, and sometime South, and sometime West, as wee might best finde the way. About three in the afternoone the gale began to fresh: about six in the afternoone the winde was at Northeast with fogge. [Sidenote: Much snow.] Here we had eighty eight fathoms: we bare saile all the same night, and it snowed very much.

The eleuenth day we were much troubled with yce, and by great force we made our way through it, which we thought a thing impossible: but extremity doth cause men to doe much, and in the weaknesse of man Gods strength most appeareth. This day we had 95. fathoms. At three in the afternoone the winde came to the Southwest, we were forced to make our shippe faste to a piece of yce, for we were inclosed with it, and taried the Lordes leasure. This night we had 97. fathoms.

The 12. day the wind was at the Southeast not very much but in a maner calme: at a 11. of the clocke the winde came to the West Southwest: all the day was very darke with snowe and fogge. At 6. in the afternoone we set saile the winde being at the North Northeast: all this night we bare away Southwest, and Southsouthwest, as well and as neere as the yce would giue vs leaue: all this night we found the yce somewhat fauourable to vs, more then it was before, wherupon we stood in good hope to get out of it.

The 13. day at 7. in the morning the winde was at the Northeast, and Northeast and by East: all this day we were much troubled with the yce, for with a blow against a piece of yce we brake the stocke of our ancre, and many other great blowes we had against the yce, that it was marueilous that the ship was able to abide them: the side of our boate was broken with our ship which did recule back, the boate being betwixt a great piece of yce, and the ship, and it perished the head of our rudder. [Sidenote: great store of snowe.] This day was a very hard day with vs: at night we found much broken yce, and all this night it blewe very much winde, so that we lay in drift with the yce, and our drift was South, for the winde was at North all this night, and we had great store of snowe.

The 14. day in the morning wee made our shippe fast to a piece of yce, and let her driue with it. In the meane time wee mended our boate and our steerage; all this day the winde continued Northerly, and here wee had threescore and two fathoms. Thus we lay a drift all the same night.

The 15. day we set saile at 6. in the morning, the winde being at Northeast. At 9. aforenoon we entred into a clear Sea without yce, whereof wee were most glad, and not without great cause, and gaue God the praise. We had 19. fathoms water, and ranne in Southwest all the morning vntill we came to 14. fathoms, and thence we halted West, til we came to 10. fathoms, and then we went Northwest, for so the land doeth trend. At 12. of the clocke we had sight of the land, which we might haue had sooner, but it was darke and foggie all the same day: for when wee had sight of the lande, wee were not passing three leagues from it. [Sidenote: 69 degrees 49 minutes.] This day we had the pole eleuated 69 degrees 49 minutes. All day we ran along the coast in ten and nine fadoms, pepered sand. It is a very goodly coast and a bolde, and faire soundings off it, without sandes or rocks.

[They are thwart against Vaigatz.] The 16 day the winde was at East: this day we were troubled againe with ice, but we made great shift with it: for we gotte betweene the shoare and it. This day at twelue of the clocke we were thwart of the Southeast part of Vaigats, all along which part there was great store of yce, so that we stood in doubt of passage, yet by much adoe we got betwixt the shoare and it: about 6 in the afternoone was found a great white beare vpon a piece of ice: all this day in the afternoone it was darke with fogge. And all the night we haled North and North by West, and sometime North and by East, for so doth the land trend;

[Sidenote: Sands.] The 17 day in the morning we haled West, for so doth the land lie. The wind was at Southeast, and it was very darke with fogge, and in running along the shoare we fell a ground, but God be praised without hurt, for wee came presently off againe. [Sidenote: The Islands.] The William came to an anker to stay for vs, and sent some of their men to help vs, but before they came we were vnder saile, and as we came, to the William we did stowe our boates, and made saile, we went within some of the Islands, and haled Westsouthwest.

About two of the clocke in the atfternoone, we set our course Southwest and by South: so we ranne Southwest vntill twelue at night, the wind came to the Northnortheast, and then we haled West.

The 18 day at 6 in the morning we had 16 fadoms red sand: at 6 in the morning 13 fadoms. At 10. 14 fadoms, and we haled Westnorthwest. At 12 a clock the winde came to the East, and East by South, we haled West and by North all the same day and night. At 6 in the afternoone we had 17 fadoms red sand.

The 19 day the wind was at Eastnortheast: at 6 in the morning wee had 19 fadoms red sand: at 12 of the clock the wind blew North and North by East, we had 17 fadoms of water, at 3 in the afternoone 15.

The 20 day the wind was at Northeast, and Northnortheast: at 7 in the morning we had 30 fadomes blacke oze: at twelue of the clocke we were vpon the suddaine in shoale water, among great sands and could find no way out. By sounding and seeking about, we came aground, and so did the William, but we had no hurt, for the wind was off the shoare, and the same night it was calme: all night we did our best, but we could not haue her afloat. [Sidenote: Shoales off Colgoyeue.] These shoales doe lie off Colgoyeue; it is very flat a great way off, and it doth not high aboue 2 or 3 foote water: it floweth Northeast and Southwest.

The 21 day the wind was at Southwest, and being very faire weather we did lighten our ships as much as was possible for vs to doe, by reason of the place. The same high water, by the helpe of God, we got both a floate, and the wind being at the Southwest did help vs, for it caused it to flow the more water.

This day we found the pole to be eleuated 68 degrees 40 min. In the afternoone we both set saile to seeke way to get out of these sands, our boate a head sounding, hauing 6, 7, and 8 fadomes all within the sand which was without vs. We bare to the Southward, and the William bare more to the Eastwards, and night being at hand the wind came to the Southeast, whereupon we layd it to the Southwards, lying Southwest, and South and by West, and ran to 19, and 12 and 14 fadoms and presently we had sixe fadoms, which was off the sands head, which we were a ground vpon the day before. Then we cast about to the Eastwards for deepe water, which we presently had, as 10, 15, and 20 and so to 23 fadoms.

[Sidenote: They lost the William here.] The 22 day at eight in the morning, we cast about to the Southward; and this day in the morning we saw the William vnder our lee as far as we could see her, and with a great fogge we lost the sight of her, and since we haue not seene her. Thus we ranne til we came to thirtie fadomes black oze, which we had at twelue of the clocke, and at three in the afternoone we had twenty and three fadoms and then we ranne Westnorthwest, and West by North, all the same night following.

The 23 day we had at 6 in the morning 27 fadoms, at 8 a clocke 28 fadoms, at 9 the winde being at East Southeast, we haled Westnorthwest: [Sidenote: The land of Hungry.] this day we had sight of the land of Hugri side. At twelue of the clocke we had two fadoms sand. [Sidenote: The bay of Morzouets.] This day we ranne West and by North, and came to fiue fadoms off the bay of Morzouets. Then we layd it to the Northwards so that we lay Northnortheast off. The wind after came to the North, and North by East, and we lay East and East by North, then we layd it to the Westward againe: and thus we lay till we came to fortie fadoms, and then we went Northwest till wee came to fourteene fadoms, and so to tenne fadoms. Then we cast about to the Eastwards and lay East, and East by North all the same night.

The 24 day at 8 in the morning we had 32 fadoms. We ran Northwest till we came to 11 fadoms, then we lay to the Northwards till 12 at night, and then we came to forty fadoms, then the wind at Northeast we lay to the Westwards, and haled Northeast along.

The 25 at 4 in the morning we had 37 fadoms, wee ranne Northwest, the winde at Northnortheast very much.

The 26 day we ran with the same winde, and found the pole to be eleuated 70 deg. 40 min.

The 27 at 7 in the morning we saw land, which we made to be Kegor, then we haled Northwest, and North by West to double the North Cape.

The 28 day at 3 in the morning we ran Northwest, and so all day. At night the wind came to the Southwest, and we ran Northwest all that night.

[Sidenote: The towne of Hungon.] The 29 day we put into a sound called Tane, and the towne is called Hungon: we came to an ancre at 5 in the afternoone, at 25 fadoms very faire sand. This sound is very large and good, and the same night we got water aboard.

The 30 day in the morning the winde at Northeast, and but litle, we set saile, and with our boate on head we got the sea about 12 of the clocke: the wind with a faire gale came to the East Southeast, and all this day and night we ran West Northwest.

[Sidenote: They double the North Cape in their return.] The 31 day at 12 of the clocke we doubled the North Cape, the wind being at Eastsoutheast, we haled West all the same day, and at night we ran Westsouthwest.

The 1 day of September the wind was at Northeast with very much fogge: all this day we ran Westsouthwest: at 2 in the afternoone the wind came North.

The second day at 3 in the morning we doubled Fowlnesse, and the wind was this day variable at all parts of the Compasse. In the afternoone we made but little way: at 6 a clocke the wind came to the Southwest, and we went Northwest. [Sidenote: Fowlenesse.] At 9 in the night there came downe so much winde by the Westsouthwest, that we were faine to lay it a hull, we haled it to Northwards for the space of 2 houres, and then we layd her head to the Southwards, and at the breake of day we saw land, which is very high, and is called by the men of the countrey Foulenesse. It is within ful of small Islands, and without full of rocks very farre out, and within the rockes you haue fayre sand at 20 fadoms.

The 3 day in the morning we bare with the sound aforesaid: Within it is but shoale water, 4 5 and 3 fadoms, sandie ground, the land is very high, and the Church that is seene is called Helike Kirke. It doeth high here not aboue 8 or 9 foote.

[Sidenote: Lowfoote.] The 12 day at 3 in the afternoone, we put into a sound by Lowfoote, where it doeth flowe Southwest, and by South, and doth high 7 or 8 foote water.

The 13 day much wind at West: we had a ledge of rocks in the wind of vs, but the road was reasonable good for all Southerly and Westerly winds. We had the maine land in the winde of vs: this day was stormie with raine.

[Sidenote: The sound of Romesal.] The 23 day at foure of the clocke in the afternoone we put into Norway, into a sound called Romesal, where it floweth Southsoutheast, and doth high 8 foote water: this place is full of low Islands, and many good sounds without the high mountaine land. Here is great store of wood growing, as firre, birch, oke, and hasell: all this night the wind was at the South, very much winde, with raine and fogge.

The 28 day in the morning the wind being at Eastnortheast we set saile at 8 of the clocke, and haled out of the bay Westsouthwest, and Southwest, hauing a goodly gale vntill one of the clocke, and then the wind came to

Southeast, and to the South with raine and fogge, and very much winde: at sixe of the clocke we came into a very good rode, where we did ride all the same night in good safetie.

The 29 day we put into a good sound, the wind by the Southwest: at three in the afternoone there came downe very much wind by the South, and all night with vehement blastes, and raine.

The 30 day all day the wind was at Westsouthwest. And in this sound the pole is eleuated 63 deg. 10 min.

The first day of October the winde was at South with very much winde, and vehement blastes.

The 7 day we set saile: for from the first of this moneth untill this 7 day, we had very foule weather, but specailly the fourth day when the wind was so great, that our cables brake with the very storme, and I do not think that it is possible that any more wind then that was should blow: for after the breaking of our cable, we did driue a league, before our ankers would take any hold: but God be thanked the storme began to slacke, otherwise we had bene in ill case.

The 7. at night we came to an anker vntil the next day, which was the 8. day of the moneth, when as the winde grew great againe, with raine, whereupon we set saile and returned into the sound againe: and at our first comming to an anker, presently there blew so much winde, that although our best anker was out, yet the extremitie of the storm droue vs vpon a ledge of rocks, and did bruse our ship in such sort, that we were constrained to lighten her to saue her, and by this meanes (by the helpe of God) we got off our ship and stopped our leakes, and moored her in good safetie abiding for a wind. We rid from this day by reason of contrary winds, with fogge and raine vntill the 24 day, which day in the morning the winde came to the Northeast, and at 8 of the clocke we set saile. [Sidenote: Moore sound.] This sound is called Moore sound, where it higheth about 5 foote water, and floweth Southsoutheast. The next day being the 25 day we put into a sound which is called Vlta sound, where was a ship of the king of Denmark put into another sound there by, being 2 leagues to the southwards of vs, that came out of Island: the wind was contrary for vs at Southsouthwest.

The 12 day of Nouember we set saile the wind being at the East Southeast, and past through the sound where the kings ship did lie: which sound is called Sloure sound. But as we did open the sound, we found the wind at the Southwest, so that we could doe no good, so that we moared our ship betweene 2. Islands vntill the 18 day, and then the weather being faire and calme, we set saile, and went to sea hoping to find a faire wind, but in the sea we found the wind at the Southwest, and Southsouthwest, so that we were constrained to returne into the same sound.

The next day being the 19 the kings ship came out also, because she saw vs put to sea, and came as farre out as we, and moared where we did moare afore: And at our returne back againe, we moared our ship in an vtter sound called Scorpe sound, because the kings ship was without victuals, and we did not greatly desire her company, although they desired ours. In this sound the pole is eleuated 62 deg. 47 min. Thus we lay stil for a wind vntil the 1 of December, which day we set saile at 6 a clocke in the morning, and at four in the afternoon we laid it to the inwards.

The 9 day we had sight of the coast of Scotland which was Buquhamnesse.

The 10 day we were open off the Frith.

The 11 day at 4 in the morning we were thwart of Barwike: at 6 we were thwart of Bamburch: the same day at 10 at night we were shot as farre as Hollyfoote. Then the wind came to the South and Southeast, so that we lay vntill the next day in the morning, and then we were constrained to put with Tinmouth. The same day at night wee haled aground to stoppe a leake, which we found to be in the skarfe afore. The wind continued by the Southeast and Southsoutheast vntill the 20 day, and then we set saile about 12 at night, bearing along the coast.

The 22 day by reason of a Southeast wind, we thought we should haue bene put into Humber, but the wind came to the West, so that we haled Southeast: and at 3 in the afternoone we haled a sea boord the sands, and had shoale water off, Lymery and Owry, and were in 4 fadomes off them. The next day we haled as we might to sease Orfordnesse.

The 24 day we came thwart of the Nase, about 8 in the morning.

The 25 day being the Natiuity of Christ, we came to an anker betweene Old hauen and Tilberie hope. The same day we turned as high as Porshet.

The 26 day we turned as high as Ratcliffe, and praised God for our safe returne. And thus I ende, 1580.

[The William with Charles Iackman arriued at a port in Norway betweene Tronden and Rostock in October 1580, and there did winter: And from thence
departed againe in February following, and went in company of a ship of the
King of Denmarke toward Island: and since that time he was neuer heard of.]

* * * * *

Instructions made by the company of English, merchants for discouery of new trades, vnto Richard Gibs, William Biggat, Iohn Backhouse, William Freeman, Iohn Haly, and Iames Woodcock, &c. masters of the 9. ships and one barke that we had freighted for a voiage with them to be made (by the grace of God) from hence to S. Nicholas in Russia, and backe againe: which ships being now in the riuer of Thames are presently ready to depart vpon the said voyage, with the next apt winds that may serue thereunto: and with this Fleet afterwards was ioned M. Christopher Carlisle with the Tyger. The 1 off Iune 1582.

Forasmuch as the number of shippes which we purpose to send in this fleete together for Saint Nicholas in Russia is greater then at any time heretofore wee haue sent thither, as also for that some speeches are giuen out that you shall be met withall by such as with force and violence will assault you as enemies, to the end that good order may be established among you for keeping together in company, and vniting your forces, as well for the better direction to be had in your nauigation, as also for your more safety and strength against the enemie, we haue thought good to appoint among you an Admirall and Viceadmirall, and that all of you and eueryone particularly shall be bound in the summe of one hundred pounds to keepe company together.

2 Because the Salomon is the biggest ship, best appointed, and of greatest force to defend or offend the enemie, we doe therefore appoint that ship Admirall, which shall weare the flag in the maine top.

3 The Thomas Allen being a good ship and well appointed, and for that the master of her is the ancientest master of the Fleete that hath taken charge that way, we doe appoint the same ship to be Viceadmirall, and to weare the flag in the foretop.

4 And for that the master of the Prudence is of great experience and knowledge in that voyage, we doe appoint that he with the master of the Admirall and Viceadmirall shall conferre, consult and agree vpon the courses and directions that shall be vsed in this voyage, and it shall be lawfull vnto the master of the Admirall, with the consent of M. Gibs, and M. Biggat, or one of them to make his courses and directions from time to time during the whole voyage, and all the fleete are to follow and obserue the same without straying or breaking of company at any time vpon the penaltie before specified.

5 The appointing of the ships for Admiral and Viceadmiral, and those men to consult and agree vpon the courses and directions of the voyage, as aforesaid, hath bene done by the consents and with the liking of you all, and therefore doubt not but that you will all carefully and willingly obserue the premisses.

6 Item, we haue thought good to put in mind, that at such times as you may conueniently from time to time, you do assemble and meete together, to consider, consult, and determine vpon such articles as you shall think necessary to be propounded touching your best safetie and defence against all forces that may be offered you in this voyage, as well outwards bound, and while you shall remaine in the roade and bay of S. Nicholas, as also homewardes hound, and that which you shall agree vpon, or that which most of you shal consent vnto, cause it to be set down in writing for record, which may serue for an acte amongst your selues to binde you all to obserue the same.

7 We haue appointed Iames Woodcock in the smal barke to attend vpon you, and to receiue his directions from you. You are therefore to remember well what conference and talke hath bene had with you here before your going touching the sayd barke, to what purposes she may best serue, and the maner how to imploy her, and thereupon to giue your order and direction vnto him, as the time and place shall require.

[Sidenote: Berozoua Vstia.] 8 Item, if you shall vnderstand as you are outwards bound, that the enemie is gone before you to S. Nicholas, remember what aduice hath bene giuen you for your stay at Berozoua Vstia, till you haue by espials viewed and vnderstood the forces, and the manner of their abode at that place.

9 And if in the sea either outwards or homewards, or in the time of your abode at anker at Saint Nicholas, you shall be assaulted by force of any, as enemie whatsoeuer, you are to defend your selues with such forces as you may or can: trust not too farre, neither giue place to inconuenience.

10 You will not forget what conference we had touching your passing outwards bound by Wardhouse, to view and vnderstand what you can at that place, and to shew your selues, to see if there be any there that haue a mind to speake with you, for that we thinke it better then, and thereabout, then afterwards or els where.

11 While you shall remaine in the road at S. Nicholas, be circumspect and carefull to haue your ships in readinesse and in good order alwaies, and vpon all suddens. The greatest danger vnto you in that place will be while you shall shift your ships: therefore you are to consider of it, but the fittest time for you to doe the same, will bee when the winde is Southerly off the shore, or calme, and at such time you may the better doe it without danger. You must take such order among you, that your companies may be alwaies willing and ready to help one the other, and appoint among your selues such ships to shift first, and such after, in such sort and forme as you shall thinke best and most conuenient. And while they shall be in discharging, shifting, and lading, let the rest of your companies which haue not then to

doe in lading or discharging, helpe those ships that shall haue labour to doe, as well for carying the barkes from ships to the shoare, or from shore to the shippe: with your boates, as also for any other helpe that they shall haue need of.

12 Remember what hath bene said vnto you touching the moring of your ships, &c. for vsing aduantage against the enemie, if you shall be assaulted in that place.

13 See that you serue God, abolish swearing and gaming, be carefull of fire and candles, &c.

14 You are to consult and agree among your selues vpon signes, tokens, and good orders for the better keeping of company together, and also the maner how and by what meanes, rescue, ayde, or helpe may be giuen by one to the other in fight, if you happen to come to it.

Thus we pray God to send you a prosperous voyage and safe returne.

* * * * *

The opinion of Master William Burrough sent to a friend, requiring his iudgment for the fittest time of the departure of our ships towards S. Nicholas in Russia.

Whereas you request me to perswade the company not to send their shippes from hence before the fine of May, I do not thinke the same so good a course for them to obserue; for you know that the sooner wee sende them hence, the sooner we may looke for their returne. [Sidenote: The Russian fleet best to be set forth in the beginning of May.] If wee sende them in the beginning of May, then may they be at Saint Nicholas by the fine of the same moneth: and by that time the greatest parte of your lading of necessitie must bee downe, especially the flaxe: but if it should fall out so lateward a breaking vp of the riuer of Duyna, that by the ende of May the goods cannot be brought to Saint Nicholas, yet this is alwayes to be accounted for certaine, that before our ships can come thither, the goods may be brought downe to that place: and if through ice the shippes be kept backe any time, the losse and charge of that time toucheth not the companie at all, but the owners of the shippes, and yet will the Owners put that in aduenture, rather than tarie longer time before their going hence.

Now seeing by sending our shippes hence in the beginning of May, their arriuall at S. Nicholas may be at the ende of the same moneth, and remaining thirtie dayes there, they may bee laden and come thence by the last of Iune, and returne home hither by the 10 of August with commodities to serue the market then, it cannot bee denied but we should reape thereby great commoditie.

But it may he obiected, that if all our shippes be sent then to returne as aforesaid, you shall not be able to send vs in so much cordage, Waxe and Oyles, as otherwise you should doe if they remained a moneth longer, neither could you by that time perfect your accounts to be sent in them as you would doe.

For answere thereunto this is my meaning: though I wish the greatest part of our shipping to go as aforesaid, yet would I haue one good ship or two at the most well furnished in al points that should depart alwaies from hence, betweene the beginning and the 10 day of Iune: and the same to be conditioned withall to remaine at S. Nicholas from the first arriuall there vntill the middest of August, or to be despatched thence sooner, at the will and liking of our factors for the same: by this order these commodities following may ensue.

1 You may haue our commodities there timely to send vp the riuer before it waxe shallow, to be dispersed in the countrey at your pleasure.

2 The greatest part of our goods may be returned thither timely to serue the first markets.

3 Our late ships remaining so long here may serue to good purpose, for returning answere of such letters as may he sent ouer land, and receiued here before their departure.

4 Their remaining so late with you shal satisfie your desire for perfecting your accounts, and may bring such cordage, Waxe, Oile, and other commodities, as you can prouide before that time: and chiefly may serue vs in stead to bring home our goods that may be sent vs from Persia.

Now seeing it may be so many wayes commodious to the commpany to obserue this order, without any charge vnto them, I wish that you put to your helping hand to further the same.

* * * * *

A copie of the Commission giuen to Sir Ierome Bowes, authorizing him her Maiesties Ambassadour vnto the Emperour of Russia, Anno 1583.

ELIZABETHA, Dei gratia, AngliŠ, FranciŠ, et HyberniŠ Regina, fidei defensatrix, &c. Vniuersis et singulis prŠsentes literas visuris et inspecturis, salutem. Cum Serenissimus Princeps, Ioannes Basilius, Rex, et magnus Dux RussiŠ, VolodimerŠ, MoscouiŠ, et NouogrodiŠ, Rex Cazani, et Astracani, Dominus PlescoŠ, et magnus Dux SmolenscoŠ, Tueri, Vgori; PermiŠ, ValeŠ, BolharŠ, et aliarum ditionum: Dominus et magnus Dux NouogrodiŠ in inferiori regione ChernigŠ, RezanŠ, PoletscoŠ, Ratsauie, Yeraslaue, Bealozeri, LiflandiŠ, Oudori, et CondensŠ, et gubernator in tota prouincia SiberiŠ, et partium Septentrionalium, et aliarum, frater, et Amicus charissimus, Nobilem virum, Feodor Andrewich Spisemski, nuper ad nos ablegauerit, ad certa quŠdam negotia nobiscum agenda, quŠ honorem vtrinque nostrum quÓm proximŔ attingunt, quŠque rectŔ definiri concludique nequeunt nisi Ambassiatorem aliquem et oratorem ad prŠfatum serenissimum principem amandauerimus: Hinc est, qu d nos de fidelitate, industria, prouida circumspectione, et satis magno rerum vsu, prŠdilecti nobis famuli nostri, Hieronimi Bowes Militis, ex nobilibus domesticis nostris vnius, plurim"m confidentes, prŠfatum Hieronimum Bowes Militem, nostrum verum et indubitatum Ambassiatorem, Oratorem, et Commissarium specialem facimus, et constituimus per prŠsentes. Dantes, et concedentes eidem Hieronimo Bowes Militi oratori nostro tenore prŠsentium, authoritatem, et mandatum, tam generale, quÓm speciate, ita qu d specialitas non deroget generalitati, nec Ŕ contra generalitas specialitati, nomine nostro, et pro nobis, cum prŠfato serenissimo principe, eiusque consiliarijs, et deputatis quibuscunque de prŠfatis negotijs et eorum singulis, tractandi, conferendi, concludendi appunctuandique, prout prŠfato Oratori nostro Šquum, et ex honore nostro videbitur: Nec non de, et super huiusmodi tractatis, conclusis, appunctuatisque, cŠterÝsque omnibus et singulis, prŠmissa quouismodo concernentibus, literas, et instrumenta valida et efficacia, nomine nostro, et pro nobis tradendi, literasque et instrumenta consimilis vigoris et effectus, ex altera parte petendi, et confici, et sigillari debitŔ procurandi, et recipiendi, et generaliter omnia, et singula prŠmissa qualitercunque concernentia, faciendi, exercendi, et expediendi, in, et eodem modo, sicut nos ipsi faceremus, et facere possemus, si essemus prŠsentes, etiamsi talia sint, quŠ de se mandatum exigant magis speciale; promittentes bona fide, et in verbo Regio, omnia et singula, quŠ per prŠdictum Ambassiatorem, et oratorem nostrum appunctuata, promissa. conuenta, concordata, et conclusa fuerint in hac parte, nos rata et grata, et firma habituras et obseruaturas, et superinde literas nostras patentes confirmatorias, et approbatortias in forma valida, et autentica, prout opus fuerit, daturas. In cuius rei testimonium, his prŠsentibus manu nostra signatis, magnum sigillum nostrum regni nostri AngleiŠ apponi fecimus. DatŠ Ŕ Regia nostra Grenwici quinto die mensis Iunij, Anno Dom. 1583. Regni ver nostri vicessimo quinto.

The same in English.

Elizabeth by the grace of God, Queene of England, France and Ireland, defender of the faith, &c. to al and singular, to whom these presents shal come to be seen and red, greeting. Whereas the most excellent prince Iohn Basiliwich king, and great duke of all Russia, Volodomer, Moscouie, and Nouogrod, king of Cazan and Astracan, lord of Plesco, and great duke of Smolensco, of Tuer, Vgor, and Permia, Valca, Bolhar and others, lord great duke of Nouogrod in the low country, of Cherniga, Rezan, Polotsco,

Rostoue, Yeraslaue, Bealozera, Liefland, Oudor, and Condensa, and gouernour of al the land of Siberia, and of the North parts and other, our most deare brother and friend, did of late send vnto vs one Feodor Andrewich Spisemsky, a noble man of his, to deale with vs in certaine speciall businesses, respecting very neerely the honour of either of vs, and being such as without the speeding of some Ambassadour of ours to the aforesaid most excellent prince, cannot be sufficiently determined and concluded: For this cause we hauing great confidence in the fidelitie, industrie, prouident circumspection and conuenient experience of our welbeloued seruant Ierome Bowes, knight, & gentleman of qualitie of our householde, do by these presents make and constitute the foresaid Ierome Bowes knight our true and undoubted Ambassadour, Orator and special commisioner, giuing and graunting to the same Ierome Bowes knight, our Orator, by the vertue of these presents authoritie and commandment, as wel general as special, so that the special shall not preiudice the generall, nor on the other side the general the special to, intreat, conferre, conclude, and appoint in our name, and for us with the foresaid most excellent prince and his counsellers and deputies whatsoeuer, concerning the foresaid businesses, and ech of them, according as it shall seeme good, and for our honour to our foresaid Orator, as also of and vpon such things intreated, concluded and appointed, as in all and singular other things, any maner of way concerning the premisses, to deliuer in our name and for vs, sufficient and effectual letters and instruments and to require letters and instruments, of the like validitie and effect of the other part, and to procure them lawfully to bee made and sealed and then to receiue them, and generally to doe, execute, and dispatch al and singular other things concerning the premisses, in, and after the same maner, as we our selues would and might do if we were present, although they be such things as may seeme of themselues to require a more speciall commandement: promising in good faith and in the word of a prince, that we will hold and obserue all and singular the things which by our Ambassador aforesayd shall be appointed, promised, agreed, accorded and concluded in this behalfe; as lawfull, gratefull, and firme, and thereupon as need shall require, will giue our letters patents, confirmatory and approbatory, in forme effectuall and autenticall. In witnesse whereof, we haue caused our great seale of our kingdome of England to be put to these presents, and signed them with our owne hand.

Giuen at our pallace of Greenewich the fourth day of Iune, in the yeere of our Lord 1583, and of our reigne the fiue and twentieth.

* * * * *

A letter sent from her Highnesse to the sayd great Duke of Russia, by sir Hierome Bowes aforesayd, her Maiesties Ambassadour.

Serenissimo Principo ac Domino, Ioanni Basilio, Dei gratia Regi et magno Duci totius Russiǣ, Volodomene, &c. Regi Cazani, &c. Domino Plescoǣ, &c.

Domino et magno Duci Nouogrodiǣ &c. et Gubernatori in tota Prouincia Siberiǣ; &c. Fratri et amico nostro charissimo.

ELIZABETHA, Dei gratia Angliǣ Franciǣ, et Hiberniǣ Regina, fidei defensatrix, &c. Serenissimo Principi ac Domino, Ioanni Basilio, eadem Dei gratia Regi et magno Duci totius Russiǣ, Volodomerǣ, Moscouiǣ, et Nouogrodiǣ, Regi Cazani et Astracani, Domino Plescoǣ; et magno Duci Smolenscoǣ, Tueri, Vgori, Permiǣ, Viatskǣ, Bolharǣ, et aliarum ditionum, Domino et magno Duci Nouogrodiǣ in inferiori regione, Chernigǣ, Rezanǣ, Polotscoǣ, Rostouǣ, Iaroslauǣ, Bealozeri, Liflandiǣ, Oudori et Condensǣ, et Gubernatori in tota prouincia Siberiǣ, et partium Septentrionalium, et aliarum, fratri, et amico suo charissimo, Salutem.

Serenissime princeps; frater et amice charissime, ex ijs que nobiscum egit S. V. illustris legatus, intelleximus, quÓm gratŔ vobis faceremus satis, si legatum aliquem cum mandatis instructum, ad S. V. ablegaremus. In quo certŔ quidem instituto adeͺ nobis ex animo placuit, quod est honestŔ postulatum, vt non nisi prǣstita re, possemus nobis quoquo modo satisfacere. Atque cum id haberemus apud nos decretum, nobis non incommodŔ incurrit in mentem et oculos Hieronimus Bowes miles, ex nobilibus nostris Domesticis, plurimum nobis dilectus, quem, inprǣsentiarum ad S. V. ablegamus, cuius prudentiǣ et fidei, totum hoc quicquid est, quod ad Serenitatum mutuͺ nostrarum dignitatem omandam pertinere posse arbitramur, commisimus. In quo munere perfungendo, quin omnem curam et diligentiam sit collaturus, neutiquam dubitamus: Ó S. autem V. rogamus, velit ei eam fidem habere in ijs persequendis quǣ habet Ó nobis in mandatis, quam nobis habendam putaret, si essemus prǣsentes. PrǣstereÓ, c¨m nobis multum charus sit Robertus Iacobus medicus, quem superiori [Marginal note: 1582.] anno, ad S. V. misimus, rogamus vt eum eo loco S. V. habeat, quo virum probatissimum, et singulari quÓm plurimarum virtutum laude ornatum habendum esse, boni principes censent. Quem Ó nobis neutiquam ablegauissemus, nisi amicitiǣ nostrǣ, et studio gratificandi S. V. plurim¨m tribuissemus. In qua dum voluntate manemus erga S. V. non nisi optimŔ de bonis vestris meritis in prǣfatum Iacobum nobis pollicemur. Et Deum Opt. Max. precamur, vt S. V. saluam conseruet, et incolumem. Datǣ Ŕ Regia nostra Grenouici 19 die mensis Iunij, Anno Domini 1583, regni verͺ nostri vicessimo quinto.

S. vestra bona soror.

The same in English.

Elizabeth by the grace of God, Queene of England, France, and Ireland, defender of the faith &c. to the most excellent Prince and Lord, Iohn Basiliwich, by the same grace of God, King and great Duke of all Russia, Volodomer, Moscouie, and Nouogrod, King of Cazan and Astracan, Lord of Plesco, and great Duke of Smolensco, of Tuer, Vgor, and Permie, Viatsca, Bolhar, and others, Lord and great Duke of Nouogrod in the lowe countrey, of Cherniga, Rezan, Polotsko, Rostoue, Iaroslaue, Bealozera, Lifland, Oudor, Obdor, and Condensa, and Gouernour of all the land of Siberia, and of the North, parts and others, her dearest brother and friend, Salutations.

Most excellent Prince, most deare brother and friend, by those things which the worthy ambassador of your excellency declared vnto vs, we haue vnderstood how kindly it would be taken, if we should send to your excellency an ambassador from vs, with commandement and instructions. In which matter your honourable request hath so much pleased vs, that we could not any maner of way satisfie our selues, except we performed the same. And hauing purposed with our selfe so to doe, we thought of, and remembred Ierome Bowes Knight, a gentleman of qualitie of our householde, a man very much beloued of vs, whom at this present we send vnto your Maiesty, and to whose wisdome and faithfulnesse we haue committed all, whatsoeuer we take to apperteine to the aduancement of both our honors indifferently. In the discharge of which seruice, we doubt not but that all care and diligence shall be vsed on his part, so that we intreat your Maiesty to giue him credence in the prosecuting of those things which he hath from vs in commandement, no lesse then to our selfe, if we were present. [Sidenote: Doctor Iacob.] And whereas Robert Iacob doctor of physicke is a man very deare vuto vs, whom, the last yere we sent vnto your excellency, we desire that he may haue that fauor and estimation with you, which good, princes thinke a most honest and vertuous man woorthy of: for had we not caried great respect to our mutual friendship, and indeuour to gratifie your Maiestie, we should in no case haue parted with him. And seeing we continue still the same, good will towards your excellency, we doe euen promise to our selfe your honourable kindnesses towards him: and we pray the almightie God to preserue your Maiesty in good, safetie and health. Giuen at our pallace of Greenewich the 19 day of Iune, in the yere of our Lord 1583, and of our reigne the fiue and twentieth.

Your Maiesties good sister.

* * * * *

A briefe discourse of the voyage of Sir Ierome Bowes knight, her Maiesties ambassadour to Iuan Vasiliuich the Emperour of Moscouia, in the yeere 1583.

[Sidenote: Pheodor Andreuich Phisemsky the Emperors ambassadour.] The Emperour of Russia that then liued, by name Iuan Vasiliwich, hauing deliberately considered how necessary it were for the strengthening of his estate, and that a sure commerce and entercourse of merchants should be againe renued betweene him and her sacred Maiesty of England, with such further immunities and priuileges for the honor and vtility of both their dominions, and subiects of the same, as with mutuall treatie of persons interposed on both sides, might be asserted vnto: sent ouer into this realme, in the yeere of our Lord 1582, as his ambassadour for that purpose, an ancient discreet gentleman of his householde called Pheodor Andreuich Phisemsky, accompanied with one of his Secretaries, for his better assistance in that expedition: and besides his many other directions, whereof part were to be deliuered by word of mouth, and the rest set downe in a letter vnder the Emperours signature, addressed to her Maiesty: he had in speciall charge to sollicit her Maiesty to send ouer with him to his maister an ambassador from her, to treat and contract of such affaires of importance as concerned both the realmes, which was the principall end of his imployments hither. Whereupon her Maiesty very graciously inclining to the Emperors motion, and at the humble sute of the English merchants trading those countreys being caried with the same princely respects, to satisfie his demands in that behalfe, made choice of sir Ierome Bowes, a gentleman of her Court, ordinarily attending vpon her Maiesties person, towards whom was apparantly expressed her princely opinion and fauor by the credit of this negociation.

After he had receiued his commission, with other speciall letters to the Emperor, with all other instructions apperteining to his charge, and that the sayd Russe ambassadour was licenced to returne home to his maister, being honorably entertained and rewarded, the English ambassador being attended upon with forty persons at the least, very honourably furnished, whereof many were gentlemen, and one M. Humfrey Cole a learned preacher, tooke his leaue of her Maiesty at the Court at Greenwich the eighteenth of Iune, and with the other ambassadour, with their seuerall companies, embarked themselues at Harwich the two and twentieth of the same, and after a stormy voyage at the Sea, they arriued both in safety in the road of S. Nicholas the three and twentieth of Iuly next following.

The Russe ambassador lodged himselfe at the abbey of S. Nicholas: and the English ambassador was lodged and well intertained by the English merchants, at their house at S. Nicholas, standing in an Island called Rose Island.

The Russe ambassador hauing reposed himselfe one whole day, took his leaue of the English ambassador, and departed towards Mosco.

The English ambassadour abode yet at S. Nicholas four or fiue dayes, when hauing made prouision of boats, and meanes to that purpose, he went forward vpon his iourney; towards Mosco, to a towne called Colmogro, about foure score miles distant from S. Nicholas.

[Sidenote: The Hollanders intrude into our trade.] You must here vnderstand that before the English ambassadors going into Russia, there were diuers strangers, but especially certaine Dutch merchants, who had intruded themselues to trade into those countreys. Notwithstanding a priuilege of the sole trade thither was long before granted to the English merchants. These Dutch men had already so handled the matter, as they had by chargeable meanes woone three of the chiefest counsellors to the Emperour to be their assured friends, namely, Mekita Romanouich, Bodan Belskoy, and Andrew Shalkan the chancellor: for besides dayly gifts that they bestowed vpon them all, they tooke so much money of theirs at interest at fiue and twenty vpon the hundred, as they payed to some one of them fiue thousand marks yeerely for the vse of his money, and the English merchants at that time had not one friend in Court.

The ambassador hauing now spent fiue weeks at S. Nicholas, and at Colmogro, there came to him then a gentleman sent from the Emperor to enterteine him, and had in charge to conduct him vp the riuers towards Mosco, and to deliuer him prouision of all kinde of victuals necessary.

This gentleman being a follower of Shalkan the chancellor, was by him (as it seemed) foisted into that seruice of purpose, as afterward appeared by the course he tooke, to offer discourtesies, and occasions of mislike to the ambassador: for you must vnderstand that the chancellor and the other two great counsellors (spoken of as friends to the Dutchmen) had a purpose to oppose themselues directly against her Maiesties ambassage, especially in that point, for the barring of all strangers from trading into the Emperors countrey.

This gentleman conducted the English ambassador a thousand miles vp the riuers of Dwina and Soughana, to a citie called Vologda, where receiued him another gentleman sent from the Emperor, a man of better countenance then the other, who presented the ambassador from the Emperor with two faire geldings well furnished after their maner.

At a citie called Yeraslaue vpon the riuer Volga there met the ambassador a duke well accompanied, sent from the Emperor, who presented him from the
Emperor a coach and ten geldings tor the more easie conueying of him to Mosco, from whence this citie was distant fiue hundred miles.

Two miles on this side Mosco there met the ambassador foure gentlemen of good account, accompanied with two hundred horse: who after a little salutation, not familiar, without imbracing, tolde him that they had to say to him from the Emperor, and would haue had him light on foot to haue heard it, notwithstanding themselues would still haue sit on horsebacke: which the ambassador soone refused to doe, and so they stood long vpon termes, whether both parties should light or not: which afterwards agreed vpon, there was yet great nicenesse whose foot should not be first on ground.

Their message being deliuered, and after hauing embraced ech other, they conducted the sayd ambassador to his lodging at Mosco, a house builded of purpose for him, themselues being placed in the next house to it, as appointed to furnish him of all prouisions, and to be vsed by him vpon all other occasions.

The ambassador hauing beene some dayes in Mosco, and hauing in all that time bene very honorably vsed from the Emperor (for such was his will) though some of his chiefest counsellors (as is sayd) had another purpose, and did often times cunningly put it in vse: He was sent for to Court, and was accompanied thither with about forty gentlemen honorably mounted, and sumptuously arayed, and in his passage from his lodging to the court, were set in a ward fiue or sixe thousand shot, that were of the Emperors gard. At the entry into the court there met him four noble men apparelled in cloth of gold and rich furres, their caps embroidred with pearle and stone, who conducted him towards the Emperor; till he was met with foure others of greater degree then they, who guided him yet further towards the Emperor, in which passage there stood along the walles, and sate vpon benches and formes in row, seuen or eight hundred persons, said to be noblemen and gentlemen, all apparelled in garments of coloured satins and cloth of golde.

These foure noblemen accompanied him to the Emperors chamber doore, where met him the Emperors herald, whose office is there held great: and with him all the great officers of the Emperors chamber, who all conducted him to the place where the Emperor safe in his state, hauing three crownes standing by him, viz. of Moscouia, Cazan and Astrakan, and also by him 4 yoong noblemen of about twenty yeres of age, of ech side, twaine, costly apparelled in white, holding vpon their shoulders ech of them a brode axe, much like to a Galloglas axe of Ireland, thin and very sharpe, the steale or handle not past halfe a yard long, and there sate about the chamber vpon benches and other low seats, aboue an hundred noblemen richly apparrelled in cloth of golde.

The ambassador being thus brought to the Emperor to kisse his hand, after some complements and inquirie of her Maiesties health, he willed him goe sit downe in a place prouided for that purpose, nigh ten pases distant from him, from whence he would haue had him to haue sent him her Maiesties letters and present, which the ambassadour thinking not reasonable stept forward towards the Emperor: in which passage the chancellor came to meet him, and would haue taken his letters: to whom the ambassador sayd, that her Maiesty had directed no letters to him, and so went on, and deliuered them himselfe to the Emperors owne hands.

And after hauing thus deliuered her Maiesties letters and what he had els to say at that time, he was conducted to the Councell chamber, where hauing had conference with the councell of matters of his ambassage, he was soone after sent for againe to the Emperour, where he dined in his presence at a side table, nere vnto him, and all his company at another boord, where also dined at other tables in the same place, all the chiefe noble men that were about the Court, to the number of an hundred. And in the time of this dinner, the Emperor vsed many fauors to the ambassadour and about the midst of dinner (standing vp) dranke a great carouse to the health of the Queene his good sister, and sent him a great bowle full of Rhenish wine and sugar to pledge him.

The ambassadour after this, was often called to Court, where he had conference both with the Emperour and his councell of the matters in question, touching both ambassages, which diuers times raised many iarres: and in the end, after sundry meetings, the Emperour finding himself not satisfied to his liking, for that the ambassadour had not power by his commission to yeeld to euery thing that he thought fit, as a man whose will was seldom wonted to be gainsayd, let loose his passion, and with a sterne and angry countenance tolde him that he did not reckon the Queene of England to be his fellow: for there are (quoth he) that are her betters.

The ambassadour greatly misliking these speeches, and being very vnwilling (how dangerous soeuer it might prooue to his owne person) to giue way to the Emperor, to derogate ought from the honour and greatness of her Maiesty: and finding also that to subiect himselfe to the angrie humour and disposition of the Emperour was not the means to winne ought at his hands, with like courage and countenance to answere his, tolde him that the Queene his Mistresse was as great a prince as any was in Christendome, equall to him that thought himselfe the greatest, well able to defend herselfe against his malice, whosoeuer, and wanted no means to offend any that either shee had or should haue cause to be enemy vnto. Yea (quoth he) How sayest thou to the French king, and the king of Spaine? Mary (quoth the ambassadour) I holde the Queene my Mistresse as great as any of them both. Then what sayest thou (quoth hee) to the Emperour of Germany?

Such is the greatnesse of the Queene my Mistresse (quoth the Ambassadour) as the King, her father had (not long since) the Emperor in his pay, in his warres against France.

This answer misliked the Emperor yet so much more, as that he tolde the Ambassadour, that were he not an ambassador, he would throw him out of the doores. Whereunto he answered that he might doe his will, for he was now fast within his countrey: but he had a Mistresse who (he doubted not) would be reuenged of any iniury that should be done vnto him. Whereupon the Emperour in great sudden bade him get him home. And he with no more reuerence then such vsage required, saluted the Emperor and went his way.

All this notwithstanding, the ambassadour was not much sooner out of the chamber, and the Emperours cholar somewhat setled, but he deliuered to his councell that stood about him many commendations in the fauor of the Ambassador, for that he would not indure one ill word to be spoken against his mistresse, and there withall wished himselfe to haue such a seruant.

The Ambassadour had not beene much more then one houre in his lodgings, but the Emperour imagining (as it seemed) by the extraordinary behauiour of the ambassador (for he wanted not wit to iudge) that he had found what was the Emperors case, sent his principall secretary vnto him, to tell him, that notwithstanding what had past, yet for the great loue that he bare to the Queene his sister, he should very shortly be called againe to Court, and haue a resolution of all the matters in question: and this secretary was now further content to impart, and sayd to the ambassadour that the Empereur was fully resolued to send a greater, noble man vnto him in ambassage to the Queene his sister, then euer he yet at any time sent out of his countrey: and that he determined also to send to the Queene a present woorth three thousand pounds, and to gratifie himselfe at his departure with a gift that should be woorth a thousand pounds: and tolde him also that the next day the Emperour would send a great noble man vnto him, to conferre with him of certaine abuses done him by Shalkan the chancellor, and his ministers.

And so the day following he sent Bodan Belskoy the chiefest counceller that he had, a man most in credit with him: this man examined all matters wherewith the ambassador had found himselfe grieued, and supplied him, with what hee wanted, and righted him in all things wherein hee had beene wronged.

Not long after the returne of this noble man, the Emperor caused to be set downe in his owne presence, a new and much larger allowance of diet for the ambassador then he had had before, and shortly after sent the same to the ambassadour by his principall Secretarie Sauio Frollo. This diet was so great, as the ambassadour oftentimes sought to haue it lessened, but the Emperour would not by any means.

The scroule of the new diet was this:

One bushel of fine meale for three dayes.
One bushel of wheate meale for a day and a halfe.
Two liue geese for one day.
Twenty hennes for the day.
Seuen sheepe for a day.
One oxe for three dayes.
One side of pork for a day.
Seuentie egges for a day.
Ten pound of butter.
Seuenty peny white loaues of bread.
Twelue peny loaues of bread.
One veather or gallon of vinegar.
Two veathers of salt cabiges.
One pecke of onions.
Ten pound of salt.
On altine, or sixe peny woorth of waxe candles.
Two altines of tallow candles.
One fourth part of a veather of cherrie mead.
As much of Malynouomead.
Halfe a veather of burnt wine.
One veather of sodden mead called Obarni.
Three veathers of sweet mead.
Ten veathers of white mead.
Fifteene veathers of ordinary mead.
Foure veathers of sweet beere.
Fiftene veathers of beere.
Halfe a pound of pepper.
Three sollitincks or ounces of saffron.
One sollitincke of mase.
One sollitincke of nutmegs.
Two sollitincks of cloues.
Three sollitincks of sinamon.

Prouender.

One bushell of oats.
One load of hay.
One load of straw.

Now he began so much to discouer his purpose and affections towards her Maiesty and her countrey, as he sent to the ambassador, intreating him that his preacher [Marginal note: M. Cole.], and doctor Iacob his English physician, might set downe the points of the religion in vse in England, which the Ambassadour caused to be done accordingly, and sent them vnto him, who seemed so well to like them, as he caused them (with much good allowance) to be publikely read before diuers of his councell, and many others of his nobility.

Now he drew hotly againe in question to marry, some kinsewoman of her Maiesties, and that he would send againe into England, to haue some one of them to wife, and if her Maiestie would not vpon his next Ambassage send him such a one as he required, himselfe would then goe into England, and cary his treasure with him, and marry one of them there.

Here you must vnderstand that the yeere before this ambassage, he had sent to her Maiesty by his ambassador to haue had the lady Mary Hastings in marriage, which intreaty by meanes of her inability of body, by occasion of much sicknesse, or perhaps, of no great liking either of herselfe or friends, or both, tooke no place.

The ambassador was now so farre growen into the Emperors fauor, and his affection so great to England, as those great councellors that were the Ambassadors great enemies before, were now desirous of some publike courtesies at his hands for their aduantage to the Emperour: neither durst they, now any more interpose themselues twixt the Emperour and him: for not long before this, the Emperor for abusing the ambassador, had (to shew his fauour towards him) beaten Shalkan the chanceller very grieuously, and had sent him word, that he would not leaue one of his race aliue.

Now whilest the ambassador was thus strongly possest of the Emperours fauor, he imployed himselfe in all he might, not onely for the speedy dispatch of the negociation he had in hand, but laboured also by all the good means he might, further to benefit his country and countreymen, and so not long after wanne at the Emperours hands not onely all those things he had in commission to treat for by his instructions, but also some other of good and great importance, for the benefit of the merchants.

Priuate sutes obteined of the Emperor by the ambassador.

Leaue for Richard Fransham an English man and apothecary to the Emperour, his wife, and children to come home into England, and to bring with him all such goods as he had gotten there.

He obteined like leaue for Richard Elmes an English man one of the Emperours surgions.

He also got leaue for Iane Ricards the widow of Doctor Bomelius a Dutchman, and physician to the Emperour, who, for treason practised with the king of Pole against the sayd Emperour, was rosted to death at the city of Mosco, in the yere 1579.

These following he obteined for the behoofe of the merchants.

He procured for the merchants promise of recompence for certaine goods taken from their factors by robbery vpon the Volga.

He obtained likewise the payment of fiue hundred marks, which was payd for ten yeeres before his going into Russia (into the Emperors receit) for a rent of a house that they had at Vologda.

He also got granted for them the repayment of fifteene hundred marks, which had bene exacted of them the two last yeres before his comming thither.

He got also for them order for the repayment of an olde and desperate debt of three thousand marks, a debt so desperate, as foure yeeres left out of their accounts, and by the opinion of them all, not thought fit to be dealt with, for too much offending the Emperour, or impeaching his other businesse, which was thought at least otherwise sufficient, and was therefore left out of his instructions from her Maiesty.

He obteined that all strangers were forbidden to trade any more into Russia, and that the passage and trade to all the Emperors Northern coasts and countries, from the Wardhouse to the riuer of Ob should be onely free to the English nation.

Lastly, of a great desire he had to do the merchants good, without motion either of themselues here, or their Agents there, or any other of them, he obtained of the Emperour the abatement of all their custome which they had long before payd, and agreed still to continue, which custome the Dutchmen and strangers being remooued, as now it was agreed, amounted to two thousand pounds yerely.

All these were granted, some already payd before his comming from Mosco, the olde priuilege ratified, newly written, signed and sealed, and was to be deliuered to the ambassadour at his next comming to Court, before when the Emperor fell sicke of a surfet, and so died.

After whose death the case was woondrously altered with the ambassador: for whereas both, in his owne conceit, and in all mens opinion els, he was in great forwardnes to haue growen a great man with the Emperor, what for the loue he bare to her Maiesty, and the particular liking he had of himselfe, he now fell into the hands of his great enemies, Mekita Romanouich and Andre Shalkan the chanceller, who, after the death of the

Emperour, tooke the speciall gouernment upon themselues, and so presently caused the Ambassadour to be shut vp a close prisoner in his owne house, for the space of nine weeks, and was so straightly guarded and badly vsed by those that attended him, as he dayly suspected some further mischiefe to haue followed: for in this time there grew a great vprore in Mosco of nigh twenty thousand persons, which remembring that his enemies reigned, somewhat amazed the ambassadour, but yet afterwards the matter fell out against that great counsellor Bodan Belskoy, whom I noted before to be a speciall man in the old Emperors fauor: who was now notwithstanding so outragiously assaulted, as that he was forced to seeke the Emperors chamber for his safety, and was afterwards sent away to Cazan, a place he had in gouernment, fiue hundred miles from Mosco, where he hath remained euer since, and neuer as yet called againe to court, at which time the ambassador expected some such like measure, and prepared himselfe aswell as he could, for his defence: yet happily after this, was sent for to court, to haue his dispatch, and to take his leaue of the Emperor: whither being conducted (not after the woonted maner) and brought to the councell chamber, came to him onely Shalkan the chanceller and a brother of his, who without more adoe, tolde him for the summe of his dispatch, that this Emperour would not treat of further amity with the Queene his mistresse, then such as was betweene his late father and her, before his comming thither: and would not heare any reply to be made by the ambassadour, but presently caused both himselfe and all his company to be disarmed of their weapons; and go towards the Emperor. In which passage there were such outrages offered him as had he not vsed more patience then his disposition afforded him, or the occasion required, he had not in likelihood escaped with life, but yet at length was brought to the presence of the Emperour who sayd nothing to him, but what the chancellor had already done, but offered him a letter to carry to her Maiesty, which the ambassadour (for that he knew it conteined nothing that did concerne his ambassage) refused till he saw his danger grow too great: neither would the Emperour suffer the ambassadour to reply ought, nor well he could, for they had now of purpose taken away his interpretor, being yet vnwilling (as it seemed, and suspecting the ambassadours purpose) that the Emperor and other should know how dishonourably he had beene handled: [Sidenote: The great friendship of L. Boris Pheodorouich.] for there, was at that time, in that presence a noble braue gentleman, one Boris Pheodorouich Godenoe, brother to the Emperor that now is, who yet after the death or the Emperour did alwayes vse the ambassadour most honorably, and would very willingly haue done him much more kindnesse, but his authority was not yet, till the coronation of the Emperor: but notwithstanding he sent often vnto him, not long before his departure, and accompanied his many honourable fauours with a present of two faire pieces of cloth of golde, and a tymber of very good sables: and desired that as there was kindnesse and brotherhood twixt the Emperor and her Maiesty, so there might be loue and brotherhood twixt him and the Ambassadour. Sauing from this man, there was now no more fauour left for the ambassadour in Moscouia: for the chanceller Shalkan had now sent him word that the English Emperor was dead: he had now nothing offered him but dangers and disgraces too many, and a hasty dispatch from the Mosco, that he might not tary the coronation of the new Emperour: offences many in his preparation for his long iourney, onely one meane gentleman appointed to accompany him to the sea side, expecting daily in his passage some sudden reuenge to be done vpon him, for so he understood it was threatned before his comming from the Mosco, and therefore with resolution prouided by all the meanes he might, by himselfe and his seruants for his defence (for now was his danger knowen such, as the English merchants did altogether leaue him, although he commanded them in her Maiesties name to accompany him) that if any such thing should happen to be offered him, as many of them as he could that should offer to execute it, should die with him for company: which being perceiued was thought to make his passage the safer. So afterward being driuen to disgest many iniuries by the way, at length he recouered S. Nicholas, where remembring his vnfortunate losse of the old Emperor and his ill vsage since then at the Mosco, he being forced to take a bare letter for the summe of his dispatch, conteyning nothing of that he came for, and the poore and disgraceful present sent him (in the name of the Emperour) in respect of that that was meant him by the old Emperor, knowing all these to be done in disgrace of her Maiestie and himselfe, determined now to be discharged of some part of them in such sort as he could, and so prouiding as he might to preuent his danger, in getting to his shippe, furnishing and placing his men to answere any assault that should be offered him, after he had bidden farewell to the vncourteous gentleman that brought him thither, by three or foure of the valiantest and discreetest men he had, he sent to be deliuered him or left at his lodging, his maisters weake letter, and worsse present, and so afterwards happily (though hardly) recouered his ship in safetie, although presently afterwards, there was great hurly burly after him, to force him to receiue the same againe, but failed of their purpose. So came the ambassadour from S. Nicholas the twelfth day of August, and arriued at Grauesend the twelfth of September following, and attended her Maiestie at the court at Otelands, where, after hauing kist her Maiesties hands, and deliuered some part of the successe of his ambassage, he presented her an Elke or Loshe, the Red deere of the countrey, and also a brace of Raine deare, Buck and Doe, both bearing very huge hornes: they in her Maiesties presence drew a sled and a man vpon it, after the maner of the Samoeds, a people that inhabite in the Northeast from Russia and were that yeere come ouer the sea in the winter season vpon the yce, in their sleds, drawen with these deere into Russia, where the ambassadour bought of them seuenteene, whereof he brought nine aliue into Kent.

* * * * *

The maner of the preferring of sutes in Russia, by the example of our English merchants bill, exhibited to the Emperour.

Iohn Basiliwich, Lord, King, and great Duke of all Russia, the English merchants, William sonne of Thomas, with his company sue vnto.

Lord, in the 7082. yeere of the worlds creation, thy Maiesties treasurer, named Gregorie Mekitowich Borozden, tooke of vs for thy vse 12. poods of loafe sugar, prised at 8. robles the pood, which sugar was sent to the Sloboda [Marginal note: The Emperours house of recreation.]. More, the sayd Gregorie treasurer, tooke of vs for thy Maiestie 200. reames of paper, prised at 20. altines the reame, for all which the money hath not bene payd which amounteth to 216. robles.

And in the 84. yeere thy diake Stephan Lighachdo tooke of vs for thy Maiesty copper plates, for the summe of 1032. robles and one fourth part vnpayd for.

Also in the said 84. yeere thy Maiesties diakes called Iuan Blasghoy, and Iuan Sobakin tooke of us for thy vse, sundry commodities and haue not payd 630. robles, the rest of the money due for the said goods.

In the 83. yeere thy Maiesties treasurer Peter Gholauen tooke of vs for thy Maiestie, cloth of sundry sorts, and hath not payd of the money due therefore 538 robles.

In the 88. yere, thy diakes Andrea Shalkan, and Istomay Yeuskoy tooke of vs lead for thy Maiestie, to the value of 267. robles and a halfe not payd.

And in the same yeere thy Maiesties diak Boris Gregoriwich had for thy vse 15. broad cloths of diuerse sorts, prised at 210. robles, whereof 90. robles are vnpayd.

Also in the said 88. yere thy diak Andrea Shalkan tooke from vs 1000. robles for thee (Lord) in ready money, yet we know not whether by thy Maiesties appointment.

And also in the 89. yeere (Lord) thy diak Andrea Shalkan tooke from vs for thy Maiesty 500. robles, we know not whether by thy Maiesties order or no, because that thy authorized people do yeerely take away from vs, neither do they giue vs right in any cause.

All the mony (Lord) which is not payd vs out of thy Maiesties treasury for our commodities or wares, with the money taken from vs by Andrea Shalkan, is 4273. robles 25. altines.

Right noble king and Lord, shew thy mercy, and cause the money to be payd vs which is owing for our goods, as also that which has beene taken from vs: extend thy fauor, King and Lord.

* * * * *

A letter of M. Henrie Lane to the worshipfull M. William Sanderson, conteining a briefe discourse of that which passed in the the Northeast discouery for the space of three and thirtie yeres.

Master Sanderson, as you lately requested mee, so haue I sought, and though I cannot finde things that heretofore I kept in writing and lent out to others, yet perusing at London copies of mine old letters to content one that meaneth to pleasure many, I haue briefly and as truely as I may, drawen out as foloweth: the rough hewing may be planed at your leasure, or as pleaseth him that shall take the paines.

First the honorable attempt to discouer by sea Northeast and Northwest named for Cathay, being chiefly procured by priuiledge from king Edward the sixt, and other his nobilitie, by and at the cost and sute of M. Sebastian Cabota, then gouernor for discoueries with sir Andrew Iudde, sir George Barnes, sir William Garrard, M. Anthonie Hussie, and a companie of merchants, was in the last yeere of his Maiesties reigne 1553. [Sidenote: Anno 1553 M. William Burrough was then yong, and with his brother in this first voyage.] The generall charge whereof was committed to one sir Hugh Willoughbie knight, a goodly Gentleman, accompanied with sufficient number of Pilots, Maisters, Merchants and Mariners, hauing three shippes well furnished, to wit, The Bona Speranša, the Edward Bonaduenture, and the Confidentia. The Edward Bonaduenture, Richard Chanceller being Pilot, and Steuen Burrough Maister, hauing discouered Wardhouse vpon the coast of Finmark, by storme or fogge departed from the rest, found the bay of S. Nicholas now the chiefe port for Russia, there wintred in safetie, and had ayde of the people at a village called Newnox. [Sidenote: Newnox is from the road of S. Nicholas Westward 35. miles.]

The other two shippes attempting further Northwards (as appeared by pamphlets found after written by Sir Hugh Willoughbie) were in September encountered with such extreame colde, that they put backe to seeke a wintring place: and missing the saide baye fell vpon a desert coast in Lappia, entring into a Riuer immediately frozen vp, since discouered, named Arzina Reca, distant East from, a Russian Monastery of Monkes called Pechingho, from whence they neuer returned, but all to the number of 70. persons perished, which was for want of experience to haue made caues and stoues. [Sidenote: Note.] These were found with the shippes the next Summer Anno 1554. by Russe fishermen: and in Anno 1555. the place sent vnto by English merchants as hereafter appeareth.

[Sidenote: Anno 1554.] Anno 1554. the sayd shippe Edward Bonaduenture (although robbed homewards by Flemings) returned with her company to London, shewing and setting foorth their entertainments and discouery of the countreys euen to the citie of Mosco, from whence they brought a priuilege written in Russe with the Kings or great Dukes seale, the other two shippes looked for and vnknowen to them where they were.

[Sidenote: Anno 1555.] An. 1555. the said company of Merchants for discouerie vpon a new supply, sent thither againe with two ships, to wit, the Edward Bonaduenture, and another bearing the name of the King and Queene, Philip and Marie, [Sidenote: The King and Queenes letters.] whose Maiesties by their letters to the said Moscouite, recommended sundry their subiects then passing, whereof certaine, to wit, Richard Chanceller, George Killingworth, Henry Lane, and Arthur Edwards, after their arriuall at the Bay, and passing vp Dwina to Vologda went first to Mosco, where, vpon knowledge of the said letters, they with their traine had speciall entertainment, with houses and diet appointed, and shortly permitted to the princes presence, they were with gentlemen brought through the citie of Mosco, to the castle and palace, replenished with numbers of people, and some gunners. They entred sundry roomes, furnished in shew with ancient graue personages, all in long garments of sundry colours, golde, tissue, baldekin, and violet, as our vestments and copes haue bene in England, sutable with caps, iewels, and chaines. These were found to be no countries, but ancient Moscouites, inhabitants, and other their merchants of credite, as the maner is, furnished thus from the Wardrobe and Treasurie, waiting and wearing this apparell for the time, and so to restore it.

Then entring into the presence, being a large roome floored with carpets, were men of more estate, and richer shew, in number aboue an hundred set square: who after the said English men came in, doing reuerence, they all stood vp, the prince onely sitting, and yet rising at any occasion, when our King and Queenes names were read or spoken. Then after speeches by interpretation, our men kissing his hande, and bidden to dinner, were stayed in another roome, and at dinner brought through, where might be seene massie siluer and gilt plate, some like and as bigge as kilderkins, and washbowles, and entring the dining place, being the greater roome, the prince was set bare headed, his crowne and and rich cappe standing vpon a pinnacle by. Not farre distant sate his Metropolitane, with diuers other of his kindred, and chiefe Tartarian Captaines: none sate ouer against him, or any, at other tables, their backes towards him: which tables all furnished with ghests set, there was for the Englishmen, named by the Russes, Ghosti Carabelski, to wit, strangers or merchants by ship, a table in the middest of the roome, where they were set direct against the prince: and then began the seruice, brought in by a number of his yoong Lordes and Gentlemen, in such rich attire, as is aboue specified: and still from the Princes table (notwithstanding their owne furniture) they had his whole messes set ouer all in massie fine golde, deliuered euery time from him by name to them, by their seuerall Christian names, as they sate, viz. Richard, George, Henry, Arthur. [Sidenote: M. Killingworths beard of a marueilous length.] Likewise bread and sundry drinkes of purified mead, made of fine white and clarified honie. At their rising, the prince called them to his table, to receiue each one a cup from his hand to drinke, and tooke in his hand Master George Killingworths beard, which reached ouer the table, and pleasantly deliuered it the Metropolitane, who seeming to blesse it, sayd in Russe, this is Gods gift. As in deede at that time it was not onely thicke, broad, and yellow coloured, but in length fiue foot and two inches of assize. Then taking leaue, being night, they were accompanied and followed with a number, carying pots of drinke, and dishes of meat dressed, to our lodging.

This yeere the two shippes, with the dead bodies of Sir Hugh Willoughbie, and his people, were sent vnto by Master Killingworth, (which remained there in Mosco Agent almost two yeeres) and much of the goods and victuals were recouered and saued.

[Sidenote: Anno 1556.] Anno 1556. The company sent two ships for Russia, with extraordinary masters and saylers to bring home the two ships, which were frozen in Lappia, in the riuer of Arzina aforesaid. The two ships sent this yeere from England sailing from Lapland to the Bay of S. Nicholas, tooke in lading with passengers, to wit, a Russe ambassador, named Ioseph Napea, and some of his men shipped with Richard Chanceller in the Edward. But so it fell out that the two which came from Lappia, with all their new Masters and Mariners, neuer were heard of, but in foule weather, and wrought seas, after their two yeeres wintring in Lapland, became, as is supposed, vnstanch, and sunke, wherein were drowned also diuers Russes merchants, and seruants of the ambassadour. A third shippe the Edward aforesayd, falling on the North part of Scotland, vpon a rocke was also lost, and Master Chanceller, with diuers other, drowned. The sayd Russe ambassadour hardly escaping, with other his men, mariners, and some goods saued, were sent for into Scotland, from the King, Queene, and Merchants (the messenger being M. Doctor Laurence Hussie, and others:) And then, as in the chronicles appeareth, honorably enterteined and receiued at London.

This yeere also the company furnished and sent out a pinnesse, named the Serchthrift, to discouer the harborowes in the North coast from Norway to

Wardhouse, and so to the Bay of S. Nicholas. There was in her Master and Pilot, Stephen Burrough, with his brother William, and eight other. Their discouery was beyond the Bay, towarde the Samoeds, people dwelling neare the riuer of Ob, and found a sound or sea with an Island called Vaigats, first by them put into the Carde or Mappe. In that place they threw snowe out of their said pinnesse, with shouels in August, by which extremitie, and lacke of time, they came backe to Russia, and wintred at Colmogro.

[Sidenote: Anno 1557.] Anno 1557. The company with foure good ships, sent backe the said Russe ambassadour, and in company with him, sent as an Agent, for further discouery, Master Anthony Ienkinson, who afterward anno 1558, with great fauour of the prince of Moscouia, and his letters passed the riuer Volga to Cazan, and meaning to seeke Cathay by land, was by many troupes and companies of vnciuil Tartarians encountred, and in danger: [Sidenote: Boghar voyage. 1560.] but keeping company with merchants of Bactria, of Boghar, and Vrgeme, trauelling with camels, he with his company, went to Boghar, and no further: whose entertainment of the king is to be had of master Ienkinson, which returned anno 1559. to Moscouie. [Sidenote: The first trade to the Narue. 1560.] And in anno 1560. he with Henry Lane, came home into England: which yeere was the first safe returne, without losse or shipwracke, or dead fraight, and burnings. And at this time was the first traffike to the Narue in Liuonia, which confines with Lituania, and all the dominions of Russia: and the markets, faires, commodities, great townes and riuers, were sent vnto by dyuers seruants: the reports were taken by Henry Lane, Agent, and deliuered to the companie, 1561. The trade to Rie, and Reuel, of old time hath bene long since frequented by our English nation, but this trade to the Narue was hitherto concealed from vs by the Danskers and Lubeckers.

Anno 1561. the said Master Anthony Ienkinson went Agent into Russia; who the next yeere after, passing all the riuer of Volga to Astracan, and ouer the Caspian sea, arriued in Persia, and opened the trade thither.

[Sidenote: Alcock slaine in Persia. Bannister died in Media. Edwards died at Astracan.] Also betweene the yeeres 1568. and 1573. sundry voyages after Master Ienkinsons, were made by Thomas Alcock, Arthur Edwards, Master Thomas Banister, and Master Geffrey Ducket, whose returne (if spoyle neere Volga had not preuented by rouing theeues) had altogether salued and recouered the companies (called the olde companies) great losse, charges, and damages: but the saying is true, By vnitie small things grow great, and by contention great things become small. This may be vnderstood best by the company. The forwardnesse of some few, euill doing of some vniust factors, was cause of muche of the euill successe.

Arthur Edwards was sent againe 1579. and died in the voyage at Astcacan. About which matters, are to be remembred the voyages of Master Thomas Randolph Esquire, Ambassador, anno 1567. And late of Sir Ierome Bowes, anno 1583. both tending and treating for further discoueries, freedomes, and priuileges, wherewith I meddle not. But in conclusion, for their paines and aduentures this way (as diuers do now adayes other wayes) as worthy Gentlemen sent from princes, to doe their countrey good, I put them in your memorie, with my hearty farewell. From S. Margarets neere Dartforth in Kent.

Yours Henry Lane.

* * * * *

The most solemne, and magnificent coronation of Pheodor [Marginal note: Or Theodor.] Iuanowich, Emperour of Russia &c. the tenth of Iune, in the yeere 1584; seene and obserued by Master Ierome Horsey gentleman, and seruant to her Maiesty, a man of great trauell, and long experience in those parts: wherewith is also ioyned the course of his iourney ouer land from Mosco to Emden.

[Sidenote: The death of Iuan Vasiliwich, 1584. Apr. 18.] When the old Emperour Iuan Vasiliwich died, (being about the eighteenth of Aprill, 1584. after our computation) in the citie of Mosco, hauing raigned 54 yeeres, there was some tumult and vprore among some of the nobilitie, and cominaltie, which notwithstanding was quickly pacified. [Sidenote: L. Boris adopted as the Emperors third sonne.] Immediately the same night, the Prince Boris Pheodorowich Godonoua, Knez Iuan Pheodorowich, Mesthis Slafsky, Knez Iuan Petrowich Susky, Mekita Romanowich and Bodan Iacoulewich Belskoy, being all noble men, and chiefest in the Emperors Will, especially the Lord Boris, whom he adopted as his third sonne, and was brother to the Empresse, who was a man very wel liked of al estates, as no lesse worthy for his valure and wisdome: all these were appointed to dispose, and settle his sonne Pheodor Iuanowich, hauing one sworne another, and all the nobilitie, and officers whosoeuer. In the morning the dead Emperor was layd into the Church of Michael the Archangel, into a hewen sepulcre, very richly decked with vestures fit for such a purpose: and present Proclamation was made, (Emperor Pheodor Iuanowich of all Russia, &c.). Throughout all the citie of Mosco was great watch and ward, with souldiers, and gunners, good orders established, and officers placed to subdue the tumulters, and mainteine quietnes: to see what speede and policie was in this case vsed was a thing worth the beholding. This being done in Mosco, great men of birth and accompt were also presently sent to the bordering Townes, as Smolensko, Vobsko, Kasan, Nouogorod &c. with fresh garrison, and the old sent vp. As vpon the 4. of May a parliament was held, wherein were assembled, the Metropolitane, Archbishops, Bishops, Priors, and chiefe clergie men, and all the nobility whatsoeuer: where many matters were determined not pertinent to my purpose, yet all tended to a new reformation in the gouernment: but especially the terme, and time was agreed vpon for the solempnizing of the new Emperors coronation. [Sidenote: The old Empresse, her father, and her yong sonne sent to Ouglets.] In the meane time the Empresse, wife to the old Emperor, was with her child the Emperors sonne, Charlewich Demetrie Iuanowich, of one yeres age or there abouts, sent with her father Pheodor Pheodorowich Nagay, and that kindred, being 5. Brothers, to a towne called Ouglets, which was giuen ynto her, and the young Prince her sonne, with all the lands belonging to it in the shire, with officers of all sortes appointed, hauing allowance of apparell, iewels, diet, horse &c. in ample maner belonging to the estate of a princesse. [Sidenote: The day of Pheodor his coronation.] The time of mourning after their vse being expired, called Sorachyn, or fortie orderlie dayes, the day of the solemnizing of this coronation, with great preparations, was come, being vpon the 10. day of Iune, 1584: and that day then Sunday; he being of the age of 25. yeres: at which time, Master Ierome Horsey was orderly sent for, and placed in a fit roome to see all the solemnitie. The Emperor comming out of his Pallace, there went before him, the Metropolitan, Archbishops, Bishops, and chiefest Monkes, and Clergie men, with very rich Copes, and Priestes garments vpon them, carying pictures of our Ladie &c. with the Emperours Angell, banners, censers, and many other such ceremonious things, singing all the way. The Emperour with his nobilitie in order entred the Church named Blaueshina, or Blessednes, where prayers, and seruice were vsed, according to the maner of their Church: that done, they went thence to the Church, called Michael the Archangell, and there also vsed the like prayers, and seruice: and from thence to our Lady Church, Prechista, being their Cathedrall Church. In the middest thereof was a chaire of maiestie placed, wherein his Auncestors vsed to sit at such extraordinarie times: his robes were then changed, and most rich and vnualuable garments put on him: being placed in this Princely seate, his nobility standing round about him in their degres, his imperiall Crowne was set vpon his head by the Metropolitane, his Scepter globe in his right hand, his sword of Iustice in his left of great riches: his 6. Crownes also, by which he holdeth his kingdomes were set before him, and the Lord Boris Pheodorowich was placed at his right hand: then the Metropolitan read openly a booke of a small volume, with exhortations to the Emperour to minister true iustice, to inioy with tranquilitie the Crowne of his auncestors, which God had giuen him, and vsed these words following.

Through the will of the almighty and without beginning God, which was before this world, whom we glorifie in the Trinitie, one onely God, the

Father, the Sonne, and the holy Ghost, maker of all things, worker of all in all euery where, fulfiller of all things, by which will, and working, he both liueth, and giueth life to man: that our only God which enspireth euery one of vs his only children with his word to discerne God through our Lord Iesus Christ, and the holy quickning spirit of life, now in these perilous times establish vs to keep the right Scepter, and suffer vs to raigne of our selues to the good profit of the land, to the subduing of the people, together with the enemies, and the maintenance of vertue. And so the Metropolitan blessed and layd his crosse vpon him. After this, he was taken out of his chaire of Maiestie, hauing vpon him an vpper robe adorned with precious stones of all sorts, orient pearles of great quantitie, but alwayes augmented in riches: it was in waight two hundred pounds, the traine, and parts thereof borne vp by 6. Dukes, his chiefe imperiall Crowne vpon his head very precious: his staffe imperiall in his right hand of an vnicornes horne of three foot and a halfe in length beset with rich stones, bought of Merchants of Ausburge by the old Emperour in An. 1581, and cost him 7000. Markes sterling. This Iewel M. Horsey kept sometimes, before the Emperor had it. His scepter globe was caried before him by the prince Boris Pheodorowich, his rich cap beset with rich stones and pearles was caried before him by a Duke: his 6. Crownes also were caried by Demetrius Iuanowich Godonoua, the Emperors vncle, Mekita Romanowich the Emperors vncle, Stephan Vasiliwich, Gregory Vasiliwich, Iuan Vasiliwich brothers of the blood royal. Thus at last the Emperor came to the great Church doore, and the people cried, God saue our Emperour Pheodor Iuanowich of al Russia, His horse was there ready most richly adorned, with a couering of imbrodered pearle, and precious stones, saddle, and all furniture agreeable to it, reported to be worth 300000. markes sterling.

There was a bridge made of 150. fadome in length, three maner of waies, three foote aboue ground and two fadome broad, for him to goe from one Church to the other with his Princes and nobles from the presse of the people, which were in number infinite, and some at that time pressed to death with the throng. As the Emperour returned out of the Churches, they were spred vnder foot with cloth of gold, the porches of the Church with red veluet, the bridges with scarlet, and stammell cloth from one church to another: and as soone as the Emperor was passed by, the cloth of gold, veluet and scarlet was cut, and taken of those that could come by it, euery man desirous to haue a piece, to reserue it for a monument: siluer and gold coyne, then mynted of purpose was cast among the people in great quantitie. The lord Boris Pheodorowich was sumptuously, and richly attired, with his garments decked with great orient pearle, beset with al sorts of precious stones. In like rich maner were appareled all the family of the Godonouaes in their degrees, with the rest of the princes, and nobilitie, whereof one named Knez Iuan Michalowich Glynsky, whose robe, horse, and furniture, was in register found worth one hundred thousand markes sterling, being of great antiquitie. The Empresse being in her pallace, was placed in her chaire of Maiesty also before a great open window: most precious, and rich were her robes, and shining to behold, with rich stones, and orient pearle beset, her crowne was placed vpon her head, accompanied with her Princesses, and Ladies of estate: then cried out the people, God preserue our noble Empresse Irenia. After all this the Emperour came into the Parliament house which was richly decked: there he was placed in his royall seat adorned as before: his 6. crownes were set before him vpon a table; the basin, and ewer royall of gold held by his knight of gard with his men standing two on each, side in white apparell of cloth of siluer, called Kindry, with scepters, and battle axes of gold in their hands: the Princes, and nobilitie were all placed according to their degrees, all in their rich roabs.

The Emperour after a short oration, permitted euery man in order to kisse his hande: which being done, he remoued to a princely seate prepared for him at the table: where he was serued by his nobles in very princely order. The three out roomes being very great, and large were beset with plate of golde, and siluer round, from the ground vp to the vaults one vpon the other: among which plate were many barrels of siluer, and golde: this solemnitie, and triumph lasted a whole weeke, wherein many royall pastimes were shewed and vsed: after which the chiefest men of the nobilitie were elected to their places of office, and dignitie, as the Prince Boris Pheodorowich was made chiefe Counseller to the Emperor, Master of the horse, had the charge of his person, Liuetenant of the Empire, and Warlike engins, Gouernor or Liuetenant of the Empire of Cazan, and Astracan and others: to this dignitie were by Parliament, and gift of the Emperor giuen him many reuenues, and rich lands, as there was giuen him, and his for euer to inherite a prouince called Vaga, of 300. English miles in length, and 250. in bredth, with many townes and great villages populous and wealthy, his yeerely reuenue out of that prouince, is 35. thousand markes sterling, being not the 5. part of his yerely reuenue. Further, he and his house be of such authoritie, and power, that in 40. days warning they are able to bring into the fielde 100. thousand Souldiers well furnished.

The conclusion of the Emperors Coronation was a peale of ordinance, called a peale royall two miles without the citie, being 170. great pieces of brasse of all sorts, as faire as any can be made, these pieces were all discharged with shot against bulwarkes made of purpose: 20. thousand hargubusers standing in 8. rankes two miles in length, appareled all in veluet, coloured silke and stammels, discharged their shot also twise ouer in good order: and so the Emperor accompanied with all his princes and nobles, at the least 50. thousand horse departed through the City to his pallace. This royall coronation would aske much time, and many leaues of paper to be described particularly as it was performed: it shal suffice, to vnderstahd that the like magnificence was neuer seen in Russia.

The coronation, and other triumphes ended, al the nobilitie, officers, and merchants according to an accustomed order euery one in his place, and degree brought rich presents vnto the Emperor, wishing him long life, and ioy in his kingdome.

[Sidenote: Iohn de Wale.] The same time also Master Ierom Horsey aforesaid, remayning as seruant in Russia for the Queenes most excellent Maiestie, was called for to the Emperor, as he sate in his imperiall seat, and then also a famous Merchant of Netherland being newly come to Mosco, (who gaue him selfe out to be the king of Spaines subiect) called Iohn de Wale, was in like sort called for. Some of the nobilitie would haue preferred this subiect of the Spaniard before Master Horsey seruant to the Queene of England, whereunto Master Horsey would in no case agree, saying, he would haue his legges cut off by the knees, before he would yeeld to such an indignitie offered to his Soueraigne the Queenes Maiesty of England, to bring the Emperor a present, in course after the King of Spaines subiect, or any other whatsoeuer. The Emperor, and the Prince Boris Pheodorowich perceiuing the controuersie, sent the Lord Treasorer Peter Iuanowich Galauyn, and Vasili Shalkan, both of the Counsell, to them, who deliuered the Emperor backe, Master Horseys speech: whereupon he was first in order (as good reason) admitted and presented the Emperor in the behalfe of the English merchants trading thither, a present wishing him ioy, and long to raigne in tranquilitie, and so kissed the Emperors hand, he accepting the present with good liking, and auouching, that for his sisters sake Queene Elizabeth of England, he would be a gracious Lord to her Merchants, in as ample maner as euer his father had ben: and being dismissed, he had the same day sent him 70. dishes of sundry kinds of meats, with 3. carts laden with al sorts of drinks very bountifully. After him was the foresayd subiect of the Spanish king admitted with his present, whom the Emperor willed to be no lesse faithfull and seruiceable vnto him, then the Queene of Englands subiects were and had bene, and then the king of Spaines subiects should receiue fauour accordingly.

All these things thus in order performed, praises were sung in all the churches. The Emperor and Empresse very deuoutly resorted on foote to many principal Churches in the Citie, and vpon Trinitie Sunday betooke themselues to a progresse in order of procession, to a famous monasterie called Sergius and the Trinitie 60. miles distant from the Citie of Mosco, accompanied with a huge armie of Noblemen, Gentlemen, and others, mounted vpon goodly horses with furniture accordingly.

The Empresse of deuotion tooke this iourney on foot all the way, accompanied with her princesses and ladies, no small number: her guard and gunners were in number 20000, her chiefe counseller or attendant, was a noble man of the blood Roial her vncle of great authoritie called Demetri Iuanowich Godonoua. All this progresse ended, both the Emperor and Empresse returned to Mosco: shortly after the Emperor by the direction of the prince Boris Pheodorowich, sent a power into the land of Siberia, where all the rich Sables and Furres are gotten. This power conquered in one yeere and a halfe, 1000. miles. [Sidenote: Chare Siberski prince of Siberia taken prisoner and brought to Mosco.] In the performance of this warre, there was taken prisoner the Emperor of the countrey called Chare Sibersky, and with him many other dukes and noble men, which were brought to Mosko with a guard of souldiers and gunners, who were receiued into the citie in very honorable maner, and do there remaine to this day.

Hereupon the corrupt officers, Iudges, Iustices, captains and lieutenants through the whole kingdom were remooued, and more honest men substituted in their places, with expresse commandement, vnder seuere punishment to surcease their old bribing and extortion which they had vsed in the old Emperors time, and now to execute true iustice without respect of persons: and to the end that this might be the better done, their lands and yeerly stipends were augmented: the great taskes, customes, and duties, which were before layd vpon the people in the old Emperors time, were now abated, and some wholy remitted, and no punishments commanded to be vsed, without sufficient and due proofe, although the crime were capitall, deseruing death: many Dukes and noble men of great houses, that were vnder displeasure, and imprisoned 20. yeeres by the old Emperor, were now set at libertie and restored to their lands: all prisoners were set at libertie and their trespasses forgiuen. In summe, a great alteration vniuersally in the gouernment folowed, and yet all was done quietly, ciuilly, peaceably, without trouble to the Prince, or offence to the Subiect: and this bred great assurance and honour to the kingdom, and all was accomplished by the wisedom especially of Irenia the Empresse.

[Sidenote: Sophet Keri Alli king of the Crimmes arriual at Mosco.] These things being reported and caried to the eares of the kings and princes that were borderers vpon Russia, they grew so fearefull and terrible to them, that the Monarch of all the Scythians called the Crimme Tartar or great Can himselfe, named Sophet Keri Alli, came out of his owne countrey to the Emperor of Russia, accompanied with a great number of his nobilitie well horsed, although to them that were Christians they seemed rude, yet they were personable men, and valiant: their comming was gratefull to the Emperor, and their entertainment was honourable, the Tartar prince hauing brought with him his wiues also, receiued of the Russe Emperor entertainment, and princely welcome according to their estates.

Not long after, 1200. Polish gentlemen, valiant Souldiors, and proper men came to Mosko offring their seruice to the Emperor, who were all entertained: and in like sort many Chirkasses, and people of other nations came and offred seruice. And assoone as the report of this new created Emperor was spred ouer other kingdoms of Europe, there were sent to him sundry Ambassadors to wish him ioy and prosperitie in his kingdom: thither came Ambassadors from the Turke, from the Persian, the Bogharian, the Crimme, the Georgian, and many other Tartar princes. There came also Ambassadors from the Emperor of Almaine, the Pole, the Swethen, the Dane, &c. And since his coronation no enemie of his hath preuailed in his attempts.

[Sidenote: The new Emperor Pheodore Iuanowich his letters and requests to the Queene.] It fell out not long after, that the Emperor was desirous to send a message to the most excellent Queene of England, for which seruice he thought no man fitter then M. Ierome Horsey, supposing that one of the Queenes owne men and subiects would be the more acceptable to her. The summe of which message was, that the Emperor desired a continuance of that league, friendship, amitie and intercourse of traffique which was betweene his father and the Queens maiestie and her subiects, with other priuate affaires besides, which are not to be made common.

[Sidenote: M. Horseis voiage from Mosco to England ouerland.] Master Horsey hauing receiued the letters and requests of the Emperor, prouided for his iourney ouer land, and departed from Mosco the fift day of September, thence vnto Otuer, to Torshook, to great Nouogrod, to Vobsky, and thence to Nyhouse in Liuonia, to Wenden, and so to Riga: (where he was beset, an brought foorthwith before a Cardinall called Rageuil, but yet suffred to passe in the end:) From thence to Mito, to Golden, and Libou in Curland, to Memel, to Koningsburgh in Prussia, to Elbing, to Dantzike, to Stetine in Pomerland, to Rostock, to Lubeck, to Hamborough, to Breme, to Emden, and by sea to London. Being arriued at her maiesties roiall court, and hauing deliuered the Emperors letters with good fauour, and gracious acceptance, he was foorthwith againe commaunded to repasse into Russia, with other letters from her maiestie to the Emperor, and prince Boris Pheodorowich, answering the Emperors letters, and withall requesting the fauour and friendship, which his father had yeelded to the English merchants: and hereunto was he earnestly also solicited by the merchants of London themselues of that company, to deale in their behalfe. [Sidenote: 1586.] Being thus dispatched from London by sea, he arriued in Mosco the 20. of April 1586. and was very honourably welcommed. And for the merchants behoofe, obtained all his requests, being therein specially fauoured by the noble prince Boris Pheodorowich, who alwayes affected M. Horsey with speciall liking, And hauing obtained priuiledges for the merchants, he was recommended from the Emperor againe, to the Queene of England his mistresse, by whom the prince Boris, in token of his honorable and good opinion of the Queens maiestie, sent her highnesse a roiall present of Sables, Luzarns, cloth of gold and other rich things. So that the companie of English merchants, next to their thankfulnes to her maiestie, are to account M. Horseis paines their speciall benefit, who obtained for them those priuileges, which in twentie yeeres before would not be granted.

The maner of M. Horseis last dispatch from the Emperor, because it was very honorable, I thought good to record. He was freely allowed post horses for him and his seruants, victuals and all other necessaries for his long iourney; at euery towne that he came vnto from Mosco to Vologda, which is by land fiue hundred miles, he receiued the like free and bountifull allowances, at the Emperors charge. New victuall and prouision were giuen him vpon the riuer Dwina at euery towne by the Kings officers, being one thousand miles in length. When he came to the new castle called Archangel, he was receiued of the Duke Knez Vasili Andrewich Isuenogorodsky by the Emperors commission into the Castle, gunners being set in rankes, after their vse, where he was sumptuously feasted: from thence hee was dispatched with bountifull prouision and allowance in the Dukes boat, with one hundred men to rowe him, and one hundred Gunners in other boats to conduct him, with a gentleman captaine of the Gunners. Comming to the road where the English, Dutch, and French ships rode, the gunners discharged, and the ships shot in like maner 46. pieces of their ordinance, and so he was brought to his lodging at the English house vpon Rose Island.

And that which was the full and complete conclusion of the fauour of the Emperor and Boris Pheodorowich toward M. Horsey, there were the next day sent him for his further prouision vpon the sea by a gentleman and a captaine the things following.

> 16. liue oxen. 70. sheepe. 600. hens. 25. flitches of Bacon. 80. bushels of meale. 600. loaues of bread. 2000. egs. 10. geese. 2. cranes. 2. Swans 65. gallons of mead. 40. gallons of AquauitŠ. 60. gallons of beere. 3. yong beares. 4. hawkes. Store of onions and garlike. 10. fresh salmons. A wild bore.

All these things were brought him downe by a Gentleman of the Emperors, and another of prince Boris Pheodorowich, and were recalled in order by Iohn Frese seruant to M. Horsey, together with an honorable present and reward from the prince Boris, sent him by M. Francis Cherry an

Englishman: which present was a whole very rich piece of cloth of gold, and a faire paire of Sables. This gentleman hath obserued many other rare things concerning those partes, which hereafter (God willing) at more conuenient time and laisure shall come to light.

* * * * *

Pheodor Iuanowich the new Emperors gracious letter of priuilege to the English Merchants word for word, obtained by M. Ierome Horsey. 1586.

Through the wil of the almightie, and without beginning God, which was before this world, whom we glorifie in the Trinitie, one only God the father, the sonne, and the holy ghost, maker of all things, worker of all in all euery where, fulfiller of all things, by which will and working, he both loueth and giueth life to man, That our onely God, which inspireth euery one of vs his onely children with his word, to descerne God through our Lord Iesus Christ, and the holy quickning spirit of life now in these perilous times, Establish vs to keep the right Scepter, and suffer vs of our selues to raigne to the good profite of the land, and to the subduing of the people, together with the enemies, and to the maintenance of virtue.

We Pheodor the ofspring of Iohn, the great Lord, Emperor, king and great prince of all Russia, of Volodemeria, Moscouia and Nouogrod, king of Cazan, king of Astracan, Lord of Plesko, and great prince of Smolensko, of Tuer, Yougoria, Permia, Viatsko, of Bolghar and others, lord and great prince of the land of the lower Nouogrod, Chernigo, Rezan, Polotsko, Rostow. Yeraslaue, the White lake, Liefland, Oudor, Condensa, and Ruler of all Siberia, and all the Northside, and lord of many other countries.

I haue gratified the merchants of England, to wit, sir Rowland Haiward, and
Richard Martin Aldermen, sir George Barnes, Thomas Smith, esquire, Ierome
Horsey, Richard Saltonstall, with their fellowes.

I haue licensed them to saile with their shippes into our dominion the land of Dwina, with all kind of commodities to trade freely, and vnto our kingdom andd the citie of Mosco, and to all the cities of our empire of Moscouia.

And the English merchants sir Rowland Haiward and his societie desired vs, that we would gratifie them to trade into our kingdom of Moscouia, and into our heritage of great Nouogrod and Plesko, and into all parts of our kingdom, to buy and sell with their wares without custome.

Therefore we for our sisters sake Queene Elizabeth, and also because that they allege that they had great losse and hinderance by the venture of the sea, and otherwise, haue gratified the said English merchants sir Rowland Haiward and his societie, freely to come into our kingdom of Moscouia, and into al our dominions with al kind of commodities, to trade, and traffique freely, and at their pleasure with al kind of their commodities: also I haue commanded not to take any maner of custome for their goods, nor other customs whatsoeuer: That is to say, neither for passing by any place by water, nor for lanching, neither for passing through any place by land, neither for the vessels or boats, nor for their heads, nor for passing ouer bridges, nor for ferying ouer at any place, neither for acknowledgment at any place where they shall come, nor any maner of custome or dutie, by what name soeuer.

Only they shall not bring with them into our dominions, neither recarie out of our dominions, or father any other mens goods but their owne, neither sell them nor barter them away for them.

Also our natural people shall not buy and sell for them, or from them, neither shal they retaine or keepe any of our naturall subiects goods, or pawnes by them to colour them.

Also they shall not send any of their Russe seruants about into any citie to ingrosse, or buy vp commodities, but into what citie they themselues shal come, they shal buy and sel, and shal sel their owne commodities and not ours.

And when they shal come into our inheritance of great Nouogrod and Plesko, and through all our dominions with their commodities, then our noblemen, and captains, and euery one of our officers shall suffer them to depart according to this our letter, and shall take no custom at all of them, for any of their commodities, neither for passing through or passing by, nor for passage ouer any bridges, nor shall take of them any other dutie whatsoeuer name they haue.

Also into what places of our dominion, or when they shal happen to come, and to proceed to buy or sell, and wheresoeuer they shall passe through with goods not buying of any commodities, neither will sell their owne, then in those cities and townes they shall take no maner of custome or dutie of them accordingly as before.

And I haue gratified them and giuen them free leaue to traffique throughout all the dominions of our kingdom in all cities with their goods, to buy and sell all maner of commodities, without any dutie or custome whatsoeuer.

And the English merchants where they are desirous to buy or sell, or barter their wares with our merchants, whole wares for wares, they shall sell their commodities whole, and not by retaile: That is to say, neither by small weight nor by the yard, to sell or barter in their owne houses, and they shal sel and barter their wares wholly, Cloth by the packe, and by the whole Cloth, and Damaske and veluet by the piece and not by the yard, and al maner of commodities that are to be sold by weight, not to sell by the small weights, as by the pound and ounce, but by whole sale: also they shall sel wines by the pipe: and by the gallon, quart or stoope they shal not sell.

And they shall buy, sell and exchange their owne commodities themselues, and the Russe merchants shall not make sales or exchange for them or from them any of their commodities, neither shal they themselues conuey or cary through any other mans goods at no place instead of their owne: and which of the English merchants will at any time sell his commodities at Colmogro or Vologda or Yeraslaue, they may, and of their commodities throughout all our cities and dominions, our noblemen, captains, and euery of our officers shall take no maner of custome, according as it is written in this our gracious letter: and throughout all our dominions and cities they shal hire carriers and vessels with men to labour, at their owne charge, to transport their goods.

So likewise, whensoeuer the English merchants are disposed to depart out of our kingdom into any other countrey or into their owne land, if our pleasure be, they shall take our goods with them from our Treasurie, and shall sell them, and exchange them for such commoditie as is commodious for our kingdom, and shall deliuer it into our Treasurie, and with those our commodities, our Noblemen and captains, and euery of our officers shall let them passe through all our cities also without custome according to these our letters.

Also whensoeuer the English merchants shall haue sold their own goods and bought themselues commodities, and wil depart out of Mosco, then they shal manifest themselues to our chiefe Secretarie Andrew Sholkaloue, in the office where the Ambassadors are alwayes dispatched.

And if the English merchants comming, haue had any mischance by the sea, insomuch that the ship be broken, or if that ship do come to any part of our country: then we will cause the goods to be sought out in true Iustice, and to be giuen to the English people, which at that time shall bee here resident in our countrey: and if so be that it so fell out that at that time there be no Englishmen within our realme: then wil we cause these goods to be laid vp in a place together, and when the people of England shall come into our realme, then we will command all those goods to be deliuered to the sayd English people.

Also we haue gratified all the English merchants with the house of one Vrie here in the Mosco right ouer against S. Maximes church behind the market, and they shal dwel in the same house according as before time, and they shall keepe one alwayes in the house to keepe it, either a Russe, or one of their owne people.

Also the English merchants shal possesse their houses, to wit, at Yeraslaue, Vologda, Colmogro, and the house at the hauen of the sea, and they shal dwel in those houses, according as our goodnes hath bene to them heretofore: and we haue commanded, that there shall not be taken of them no yeerely rent, nor no maner of custome, taxe, rent or any other dutie whatsoeuer for those houses, neither shal they pay any dutie or taxe with any of the townsmen of those places, and in euery one of those houses, to wit, at Yeraslaue, Vologda, and Colmogro, they shall haue men to keepe their houses, two or three of their owne countrey people, strangers or els Russes, men of the meanest sort, which shall be no merchants, that they may lay their goods in those houses, and they may sell the commodities out of those their houses to whom they please, according to this our gracious letter: and those that keepe their houses shall not sell or buy no part of their commoditie, except they be there or giue order, whereby they be not deceiued by them.

So likewise I haue gratified them with their house at the sea hauen, at the mouth of Podezemsky, and we haue commanded that they shal not cary their goods from thence to the new castle S. Michael the archangel, but shall arriue, and doe as they haue done heretofore with their wares at that their house, and shall vnlade their commodities out of their ships, and shal lade them againe with Russe commodities, euen there at that their house without interruption: onely they shal permit our officers of Colmogro and sworn men to write vp those commodities, both the commodities of England, and those of Russeland, what the merchants shal declare themselues, and no otherwise, but they shal not ouerlooke their commodities, neither shal they vnbind any of their packs.

And when the English merchants are disposed to send into their owne countrey, to wit, any of their owne people on land through any other kingdom whatsoeuer, they shall not send their people without our kingly knowledge, and commandement, and which of their people so euer they do meane to send out of our kingdom into their owne countrey, then they shal send those their people, not without our kingly maiesties knowledge, to wit, those that go of pleasure without carying any commodities with them, and they shal haue a letter of passe giuen vnto them, out of the office where the Ambassadors haue alwayes their dispatch.

And whosoeuer hath anything to doe with them in matters of controuersie, either concerning merchandize or iniuries, then they are to be iudged by our treasurers and Secretarie of the Ambassadors office to do iustice between both parties, and to seek out the trueth of matters in al things, and whatsoeuer cannot be found out by the Law, shalbe tried by othe and lots: whose lot soeuer is taken foorth, him to haue right.

And in what place of all our kingdom, in what citie soeuer they or their people shall bee, and that there happen any matter of controuersie, either concerning merchandise, iniuries or otherwise, that they haue occasion to set vpon any man by lawe, or that any seeke vpon them, concerning what matter soeuer in all our kingdom and cities, then our lieutenants, captains, and our officers shall giue them Iustice, and shall minister all true iustice betweene them, seeking out the trueth: and what cannot be truly sought by law, shalbe sought out by othe and lot; whose lot soeuer is taken out, him to haue right accordingly as before, and the Iudges or Iustices shall take of them no kind of dutie, for matters of law no where throughout all our realmes. This letter is giuen in our princely palace within the citie of Mosco, in the yeere from the foundation of the world, seuen thousand fourescore and fifteene in the moneth of February.

* * * * *

The Ambassage of M. Giles Fletcher, Doctor of the Ciuil Law, sent from her
  Maiestie to Theodor the Emperor of Russia. Anno 1588.

In the yeere 1588. was sent Ambassador from her highnesse into the countrey of Russia, Giles Fletcher Doctor of the Ciuil Lawe, as well to treat with the new Emperor Pheodor Iuanowich, about league and amitie, in like maner as was before with his father Iuan Vasilowich, as also for the reestablishing and reducing into order the deciad trade of our Englishmen there. Who notwithstanding at his first arriuall at the Mosco, found some parts of hard entertainment, by meanes of certaine rumors concerning the late nauall victory which was there reported to haue fallen on the Spanish side, as also for some dislike conceiued against the priuileged trade of our English merchants. Yet in the end he obtained of the Emperour many good and equall conditions, and was curteously and honourably dismissed by him. The principall points which he entreated of, and were granted vnto him by the said Emperor were these:

1 A continuation of league and amitie betweene her Highnesse and the sayd Emperour Pheodor Iuanowich, in like maner as was before with his father Iuan Vasilowich.

2 A confirmation and reestablishment of the former priuileges of the Companie of our English merchants, which were infringed and annulled in the principal points, with diuers necessary additions to the same, for the better ordering of their trade in those countreys hereafter, viz. That the state of the priuilege granted before in the names of some priuate and

- 188 -

particular men, be altered in that point, and the same granted by the name and stile of their incorporation, viz. To the felowship of English merchants for the discouerie of new trades.

3 That vpon euery surmise and light quarel, the said priuilege be not reuoked and annulled, as before time it hath bene.

4 That iustice shall be administred to the said Companie and their Agent without delay, vpon such as shal offer them any despite or iniurie, or shal exact or impose vpon them any paiment, taxation or imposition whatsoeuer, contrary to the freedome of the said grant.

5 That the goods and commodities of the said Companie, be not forcibly taken as before time they had bene by the Emperors officers or people of authoritie, either for the vse of the said Emperor or of his officers. But in case they haue need of the said commodities, the same to be taken at reasonable prices, and for ready money.

6 That the said Companie be not charged hereafter with the answering of such debts as are made by any Englishman not being of the societie.

7 That the Emperors authorized people shall not hereafter repute any Englishman residant in that countrey, to be any factor, seruant, or dealer, in the said Companies affaires, but such as the Agents shall inregister by name, within the offices where custome is entered in all such places of the land where the sayd Companie haue residences to traffike.

8 That the names of such as shall so be inregistred be no longer continued in record, nor themselues reputed as factors or dealers for the said Companie, then the Agent shall thinke good. But in case the said Agent in his discretion shall thinke meete to strike out of the Register any name of such as haue bene employed in the Companies seruice, the said person to be held as priuate, and whose acte in bargaining or otherwise, shall not charge the said Companie.

9 That if any English man within the countrey of Russia be suspected for any notorious crime, as felony, treason, &c. the same be not straightwaies set vpon the Pudkey, [Marginal note: It is rosting to death.] nor otherwise tormented, till such time as he shall be conuicted by plaine and euident proofes: which being done, the whole proceeding to be sent ouer to the Queene of England.

10 That the said priuilege with the additions, shall be published in all townes and partes of the Emperors dominions, where the said Companie haue traffike.

11 That the said Companie shall be permitted to vse a sole trade through the Emperours countries, by the riuer Volga into Media, Persia, Bogharia, and the other the East countries.

12 Whereas there was claimed of the said Companie the summe of 23553. markes of debt, made by certaine of their factors for the said company, for paiment whereof their whole stocke was in danger of arrest, by publike authoritie: Futher also 2140. rubbles for custome and houserent, he obtained a rebatement of eighteene thousand, one hundred fiftie and three marks of the sayd debt.

The sayd Ambassador M. Giles Fletcher, as I vnderstand, hath drawen a booke intituled, Of the Russe Common wealth, containing:

First, a Cosmographicall description, of the countrey, which hath these chapters.

1 Of the length and bredth of the countrey of Russia, with the names of the shires.

2 Of the soile and climate.

3 Of the natiue commodities of the countrey.

Secondly, a description of their policie contained in these Chapters, viz.

1 Of the constitution or state of the Russe Common wealth.

2 Of their Parliaments, and maner of holding them,

3 Of the Russe Nobilitie and meanes whereby it is kept in an vnder proportion agreeable to that state.

4 Of the maner of gouerning their prouinces of shires.

5 Of the Emperours priuie counsell.

6 Of the Emperors customs and their reuenues, with the practises for the increase of them.

7 Of the Russe communaltie and their condition.

8 Of their publike iustice and maner of proceeding therein.

9 Of the Emperors forces for his warres, with the chiefe officers, and their salarie or pay.

10 Of their maner of mustering, armour, and prouision for victuall.

11 Of their ordering, marching, charging, and their martiall discipline.

12 Of their colonies and policie in maintaining their purchases by conquest.

13 Of their borderers with whom they haue most to doe in warre and peace.

14 Of their church officers and degrees.

15 Of their liturgie or forme of Church seruice.

16 Of their maner of administring the Sacraments.

17 Of the doctrine of the Russe church.

18 Of the maner of solemnizing their marriages.

19 Of the other ceremonies of the Russe church.

Thirdly, the Oeconomie or priuate behauiour of the Russe containing these chapters.

1 Of the Emperors houshold officers, and order of his house.

2 Of the priuate behauiour and maner of the Russe people.

The description of the countrey of Russia, with the bredth, length, and names of the Shires.

The countrey of Russia was sometimes called Sarmatia. It changed the name (as some do suppose) for that it was parted into diuers smal, and yet absolute gouernments, not depending, nor being subiect the one to the other. For Russe in that tongue doeth signifie as much as to part, or diuide. The Russe reporteth that foure brethren, Trubor, Rurico, Sinees, and Variuus deuided among them the North parts of the country. Likewise that the South parts were possessed by 4. other, Kio, Scieko, Choranus, and their sister Libeda: each calling his territorie after his owne name. Of this partition it was called Russia, about the yere from Christ 860. [Sidenote: Strabo in his 7. booke of Geogr.] As for the coniecture which I find in some Cosmographers, that the Russe nation borowed the name of the people called Roxellani, and were the very same nation with them, it is without all good probabilitie, both in respect of the etymologie of the word (which is very far fet) and especially for the seat and dwelling of that people, which was betwixt the two ruiers of Tanais and Boristhenes, (as Strabo reporteth) quite another way from the countrey of Russia.

When it bare the name of Sarmatia, it was diuided into two chiefe parts: the White and the Black. The white Sarmatia was all that part that lieth towards the North, and on the side of Liefland: as the prouinces now called Dwina, Vagha, Vstiug, Vologda, Cargapolia, Nouogrodia, &c whereof Nouogrod velica was the Metropolite or chiefe citie. Black Sarmatia was al that countrey that lieth Southward towards the Euxin or Black sea: as the dukedome of Volodemer, of Mosco, Rezan, &c. Some haue thought that the name of Sarmatia was first taken, from one Sarmates, whom Moses and Iosephus cal Asarmathes sonne to Ioktan, and nephew to Heber, of the posteritie of Sera. [Sidenote: Gen, 10. Ioseph. l. 1. ca, 14.] But this seemeth to be nothing but a coniecture taken out of the likenes of the name Asarmathes. For the dwelling of all Ioktans posteritie is described by Moses to haue bene betwixt Mescha or Masius (an hil of the Ammonites) and Sephace, nere to the riuer Euphrates: which maketh it very vnlikely that Asarmathes should plant any colonies so far off in the North and Northwest countries. [Sidenote: The borders of Russia.] It is bounded northward by the Lappes and the North Ocean. On the Southside by the Tartars called Crimmes. Eastward they haue the Nagaian Tartar, that possesseth all the countrey on the East side of Volga towards the Caspian sea. On the West and Southwest border lieth Lituania, Liuonia and Polonia.

[Sidenote: The Shires of Russia.] The whole Countrey being nowe reduced vnder the gouernment of one, conteineth these chiefe Prouinces or Shires. Volodemer, (which beareth the first place in the Emperours stile, becauce their house came of the Dukes of that Countrey) Mosco, Nisnouogrod, Plesko, Smolensko, Nouogrod velica (or Nouogrod of the low Countrey) Rostoue, Yeraslaue, Bealozera, Rezan, Duyna, Cargapolia, Meschora, Vagha, Vstuga, Ghaletsa. These are the naturall shires perteyning to Russia, but farre greater and larger then the shires of England, though not so well peopled. [Sidenote: The Prouinces or Countries got by conquest.] The other Countreys or prouinces to which the Russe Emperours haue gotten perforce added of late to their other dominion, are these which followe, Twerra, Youghoria, Permia, Vadska, Boulghoria, Chernigo, Oudoria, Obdoria, Condora, with a great part of Siberia: where the people though they be not naturall Russes, yet obey the Emperour of Russia, and are ruled by the Lawes of his Countrey, paying customes and taxes, as his owne people doe. Besides these he hath vnder him the kingdomes of Cazan and Astracan, gotten by conquest not long since. As for all his possession in Lituania (to the number of 30. great Townes and more,) with Narue and Dorp in Liuonia, they are quite gone, being surprised of late yeeres by the Kings of Poland and Sweden. These Shires and Prouinces are reduced into foure Iurisdictions, which they call Chetfyrds (that is) Tetrarchies, or Fourth parts.

[Sidenote: The breadth and length of the Countrey.] The whole Countrey is of great length and breadth. From the North to the South (if you measure from Cola to Astracan which bendeth somewhat Eastward) it reacheth in length about 4260. verst, or miles. [Sidenote: Pechinga.] Notwithstanding the Emperour of Russia hath more territorie Northward, farre beyond Cola vnto the Riuer of Tromschua, that runneth a hundred verst, welnigh beyond Pechingna, neere to Wardhouse but not intire nor clearely limited, by reason of the kings of Sweden and Denmarke, that haue diuers townes there, aswell as the Russe, plotted together the one with the other; euery one of them clayming the whole of those North parts as his owne right. The breadth (if you go from that part of his territorie that lyeth farthest Westward on the Narue side, to the parts of Siberia Eastward, where the Emperour hath his garrisons) is 4400. verst or thereabouts. A verst (by their reckoning) is a 1000. pases, yet lesse by one quarter than an English mile. If the whole dominion of the Russe Emperour were all habitable, and peopled in all places, as it is in some, he would either hardly holde it all within one regiment, or be ouer mightie for all his neighbour Princes.

Of the Soile and Climate.

The soyle of the Countrey for the most part is of a sleight sandie moulde, yet very much different one place from another, for the yeeld of such things as grow out of the earth. The Countrey Northwards towards the parts of S. Nicholas and Cola, and Northeast towards Siberia, is all very barren, and full of desert woods by reason of the Climate, and extremitie of the colde in Winter time. So likewise along the Riuer Volgha betwixt the countreys of Cazan, and Astracan: where (notwithstanding the soyle is very fruitfull) it is all vnhabited, sauing that vpon the riuer Volgha on the Westside, the Emperour hath some fewe Castels with garisons in them. This happeneth by meanes of the Crimme Tartar, that will neither himselfe plant Townes to dwel there, (liuing a wild and vagrant life) nor suffer the Russe (that is farre off with the strength of his Countrey) to people those parts. From Vologda (which lieth almost 1700. verst from the port of S. Nicholas) downe towards Mosco, and so towards the South part that bordereth vpon the Crimme, (which conteineth the like space of 1700. verst or there abouts) is a very fruitfull and pleasant countrey, yeelding pasture, and corne, with woods and waters in very great plentie. The like is betwixt Rezan (that lieth Southeast from Mosco) to Nouogrod and Vobsko, that reach farthest towards the Northwest. So betwixt Mosco, and Smolensko (that lyeth Southwest towards Lituania) is a very fruitfull and pleasant soile.

The whole countrey differeth very much from it selfe, by reason of the yeere: so that a man would marueile to see the great, alteration and difference betwixt the Winter, and the Summer Russia. The whole Countrey in the Winter lieth vnder snow, which falleth continually, and is sometime of a yard or two thicke, but greater towards the North. [Sidenote: The colde of Russia.] The riuers and other waters are all frosen vp a yard or more thicke, how swift or broade soeuer they bee. And this continueth commonly fiue moneths, viz. from the beginning of Nouember till towardes the ende of March, what time the snow beginneth to melt. So that it would breede a frost in a man to looke abroad at that time, and see the Winter face of that Countrey. The sharpenesse of the aire you may iudge of by this: for that water dropped downe or cast vp into the air congealeth into yce before it come to the ground. In the extremitie of Winter, if you holde a pewter dish or pot in your hand, or any other metall (except in some chamber where their warme stoaues bee) your fingers will friese fast vnto it, and drawe off the skinne at the parting. When you passe out of a warme roome into a colde, you shall sensibly feele your breath to waxe starke, and euen stifeling with the colde, as you drawe it in and out. Diuers not onely that trauell abroad, but in the very markets and streetes of their Townes, are mortally pinched and killed withall: so that you shall see many drop downe in the streetes; many trauellers brought into the Townes sitting dead and stifle in their Sleds. Diuers lose their noses, the tips of their eares, and the bals of their cheeks, their toes, feete, &c. Many times (when the Winter is very hard and extreeme) the beares and woolfes issue by troopes out of the woods driuen by hunger, and enter the villages, tearing and rauening all they can finde: so that the inhabitants are faine to flie for safegard of their liues. And yet in the Sommer time you shal see such a new hiew and face of a Countrey, the woods (for the most part which are all of firre and birch) so fresh and so sweete, the pastures and medowes so greene and well growen, (and that vpon the sudden) such varietie of flowers, such noyse of birdes (specially of Nightingales, that seeme to be more lowde and of a more variable note then in other Countreys) that a man shall not lightly trauell in a more pleasant Countrey.

And this fresh and speedy growth of the spring there seemeth to proceede from the benefite of the snow: which all the Winter time being spread ouer the whole Countrey as a white robe, and keeping it warme from the rigour of the frost, in the Spring time (when the Sunne waxeth wanme, and dissolueth it into water) doeth so throughly drench and soake the ground, that is somewhat of a sleight and sandie mould, and then shineth so hotely vpon it againe, that it draweth the hearbes and plants foorth in great plentie and varietie, in a very short time. As the Winter exceedeth in colde, so the Sommer inclineth to ouer much heat, specially in the monethes of Iune, Iuly and August, being much warmer then the Sommer aire in England.

The countrey throughout is very well watered with springs, riuers, and Ozeraes, or lakes. Wherein the prouidence of God is to be noted, for that much of the Countrey being so farre inland, as that some part lieth a thousand miles and more euery way from any sea, yet it is serued with faire Riuers, and that in very great number, that emptying themselues one into another, runne all into the Sea. Their lakes are many and large, some of 60. 80. 100. and 200. miles long with breadth proportionate.

[Sidenote: The chiefe Riuers of Russia.] The chiefe Riuers are these, First, Volgha, that hath his head or spring at the route of an Aldertree, about 200. verst aboue Yaruslaue, and groweth so bigge by the encrease of other

Riuers by that time it commeth thither, that it is broad an English mile and more, and so runneth into the Caspian sea, about 2800. verst or miles of length.

The next is Boristhenes (now called Neper) that diuideth the Countrey from
Lituania, and falleth into the Euxin sea.

The third Tanais or Don, (the ancient bounder betwixt Europe and Asia) that taketh his head out of Rezan Ozera, and so running through the Countrey of the Chrim Tartar, falleth into the great Sea, lake, or meare, (called Maeotis) by the citie of Azou. By this Riuer (as the Russe reporteth), you may passe from their Citie Mosco to Constantinople, and so into all those parts of the world by water, drawing your boate (as their maner is) ouer a little Isthmus or narrowe slip of land, a few versts ouerthwart. Which was proued not long since by an Ambassadour sent to Constantinople, who passed the riuer of Moscua, and so into another called Ocka, whence hee drew his boat ouer into Tanais, and thence passed the whole way by water.

The fourth is called Duyna, many hundred miles long, that falleth Northward into the bay of S. Nicholas, and hath great Alabaster rockes on the bankes towards the sea side.

The fifth Duna, that emptieth into the Baltick sea by the towne Riga.

The sixt Onega, that falleth into the Bay at Solouetsko 90. verst from the port of S. Nicholas. This riuer below the towne Cargapolia, meeteth with the Riuer Volock, that falleth into the Finland Sea by the towne Yama. So that from the port of S. Nicholas into the Finland sea, and so into the Sound, you may passe all by water, as hath bene tried by the Russe.

The seuenth Suchana, that floweth into Duyna, and so into the North Sea.

The eight Ocka, that fetcheth his head from the borders of the Chrim, and streameth into Volgha.

The ninth Moscua, that runneth thorough the Citie Mosco, and giueth it the name.

There is Wichida also a very large and long riuer that riseth out of Permia, and falleth into Volgha. All these are riuers of very large streames, the least to be compared to the Thames in bignesse, and in length farre more, besides diuers other. The Pole at Mosco is 55. degrees 10. minutes. At the port of S. Nicholas towards the North 63. degrees and 50. minutes.

The natiue commodities of the Countrey.

[Sidenote: The fruits and graine of Russia.] For kindes of fruites, they haue Apples, peares plummes, cherries, red and blacke, (but the blacke wilde) a deene like a muske millian, but more sweete and pleasant, cucumbers and goords (which they call Arbouse) rasps, strawberies, and hurtilberies, with many other beries in great quantitie in euery wood and hedge. Their kindes of graine are wheat, rie, barley, oates, pease, buckway, psnytha, that in taste is somewhat like to rice. Of all these graines the Countrey yeeldeth very sufficient with an ouerplus quantitie, so that wheate is solde sometime for two alteens or ten pence starling the Chetfird, which maketh almost three English bushels.

Their rie is sowed before the Winter, all their other graine in the Spring time, and for the most part in May. The Permians and some other that dwell farre North, and in desert places, are serued from the parts that lye more Southward, and are forced to make, bread sometimes of a kinde of roote (called Vaghnoy) and of the middle rine of the firre tree. If there be any dearth (as they accompted this last yeere Anno 1588. wheat and rie being 13. alteens, or 5. shillings fiue pence starling the Chetfird) the fault is rather in the practise of their Nobilitie that vse to engrosse it, then in the Countrey it selfe.

[Sidenote: The chiefe commodities of the countrey. 1. Furres.] The natiue commodities of the Countrey (wherewith they serue both their owne turnes, and send much abroad to the great enriching of the Emperor, and his people) are many and substantiall. First, furres of all sorts. Wherein the prouidence of God is to be noted, that prouideth a naturall remedie for them, to helpe the naturall inconuenience of their Countrey by the cold of the Climat. Their chiefe furres are these, Blacke fox, Sables, Lusernes, dun fox, Martrones, Gurnestalles or Armins, Lasets or Miniuer, Beuer, Wuluerins, the skin of a great water Rat that smelleth naturally like muske, [Sidenote: These rats are in Canada.] Calaber or gray squirel, red squirel, red and white fox. Besides the great quantitie spent within the Countrey (the people being clad al in furres the whole winter) there are transported out of the Countrey some yeeres by the merchants of Turkie, Persia, Bougharia, Georgia, Armenia, and some other of Christendom, to the value of foure or fiue hundred thousand rubbles, as I haue heard of the merchants. [Sidenote: Momgosorskoy perhaps Molgomzaia.] The best Sable furre groweth in the countrey of Pechora, Momgosorskoy and Obdorskoy, the worser sort in Siberia, Perm, and other places. The blacke foxe and red come out of Siberia, white and dunne from Pechora, whence also come the white wolfe, and white Beare skin. The best Wuluerin also thence and from Perm. The best Martrons are from Siberia, Cadamo, Morum, Perm, and Cazan. Lyserns, Mineuer, and Armins, the best are out of Gallets, and Ouglits, many from Nouogrod and Perm. The Beauer of the best sort breedeth in Murmonskey by Cola. Other common furres and most of these kindes grow in many, and some in all parts of the Countrey.

[Sidenote: 2. Waxe.] The second commoditie is of Waxe, whereof hath bene shipped into forreigne countreys (as I haue heard it reported by those that best know it) the summe of 50000. pood yeerely, euery pood conteyneth 40. pound, but now about 10000. pood a yeere.

[Sidenote: 3. Hony.] The third is their Honie, whereof besides an exceeding great quantitie spent in their ordinary drinkes (which is Mead of all sorts) and their other vses, some good quantitie is caried out of the countrey. The chiefe encrease of hony is in Mordua and Cadam neere to the Cheremissen Tartar: much out of Seuerskoy, Rezan, Morum, Cazan, Dorogobose, and Vasma.

[Sidenote: 4. Tallow.] Fourthly, of Tallow they afoord a great waight for transportation: not onely for that their countrey hath very much good ground apt for pasturage of cattell, but also by reason of their many Lents and other fastes: and partly because their greater men vse much waxe for their lights, the poorer and meaner sort birch dried in their stoaues, and cut into long shiuers, which they call Luchineos. Of tallow there hath bene shipped out of the Realme a few yeeres since about 100000. pood yerely, now not past 30000. or thereabouts. The best yeeld of tallow is in the parts and territories of Smolensko, Yaruslaue, Ouglits, Nouogrod, and Vologda, Otfer, and Gorodetskey.

[Sidenote: 5. Hide.] An other principall commoditie is their Losh and Cow hide. Their Losh or Buffe hide is very faire and large. Their bull and cowe hide (for oxen they make none, neither yet weather) is of a small sise. There hath bene transported by merchants strangers some yeres 100000. hides. Now it is decreased to 30000. or thereabouts. Besides great store of goates skinnes, whereof great numbers are shipped out of the countrey. The largest kinde of Losh or Buffe breedeth about Rostoue, Wichida, Nouogrod, Morum, and Perm. The lesser sort within the kingdome of Cazan.

[Sidenote: 6. Trane oyle.] Another very great and principall commoditie is their Trane oyle, drawen out of the Seal fish. Where it will not be impertinent to shewe the maner of their hunting the Seal, which they make this oyle of: which is in this sort. [Sidenote: The maner of hunting the Seale fish.] Towards the ende of Sommer (before the frost beginne) they goe downe with their boates into the bay of S. Nicholas, to a cape called Cusconesse or Foxnose, where they leaue their boats till the next spring tide. When the Sunne waxeth warme toward the spring, and yet the yce not melted within the Bay, they returne thither againe. Then drawing their boates ouer the sea yce, they vse them for houses to rest and lodge in. There are commonly about 17. or 18. fleete of them, of great large boates, which diuide themselues into diuers companies, fiue or sixe boats in a consort.

They that first finde the haunt, fire a beacon, which they carry with them for the nonce. Which being espied by the other companies, by such among them as are appointed of purpose, they come altogether and compasse the Seales round about in a ring, that lie sunning themselues together vpon the yce, commonly foure or fiue thousand in a shoale, and so they inuade them euery man with his club in his hand. If they hit them on the nose they are soone killed. If on the sides or backe they beare out the blow, and many times so catch and holde downe the clubbe with their teeth by maine force, that the partie is forced to call for helpe to his fellowes.

The maner of the Seals is when they see themselues beset, to gather all close together in a throng or plumpe, to sway downe the yce, and to breake it (if they can) which so bendeth the yce that many times it taketh the sea water vpon it, and maketh the hunters to wade a foote or more deepe. After the slaughter when they haue killed what they can, they fall to sharing euery boate his part in equall portions: and so they flay them, taking from the body the skin, and the lard or fat with all that cleaueth to the skin. This they take with them, leauing the bodies behind, and so go to shore. Where they digge pits, in the grounde of a fadome and an halfe deepe, or thereabout, and so taking the fat or lard off from the skinne, they throw it into the pit, and cast in among it boat burning stones to melt it withall. The vppermost and purest is sold, and vsed to oile wool for cloth, the grosser (that is of a red colour) they sell to make sope.

[Sidenote: 7. Ickary.] Likewise of Ickary or Cauery, a great quantitie is made vpon the riuer of Volgha out of the fish called Bellougina, the Sturgeon, the Seueriga and the Sterledey. Whereof the most part is shipped by French and Netherlandish merchants for Italy and Spaine, some by English merchants.

[Sidenote: 8. Hempe and Flaxe.] The next is of Flax and Hempe, whereof there hath bene shipped (as I haue heard merchants say) at the port of Narue a great part of 100. ships small and great yerely. Now, not past fiue. The reason of this abating and decrease of this and other commodities, that were wont to be transported in a greater quantitie, is the shutting vp of the port of the Narue towards the Finland sea, which now is in the handes and possession of the Sweden. Likewise the stopping of the passage ouerland by the way of Smolensko, and Plotsko, by reason of their warres with the Polonian, which causeth the people to be lesse prouident in mainteining and gathering these and like commodities, for that they lacke sales. For the growth of flaxe the prouince of Vobsko, and the countrey about is the chiefe and onely place. For Hempe Smolensko, Dorogobose and Vasma.

[Sidenote: 9. Salt.] The countrey besides maketh great store of salt. Their best salt is made at Stararouse in very great quantitie, where they haue great store of salt wels, about 250. verst from the sea. At Astracan salt is made naturally by the sea water, that casteth it vp into great hils, and so it is digged down, and caried away by the merchants and other that wil fetch it from thence. They pay to the Emperor for acknowledgement or custome 3. d. Russe vpon euery hundred weight. [Sidenote: Nonocks.] Besides these two, they make salt in many other places of the Realme, as in Perm, Wichida, Totma, Kenitsma, Solouetsky, Ocona, Bombasey, and Nonocks, all out of salt pits, saue at Solouetsky, which lieth neere to the sea.

[Sidenote: 10. Tarre.] Likewise of Tarre they make a great quantitie out of their firre trees in the conntrey of Duyna and Smolensko, whereof much is sent abroad. [Sidenote: 11. Ribazuba.] Besides these (which are all good and substantiall commodities) they haue diuers other of smaller accompt, that are naturall and proper to that countrey: as the fish tooth (which they call Ribazuba) which is vsed both among themselues, and the Persians and Bougharians that fetch it from thence for beads, kniues, and sword hafts of Noblemen and gentlemen, and for diuers other vses. Some vse the powder of it against poison, as the Vnicornes horne. The fish that weareth it is called a Morse, and is caught about Pechora. These fish teeth some of them are almost 2. foote of length, and weigh 11. or 12. pound apiece.

[Sidenote: 12. Slude.] In the prouince of Corelia, and about the riuer Duyna towards the North sea, there groweth a soft rocke which they call Slude. This they cut into pieces, and so teare it into thin flakes, which naturally it is apt for, and so vse it for glasse-lanthorns and such like. It giueth both inwards and outwards a clearer light then glasse, and for this respect is better then either glasse or horne: for that it neither breaketh like glasse nor yet will burne like the lanthorne. [Sidenote: 13. Saltpeter and brimstone.] Saltpeter in many places, as at Ouglits, Yaruslaue, and Vstiug, they make and some smal store of brimstone vpon the riuer Volgha, but want skil to refine it. [Sidenote: 14. Iron.] Their iron is somewhat brittle, but a great weight of it is made in Corelia, Cargapolia, and Vstiug Thelesna. Other mine they haue none gowing within the realme.

[Sidenote: The strange beastes, fish, foule, &c., that breed in Russia.] Their beasts of strange kinds are the Losh, the Ollen, the wild horse, the beare, the wolueing, or wood dog, the Lyserne, the Beauer, the Sable, the Martron, the black and dunne fox, the white Beare towards the sea coast of Pechora, the Gurnstale, the Laset or Mineuer. They haue a kinde of Squirrell that hath growing on the pinion of the shoulder bone a long tuft of haire, much like vnto feathers with a far broader taile than haue any other squirrels, which they moue and shake as they leape from tree to tree, much like vnto a wing. They skise a large space, and seeme for to flie withal, and therefore they cal them Letach Vechshe, that is, the flying squirrels. Their hares and squirrels in sommer are of the same colour with ours, in Winter the hare changeth her coate into milke white, the squirrel into gray, whereof cometh the Calaber.

They haue fallow deere, the roe bucke, and goats very great store. Their horses are but smal, but very swift and hard, they trauell them vnshod both winter and Sommer, without all regard of pace. Their sheepe are but smal and beare course and harsh wool. Of foule they haue diuers of the principal kinds: First, great store of hawks, the eagle, the gerfaulcon, the slightfaulcon, the goshawk, the tassel, the sparhawk, &c. But the principal hawke that breedeth in the country, is counted the gerfaulcon. Of other fowles their principal kinds are the swan tame and wilde, (whereof they haue great store) the storke, the crane, the tedder of the colour of a feasant, but far bigger and liueth in the firre woods. Of feasant and partridge they haue very great plentie. An owle there is of very a great bignesse more vgly to behold then the owles of this country, with a broad face, and eares much like vnto a man.

For fresh water fish, besides the common sorts (as carpe, pikes, pearch, tench, roach, &c.) they haue diuers kinds very good and delicate: as the Bellouga or Bellougina of 4. or 5. elnes long, the Ositrina or Sturgion, the Seueriga and Sterledy somewhat in fashion and taste like to the Sturgion, but not so thick nor long. These 4. kindes of fish breed in the Volgha, and are catched in great plenty, and serued thence into the whole Realme for a great food. Of the Roes of these foure kinds they make very great store of Icary or Caueary as was said before.

They haue besides these that breed in the Volgha a fish called the Riba bela, or white salmon, which they account more delicate then they do the red salmon, whereof also they haue exceeding great plentie in the Riuers Northward, as in Duyna, the riuer of Cola, &c. In the Ozera or lake neere a towne called Perislaue, not far from the Mosco, they haue a smal fish which they cal the fresh herring, of the fashion, and somewhat of the taste of a sea-herring. Their chiefe townes for fish are, Yaruslaue, Bealozera, Nouogrod, Astracan, and Cazan: which all yeeld a large custome to the Emperour euery yeere for their trades of fishing, which they practise in Sommer, but sende if frozen in the Winter time into all parts of the Realme.

The chiefe Cities of Russia.

The chiefe cities of Russia are Mosco, Nouogrod, Rostoue, Volodomer, Plesko, Smolensko, Iaruslaue, Perislaue, Nisnouogrod, Vologda, Vstiug, Colmogro, Cazan, Astracan, Cargapolia, Columna. [Sidenote: Mosco] The city, of Mosco is supposed to be of great antiquitie, though the first founder be vnknowen to the Russe. It seemeth to haue taken the name from the riuer that runneth on the one side of the towne. Berosus the Chaldean in his 5. booke telleth that Nimrod (whom other profane stories cal Saturne) sent Assyrius, Medus, Moscus, and Magog into Asia to plant colonies there, and that Moscus planted both in Asia and Europe. Which may make some probabilitie, that the citie, or rather the riuer whereon it is built tooke, the denomination from this Moscus: the rather because of the climate or situation, which is in the very farthest part and list of Europe, bordering vpon Asia. The Citie was much enlarged by one Iuan or Iohn, sonne to Daniel, that first changed his tide of duke into King: though that honour continued not to his posteritie: the rather because he was inuested into it by the Popes Legate, who at that time was Innocentius the 4. about the yeere 1246. which was very much misliked by the Russe people, being then a part of the Easterne or Greeke Church. Since that time the name of this city hath growen more famous, and better knowen to the world: insomuch that, not only the prouince, but the whole countrey of Russia is termed by some by the name of Moscouia the Metropolite city. The forme of this city is in maner round with 3. strong wals, circuling the one within the other, and streets lying betwene, whereof the inmost wall, and the buildings closed within it (lying safest as the heart within the body, fenced and watred with the riuer Moscoua, that runneth close by it) is all accompted the Emperors castle. The number of houses (as I haue heard) through the whole Citie (being reckoned by the Emperor a little before it was fired by the Crim) was 41500. in all. Since the Tartar besieged and fired the towne, (which was in the yere 1571.) there lieth waste of it a great breadth of ground, which before was wel set and planted with buildings, specially that part on the South side of Moscua, built not long before by Basilius the Emperor for his garison of souldiers, to whom he gaue priuiledge to drinke Mead, and beere at the dry or prohibited times, when other Russes may drinke nothing but water, and for that cause called this new city by the name of Naloi, that is skinck [Footnote: From *Scenc*—drink, SAX.

> Where every iovial tinker for his chink,
> May cry, mine host, to crambe giue us drink,
> And do not slink, but skink, or else you stink.
>   (B. JONSON, *New Inn*, I. 3.)]

or poure in. So that now the city of Mosco is not much bigger then the city of London. [Sidenote: Nouograd.] The next in greatnes, and in a maner as large, is the citie Nouograd: where was committed (as the Russe saith) the memorable warre so much spoke of in stories of the Scythians seruants, that tooke armes against their Masters: which they report in this sort: viz. That the Boiarens or gentlemen of Nouograd and the territory about (which only are souldiers after the discipline of those countreis) had war with the Tartars. Which being wel performed and ended by them, they returned homewards. Where they vnderstood by the way that their Cholopey or bondslaues whom they left at home, had in their absence possessed their townes, lands, houses, wiues and all. At which newes being somewhat amased, and yet disdeining the villany of their seruants, they made the more speed home: and so not far from Nouograd met them in warlike maner marching against them. Whereupon aduising what was best to be done, they agreed all to set vpon them with no other shew of weapon but with their horse whips, (which as their maner is euery man rideth withal) to put them in remembrance of their seruile condition, thereby to terrifie them, and abate their courage. And so marching on and lashing al together with their whips in their hands they gaue the onset. Which seemed so terrible in the eares of their villaines, and stroke such a sense into them of the smart of the whip which they had felt before, that they fled altogether like sheepe before the driuers. In memory of this victory the Nouogradians euer since haue stamped their coine (which they cal a dingoe Nouogrodskoy currant through al Russia) with the figure of a horsman shaking a whip aloft in his hand. These 2. cities exceed the rest in greatnes. For strength their chiefe townes are Vobsko, Smolensko, Cazan and Astracan, as lying vpon the borders. [Sidenote: Iaruslaue.] But for situation Iaruslaue far exceedeth the rest. For besides the commodities that the soile yeeldeth of pasture and corne, it lieth vpon the famous riuer of Volgha, and looketh ouer it from a high banke very faire and stately to behold: whereof the towne taketh the name. For Iaraslaue in that tongue signifieth as much as a faire or famous banke. [Sidenote: Saxo Grammaticus lib. II. pag. 187.] In this towne (as may be ghessed by the name) dwelt the Russe king Vladimer sirnamed Iaruslaue, that maried the Daughter of Harald king of England, by mediation of Sweno the Dane, as is noted in the Danish story about the yere 1067.

The other townes haue nothing that is greatly memorable, saue many ruines within their wals. [Sidenote: The manner of Russe building.] The streets of their cities and townes in stead of pauing are planked with fir trees, plained and layd enen close the one to the other. Their houses are of wood without any lime or stone, built very close and warme with firre trees plained and piled one vpon another. They are fastened together with dents or notches at euery corner, and so clasped fast together. Betwixt the trees or timber they thrust in mosse (whereof they gather plenty in their woods) to keep out the aire. Euery house hath a paire of staires that lead vp into the chambers out of the yard or streat after the Scottish maner. This building seemeth far better for their countrey, then that of stone or bricke; as being colder and more dampish then their wooden houses, specially of firre, that is a dry and warme wood. Whereof the prouidence of God hath giuen them such store, as that you may build a faire house for 20. or 30. rubbles or litle more, where wood is most scant. The greatest inconuenience of their wodden building is the aptnesse for firing, which happeneth very oft and in very fearful sort, by reason of the drinesse and fatnes of the fir, that being once fired, burneth like a torch, and is hardly quenched til all be burnt vp.

Of the maner of Crowning or Inauguration of the Russe Emperours.

The solemnities vsed at the Russe Emperors coronation, are on this maner. In the great church of Precheste (or our Lady) within the Emperors castle is erected a stage whereon standeth a scrine that beareth vpon it the Imperial cap and robe of very rich stuffe. When the day of the Inauguration is come, there resort thither, first the Patriarch with the Metropolitanes, archbishops, bishops, abbots and priors, al richly clad in their pontificalibus. Then enter the Deacons with the quier of singers. Who so soone as the Emperor setteth foot into the church, begin to sing: Many yeres may liue noble Theodore Iuanowich, &c: Wereunto the patriarch and Metropolite with the rest of the cleargy answere with a certaine hymne, in forme of a praier, singing it altogether with a great noise. The hymne being ended, the patriarch with the Emperor mount vp the stage, where standeth a seat ready for the Emperor. Whereupon the patriarch willeth him to sit downe, and then placing himself by him vpon another seat prouided for that purpose, boweth downe his head towards the ground, and saith this prayer: O Lord God king of kings, Lord of Lords, which by thy prophet Samuel didst chose thy seruant Dauid, and annoynt him for King ouer thy people Israel, heare now our prayer, and looke from thy sanctuary vpon this thy seruant Theodore, whom thou hast chosen and exalted for king ouer these thy holy nations anoint him with the oile of gladnes, protect by thy power, put vpon his head a crowne of gold and precious stones, giue him length of dayes, place him in the seat of Iustice, strengthen his arme, make subiect vnto him all the barbarous nations. Let thy feare be in his whole heart, turne him from an euill faith, and all errour, and shewe him the saluation of thy holy and vniuersal Church, that he may iudge thy people with iustice, and protect the children of the poore, and finally atteine euerlasting life. This prayer he speaketh with a low voice, and then pronounceth aloud: Al praise and power to God the Father, the Sonne, and the holy Ghost. The prayer, being ended, he commandeth certaine Abbots to reach the imperiall roabe and cap: which is done very decently, and with great solemnitie, the Patriarch withal pronouncing aloud: Peace be vnto all. And so he beginneth another prayer to this effect: Bow your selues together with vs, and pray to him that reigneth ouer all. Preserue him (oh Lord) vnder thy holy protection, keepe him that hee may doe good and holy things, let Iustice shine forth in his dayes, that we may liue quietly without strife and malice. This is pronounced somewhat softly by the Patriarch, whereto hee addeth againe aloud: Thou art the king of the whole world and the sauiour of our soules, to thee the Father, sonne and Holy ghost be al praise for euer and euer. Amen. Then putting on the roabe and the cap, he blesseth the Emperour with the signe of the crosse, saying withall: In the name of the Father, the Sonne and the Holy ghost. The like is done by the Metropolites, Archbishops, and Bishops: who all in their order come to the chaire, and one after another blesse the Emperour with their two forefingers. Then is sayd by the Patriarch another prayer, that beginneth: Oh most holy virgin, mother of God &c. After which a Deacon pronounceth with a loude voice: Many yeres to noble Theodore, good, honourable, beloued of God, great Duke of Volodemer, of Mosco, Emperour, and Monarch of all Russia, &c. Whereto the other Priests and Deacons that stand somewhat farre of by the altar or table, answere singing: Many yeres, many yeres to the noble Theodore. The same note is taken vp by the Priests and Deacons, that are placed at the right and left side of the Church, and then altogether, they channt and thunder out, singing: Many yeres to the noble Theodore, good, honourable, beloued of God, great Duke of Volodomer, Mosco, Emperour of all Russia, &c. These solemnities being ended, first commeth the Patriarch with the Metropolites, Archbishops, and Bishops; then the Nobility, and the whole company in their order, to doe homage to the Emperour, bending downe their heads, and knocking them at his feete to the very ground.

The stile wherewith he is inuested at his Coronation, runneth after this maner.

Theodore Iuanowich, by the grace of God great Lord and Emperour of all Russia, great Duke of Volodomer, Mosco, and Nouogrod, King of Cazan, King
of Astracan, Lord of Plesco, and great Duke of Smolensco, of Twerria, Ioughoria, Permia, Vadska, Bulghoria, and others; Lord and great Duke of Nouogrod of the Low countrey, of Chernigo, Rezan, Polotskoy, Rostoue, Yaruslaueley, Bealozera, Liefland, Oudoria, Obdoria, and Condensa, Commander of all Siberia, and of the North parts, and Lord of many other Countreis, &c.

This stile conteineth in it all the Emperours Prouinces, and setteth foorth his greatnesse. And therefore they haue a great delight and pride in it, forcing not onely their owne people but also strangers (that haue any matter to deliuer to the Emperour by speech or writing) to repeate the whole forme from the beginning to the end. Which breedeth much cauill, and sometimes quarell betwixt them and the Tartar, and Poland Ambassadours: who refuse to call him Czar, that is Emperor, and to repeate the other parts of his long stile. My selfe when I had audience of the Emperour, thought good to salute him only with thus much viz. Emperour of all Russia, great Duke of Volodomer, Mosco and Nouogrod, King of Cazan, King of Astracan. The rest I omitted of purpose, because I knew they gloried, to haue their stile appeare to be of a larger volume then the Queenes of England. But this was taken in so ill part, that the Chancelour (who then attended the Emperour, with the rest of the nobility) with a loude chafing voice, called still vpon me to say out the rest. Whereto I answered, that the Emperors stile was very long, and could not so well be remembred by strangers, that I had repeated so much of it, as might shew that I gaue honour to the rest &c. But all would not serue till I commanded my interpreter to say it all out.

Their forces for the wars, with the chief officers and their salaries.

The Souldiers of Russia are called Sinaboyarskey, or the sons of Gentlemen: because they are all out of that degree, by vertue of their military profession. [Sidenote: Souldiers by birth and inheritance.] For euery souldier in Russia is a gentleman, and none are gentlemen, but only the souldiers, that take it by discent from their ancestors: so that the sonne of a gentleman (which is borne a souldier) is euer a gentleman, and a souldier withall, and professeth nothing els but military matters. When they are of yeres able to beare armes, they come to the office of Roserade, or great Constable, and there present themselues: who entreth their names, and allotteth them certaine lands to maintaine their charges, for the most part the same their fathers enioyed. For the lands assigned to maintaine the army, are euer certain, annexed to this office without improuing, or detracting one foot. But that if the Emperor haue sufficient in wages, the roomes being full so farre as the land doeth extend already, they are many times deferred, and haue nothing allowed them, except some one portion of the land be deuided into two. The whole number of his souldiers in continuall pay, is this. First he hath his Dworaney, that is, Pensioners, or Gard of his person, to the number of 15000 horsemen, with their captaines and other officers, that are alwaies in a readines.

[Sidenote: Degrees of horsemen. 1. PrŠtoriani or such as attend the Emperors person.] Of these 15000 horsemen, there are three sorts or degrees, which differ as well in estimation as in wages, one degree from another. The first sort of them is called Dworaney Bulshey, or the company of head Pensioners, that haue some an hundred, some fourescore rubbles a yeare, and none vnder 70. The second sort are called Seredney Dworaney, or the middle rank of Pensioners. These haue sixty or fifty rubbles by the yeare, none vnder fortie. The third and lowest sort, are the Dyta Boiarskey, that is the low Pensioners. Their salary is thirty rubbles a yere for him that hath most, some haue but 25, some 20, none vnder 12. Whereof the halfe part is paid them at the Mosco, the other halfe in the field by the general, when they haue any wars, and are imploied in seruice. When they receiue their whole pay it amounteth to 55000 rubbles by the yere.

And this is their wages, besides lands allotted to euery one of them, both to the greater and the lesse, according to their degrees. Whereof he that hath least, hath to yeelde him twentie rubbles or markes by the yeare. [Sidenote: Two other troupes to the number of 65000.] Besides these 15000 horsemen, that are of better choyce (as being the Emperors owne gard when himselfe goeth to the wars, not vnlike the Romane souldiers called PrŠtoriani) are a hundred and ten men of speciall account for their Nobilitie, and trust, which are chosen by the Emperor, and haue their names registred, that find among them for the Emperors wars, to the number of 65000. horsemen, with all necessaries meet for the wars after the Russe maner.

To this end they haue yerely allowance made by the Emperor for themselues, and their companies, to the summe of 40000 rubbles. And these 65000 are to repayre to the field euery yeare on the borders towards the Crim Tartar, (except they be appointed for some other seruice) whether there be wars with the Tartars, or not. This might seeme peraduenture somewhat dangerous for some state, to haue so great forces vnder the command of Noblemen to assemble euery yere to one certain place. But the matter is so vsed, as that no danger can growe to the Emperor, or his state by this means. First, because these noblemen are many, to wit, an 110. in al, and changed by the Emperor so oft as he thinketh good. Secondly, because they haue their liuings of the Emperor, being otherwise but of very small reuenue, and receiue this yerely pay of 46000 rubbles, when it is presently to be payd forth againe to the souldiers that are vnder them. Thirdly, because for the most part they are about the Emperors person being of his Counsel, either speciall or at large. Fourthly, they are rather as paymasters, then Captaines to their companies, themselues not going forth ordinarily to the wars, saue when some of them are appointed by speciall order from the Emperor himselfe. [Sidenote: Horsemen in continuall pay 80000.] So the whole number of horsemen that are euer in a readinesse, and in continuall pay, are 80000, a few more or lesse.

If he haue neede of a greater number (which seldome falleth out) then he enterteineth of those Sinaboiarskey, that are out of pay, so many as be needeth: and if yet he want of his number, he giueth charge to his Noblemen, that hold lands of him to bring into the field euery man a proportionable number of his seruants (called Kolophey, such as till his lands) with their furniture, according to the iust number that he intendeth to make. Which the seruice being done, presently lay in their weapons, and returne to their seruile occupations againe.

[Sidenote: Footmen in continuall pay 12000.] Of footemen that are in continuall pay he hath to the number of 12000 all gunners, called Strelsey: Whereof 5000 are to attend about the citie of Mosco, or any other place where the Emperor shall abide, and 2000 (which are called Stremaney Strelsey, or gunners at the stirrop) about his owne person at the very Court or house where himselfe lodgeth. The rest are placed in his garison townes, till there be occasion to haue them in the field, and receiue for their salarie or stipend euery man seuen rubbles a yeare, besides twelue measures a piece of Rye, and Oates. [Sidenote: Strangers mercenaries in pay 4300.] Of mercenary Souldiers, that are strangers (whom they call Nimschoy) they haue at this time 4300 of Polonians: of Chirchasses (that are vnder the Polonians) about 4000, whereof 3500 are abroad in his garisons: of Doutches and Scots about 150: of Greekes, Turks, Danes and Swedens, all in one band, an 100 or thereabouts. But these they vse onely vpon the Tartar side, and against the Siberians: as they doe the Tartar souldiers (whom they hire sometimes, but only for the present) on the other side against the Polonian and Sweden: thinking it best policie to vse their seruice vpon the contrary border.

[Sidenote: The chief captains or leaders.] The chiefe Captaines or leaders of these forces, according to their names and degrees, are these which follow. [Sidenote: 1. The Voiauod or general.] First, the Voyauoda Bulshaia, that is, the Great Captaine, or Lieutenant general vnder the Emperor. This commonly is one of the foure houses of the chiefe Nobility of the land. Their great Voiauod or general at this present in their wars, is commonly one of these foure: Knez Feodor Iuanowich Methisloskey, Knez Iuan Michalowich Glinskoy, Cherechaskoy, and Trowbetskoy, all of great nobilitie. [Sidenote: 2. Lieutenant general.] Next vnto the Voiauod or general there is some other placed as Lieutenant general, being a man of great valour and experience in the wars, who ordereth all things that the other countenanceth. At this time their principal man, and most vsed in their wars, is one Knez Demetrie Iuanowich Forestine, an ancient and expert captaine, and one that hath done great seruice (as they say) against the Tartar and Polonian. [Sidenote: 3. Marshals of the field foure.] Next under the Voiauod and his Lieutenant general are foure other that haue the marshalling of the whole army deuided among them, and may be called the marshals of the field.

Euery man hath his quarter, or fourth part vnder him. Whereof the first is called the Praua Polskoy, or right wing. The second is the Leuoy Polskoy, or left wing. The third is Rusnoy Polskoy, or the broken band, because out of this there are chosen to send abroad vpon any sodaine exploit, or to make a rescue or supplie, as occasion doth require. The fourth Storoshouoy Polskoy, or the warding band. [Sidenote: Foure marshals: deputies eight.] Euery one of these foure Marshals haue two other vnder them (eight in all) that twise euery weeke at the least must muster and traine their seueral wings or bands, and hold and giue iustice for all faults, and disorders committed in the campe.

And these eight are commonly chosen out of the 110. (which I spake of before) that receiue and deliuer the pay to the souldiers. [Sidenote: Fiue Coronels vnder Captaines.] Vnder these eight are diuers other Captaines, as the Gulauoy, Captaines of thousands fiue hundreds and 100. The Petyde Setskoy or Captains of fifties, and the Decetskies or Captains of tennes.

[Sidenote: Sixe Masters of the Artillery.] Besides the Voiauoda or general of the armie (spoken of before) they haue two other that beare the name of Voiauoda, whereof one is the master of the great Ordinance (called Naradna voiauoda) who hath diuers vnder officers, necessary for that seruice. [The walking Captaine.] The other is called the Voiauoda gulauoy, or the walking Captaine, that hath allowed him 1000 good horsemen of principall choyce, to range and spie abroad, and hath the charge of the running Castle, which we are to speake of in the Chapter following. Al these Captains, and men of charge must once euery day resort to the Bulsha voiauoda, or General of the armie, to know his pleasure, and to informe him, if there be any requisite matter pertaining to their office.

Of their mustering, and leuying of forces, maner of armour, and prouision of victuall for the warres.

[Sidenote: Their order of mustering.] When wars are towards (which they faile not of lightly euery yere with the Tartar, and many times with the Polonian and Sweden) the foure Lords of the Chetfirds send forth their summons in the Emperors name, to all the Dukes and Dyacks of the Prouinces, to be proclaimed in the head townes of euery Shire: that al the Sinaboiarskey, or sonnes of gentlemen make their repaire to such a border where the seruice is to be done, at such a place, and by such a day, and there present themselues to such, and such Captaines. When they come to the place assigned them in the summons or proclamation, their names are taken by certaine officers that haue commission for that purpose from the Roserade, or high Constable, as Clarkes of the bands. If any make default or faile at the day, he is mulcted, and punished very seuerely. As for the General and other chief Captaines, they are sent thither from the Emperors owne hand, with such Commission and charge as he thinketh behoofull for the present seruice. When the souldiers are assembled, they are reduced into their bands, and companies, vnder their seueral Captaines of tennes, fifties, hundreds, thousands, &c. and these Bands into 4 Polskeis, or Legions (but of farre greater numbers then the Romane legions were) vnder their foure great Leaders, which also haue the authoritie of Marshals of the field (as was sayd before.)

[Sidenote: The horsemans furniture.] Concerning their armour they are but slightly appointed. The common horseman hath nothing els but his bow in his case vnder his right arme, and his quiuer and sword hanging on the left side: except some fewe that beare a case of dagges, or a Iauelin, or short staffe along their horse side. The vnder captains wil haue commonly some piece of armour besides, as a shirt of male, or such like. The General with the other chiefe captaines and men of Nobilitie wil haue their horse very richly furnished, their saddles of cloth of gold, their bridles fair bossed and tasselled with gold, and silk fringe, bestudded with pearle and precious stones, themselues in very faire armor, which they cal Bullatnoy, made of faire shining steele, yet couered commonly with cloth of golde, and edged round with armin furre, his steele helmet on his head of a very great price, his sword bow and arrowes at his side, his speare in his hand, with another faire helmet, and Shesta pera, or horsemans scepter carried before him. Their swords, bowes, and arrowes are of the Turkish fashion. They practise like the Tartar to shoote forwards and backwards, as they flie and retire.

[Sidenote: The footmans furniture.] The Strelsey or footeman hath nothing but his piece in his hand, his striking hatchet at his back, and his sword by his side. The stock of his piece is not made calieuerwise, but with a plaine and straite stocke (somewhat like a fouling piece) the barrel is rudely and vnartificially made, very heauie, yet shooteth but a very small bullet. [Sidenote: Prouision of victual.] As for their prouision of victual, the Emperor alloweth none, either for Captaine or souldiour, neither prouideth any for them except peraduenture some come for their money. Euery man is to bring sufficient for himselfe, to serue his turne for foure monethes, and if neede require to giue order for more to be brought vnto him to the Campe from his tenant that tilleth his land, or some other place. One great helpe they haue, that for lodging and diet euery Russe is prepared to be a souldier beforehand. Though the chiefe Captains and other of account cary tents with them after the fashion of ours, with some better prouision of victual then the rest. They bring with them commonly into the Campe for victuall a kind of dried bread, (which they call Suchary) with some store of meale, which they temper with water, and so make it into a ball, or small lumpe of dowe, called Tollockno. And this they eate rawe in stead of bread; Their meat is bacon, or some other flesh or fish dryed, after the Dutch maner. If the Russe soldier were as hardy to execute an enterprise, as he is hard to beare out toyle and trauell, or were otherwise as apt and well trained for the warres, as he is indifferent for his lodging and diet bee would farre exceede the souldiers of our parts.

Of their marching, charging, and other Martial discipline.

The Russe trusteth rather to his number, then to the valure of his souldiers, or good ordering of his forces. Their marching or leading is without al order, saue that the foure Polskey or Legions, (whereinto their armie is deuided) keepe themselues seuerall vnder their ensignes, and so thrust all on together in a hurrey, as they are directed by their Generall. Their Ensigne is the image of S. George. [Sidenote: Horsemen drummes.] The Bulsha Dworaney or chiefe horsemen, haue euery man a small drum of brasse at his saddle bowe, which he striketh when he giueth the charge, or onset.

[Sidenote: The horsemans maner of charging.] They haue drummes besides of a huge bignes, which they cary with them vpon a boord layde on foure horses, that are sparred together with chaines, euery drumme haning eight strikers, or drummers, besides trumpets and shawmes, which they sound after a wilde maner, much different from ours. When they giue any charge, or make any inuasion, they make a great hallow or shoute altogether, as lowd as they can, which with the sound of their trumpets, shawmes and drummes, maketh a confused and horrible noyse. So they set on first discharging their arrowes, then dealing with their swordes, which they vse in a brauerie to shake, and brandish ouer their heads, before they come to strokes.

[Sidenote: The footmans charge.] Their footmen (because otherwise they want order in leading) are commonly placed in some ambush or place of aduantage, where they most annoy the enemie, with least hurt to themselues. [Sidenote: The walking Castle.] If it be a set battell, or if any great inuasion be made vpon the Russe borders by the Tartar, they are set within the running or mouing Castle (called Bexa, or Gulaygorod) which is caried about with them by the Voiauoda golauoy (or the walking General) whom I spake of before. This walking or moouing Castle is so framed, that it may be set vp in length (as occasion doeth require) the space of one, two, three, foure, fiue, sixe, or seuen miles: for so long will reach. It is nothing els but a double wall of wood to defend them on both sides behinde and before, with a space of three yards or thereabouts, betwixt the two sides: so that they may stand within it, and haue roome enough to charge and discharge their pieces, and to vse their other weapons. It is closed at both ends, and made with loope holes on either side, to lay out the nose of their piece, or to push foorth any other weapon. It is caried with the armie wheresoeuer it goeth, being taken into pieces, and so layde on cartes sparred together, and drawen by horse that are not seene, by reason that they are couered with their cariage as with a shelfe or penthouse. When it is brought to the place where it is to be vsed (which is deuised and chosen out before by the walking Voiauod) it is planted so much as the present vse requireth, sometime a mile long, sometimes two, sometimes three or more: Which is soone done without the helpe of any Carpenter, or instrument: because the timber is so framed to claspe together one piece with in another: as is easily vnderstoode by those that know the maner of the Russe building.

In this Castle standeth their shot wel fenced for aduantage, especially against the Tartar, that bringeth no ordinance, nor other weapon into the field with him, saue his sword, and bow, and arrowes. They haue also within it diuers field pieces, which they vse as occasion doth require. Of pieces for the field they carie no great store, when they warre against the Tartar: but when they deale with the Polonian (of whose forces they make more account) they go better furnished with all kind of munition, and other necessarie prouisions. It is thought that no Prince of Christendome hath better store of munition, then the Russe Emperour. And it may partly appeare by the Artillery house at Mosco, where are of all sortes of great Ordinance, all brasse pieces, very faire, to an exceeding great number.

The Russe souldier is thought to be better at his defence within some castle or towne, then he is abroad at a set pitched field. Which is euer noted in the practise of his warres, and namely at the siege of Vobsco, about eight yeres since: [Sidenote: 1580.] where he repulsed the Polonian king Stepan Batore, with his whole armie of 100000 men, and forced him in the end to giue ouer his siege, with the losse of many of his best Captaines and souldiers. But in a set field the Russe is noted to haue euer the worse of the Polonian and Sweden.

[Sidenote: Reward for valure.] If any behaue himselfe more valiantly then the rest, or do any special piece of seruice, the Emperor sendeth him a piece of golde, stamped with the Image of Saint George on horsebacke: Which they hang on their sleeues, and set in their caps. And this is accounted the greatest honour they can receiue, for any seruice they doe.

Of their Colonies, and maintaining of their conquests, or purchases by force.

The Russe Emperors of late yeres haue very much enlarged their dominions, and territories. Their first conquest after the Dukedome of Mosco, (for before that time they were but Dukes of Volodomer, as before was said) was the citie, and Dukedome of Nouogrod on the West, and Northwest side: which was no smal enlargement of their dominion, and strengthening to them for the winning of the rest. This was done by Iuan great grandfather to Theodor now Emperor, about the yere 1480. The same began likewise to encroach vpon the countries of Lituania and Liuonia, but the conquest only intended, and attempted by him vpon some part of those countries, was pursued and performed by his sonne Basileus, who first wan the citie and dukedom of Plesko, afterwards the citie and dukedome of Smolensco, and many other faire towns, with a large territory belonging vnto them, about the yere 1514. [Sidenote: 1580.] These victories against the Lettoes or Lituanians in the time of Alexander their duke, he atchieued rather by aduantage of ciuil dissentions, and treasons among themselues, then by any great policie, or force of his own. But al this was lost againe by his son Iuan Vasiliwich about 8 or 9 yeres past, vpon composition with the Polonian king Stephan Batore: whereunto he was forced by the aduantages which the Pole had then of him, by reason of the foile he had giuen him before, and the disquietnes of his own state at home. Onely the Russe Emperor, at this time hath left him on that side his countery, the cities of Smolensco, Vobsco, Chernigo, and Bealagorod in Lituania. In Liuonia, not a towne nor one foot of ground.

[Sidenote: Lituania.] When Basilius first conquered those countries, he suffered then the natiues to keepe their possessions, and to inhabite all their townes, onely paying him a tribute, vnder the gouerment of his Russe Captaines. But by their conspiracies and attempts not long after, he was taught to deale more surely with them. And so comming vpon them the second time, he killed and caried away with him, three parts of foure, which he gaue or sold to the Tartars that serued him in those wars, and in stead of them placed there his Russes, so many, as might ouermatch the rest, with certaine garisons of strength besides. Wherein notwithstanding this ouersight was committed, for that (taking away with him the vpland, or countrey people that should haue tilled the ground, and might easily haue bene kept in order without any danger, by other good policies) he was driuen afterwards many yeres together, to vitaile the countrey (specially the great townes) out of his owne countrey of Russia, the soile lying there in the meane while wast and vntilled.

[Sidenote: Narue.] The like fell out at the port of Narue in Liefland, where his sonne Iuan Vasiliwich deuised to build a towne, and a castle on the other side the riuer, (called Iuanogrod) to keepe the towne and countrey in subiection. The castle he caused to be so built and fortified, that it was thought to be inuincible. And when it was furnished, for reward to the Architect (that was a Polonian) he put out both his eyes, to make him vnable to build the like againe. But hauing left the natiues all within their owne countrey, without abating their number or strength, the towne and castle not long after was betraied, and surrendred againe to the king of Sweden.

On the Southeast side they haue got the kingdomes of Cazan, and Astracan. These were wonne from the Tartar, by the late Emperour Iuan Vasiliwich, the one about thirtie fiue, the other about thirtie and three yeares agoe. [Sidenote: Siberia and Ob. Conquest of a 1000 miles.] Northward out of the countrey of Siberia, he hath layed vnto his realme a great breadth and length of ground, from Wichida to the riuer of Obba, about a thousand miles space: so that he is bolde to write himselfe now, The great

Commander of Siberia. [Sidenote: Premia and Pechora] The countries likewise of Permia, and Pechora are a diuers people and language from the Russe, ouercome not long since, and that rather by threatning, and shaking of the sword, then by any actual force: as being a weake and naked people, without meanes to resist.

That which the Russe hath in his present possession, he keepeth on this sort. [Sidenote: Means of holding chief townes.] In his foure chief border townes of Vobsko, Smolensko, Astracan, and Cazan, he hath certaine of his counsel not of the greatest nobility, but of greatest trust, which haue more authoritie within their precincts, (for the countenancing and strengthening of their gouernment there) then the other Dukes that are set to gouerne in other places, as was noted before, in the maner of ordering their Prouinces. These he changeth sometimes euery second or third yere, but exceedeth not that time, except vpon very speciall trust, and good liking of the party, and his seruice: least by enlarging of their time, they might grow into some familiaritie with the enemie (as some haue done) being so farre out of sight.

The townes besides are very strongly fenced with trenches, castles, and store of munition, and haue garisons within them, to the number of two or three thousand a piece. They are stored with victual if any seige should come vpon them, for the space of two or three yeres before hand. The foure castles of Smolensko, Vobsko, Cazan and Astracan, he hath made very strong to beare out any siege: so that it is thought that those townes are impregnable.

[Sidenote: Meanes of holding the countries of Pechora, Permia and Siberia.] As for the countries of Pechora and Permia, and that part of of Siberia, which he hath now vnder him, they are kept by as easie meanes, as they were first got, viz. rather by shewing, then by vsing of armes. First, he hath stored the countrie with as many Russes as there are natiues, and hath there some few souldiers in garison, inough to keepe them under. Secondly, his officers and Magistrates there are of his own Russe people, and he changeth them very often, viz. euery yere twise or thrise: notwithstanding there be no great feare of any innouation. Thirdly, he deuideth them into many smal gouernments, like a staffe broke in many small pieces: so that they haue no strength being seuered, which was but litle neither when they were al in one. Fourthly, he prouideth that the people of the countrie haue neither armor nor money, being taxed and pilled so often as he thinketh good: without any meanes to shake off that yoke, or to relieue themselues.

[Sidenote: Siberia.] In Siberia (where he goeth on in pursuing his conquest) he hath diuers castles and garisons to the number of 6000 souldiers of Russes and Polonians, and sendeth many new supplies thither, to plant and inhabite, as he winneth ground. [Sidenote: The kings brother of Siberia.] At this time besides he hath gotten the kings brother of Siberia, allured by certaine of his captaines, to leaue his own country by offers of great entertainment and pleasanter life with the Russe Emperor, then he had in Siberia. [Sidenote: 1588.] He was brought in this last yere, and is now with the Emperor at Mosco well enterteined.

Of the Tartars, and other borderers to the country of Russia, with whom they haue most to doe in warre, and peace.

Their neighbors with whom they haue greatest dealings and intercourse, both in peace and war, are first the Tartar. [Sidenote: The Polonians called Laches by the Russe.] Secondly the Polonian whom the Russe calleth Laches, noting the first author or founder of the nation, who was called Laches or Leches, whereunto is added Po, which signifieth People, and is so made Polaches, that is, the People or posterity of Laches: which the Latins after their maner of writing cal Polonos. The third are the Swedens. The Polonians and Swedens are better knowen to these parts of Europe then are the Tartars, that are farther off from vs (as being of Asia) and diuided into many tribes, different in name, and gouernment one from another. [Sidenote: The Chrim Tartar.] The greatest and mightiest of them is the Chrim Tartar, (whom some call the Great Can) that lieth South, and Southeastward from Russia, and doth most annoy the country by often inuasions, commonly once euery yere, sometimes entring very farre within the inland parts. [Sidenote: The firing of Mosco by the Chrim Tartar in the yere 1571.] In the yere 1571 he came as farre as the citie of Mosco, with an armie of 200000 men, without any battel, or resistance at al, for that the Russe Emperor (then Iuan Vasiliwich) leading forth his armie to encounter with him, marched a wrong way. The citie he tooke not, but fired the suburbs, which by reason of the buildings (which are all of wood without any stone, brick, or lime, saue certaine out roomes) kindled so quickly, and went on with such rage, as that it consumed the greatest part of the citie almost within the space of foure houres, being of 30 miles or more of compasse. Then might you haue seene a lamentable spectacle: besides the huge and mighty flame of the citie all on light fire, the people burning in their houses and streetes, but most of all of such as laboured to passe out of the gates farthest from the enemie, where meeting together in a mightie throng, and so pressing euery man to preuent another, wedged themselues so fast within the gate, and streetes neere vnto it, as that three rankes walked one vpon the others head, the vppermost treading downe those that were lower: so that there perished at that time (as was said) by the fire and the presse, the number of 800000 people or more.

The principall cause of this continual quarell betwixt the Russe and the Chrim is for the right of certaine border partes claimed by the Tartar, but possessed by the Russe. The Tartar alleageth that besides Astracan and

Cazan (that are the ancient possession of the East Tartar) the whole countrey from his bounds North and Westward so farre as the citie of Mosko, and Mosko it selfe perteineth to his right. [Sidenote: Homage done by the Russe to the Chrim Tartar.] Which seemeth to haue bene true by the report of the Russes them selues, that tell of a certaine homage that was done by the Russe Emperour euery yeere to the great Chrim or Can, the Russe Emperour standing on foot and feeding the Chrims horse, (himselfe sitting on his backe) with oates out of his owne cappe, in stead of a bowle or manger, and that within the castle of Mosko. And this homage (they say) was done till the time of Basileus grandfather to this man. Who surprising the Chrim Emperour by a stratageme done by one of his nobilitie (called Iuan Demetrowich Belschey) was content with this raunsome, viz. with the changing of this homage into a tribute of furrres: which afterwards also was denied to be paide by this Emperors father.

Hereupon they continue the quarrel, the Russe defending his countrey, and that which he hath won, the Chrim Tartar inuading him once or twise euery yere, sometime about Whitsontide, but oftner in haruest. What time if the great Can or Chrim come in his owne person, he bringeth with him a great armie of 100000. or 200000. men. Otherwise they make short and sudden rodes into the countrey with lesser numbers, running about the list of the border as wild geese flie, inuading and retiring where they see aduantage.

Their common practise (being very populous) is to make diuers armies, and so drawing the Russe to one or two places of the frontiers, to inuade at some other place, that is left without defence. [Sidenote: The maner of the Tartars fight and armour.] Their maner of fight, or ordering of their forces is much after the Russe maner (spoken of before) saue that they are all horsemen, and carie nothing els but a bowe, a sheafe of arrowes, and a falcon sword after the Turkish fashion. They are very expert horsemen, and vse to shoote as readily backward, as forward. Some will haue a horsemans staff like to a bore speare, besides their other weapons. The common souldier hath no other armour than his ordinary apparell, viz. a blacke sheeps skin with the wool side outward in the day time, and inwarde in the night time, with a cap of the same. But their Morseys or noblemen imitate the Turk both in apparel and armour. When they are to passe ouer a riuer with their armie, they tie three or four horses together and taking long poles or pieces of wood, bind them fast to the tailes of their horse: so sitting on the poles they driue their horse ouer. At handie strokes, (when they ioyne battell) they are accounted farre better men then the Russe people, fierce by nature, but more hardy and bloody by continuall practise of warre: as men knowing no artes of peace, nor any ciuil practise.

[Sidenote: The subtilitie of the Tartar.] Yet their subtility is more than may seeme to agree with their barbarous condition. By reason they are practised to inuade continually, and to robbe their neighbours that border about them, they are very pregnant, and ready witted to deuise stratagems vpon the sudden for their better aduantage. As in their warre against Beala the fourth, king of Hungarie, whome they inuaded with 500000. men, and obtained against him a great victorie. Where, among other, hauing slaine his Chancelor called Nicholas Schinick, they found about him the kings priuy seale. Whereupon they deuised presently to counterfeit letters in the kings name, to the cities and townes next about the place, where the field was fought: with charge that in no case they should conuey themselues, and their goods out of their dwellings, where they might abide safely without all feare of danger, and not leaue the countrey desolate to the possession of so vile and barbarous an enemie, as was the Tartar nation, terming themselues in all reproachful maner. For notwithstanding he had lost his carriages, with some few straglers that had marched disorderly, yet he doubted not but to recouer that losse, with the accesse of a notable victorie, if the sauage Tartar durst abide him in the field. To this purpose hauing written their letters in the Polish character, by certain yong men whom they tooke in the field, and signed them with the Kings seale, they dispatched them forth to all the quarters of Hungaria. that lay neere about the place. Wherevpon the Vngarians that were now flying away with their goods, wiues, and children, vpon the rumour of the kings ouerthrow, taking comfort of these counterfeit letters, staid at home. And so were made a pray, being surprised on the sudden by this huge number of these Tartars, that had compassed them about before they were aware.

When they besiege a towne or fort, they offer much parle, and send many flattering messages to perswade a surrendry: promising all things that the inhabitants will require: but being once possessed of the place, they vse all maner of hostilitie, and crueltie. This they doe vpon a rule they haue, viz, that iustice is to bee practised but towards their owne. They encounter not lightly, but they haue some ambush, whereunto (hauing once shewed themselues, and made some short conflict) they retire as repulsed for feare, and so draw the enemie into it if they can. But the Russe beeing well acquainted with their practise is more warie of them. When they come a rouing with some small number, they set on horsebacke counterfaite shapes of men, that their number may seeme greater.

When they make any onset, their maner is to make a great shoute, crying out altogether Olla Billa, Olla Billa, God helpe vs, God help vs. They contemne death so much, as that they chuse rather to die, then to yeeld to their enemie, and are seene when they are slain to bite the very weapon, when they are past striking or helping of themselues. Wherein appeareth how different the Tartar is in his desperate courage from the Russe and Turke. For the Russe souldier, if he begin once to retire, putteth all his safetie in his speedy flight. And if once he be taken by his enemy, he neither defendeth himselfe, nor intreateth for his life, as reckoning straight to die. The Turk commonly, when he is past hope of escaping, falleth to intreatie, and casteth away his weapon, offereth both his hands, and holdeth them, as it were to be tied: hoping to saue his life by offering himselfe bondslaue.

The chiefe bootie the Tartars seeke for in all their warres is to get store of captiues; specially young boyes, and girles, whome they sell to the Turkes, or other their neighbours. To this purpose they take with them great baskets make like bakers panniers, to carry them tenderly, and if any of them happen to tire, or to be sicke by the way, they dash him against the ground, or some tree, and so leaue him dead. The Souldiers are not troubled with keeping the captiues and the other bootie, for hindering the execution of their warres, but they haue certaine bandes that intend nothing else, appoynted of purpose to receiue and keepe the captiues and the other praye.

[Sidenote: The Tartar religion.] The Russe borderers (being vsed to their inuasions lightly euery yeere in the Sommer) keepe fewe other cattell on the border partes, saue swine onely which the Tartar will not touch, nor driue away with him: for that he is of the Turkish religion, and will eate no swines flesh. Of Christ our Sauiour they confesse as much as doeth the Turke in his Alkaron, viz. that he came of the Angel Gabriel and the Virgin Marie, that he was a great Prophet, and shall be the Iudge of the worlde at the last day. In other matter likewise, they are much ordered after the manner and direction of the Turke: hauing felt the Turkish forces when hee wonne from them Azou and Caffa, with some other townes about the Euxine or blacke Sea, that were before tributaries to the Crim Tartar. So that now the Emperor of the Crims for the most part is chosen one of the Nobility whom the Turke doeth commend: whereby it is brought nowe to passe, that the Crim Tartar giueth to the Turke the tenth part of the spoyle which hee getteth in his warres against the Christians.

Herein they differ from the Turkish religion, for that they haue certaine idole puppets made of silke, or like stuffe, of the fashion of a man, which they fasten to the doore of their walking houses, to be as Ianusses or keepers of their house. And these idoles are made not by all, but by certaine religious women which they haue among them for that and like vses. They haue besides the image of their King or great Can, of an huge bignesse, which they erect at euery stage when the army marcheth: and this euery one must bend and bowe vnto as he passeth by it, be he Tartar or stranger. They are much giuen to witchcraft, and ominous coniectures vpon euery accident which they heare or see.

In making of mariages they haue no regard of alliance or consanguinitie. Onely with his mother, sister, and daughter a man may not marrie, and though he take the woman into his house, and accompany with her, yet be accounteth her not for his wife till he haue a childe by her. Then hee beginneth to take a dowry of her friends, or horse, sheepe, kine, &c. If she be barren after a certaine time, be turneth her home againe.

[Sidenote: The Tartar nobilitie.] Vnder the Emperour they haue certaine Dukes, whome they call Morseis or Diuoymorseis, that rule ouer a certaine number of 10000, 20000, or 40000, a piece, which they call Hoords. When the Emperour hath any vse of them to serue in his warres, they are bound to come, and to bring with them in their Souldiers to a certain number, euery man with his two horse at the least, the one to ride on, the other to kill, when it commmeth to his turne to haue his horse eaten. [Sidenote: The tartar diet.] For their chiefe vitaile is horse flesh, which they eate without bread, or any other thing with it. So that if a Tartar be taken by a Russe, he shall he sure lightly to finde a horse-legge, or some other part of him at his saddle bowe.

[Sidenote: 1588.] This last yeere when I was at the Mosco, came in one Kiriach Morsey, nephew to the Emperour of the Crims that nowe is (whose father was Emperour before) accompanied with 300. Tartars, and his two wiues, whereof one was his brothers widow. Where being intertained in very good sort after the Russe maner, hee had sent vnto his lodging for his welcome, to bee made ready for his supper and his companies, two very large and fat horses, ready flayed in a shed. They prefer it before other flesh, because the meate is stronger (as they say) then Beefe, Mutton, and such like. And yet (which is marueile) though they serue all as horsemen in the warres, and eate all of horse flesh, there are brought yeerely to the Mosco to bee exchanged for other commodities 30. or 40. thousand Tartar horse, which they call Cones. They keepe also great heards of kine, and flocks of blacke sheepe, rather for the skins and milke (which they carie with them in great bottels) then for the vse of the flesh, though sometimes they eate of it. Some vse they haue of ryse, figs, and other fruits. They drinke milke or warme blood, and for the most part card them both together. They vse sometime as they trauel by the way to let their horse blood in a vaine, and to drinke it warme, as it commeth from his bodie.

[Sidenote: The Tartars dwelling.] Townes they plant none, nor other standing buildings, but haue walking houses, which the latines call Veij, built vpon wheeles like a shepheards cottage. These they drawe with them whithersoeuer they goe, driuing their cattell with them. And when they come to their stage, or standing place, they plant their carte houses verie orderly in a ranke: and so make the forme of streetes, and of a large towne. And this is the manner of the Emperor himselfe, who hath no other seat of

Empire but an Agora, or towne of wood, that moueth with him whithersoeuer he goeth. As for the fixed and standing buildings vsed in other countreyes, they say they are vnwholesome and unpleasant.

They begin to mooue their houses and cattell in the Spring time from the South part of their countrey towards the North partes. And so driuing on till they haue grased all vp to the first farthest part Northward, they returne backe againe towards their South countrey (where they continue all the Winter) by 10. or 12. miles a stage: in the meane while the grasse being sprung vp againe, to serue for their cattell as they returne. From the border of the Shelcan towards the Caspian sea, to the Russe frontiers, they haue a goodly Countrey, specially on the South and Southeast parts, but lost for lack of tillage.

Of money they haue no vse at all, and therefore prefer brasse and steele before other metals, specially bullate, which they vse for swordes, kniues, and other necessaries. As for golde and siluer they neglect it of very purpose, (as they doe all tillage of their ground) to bee more free for their wandering kinde of life, and to keepe their Countrey lesse subiect to inuasions. Which giueth them great aduantage against all their neighbors, euer inuading and neuer being inuaded. Such as haue taken vpon them to inuade their Countrey (as of olde time Cyrus and Darius Hystaspis, on the East and Southeast side) haue done it with very ill successe: as wee finde in the stories written of those times. For their manner is when any will inuade them, to allure and drawe them on by flying and reculing (as if they were afraide) till they haue drawen them some good way within their countrey. Then when they begin to want victuall and other necessaries (as needes they must where nothing is to be had) to stoppe vp the passages, and inclose them with multitudes. By which stratagem (as we reade in Laonicus Chalcacondylas in his Turkish storie) they had welnigh surprised the great and huge armie of Tamerlan, but that hee retired with all speede hee could towardes the riuer Tanais or Don, not without great losse of his men, and cariages.

[Sidenote: Pachymerius.] In the storie of Pachymerius the Greek (which he wrote of the the elder) I remember he telleth to the same purpose of one Nogas a Tartarian captaine vnder Cazan the Emperor of the East Tartars (of whom the citie and kingdome of Cazan may seeme to Emperors of Constantinople from the beginning of the reigne of Michael PalŠologus to the time of Andronicus haue taken the denomination) who refused a present of Pearle and other iewels sent vnto him from Michael PalŠologus: asking withall, for what vse they serued, and whether they were good to keepe away sicknesse, death, or other misfortunes of this life, or no. So that it seemeth they haue euer, or long time bene of that minde to value things no further, then by the vse and necessitie for which they serue.

For person and complexion they haue broade and flatte visages, of a tanned colour into yellowe and blacke, fierce and cruell lookes, thinne haired vpon the upper lippe, and pitte of the chinne, light and nimble bodied, with short legges, as if they were made naturally for horsemen: whereto they practise themselues from their childhood, seldome going afoot about anie businesse. Their speech is verie sudden and loude, speaking as it were out of a deepe hollowe throate. When they sing you would thinke a kowe lowed, or some great bandogge howled. Their greatest exercise is shooting, wherein they traine vp their children from their verie infancie, not suffering them to eate till they haue shot neere the marke within a certaine scantling. They are the very same that sometimes were called ScythŠ Nomades, or the Scythian shepheards, by the Greekes and Latines. Some thinke that the Turks took their beginning from the nation of the Crim Tartars. [Sidenote: Laonicus Calcocondylas.] Of which opinion is Laonicus Calcocondylas the Greek Historiographer, in his first booke of his Turkish storie. Wherein hee followeth diuers verie probable coniectures. [Sidenote: 1.] The first taken from the verie name it selfe, for that the worde Turke signifieth a Shepheard or one that followeth a vagrant and wilde kinde of life. By which name these Scythian Tartars haue euer beene noted, being called by the Greekes [Greek: skythai nomades] or the Scythian shepheards. [Sidenote: 2.] His second reason because the Turkes (in his time) that dwelt in Asia the lesse, to wit, in Lydia, Caria, Phrygia and Cappadocia, spake the very same language that these Tartars did, that dwelt betwixt the riuer Tanais or Don, and the countrey of Sarmatia, which (as is knowen) are these Tartars called Crims. At this time also the whole nation of the Turkes differ not much in their common speech from the Tartar language. [Sidenote: 3.] Thirdly because the Turke and the Crim Tartar agree so well together, as well in religion, as in matter of Traffique neuer inuading, or iniurying one another: saue that the Turke (since Laonicus his time) hath encroached vpon some Townes vpon the Euxin Sea, that before perteined to the Crim Tartar. [Sidenote: 4.] Fourthly, because Ortogules sonne to Oguzalpes, and father to Ottoman the first of name of the Turkish nation made his first roads out of those pans of Asia, vpon the next borderers, till hee came towardes the countreys about the hill Taurus where he ouercame the Greekes that inhabited there: and so enlarged the name and territorie of the Turkish nation, till hee came to EubŠa and Attica and other partes of Greece. [Sidenote: 1400.] This is the opinion of Laonicus, who liued among the Turkes in the time of Amurat the sixt Turkish Emperour, about the yeere 1400. when the memorie of their originall was more fresh: and therefore the likelier hee was to hit the trueth.

[Sidenote: The Nagay Tartar the cruellest, The Chircase the ciuillest Tartar.] There are diuers other Tartars that border vpon Russia, as the Nayages, the Cheremissens, the Mordwites, the Chircasses, and the Shalcans, which all differ in name more then in regiment, or other condition, from the Crim Tartar, except the Chircasses that border Southwest, towardes Lituania, and are farre more ciuill than the rest of the Tartars, of a comely person, and of a stately behauiour, as applying themselues to the fashion of the Polonian. Some of them haue subiected themselues to the Kings of Poland, and professe Christianitie. The Nagay lieth Eastwarde, and is reckoned for the best man of warre among all the Tartars, but verie sauage, and cruell aboue all the rest. [Sidenote: The Cheremissen Tartar of two sorts: the Lugauoy and the Nagornay.] The Cheremessen Tartar, that lieth betwixt the Russe and the Nagay, are of two sorts, the Lugauoy (that is of the valley) and the Nagornay, or of the hilly countrey. These haue much troubled the Emperours of Russia. And therefore they are content now to buy peace of them, vnder pretence of giuing a yeerely pension of Russe commodities to their Morseys, or Diuoymorseis, that are chiefe of their tribes. For which also they are bound to serue them in their wars, vnder certaine conditions. They are said to be iust and true in their dealings: and for that cause they hate the Russe people, whom they account to be double, and false in al their dealing. And therefore the common sort are very vnwilling to keepe agreement with them, but that they are kept in by their pensions sake.

[Sidenote: The Mordwit Tartar the most barbarous of the rest.] The most rude and barbarous is counted the Mordwit Tartar, that hath many selfe-fashions and strange kinds of behauiour, differing from the rest. For his religion, though he acknowledge one God, yet his manor is to worship for God, that liuing thing that he first meeteth in the morning; and to sweare by, it all that whole day, whether it be horse, dog, cat, or whatsoeuer els it bee. When his friend dieth, he killeth his best horse, and hauing flayed off the skinne hee carieth it on high vpon a long pole before the corpes to the place of buriall. This hee doeth (as the Russe saieth) that his friend may haue a good horse to carie him to heauen: but it is likelier to declare his loue towards his dead friend, in that he will haue to die with him the best thing that he hath.

Next to the kingdome of Astracan, that is the farthest part Southeastward of the Russe dominion, lyeth the Shulcan, and the countrey of Media: whither the Russe marchants trade for rawe silkes, syndon, saphion, skinnes, and other commodities. The chiefe Townes of Media where the Russe tradeth, are Derbent (built by Alexander the great, as the inhabitants say) and Zamachi where the staple is kept for rawe silkes. [Sidenote: The reuiuing of silkwormes.] Their maner is in the Spring time to reuiue the silke-wormes (that lie dead all the Winter) by laying them in the warme sunne, and (to hasten their quickening that they may the sooner goe to worke) to put them into bags, and so to hang them vnder their childrens armes. [Sidenote: Chrinisin a kind of silkworme.] As for the woorme called

Chrinisin (as wee call it Chrymson) that maketh coloured silke, it is bred not in Media, but in Assyria. [Sidenote: Liberty to trade downe the Caspian Sea.] This trade to Derbent and Samachi for rawe silkes, and other commodities of that Countrey, as also into Persia, and Bougharia downe the riuer of Volga, and through the Caspian sea, is permitted aswell to the English as to the Russe merchants, by the Emperours last grant at my being there. Which he accounteth for a very speciall fauour, and might proue indeede very beneficiall to our English merchants, if the trade were wel and orderly vsed.

The whole nation of the Tartars are vtterly voide of all learning, and without written Law: yet certaine rules they haue which they hold by tradition, common to all the Hoords for the practise of their life. Which are of this sort. First, To obey their Emperour and other Magistrates, whatsoeuer they commaund about the publike seruice. 2 Except for the publike behoofe, euery man to be free and out of controlment. 3 No priuate man to possesse any lands, but the whole countrey to be as common. 4 To neglect all daintinesse and varietie of meates, and to content themselues with that which commeth next to hand, for more hardnesse, and readines in the executing of their affaires. 5 To weare any base attire, and to patch their clothes whether there be any neede or not: that when there is neede, it be no shame to weare a patcht coate. 6 To take or steale from any stranger whatsoeuer they can get, as beeing enemies of all men, saue to such as will subiect themselues to them. 7 Towards their owne hoorde and nation to be true in worde and deede. 8 To suffer no stranger to come within the Realme. [Sidenote: No stranger without pasport admitted.] If any doe, the same to be bondslaue to him that first taketh him, except such merchants and other as haue the Tartar Bull, or passport about them.

Of the Permians, Samoites, and Lappes.

The Permians and Samoites that lye from Russia, North and. Northeast, are thought likewise to haue taken their beginning from the Tartar kinde. And it may partly bee gessed by the fashion of their countenance, as hauing all broade and flat faces as the Tartars haue, except the Chircasses. [Sidenote: The Permians.] The Permians are accounted for a very ancient people. They are nowe subiect to the Russe. They liue by hunting, and trading with their furres, as also doeth the Samoit, that dwelleth more towardes the North Sea. [Sidenote: The Samoits.] The Samoit hath his name (as the Russe saith) of eating himselfe: as if in times past, they liued as the Cannibals, eating one another. [Footnote: *Samoyed* means "self-eater", while *Samodin* denotes "an individual". Nordenski÷ld considers it probable, however, that the old tradition of man-eaters *androphagi*, living in the north, which originated with Herodotus, reappears in a Russianised form in the name "Samoyed".]

Which they make more probable, because at this time they eate all kind of raw flesh, whatsoeuer it be, euen the very carion that lieth in the ditch. But as the Samoits themselues will say, they were called Samoie, that is, of themselues, as though they were IndigenŠ, or people bred vpon that very soyle, that neuer changed their seate from one place to another, as most nations haue done. They are subiect at this time to the Emperour of Russia.

[Sidenote: The Samoits religion.] I talked with certaine of them, and finde that they acknowledge one God: but represent him by such things as they haue most vse and good by. And therefore they worship the Sunne, the Ollen, the Losh, and such like. [Sidenote: Slata Baba or the golden Hag.] As for the story of Slata Baba, or the Golden hagge, which I haue read in some mappes, and descriptions of these countries, to be an idole after the forme of an old woman that being demanded by the Priest, giueth them certaine Oracles, concerning the successe, and euent of things, I found it to be a very fable. [Sidenotes: A fable. The Sea.] Onely in the Prouince of Obdoria vpon the sea side, neare to the mouth of the great riuer Obba, there is a rocke, which naturally (being somewhat helped by imagination) may seeme to beare the shape of a ragged woman, with a child in her armes (as the rocke by the North Cape the shape of a Frier) where the Obdorian Samoites vse much to resort, by reason of the commoditie of the place for fishing: [Sidenote: Fishing or sea.] and there, sometime (as their manner is) conceiue, and practise their sorceries, and ominous coniecturings about the good or bad speede of their iourneies, fishings, huntings and such like.

[Sidenote: The Samoits habit and behauiour.] They are clad in Seale skins, with the hairie side outwards downe as low as the knees, with their breeches and netherstockes of the same, both men and women. They are all blacke haired, naturally beardlesse. And therefore the men are hardly discerned from the women by their lookes: saue that the women weare a locke of haire downe along both their eares. [Sidenote: The people of Meta Incognota such.] They liue in a manner a wilde and sauage life, rouing still from one place of the countrey to another, without any property of house or land more to one then to another. Their leader or directer in euery companie, is their Papa or Priest.

[Sidenote: The Lappes.] On the North side of Russia next to Corelia, lieth the countrey of Lappia, which reacheth in length from the farthest point Northward, (towards the Northcape) to the farthest part Southeast (which, the Russe calleth Sweetnesse or Holy nose, the English men Capegrace) about 345. verst or miles. From Sweetnesse to Candelox by the way of Versega (which measureth the breadth of that countrey) is 90. miles or thereabouts. The whole countrey in a maner is either lakes, or mountaines, which towardes the Sea side are called Tondro, because they are all of harde and craggy rocke, but the inland partes are well furnished with woods that growe on the hilles sides, the lakes lying betweene. Their diet is very bare and simple. Bread they haue none, but feede onely vpon fish and foule. They are subiect to the Emperor of Russia, and the two kings of Sweden and Denmarke: which all exact tribute and custome of them (as was saide before) but the Emperor of Russia beareth the greatest hand ouer them, and exacteth of them farre more then the rest. The opinion is that they were first termed Lappes of their briefe and short speech. The Russe diuideth the whole nation of the Lappes into two series. The one they call Nowremanskoy Lapary, that is, the Norwegian Lappes because they be of the Danish religion. For the Danes and Noruegians they account for one people. The other that haue no religion at all but liue as bruite and heathenish people, without God in the worlde, they cal Dikoy Lapary, or the wilde Lappes.

The whole nation is vtterly vnlearned, hauing not so much as the vse of any Alphabet, or letter among them. For practise of witchcraft and sorcerie they passe all nations in the worlde. Though for enchanting of ships that saile along their coast, (as I haue heard it reported) and their giuing of winds good to their friends, and contrary to other, whom they meane to hurt by tying of certaine knots vpon a rope (somewhat like to the tale of Aeolus his windbag) is a very fable, deuised (as may seeme) by themselues, to terrifie sailers for comming neere their coast. Their weapons are the long bow, and handgunne, wherein they excell, as well for quicknesse to charge and discharge, as for neerenesse at the marke by reason of their continuall practise (whereto they are forced) of shooting at wild fowle. Their maner is in Sommer time to come downe in great companies to the sea side, to Wardhuyse, Cola, Kegor, and the bay of Vedagoba, and there to fish for Codde, Salmon, and But-fish, which they sel to the Russes, Danes, and Noruegians, and nowe of late to the English men that trade thither with cloth, which they exchange with the Laps and Corelians for their fish, oyle, and furres, whereof also they haue some store. [Sidenote: The mart at Cola.] They hold their mart at Cola on S. Peter's day: what time the captaine of Wardhuyse (that is resident there for the king of Denmark) must be present, or at least send his deputie to set prices vpon their stockfish, train oile, furres, and other commodities: as also the Russe Emperors customer, or tribute taker, to receiue his custome, which is euer paide before any thing can bee bought or solde. When their fishing is done, their manner is to drawe their carbasses Or boates on shore, and there to leaue them with the keele turned vpwardes, till the next spring tide. [Sidenote: Sleds drawen with Deere.] Their trauaile to and fro is vpon sleddes drawen by the Olen Deere: which they vse to turne a grasing all the Sommer time in an Island called Kildyn, (of a verie good soyle compared with other partes of that Countrey) and towards the Winter time, when the snowe beginneth to fall they fetch them home againe for the vse of their sledde.

The description of the regions, people, and riuers lying North and East from Moscouia: as the way from Moscouia to the riuer Petzora, and the Prouince Iugaria or Iuhra, and from thence to the riuer Obi. Likewise the description of other countreys and regions, euen vnto the Empire of the great Can of Cathay, taken out of Sigismundus ab Herberstein.

[Sidenote: The dominion of the Duke of Moscouia.] The dominion of the Prince of Moscouia, reacheth farre toward the East and North, vnto the places which we will now describe. As concerning which thing, I translated a book that was presented vnto me in the Moscouites tongue, and haue here made a briefe rehearsall of the same. I will first therefore describe the iourney from Moscouia to Petzora, and so to Iugaria and Obi. From Moscouia to the citie of Vologda, are numbered fiue hundred versts, one verst, conteyning almost the space of an Italian myle. From Vologda to Vsting toward the right hand, descending with the course of the riuer of Vologda and Suchana with whom it ioyneth, are counted fiue hundred verstes, where within two versts of the towne called Strelze, and hard by the citie of Vsting, Suchana ioyneth vnto Iug which runneth from the South: from whose mouth vnto the springs of the same, are numbred fiue hundred versts.

[Sidenote: Iug. So called of his swift and pleasant streame.] But Suchana and Iug, after they ioyne together, lose their first names, and make but one riuer named Dwina, by the which the passage to the citie of Colmogro conteineth fiue hundred versts, from whence, in the space of sixe dayes iourney, Dwina entreth into the North Ocean at sixe mouthes. And the greatest part of this iourney consisteth by Nauigation. For by lande from Vologda vnto Colmogro, passing ouer the riuer Vuaga, are a thousand verstes. Not farre from Colmogro, the riuer Pinega running from the East on the right hand for the space of seuen hundred versts, falleth into Dwina. From Dwina by the riuer Pienega, by the space of two hundred versts, they come to a place called Nicholai, from whence within halfe a verst ships haue passage into the riuer Kuluio, which hath his originall from a lake of the same name towarde the North, from whose springs is eight daies viage to the mouth of the same, where it entreth into the Ocean.

[Sidenote: The regions by the North sea.] Sayling by the coasts of the right hand of the sea, they passe by the regions of Stanuwische, Calunczcho, and Apnu: And sayling about the promontorie or cape of Chorogoski Nose, Stanuwische, Camenckh, and Tolstickh, they come at length into the riuer Mezen, and from thence in the space of sixe dayes, to a village of the same name, standing in the mouth of the riuer Pieza, by the which againe ascending toward the left hand and sommer East, they come to the riuer Piescoia: from whence sayling for the space of fiue versts, they come into two lakes, in the which are seene two wayes: whereof one on the right side, goeth to the riner Rubicho, by the which they passe to the riuer Czircho. Other, by an other and shorter way, bring their ships from the lake directly into Czirchor: from whence, except they be hindered by tempest, they come in the space of three weekes to the riuer and mouth of Czilma, flowing into the great riuer Petzora, which in that place is two versts in breadth. Sayling from thence, they come in the space of sixe dayes to the Towne and castle of Pustosero, neare vnto the which Petzora entreth into the North Ocean at sixe monthes. The inhabitants of this place, are men of simple wit: they receiued the faith of Christ, and were baptised in the yeare M. D. xviii.

From the mouth of Czilma vnto the mouth of the riuer Vssa, going by Petzora, is one moneths viage. Vssa hath his springs in the mountaine [Marginal Note: Cingulus mundi.] Poyas Semnoi, being on the left hand toward the sommer East, and springeth out of a great stone of the same mountaine, called Camen Bolschoi. From the springs of Vssa to the mouthes of the same, are numbered more then a thousand versts. Furthermore, Petzora runneth from this south winter part, from whence ascending from the mouthes of Vssa, vnto the mouthes of the riuer Stzuchogora, is three weekes viage. They that described this vyage sayd that they rested betweene the mouthes of the riuers Stzuchogora and Potzscheriema, and left their victuals there which they brought with them from Russia. Beyond the riuers of Petzora and Stzuchogora toward the mountaine Camenipoias, and the sea with the Ilands thereabout, and the Castle of Pustosero, are diuers and innumerable nations, which by one common name are called Samoged (that is) such as eate themselues. They haue great increase of foules, birdes, and diuers kindes of beastes: as Sables. Marternes, Beuers, Otters, Hermelines, Squirrels: and in the Ocean the beast called a Morse: Also Vesse, white Beares, Wolues, Hares, Equiwoduani, great Whales, and a fish called Semfi, with diuers other. [Sidenote: Wilde people.] The people of these nations come not to Moscouia: For they are wilde, and flee the company and society of other men.

From the mouthes of Stzuchogora, sayling vp the riuer vnto Poiassa, Artawische, Cameni, and Poiassa the greater, is three weekes vyage. Furthermore, the ascending to the mount Camen, is three dayes iourney: from the which descending they come to the riuer Artawischa, and from thence to the riuer Sibut, from whence they passe to the Castle of Lepin, and from Lepin to the riuer Sossa. The people that inhabite the region by this riuer, are called Vuogolici. Leauing Sossa on the right hande, they come to the great riuer Obi, that springeth out of the lake Kitaisko, the which, with all the haste they could make, they could scarcely passe ouer in one day, the riuer being of such breadth that it reacheth fourescore versts. The people also that dwell about the riuer, are called Vuogolici and Vgritzschi. From the Castle of Obea, ascending by the riuer of Oby, vnto the riuer Irtische, into the which Sossa entereth, is three moneths iourney. In these places are two Castles named Ierom and Tumen, kept by certaine Lords called Knesi Iuhorski, being tributaries to the great Duke of Moscouia, as they say. Here are diuers kinds of beasts and furres.

From the mouth of the riuer Irtische to the Castle of Grustina, is two moneths iourney: from whence to the lake Kitai, by the riuer Oby (which I said to haue his springs in this lake) is more then three moneths iourney. [Sidenote: Blacke men without speech.] From this lake come many blacke men; lacking the vse of common speech. They bring with them diuers wares, and especially pearles and precious stones, which they sell to the people called Grustintzi and Serponowtzi. These haue their name of the Castle Serponow, situate in the mountaines of Lucomoria, beyond the riuer Obi. [Sidenote: Men that yeerely die and reuiue.] They say that to the men of Lucomoria chauncheth a marueilous thing and incredible: For they affirme, that they die yeerely at the xxvii. day of Nouember, being the feast of S. George among the Moscouites: and that the next spring about the xxiii. day of Aprill, they reuiue as doe Frogges.

[Sidenote: A strange trade of merchandise.] With these also, the people of Grustintzi and Serponowtzi exercise a new and strange kinde of trade. For when the accustomed time of their dying, or rather of sleeping, approcheth, they leaue their wares in certaine places appointed, which the Grustintzi and Serponowtzi carry away, leauing other wares of equall value in their places: which if the dead men at the time of their reuiuing perceiue to be of vnequal price, they require their owne againe: by reason whereof, much strife and righting is betweene them.

From the riuer of Obi descending toward the left hand, are the people called Calami, which came thither from Obiowa and Pogosa. Beneath Obi, about Aurea Anus (that is the golden old wife) are the riuers Sossa, Berezuua, and Danadim, all which spring out of the mountaines Camen, Bolschega, Poiassa, and the rockes ioyning to the same. All the nations that inhabite from these riuers to Aurea Anus, are subiect to the prince of Moscouia.

Aurea Anus, called in the Moscouites tongue, Slata Baba, is an Idol at the mouthe of Obi in the prouince of Obdora, standing on the furthest banke toward the sea. Along by the bankes of Obi, and the riuers neare there about, are here and there many castles and fortresses: all the lordes whereof are subiect to the prince of Moscouia, as they say. They say also, or rather fable, that the idol called Aurea anus, is an image like vnto an old wife, hauing a child in her lap, and that there is now seene another infant, which they say to be her nephew: Also that there are certaine instruments that make a continuall sound like the noyse of Trumpets, the which, if it so be, I thinke it to be by reason of the winde, blowing continually into the holow places of those instruments.

The riuer Cossin falleth out of the mountaines of Lucomoria: In the mouth of this is a castle, whither from the springs of the great riuer Cossin, is two moneths viage. [Sidenote: Tachnin a great riuer. People of monstrous shape. A fish like a man. Plinie writeth of the like fish.] Furthermore, from the springs of the same riuer, the riuer Cassima hath his originall, which running through Lucomoria, falleth into the great riuer Tachnin, beyond the which (as is said) dwell men of prodigious shape, of whom some are ouergrowen with haire like wilde beastes, other haue heads like dogges, and their faces in their breasts, without neckes, and with long hands also, and without feete. There is likewise in the riuer Tachnin a certaine fish, with head, eyes, nose, mouth, hands, feete, and other members vtterly of humane shape, and yet, without any voyce, and pleasant to be eaten, as are other fishes.

[Sidenote: The end of the iournall.] All that I haue hitherto rehearsed, I haue translated out of the saide iourney which was deliuered me in the Moscouites tongue: In the which, perhaps some things may seeme fabulous, and in maner incredible, as of the double men, and the dead reuiuing, the Aurea Anus also, and the monstrous shapes of men, with the fish of humane fourme: whereof although I haue made diligent inquisition, yet could I know nothing certaine of any that had seene the same with their eyes: neuerthelesse, to giue farther occasion to other to search the truth of these things, I haue thought good to make mention hereof.

Noss in the Moscouites tongue signifieth a nose, and therefore they call all capes or points that reach into the sea by the same name.

The mountaines about the riuer of Petzora are called Semnoy Poyas, or Cingulus mundi, that is, the girdle of the world, or of the earth.

Kithai is a lake, of which the great Can of Cathay, whom the Moscouians cal
Czar Kithaiski, hath his name: For Can in the Tartars language signifieth, A King.

[Sidenote: Moria is the sea.] The places of Lucomoria, neare vnto the sea, are saluage full of woods, and inhabited without any houses. And albeit, that the author of this iourney, said, that many nations of Lucomoria are subiect to the prince of Moscouia, yet for asmuch as the kingdome of Tumen is neare thereunto, whose prince is a Tartar, and named in their Tongue, Tumenski Czar, that is, a king in Tumen, and hath of late done great domage to the prince of Moscouia: It is most like that these nations should be rather subiect vnto him.

Neare vnto the riuer Petzora (whereof mention is made in this iourney) is the citie and castle of Papin or Papinowgorod, whose inhabitants are named Papini, and haue a priuate language, differing from the Moscouites. [Sidenote: High mountaines, supposed to be Hyperborei, and Rhiphei.] Beyond this riuer are exceeding high mountaines, reaching euen vnto the bankes, whose ridges or tops, by reason of continuall windes, are in maner vtterly barren without grasse or fruits. And although in diuers places they haue diuers names, yet are they commonly called Cingulus mundi, that is, the girdle of the world. In these mountaines doe Ierfalcons breede, whereof I haue spoken before. There growe also Cedar trees, among the which are found the best and blackest kinde of Sables: and onely these mountaines are seene in all the dominions of the prince of Moscouia which perhaps are the same that the old writers call Rhipheos or Hyperboreos, so named of the Greeke word, Hyper, that is, Aboue, and Boreas, that is, the North; for by reason they are couered with continuall snow and frost, they can not without great difficultie be trauayled, and reach so farre into the North, that they make the vnknown land of Engronland. The Duke of Moscouia, Basilius the sonne of Iohn, sent on a time two of his Captaines, named Simeon Pheodorowich Kurbski, & Knes Peter Vschatoi, to search the places beyond these mountaines, and to subdue the nations thereabout. Kurbski was yet aliue at my being in Moscouia, & declared vnto me that he spent xvii. daies in ascending the mountaine, & yet could not come to the top thereof, which in their tongue is called Stolp, that is, a piller. This mountaine is extended into the Ocean vnto the mouthes of the riuers of Dwina and Petzora.

But now hauing spoken thus much of the said iourney, I will returne to the dominions of Moscouia, with other regions lying Eastward and South from the same, toward the mighty Empire of Cathay. But I will first speake somewhat briefly of the prouince of Rezan, and the famous riuer of Tanais.

[Sidenote: The fruitfull prouince of Rezan.] The prouince of Rezan, situate betweene the riuers of Occa and Tanais, hath a citie builded of wood, not far from the bank of Occa: there was in it a castle named Iaroslaue, whereof there now remainethr nothing but tokens of the old ruine. Not farre from that citie the riuer Occa maketh an Iland named Strub, which was sometime a great Dukedome, whose prince was subiect to none other. This prouince of Rezan is more fruitful then any other of the prouinces of Moscouia: Insomuch that in this (as they say) euery graine of wheat bringeth forth two, and sometimes more eares: whose stalkes or strawes grow so thicke that horses can scarsely go through them, or Quayles flie out of them. There is great plenty of hony, fishes, foules, hirdes, and wilde beasts. The fruits also due farre exceede the fruits of Moscouia. The people are bolde and warlike men.

A speciall note gathered by the excellent Venetian Cosmographer M. Iohn Baptista Ramusius out of the Atabian Geographie of Abilfada Ismael, concerning the trending of the Ocean sea from China Northward, along the coast of Tartarie and other vnknowen lands, and then running Westwards vpon the Northerne coasts of Russia, and so farther to the Northwest.

Descriuendo poi il predetto Abilfadai Ismael luoghi della terra habitabile, che circuendo il mar Oceano tocca, dice cosi.

[Sidenote: La regione delle Cine. Contini delli vltimi Tartari. Alcune Terre Incognite. Contini Settentrionali della Rosia.] Riuoltasi l'Oceano da leuante verso la regione delle Cine, et vÓ alla volta di Tramontana, et passata finalmente la detta regione, se ne giunge a Gogi et Magogi, cio Ŕ alli confini de gli Vltimi Tartari, et di quiui ad Alcune Terre che sono Incognite: Et correndo sempre per Ponente, passa sopra li confini Settentrionali della Rossia, et vÓ alla volta di Maestro.

The same in English.

The aforesaid Abilfada Ismael describing afterward the habitable places of the earth, which the Ocean sea in his circuit toucheth, sayth in this manner following.

[Sidenote: The Countrey of China. The coasts of the vttermost Tartars. Certaine vnknowne Countreys. The Northern coasts of Russia. The Northwest.] The Ocean sea turneth from the East toward the Countrey of the Chinaes, and stretcheth toward the North, and at length hauing passed the sayd Countrey, it reacheth vnto the Gogi and Magogi, that is, to the confines of The vttermost Tartars, and from thence vnto certaine vnknowen Countreys: and running still Westward it passeth vpon the Northerne coasts of Russia, and from thence it runneth toward Northwest, (which it doth indeede vpon the coast of Lappia.) By this most notable testimony it appeareth, that the Ocean sea compasseth and enuironeth all the East, Northeast, and North parts of Asia and Europe.

The Emperors priuate or houshold Officers.

The chiefe Officers of the Emperors houshold are these which follow. [Sidenote: Master of the Horse.] The first is the office of the Boiaren Conesheua, or master of the Horse. Which conteineth no more then is expressed by the name, that is to be ouerseer of the Horse, and not Magister equitum, or Master of the Horsemen. For he appointeth other for that seruice, as occasion doth require, as before was sayd. He that beareth that office at this time, is Boris Pheodorowich Godonoe, brother to the

Empresse. Of Horse for seruice in his warres (besides other for his ordinary vses) he hath to the number of ten thousand which are kept about Mosco.

The next is the Lord Steward of his houshold at this time, one Gregory Vasilowich Godonoe. The third is his Treasurer, that keepeth all his monies, iewels, plate, &c. now called Stephan Vasilowich Godonoe. The fourth his Controller, now Andreas Petrowich Clesinine. The fift his Chamberlaine. He that attendeth that office at this time, is called Estoma Bisabroza Pastelnischay. The sixt his Tasters, now Theodor Alexandrowich, and Iuan Vasilowich Godonoe. The seuenth his Harbingers, which are three Noble men, and diuers other Gentlemen that do the office vnder them. These are his ordinary officers and offices of the chiefest account.

Of Gentlemen besides them that waite about his chamber, and person (called Shilsey Strapsey) there are two hundred, all Noblemens sonnes. His ordinary Garde is two thousand Hagbutters readie with their pieces charged, and their match lighted, with other necessarie furniture continually day and night: which come not within the house, but waite without in the court or yard, where the Emperour is abiding. In the night time there lodgeth next to his bedchamber the chiefe Chamberlaine with one or two more of best trust about him. A second chamber off there lodge sixe other of like account for trust and faithfulnesse. In the thirde chamber lie certaine young Gentlemen, of these two hundred, called Shilsey Strapsey that take their turnes by forties euery night. There are groomes besides that watch in their course, and lie at euery gate and doore of the Court, called Estopnick.

The Hagbutters or Gunners, whereof there are two thousand (as was sayd before) watch about the Emperours lodgings, or bedchamber by course 250. euery night, and 250. more in the Courtyarde, and about the Treasure house. His Court or house at the Mosco is made castle wise, walled about, with great store of faire ordinance planted vpon the wall, and conteyneth a great breadth of ground within it, with many, dwelling houses: Which are appointed for such as are knowen to be sure, and trustie to the Emperor.

Of the priuate behauiour, or qualitie of the Russe people.

The priuate behauiour and qualitie of the Russe people, may partly be vnderslood by that which hath beene sayd concerning the publique state and vsage of the Countrey. [Sidenote: Constitution of their bodies.] As touching the naturall habite of their bodies, they are for the most part of a large size, and of very fleshly bodies: accounting it a grace to be somewhat grosse and burley, and therefore they nourish and spread their beards, to haue them long and broad. But for the most part, they are very vnwieldy and vnactiue withall. Which may be thought to come partly of the climate, and the numbnesse which they get by the cold in winter, and partly of their diet that standeth most of routes, onions, garlike, cabbage, and such like things that breede grosse humors, which they vse to eate alone, and with their other meates.

[Sidenote: Their diet.] Their diet is rather much then curious. At their meales they beginne commonly with a Charke or small cuppe of Aqua vitae, (which they call Russe wine) and then drinke not till towardes the end of their meales, taking it in largely, and all together, with kissing one another at euery pledge. And therefore after dinner there is no talking with them, but euery man goeth to his bench to take his afternoones sleepe, which is as ordinary with them as their nights rest. When they exceede, and haue varietie of dishes, the first are their baked meates (for roste meates they vse little) and then their broathes or pottage. Their common drinke is Mead, the poorer sort vse water and a third drinke called Quasse, which is nothing else (as we say) but water turned out of his wits, with a litle branne meashed with it.

This diet would breed in them many diseases, but that they vse bathstoues or hote houses in steade of all Phisicke, commonly twise or thrise euery weeke. All the winter time, and almost the whole Semmer, they heat their Peaches, which are made like the Germane bathstoues, and their Poclads like ouens, that so warme the house that a stranger at the first shall hardly like of it. These two extremities, specially in the winter of heat within their houses, and of extreame cold without, together with their diet, make them of a darke, and sallow complexion, their skinnes being tanned and parched both with cold and with heate: specially the women, that for the greater part are of farre worse complexions, then the men. Whereof the cause I take to be their keeping within the hote houses, and busying themselues about the heating, and vsing of their bathstoues, and peaches.

The Russe because that he is vsed to both these extremities of heat and of cold, can beare them both a great deale more patiently, then strangers can doe. [Sidenote: An admirable induring of extreme heat and colde at one and the same time.] You shall see them sometimes (to season their bodies) come out of their bathstoues all on a froth, and fuming as hoat almost as a pigge at a spit, and presently to leape into the riuer starke naked, or to powre colde water all ouer their bodies and that in the coldest of all the winter time. The women to mende the bad hue of their skinnes vse to paint their faces with white and red colours, so visibly, that euery man may perceiue it. Which is made no matter because it is common and liked well by their husbands: who make their wiues and daughters an ordinarie allowance to buy them colours to paint their faces withall, and delight themselues much to see them of fowle women to become such faire images. Thin parcheth the skinne, and helpeth to deforme them when their pinting is of.

They apparell themselues after the Greeke manner. [Sidenote: The Noblemans attire.] The Noblemans attire is on this fashion. First a Taffia, or little nightcappe on the head, that couereth litle more then his crowne, commonly verie rich wrought of silke and golde threede, and set with pearle and precious stone. His head he keepeth shauen close to the very skinne, except he be in some displeasure with the Emperour. Then hee suffereth his haire to growe and hang downe vpon his shoulders, couering his face as ugly and deformedly as he can. Ouer the Taffia hee weareth a wide cappe of blacke Foxe (which they account for the best furre) with a Tiara or long bonnet put within it, standing vp like a Persian or Babilonian hatte. About his necke (which is seene all bare) is a coller set with pearle and precious stone, about three or foure fingers broad. Next ouer his shirt, (which is curiously wrought, because he strippeth himselfe into it in the Sommer time, while he is within the house) is a Shepon, or light garment of silke, made downe to the knees, buttoned before: and then a Caftan or a close coat buttoned, and girt to him with a Persian girdle, whereat he hangs his kniues and spoone. This commonly is of cloth of gold, and hangeth downe as low as his ankles. Ouer that he weareth a lose garment of some rich silke, furred and faced about with some golde lace, called a Ferris. An other ouer that of chainlet, or like stufle called an Alkaben, sleeued and hanging lowe, and the cape commonly brooched, and set all with pearle. When hee goeth abroad, he casteth ouer all these (which are but sleight, though they seeme to be many) an other garment tailed an Honoratkey, like to the Alkaben, saue that it is made without a coller for the necke. And this is commonly of fine cloth or Camels haire. His buskins (which he weareth in stead of hose, with linnen folles vnder them in stead of boot hose) are made of a Persian leather called Saphian, embrodered with pearle. His vpper stockes commonly are of cloth of golde. When he goeth abroad, hee mounteth on horsebacke, though it be but to the next doore: which is the maner also of the Boiarskey, or Gentlemen.

[Sidenote: The Gentlemans apparel.] The Boiarskey or Gentlemans attire is of the same fashion, but differeth in stuffe: and yet he will haue his Caftan or vndercoat sometimes of cloth of golde, the rest of cloth, or silke.

[Sidenote: The Noble woman's attire.] The Noble woman (called Chyna Boiarshena) weareth on her head, first a cauil of some soft silke (which is commonly redde) and ouer it a fruntlet called Obrosa, of white colour. Ouer that her cappe (made after the coife fashion of cloth of gold) called Shapka Zempska, edged with some rich furre, and set with pearle and stone. Though they haue of late begunne to disdaine embrodering with pearle aboue their cappes, because the Diacks, and some Marchants wiues haue taken vp the fashion. In their ears they weare earerings (which they call Sargee) of two inches or more compasse, the matter of gold set with

Rubies or Saphires, or some like precious stone. In Sommer they goe often with kerchiefffes of fine white lawne, or cambricke, fastned vnder the chinne, with two long tassels pendent. The kerchiefe spotted and set thicke with rich pearle. When they ride or goe abroad in raynie weather, they weare white hattes with coloured bandes called Stapa Zemskoy. About their neckes they weare collers of three or foure fingers broad, set with rich pearle and precious stone. Their vpper garment is a loose gowne called Oposhen commonly of scarlet, with wide loose sleeues, hanging downe to the ground buttened before with great golde buttons or at least siluer and guilt nigh as bigge as a walnut. Which hath hanging ouer it fastned vnder the cappe, a large broad cape of some rich furre, that hangeth downe almost to the middes of their backes. Next vnder the Oposken [Trascriber's note: sic] or vpper garment, they weare another called a Leitnich that is made close before with great wide sleeues, the cuffe or halfe sleeue vp to the elbowes, commonly of cloth of golde: and vnder that a Ferris Zemskoy, which hangeth loose buttoned throughout to the very foote. On the hande wrests they weare very faire braselets, about two fingers broad of pearle and precious stone. They goe all in buskins of white, yellow, blew, or some other coloured leather, embrodered with pearle. This is the attire of the Noblewoman of Russia, when she maketh the best shewe of herselfe. The Gentlewomans apparell may differ in the stuffe, but is all one for the making or fashion.

[Sidenote: The Mousicks or common man attire.] As for the poore Mousick and his wife they goe poorely cladde. The man with his Honoratkey, or loose gowne to the small of the legge, tyed together with a lace before, of course white or blew cloth, with some Shube or long wastcoate of furre, or of sheepeskinne vnder it, and his furred cappe, and buskins. The poorer sort of them haue their Honoratkey, or vpper garment, made of Kowes haire. This is their winter habite. In the sommer time, commonly they weare nothing but their shirts on their backes, and buskins on their legges. The woman goeth in a red or blewe gowne, when she maketh the best shewe, and with some warme Shube of furre vnder it in the winter time. But in the sommer, nothing but her two shirts (for so they call them) one ouer the other, whether they be within doores, or without. On their heads, they weare caps of some coloured stuffe, many of veluet, or of cloth of gold: but for the most part kerchiefs. Without earings of siluer or some other mettall, and her crosse about her necke, you shall see no Russe woman, be she wife or maide.

* * * * *

The Lord Boris Phcodorowich his letter to the Right Honorable William Burghley Lord high Treasurer of England. &c.

[Sidenote: The Emperors stile increased.] By the grace of God the great Lord Emperor, and great Duke Theodore Iuanowich, great Lord, King, and great Duke of all Russia, of Volodemer, Mosco, and Nouogorod, king of Cazan, and Astracan, Lord of Vobsko, and great Duke of Smolensco, Tuer, Vghori, Permi, Viatsko, Bolgorie, and other places, Lorde and great Duke of
Nouogrod in the Lowe Countrey, of Chernigo, Rezan, Polotsky, Rostoue, Yeroslaue, Bealozera, and Liefland, of Oudorski, Obdorski, Condinski, and commander of all Sibierland, and the North coasts, great Lorde ouer the Countrey of Iuerski, Grisinski, Emperor of Kabardinski, and of the Countrey
Charchaski, and the Countrey of Gorsky, and Lord of many other regions.

From Boris Pheodorowich his Maiesties brother in law, master of his horses, gouernour of the territories of Cazan and Astracan, to William Lord Burghley, Lord high Treasurer to the most vertuous Ladie Elizabeth, Queene of England. France, and Ireland, and other dominions: I receiued your Lordships letters, wherein you write that you haue receiued very ioyfully my letters sent vnto you, and aduisedly read them, and imparted the same vnto her Maiestie: [Sidenote: The English Marchants complaints.] and that your Merchants finde themselues agreeued, that when they approch these parts, and are arriued here, they are not permitted to enter into a free and liberall course of barter, traffike, and exchange of their commodities, as heretofore they haue done, but are compelled before they can enter into any traffike to accept the Emperours waxe, and other goods, at high rates farre aboue their value, to their great losse: and that they are by reason of this restraint long holden vpon these coasts to the danger of wintering by the way. Hereafter there shalbe no cause of offence giuen to the Marchants of the Queenes Maiestie Queene Elizabeth: they shall not be forced to any thing, nether are there or shall be any demands made of custome or debts. Such things as haue beene heretofore demaunded, all such things haue beene already vpon their petition and supplication commaunded to be discharged. I haue sollicited his Maiestie for them, that they be not troubled hereafter for those matters, and that a fauourable hand be caried ouer them. And according to your request I will be a meane to the Emperour for them in all their occasions, and will my selfe shew them my fauorable countenance. And I pray you (William Burghley) to signifie to her Maiesties Merchants that I promise to haue a care of them, and for the Queenes Maiestie of Englands sake, I will take her Merchants into my protection, and will defend them as the Emperours selected people vnder the Emperors commission: and by mine appointment all his Maiesties officers and authorized people shall be careful ouer them. [Sidenote: English Marchants in great fauour with the Emperor.] The Emperors gracious fauor towards them was neuer such as it is now. And where you write that at the

Port the Emperors officers sell their waxe by commission at a set rate giuen them, farre aboue the value and that they enforce your Marchants to accept it, they deny that they take any such course, but say they barter their waxe for other wares, and also put their waxe to sale for readie money to your Merchants, according to the worth thereof, and as the price goeth in the custome house here. It hath beene heretofore deare, and now is sold as good cheape as in any other place, and as they can best agree: they enforce no man to buy it, but rather kepe it: therefore your Marchants haue no iust cause to make any such report. I haue expressely giuen order, that there shall be no such course vsed to enforce them, but to buy according to their owne willes, and to tarrie at the port or to depart at their pleasure. [Sidenote: Halfe the debt of Antony Marsh remitted.] And as touching the customes alreadie past, and debts demanded at your Merchants hands, whereof you write: Our Lord great Emperour and great Duke Theodore Iuanowich of all Russia of famous memory hath shewed his Maiesties especial fauour and loue, for the great loue of his welbeloued sister Queene of England, and by my peticion and mediation, whereas there was commandement giuen to take Marshes whole debt of your Merchants and factors, it is moderated to the halfe, and for the other halfe, commandement giuen it should not be taken, and the Merchants billes to be deliuered them. And to the end hereafter that her Maiesties Merchants moue no contention betwixt our Lord the Emperor and great Duke of Russia, and his welbeloued sister Queene Elizabeth, his Maiestie desireth order to be giuen, that your Marchants doe deale iustly in their traffike, and plainely without fraud or guile. And I will be a fauourer of them aboue all others, vnder his Maiesties authoritie: themselues shall see it. [Sidenote: Ann. Dom. 1590.] Written in our great Lorde the Emperours citie of Mosco in the moneth of Iuly. 7099.

* * * * *

The Queenes Maiesties letter to Theodore Iuanouich Emperour of Russia, 1591.

Elizabeth by the grace of God Queene of England, France, and Ireland, defender of the faith, &c. to the right high, mighty, and right noble prince Theodore Iuanouich great Lord, King, and great Duke of all Russia, Volodemer, Mosco, Nouogrod, King of Cazan, and Astracan, Lord of Vobsko, and great Duke of Smolensko, Otuer, Vghory, Perme, Viatski, Bolgory, and other places: Lord and great Duke of Nouogrod in the low countrey, of Chernigo, Rezan, Polotsky, Rostoue, Yeraslaue, Bealozero, and Lifland, of Oudorsky, Obdorsky, Condinsky, and commander of all Sibierland and the North coasts, great Lord ouer the country of Tuersky, Grisinsky, Emperor of Kabardinsky, and of the countrey of Charkasky, and of the countrey of Gorsky, and Lord of many other countreys, our most deare and louing brother, greeting. Right noble and excellent prince, we haue receiued your Maiesties letters brought ouer by our merchants in their returne of their [Marginal note: 1590.] last voyage from your port of S. Nicholas: which letters we haue aduisedly read and considered, and thereby perceiue that your Maiesty doth greatly mislike of our late employment of Ierome Horsey into your dominions as our messenger with our Highnesse letters and also that your Maiesty doth thinke that we in our letters sent by the sayd messenger haue not obserued that due order or respect which apperteined to your princely maiesty, in the forme of the said letter, aswel touching the inlargement of your Maiesties stile and titles of honor which your Maiesty expected to haue bene therein more particularly expressed, as also in the adding of our greatest seale or signet of armes to the letters which we send to so great a Prince as your Maiesty is: in any of which points we would haue bene very loth willingly to haue giuen iust cause of offence thereby to our most deare and louing brother. And as touching the sayd messenger Ierome Horsey we are sory that contrary to our expectation he is fallen into your Maiesties displeasure, whom we minde not to mainteine in any his actions by which he hath so incurred your Maiesties mislike: yet that we had reason at such time as we sent him to your Maiesty to use his seruice as our messenger, we referre our selues to your princely iudgement, praying your Maiesty to reduce into your minde the especiall commendation, which in your letters written vnto vs in the yeere 1585, you made of the sayd Ierome Horsey his behauiour in your dominions: at which time your Maiesty was pleased to vse his seruice as your messenger to vs, requiring our answere of your letters to be returned by him and by none other. That imployment, with other occasions taken by your Maiesty to vse the seruice of the sayd Ierome Horsey (as namely in the yeere 1587) when your Maiesty sent him to vs againe with your letters, and your liberall and princely priuiledge at our request granted to our merchants (for which we haue heretofore giuen thanks to your Maiesty, so doe we hereby reiterate our thankfulnesse for the same) mooued vs to be of minde, that we could not make choise of any of our subiects so fit a messenger to your Maiesty as he, whom your Maiesty had at seuerall times vsed vpon your owne occasions into this our Realme. But least your highnesse should continue of the minde that the letters which you sent by our ambassador Giles Fletcher (wherein some mention was made of your conceiued displeasure against the sayd Horsey) came not to our hands, and that wee were kept ignorant of the complaint which your Maiesty made therein against the sayd Horsey, we do not deny but that we were acquainted aswell by our ambassadour as by those letters of some displeasure conceiued against him by your Maiesty: but your sayd letters giuing onely a short generall mention of some misdemeanour committed by him, expressing no particulars, we were of opinion that this offence was not so hainous, as that it might vtterly extinguish all your former princely fauour towards him, but that vpon his humble submission to your Maiesty, or vpon better examination of the matter of the displeasure conceiued against him, the offence might haue beene either remitted, or he thereof might haue cleared himselfe. And to that end we were not onely by his great importunity long sollicited, but by the intercession of some of our Nobility giuing credit to his owne defence, we were intreated on his behalfe to vse his seruice once againe into Russia as our messenger to your Maiestie, whereby he might haue opportunity to cleare himselfe, and either by his answere or by his submission recouer your Maiesties former fauour: whereunto our princely nature was mooued to yeeld, wishing the good of our subiect so farre foorth as his desert might carry him, or his innocencie cleare him.

Thus noble Prince, our most louing and dearest brother, it may appeare vnto your Maiesty how we were induced to vse the seruice of the sayd messenger, aswell for the recouery of your Maiesties fauour towards him (if he had been found woorthy of it) as for experience of the maners and fashions of your countrey, where he hath bene much conuersant. But sith by your Maiesties letters it appeareth that he hath not cleared himselfe in your Maiesties sight, we meane not to vse him in any such price hereafter.

And as touching your Maiesties conceit of the breuitie which we vsed in the setting downe of your Maiesties stile and titles of honour: as nothing is further from vs, then to abridge so great and mighty a Prince of the honour due vnto him (whom we holde for his greatnesse to deserue more honour then we are able to giue him) so shall we need no further nor surer argument to cleare vs of the suspicion of the detracting from your Maiesty any part of your iust and princely honor and greatnesse, then the consideration of our owne stile, which is thus contracted, videlicet, Elizabeth by the grace of God Queene of England, France, and Ireland, defender of the faith &c. which kingdomes and dominions of ours are expressed by these generall words, videlicet, England, France, and Ireland: in euery of which there are seuerall principalities, dukedomes, earledomes, prouinces and countreys: which being seuerally expressed would enlarge much our stile, and make it of great length: which by our progenitours hath not bene vsed: notwithstanding, we thinke it no dishonour to vs, compendiously to abridge the same in all our writings and letters written to what Prince, King, or Potentate soeuer. Whereupon we inferre, that holding your Maiesties generall stile, we offer your Highnesse no dishonour in not expressing all the particular prouinces: albeit we can willingly content our selfe, upon the knowledge of your vsages and customes, to obserue that course, which your selfe shall thinke most honourable. And for the sealing vp of our letters which we write to all our allies, kinsmen, and friends, Kings and Princes, we haue in vse two seuerall seales: both which we esteeme alike honourable, being our princely seales. And as the volume of our letters falleth out to be great or small, so accordingly is our greater or lesser seale annexed to the sayd letters, without esteeming either of them more or lesse honourable then the other. So as, our most louing and dearest brother, in the said letters there was nothing done of purpose to detract from your Maiesty any thing, of the vsuall regard, which our Highnesse was woont to yeeld vnto your most noble father of famous memory Iuan Basiliuich Emperor of al Russia, or to your selfe, our dearest brother. For the residue of the points of your Maiesties letters concerning the entertainement of our ambassadour, and proceeding in the cause of Anthonie Marsh we holde our selfe satisfied with your princely answere, and doe therein note an honourable and princely care in your Maiestie to preuent the like troubles, controuersies and sutes, that Marshes cause stirred vp betweene our merchants and your subiects, which is, that your Maiestie doeth purpose from time to time to purge your Countrey of such straglers of our subiects, as doe or shall hereafter abide there, and are not of the Company of our merchants, but contemptuously depart out of our land without our Highnesse licence: of which sort there are presented vnto vs from our merchants the names of these seuerall persons, videlicet, Richard Cocks, Bennet Iackman, Rainold Kitchin, Simon Rogers, Michael Lane, Thomas Worsenham: whom it may please your Maiesty by your princely order to dismisse out of your land, that they may be sent home in the next shippes, to auoid the mislike which their residence in those parts might breed to the disturbance of our brotherly league, and the impeaching of the entercourse.

And whereas, most louing and dearest brother, one William Turnebull a subiect of ours is lately deceased in your kingdome, one with whom our merchants haue had much controuersie for great summes of money due vnto them by him while he was their Agent in their affayres of merchandises: which differences by arbitrable order were reduced to the summe of 3000 rubbles, and so much should haue beene payed by him as may appeare by your Maiesties councell or magistrates of iustice by very credible information and testimony: and whereas also the sayd Turnbull was further indebted by billes of his own hand to diuers of our subiects, amounting in the whole, to the summe of 1326 pounds, which billes are exemplified vnder our great seale of England, and to be sent ouer with this bearer: of which summes he hath often promised payment: it may please your most excellent Maiestie in your approoued loue to iustice, to giue order to your fauourable councell and magistrates, that those seuerall debts may be satisfied to our merchants and subiects out of the goods, merchandise, and debts which are due to the state of the sayd Turnbull: whereof your Maiesties councell shalbe informed by the Agent of our merchants.

[Sidenote: The Emperour seised our merchants goods.] We trust we shall not need to make any new request by motion to your Maiesty that some order might be taken for the finding out of the rest of our merchants goods seised to your maiesties vse in the hands and possession of Iohn Chappel their seruant, being a thing granted, and no doubt already performed by your Maiesties order. We therfore intreat your Maiesty, that as conueniently as may be, satisfaction or recompense be giuen to our said merchants towards the repairing of their sundry great losses aswell therein as otherwise by them of late sundry wayes sustained. And lastly, our most deare and louing brother, as nothing in all these our occasions is to be preferred before our entire league and amitie, descending vpon vs as an inheritance, in succession from both our ancestours and noble progenitours: so let us be carefull on both sides by all good meanes to holde and continue the same to our posterity for euer. And if any mistaking or errour of either side do rise, in not accomplishing of circumstances agreeable to the fashion of either of our countreys and kingdomes, let the same vpon our enterchangeable letters be reconciled, that our league and amitie be no way impeached for any particular occasion whatsoeuer. And thus we recommend your Maiesty to the tuition of the most High. From our royall Palace of Whitehall the 14 of Ianuary, anno Domini 1591.

* * * * *

The Queenes Maiesties letters to the Lord Boris Pheodorowich.

Elizabeth by the grace of God Queene of England, France, and Ireland, defendour of the faith, &c. to the right honourable and noble prince Lord Boris Pheodorowich Godonoua, Master of the horses to the great and mightie Emperour of Russia, his highnesse lieutenant of Cazan and Astracan, our most deare and louing cousin, greeting. Right honourable, it hath appeared vnto vs vpon the reading and perusing of the Letters lately sent vnto our Highnesse from our deare and louing brother the Emperour, in what part his Maiestie tooke the late employment of our messenger Ierome Horsey in our affaires into Russia: wherein we doe also finde the honourable endeuour vsed by your Lordship to appease his Highnesse mislike and exception taken aswell to the person of our Messenger, as to our princely letters sent by him: both of which points we haue answered in our letters sent by this bearer directed to our sayd louing brother the Emperour: vpon perusing whereof we doubt not but his Maiestie will be well satisfied touching our sayd Messenger and former letters. And for the honourable course holden by your Lordship in the interposing of your opinion and fauourable construction in a thing which might grow to the offence of the league and amitie standing betweene your Soueraigne Lord and vs (wherein your Lordship performed the office of an honourable and graue Councellour) we take our selfe beholding to your Lordship for your readinesse in that behalfe, and doe assure our selfe that the same did proceed of the especiall loue and kinde affection that your Lordship hath euer borne and continued towards vs, whereof our princely nature will neuer be vnmindfull. We haue bene also from time to time made acquainted by our chiefe and principall Councellour William Lord Burghley, Lord high Treasurour of our Highnesse Realme of England, of your letters which haue passed betweene your Lordship and him, concerning the entercourse of our Merchants trafficke in your Countreys, and of the honourable offices done by your Lordship with the Emperpur in fauour of our sayd Marchants. And lastly (which wee take a most assured argument of your vndoubted loue and affection towards vs) that your Lordship hath vouchsafed, of purpose taken into your hands the protection of our sayd Merchants, and the hearing and determining of all their causes and occasions whatsoeuer, which shall concerne them or their trade. All which wee conceiue to be done for our sake, and therefore do acknowledge ourselues to be, and still will continue beholding vnto you for the same.

And whereas we haue made mention in our sayd letters written to our louing brother the Emperour of certeine debts due aswell to our merchants, as to other of our subiects by one William Turnebull a subiect of ours late deceased in Russia, wee pray you to be referred to the sayd letter. And forasmuch as the sayd cause will fall vnder your Lordships iurisdiction by reason of your acceptation of all their causes into your patronage and protection: we are so well assured of your honourable inclination to iustice, and your good affection towards our merchants for our sake, that we shall not need to intreat your honourable furtherance either of iustice or expedition in the sayd cause. And lastly considering that your noble linage together with your great wisedome and desert hath made you a principall Councellour and directour of the state of so great a Monarchie, whereby your aduice and direction is followed in all things that doe concerne the same, we haue giuen order to our sayd principall Counsellonr William Lord Burghley, treasurour of our Realme of England, that as any occasion shall arise to the hinderance of the entercourse betweene these Countreyes, or of the priuiledges graunted by his Maiestie to our merchants, that he may by aduertisement treat with your Lordshippe thereupon: which we by reason of our great princely affayres can not so conueniently at all times doe with such expedition as the cause may require. And thus with our princely commendations we bidde you farewell. From our royall Pallace of Whitehall the foureteenth day of Ianuarie, Anno Domini 1591.

* * * * *

To the right honourable my very good Lord, the Lord Boris Pheodorowich, Master of the horses to the great and mighty Emperour of Russia, his Highnesse Lieutenant of Cazan and Astracan, William Cecil Lord

Burghley,
Knight of the noble Order of the Garter, and Lord high Treasurer of England sendeth greeting.

Right honourable my very good Lord, vpon the last returne of our merchants shippes out of Russia, there was brought vnto my handes, by one Francis Cherrie an English merchant, a letter directed to the Queenes Maiestie, from the great and mightie Emperour of Russia, and another letter from your Lordship directed to me: which sayd letter written from the Emperor to her Maiesty hath beene considerately and aduisedly by her Highnesse read and perused, and the matter of complaint against Ierome Horsey therein comprised thorowly examined: which hath turned the same Horsey to some great displeasure. I did also acquaint our Maiesty with the contents of your Lordships letters written to mee, and enformed her of your Lordships honourable fauour shewed to her Highnesse merchants from time to time: who tooke the same in most gracious part, and confessed her selfe infinitly beholding vnto your Lordship for many honourable offices done for her sake, the which she meant to acknowledge by her letters to be written to your Lordship vnder her princely hand and seale. And forasmuch as it hath pleased your good Lordshippe to take into your handes the protection of her Maiesties merchants, and the redresse of such iniuries as are, or shall be offered vnto them contrary to the meaning of the priuiledges and the free liberty of the entercourse, wherein some points your Lordship hath already vsed a reformation, as appeareth by your sayd letters: yet the continuance of traffique moouing, new occasions and other accidents tending to the losse of the sayd merchants, whereof some particulars haue beene offered vnto me to treat with your lordship vpon: I thought it good to referre them to your honourable consideration, that order might be taken in the same, for that they are apparantly repugnant to the Emperours letters written to her Maiestie, and doe much restraine the liberty of the trade: one is, that at the last comming of our merchants to the port of Saint Michael the Archangel, [Sidenote: This is a new port.] where the mart is holden, their goods were taken by the Emperours officers for his Highnesse seruice at such rates, as the sayd officers were disposed to set vpon them, so farre vnder their value, that the merchants could not assent to accept of those prices: [Sidenote: The English merchants 3 weeks restrained from their Mart.] which being denied, the sayd officers restrained them of all further traffique for the space of three weekes, by which meanes they were compelled to yeeld vnto their demaund how vnwillingly soeuer. Another is, that our sayd merchants are driuen to pay the Emperours officers custome for all such Russe money as they bring downe from the Mosco to the Sea side to employ there at the Mart within the Emperours owne land; which seemeth strange vnto me, considering the same money is brought from one place of the Countrey to another, and there imployed without any transport ouer the borders [Footnote: The original reads: *ouer the sayd of money*. As this is unintelligible, I have ventured to insert a new reading.] of the sayd country. These interruptions and impositions seeme not to stand with the liberties of the Emperours priuileges and freedome of the entercourse, which should be restrained neither to times or conditions, but to be free and absolute: whereof it may please your Lordship to be aduised, and to continue your honourable course holden betweene the Emperour and her Maiesty, to reconcile such differences as any occasion doth offer to their league or trafficke. Thus not doubting of your Lordships furtherance herein, I humbly take my leaue of your good Lordship. From her Maiesties royall palace of Whitehall this 15 of Ianuary 1591.

* * * * *

A letter from the Emperour of Russia, Theodore Iuanouich to the Queenes Maiestie.

Through the tender mercie of our God, whereby the day-spring from on high hath visited vs, thereby to guide our feet into the way of peace. Euen this our God by mercy we glorifie in Trinitie.

[Sidenote: The emperours stile lately enlarged.] We the great Lord, King and great Duke Theodore Iuanowich, gouernour of all Russia, of Volodimer, Mosco, and Nouogrod, King of Cazan and Astracan, Lord of Vobsco, and great Duke of Smolensco, Otuer, Vghori, Perme, Viatsky, Bulgary, and other regions, Lord and great Duke also of Nouogrod in the low countrey, of Chernigo, of Rezan, Polotsko, Rostoue, Yeroslaue, Bealozera, and of Lifland, of Vdorsky, Obdorsky, Condinsky, and all the countrey of Siberia, and commander of all the North parts, and Lord ouer the countrey of Iuersky, and King of Grusinsky, and of the countrey of Kabardinsky, Cherchasky, and Duke of Igorsky, Lord and ruler of many countreys more etc. To our louing sister Elizabeth Queene of England, France, and Ireland, &c. Louing sister, your letters sent by your seruant Thomas Lind, we haue receiued, and read what you haue written in the same touching our title, and touching your order holden in your letters heretofore sent vs by your seruant Ierome Horsey: wherein you haue answered vs sufficiently and most graciously.

And whereas your Maiestie hath written in your letter concerning the goods of William Turnebull late deceased in our kingdome, that your subiects, for whom he was factour, should haue debts growing vnto them from him by account: we at your Maiesties request haue caused not onely order to be taken, but for your Highnesse sake, louing sister, we haue caused the goods to be sought out and deliuered to your merchants Agent and his company, together with his stuffe, bookes, billes and writings, as also money to the value of sixe hundred rubbles, which Christopher Holmes and Francis

Cherry are to pay for ycarie [Footnote: Caviare.]: [Marginal note: This is a dainty meat made of the roas of Sturgeons.] and we haue set at libertie the said Turnebulles kinseman Raynold Kitchin and his fellowes, and deliuered them to your merchants Agent.

And further, where you write vnto vs for such your subiects as letting, either in the Mosco, the Treasurehouse, or else where by any of our authorised people, but absolutely to bee at free libertie at their owne will and pleasure. And also I will continue to be their protectour and defendour in all causes, by our Lorde and kings Maiesties order and commaundement: as it shall be knowen and certified you by your people resident here in the Mosco.

[Sidenote: Anno Domini 1592.] Written in our kings Maiesties royall citie of Mosco from the beginning of the world, 7101. yeere, in the moneth of Ianuary.

* * * * *

A most gracious Letter giuen to the English Merchants Sir Iohn Hart and his company, by Theodore Iuanowich, the King, Lord, and great duke of all Russia, the onely vpholder thereof.

The onely God omnipotent before all eternitie, his will be done without ende: the Father, Sonne, and holy Ghost we glorifie in Trinitie. Our onely God the maker of all things and worker of all in all euery where with plentifull increase: for which cause he hath giuen life to man to loue him, and to trust in him: Our onely God which inspireth euery one of vs his holy children with his word to discerne good through our Lord Iesus Christ, and the holy quickning spirit of life now in these perilous times establish vs to keepe the right scepter, and suffer vs to reigne of our selues to the good profit of the land, and to the subduing of the people together with the enemies, and to, the mainteinance of vertue.

We the great Lord, king and great duke Theodore Iuanowich, of all Russia the onely vpholder, of Volodimer, Mosco, and Nouogrod, King of Cazan, and king of Astracan, Lord of Vobsco, and great duke of Smolensko, of Otuer, Vghorie, Permia, Viatski, Bulgari, and other regions, great duke also of Nouogrod in the lowe Countrey, of Chernigo, of Rezan, Polotski Rostoue, Yaruslaue, Bealozero, and of Liefland, of Vdorski, Obdorski, Condenski, and commaunder of all the Countrey of Siberi and of the North parts, and Lord ouer the Countrey of Iuerski, Grusinski, and King ouer the Countrey of Igorski, and ruler ouer many other kingdomes and Lordships more.

Our princely Maiestie at the request of our brother in lawe Boris Feodorowich Godenoua our seruant, and Master of our horses, generall

Comptroller of our house, and gouernour of the Lordships and kingdomes of Casan and Astracan: vnto the English merchants Sir Iohn Hart knight, sir William Webbe knight, Richard Salkenstow Alderman, Nicholas Mosely alderman, Robert Doue, Wil. Garrowe, Iohn Harbey, Robert Chamberlaine, Henry Anderson, Iohn Woodworth, Francis Cherry, Iohn Merrick, and Cristopher Holmes; hath gratiously giuen leaue to come and go with their ships into our kingdome and territories of Duina with all kind of commodities at their pleasures to trafficke from the seaside to our roial city of Mosco, and in all other cities, townes, countries and territories of our whole kingdom of Mosco: vpon the humble petition and sute of the saide English merchants sir Iohn Hart and his company, wee haue giuen them leaue to passe and trafficke into all parts of our dominions and territories of Mosco, and to our inheritance of Nougrod and Plesco with their wares and commodities without paying any custome or dueties.

We the great Lord, king, and great Duke Theodore Iuanowich of all Russia, haue firmely giuen and graunted vnto the aforesaide English merchants Sir Iohn Hart and his company, for the loue we beare to our deare sister Queene Elizabeth, we I say of our gracious goodnes haue giuen leaue to trauel and passe to our royall seat of Mosco, and to all the parts of our kingdome with all kinde of commodities, and to trafficke with all kinde of wares at their owne pleasure, without paying any custome of their said wares.

To you our Customers we wil and command not to take any maner of custome of the said merchants and their company, neither for entering, weying nor passing by or through any place of our territories, nor for custome, of iudgement by Lawe, or for their person or persons: nor any duties ouer bridges, or for certificats or processes, or for conducting ouer any streames or waters, or for any other customes or dueties that may be named: we wil and straitly commaund you not to take any of them in any wise.

Prouided alwayes, that the saide merchants shall not colour any strangers wares, nor bring them into our countrey, nor fauour them colourably, nor sel for any stranger. To you our subiects also we command, not to meddle or deale with any wares of strangers colourably, nor to haue them by you in keeping, nor to offer to sel their commodities: but themselues to sel their owne commodities in change or otherwise as they may or can. And in al townes, cities, countreys, or any part of our dominions and territories it shalbe lawful for the foresaid merchants and their the sayd Turnebulles stuffe and other things, as billes, books and writings. All which shall be deliuered to your merchants Agent and his fellowes, and in money 600 rubbles of the sayd Turnebulles.

And touching your merchants, I will haue a great care ouer them, and protect them, whereby they shall suffer no damages in their trade: and all kinde of trafficke in merchandise shall be at their libertie.

Written in our Lord and Kings Maiesties royall citie of Mosco, in the yeere from the beginning of the world 7101, in the moneth of Ianuarie.

* * * * *

A letter from the Lord Boris Pheodorowich to the right honourable Lord William Burghley, Lord high Treasurer of England.

By the grace of God great Lord, King, and great Duke Theodor Iuanowich, gouernour of Russia, Volodimer, Mosco, and Nouogrod, King of Cazan and Astracan, Lord of Vobsco, and great Duke of Smolensco, Otuer, Vghory, Perme, Viatsky, Bulgary, and other regions, Lord and great Duke of all Nouogrod in the low countreys, of Chernigo, of Liffeland, of Vdorsky, Obdorsky, Condinsky, and all the countrey of Sibery, and commaunder of all the North parts, and Lord ouer the countrey of Iuersky, and King of Grusinsky, and of the countreys of Kabardinsky, Cherchasky, and Duke of Igorsky, Lord and ruler of many Countreys more &c. His princely Maiesties seruant, Lord and Master of his horses, and high Steward of his house, President of the territories of Cazan and Astracan, Boris Pheodorowich Godonoua, to the most honourable Counsellor of the most resplendent mightie great Lady Elizabeth Queene of England, France, and Ireland, William Burghley, Lord, and Knight of the Garter, high Treasurour of England, sendeth greeting.

[Sidenote: M. Francis Cherie.] I perceiue by your letter that your merchants last shippes came home in saftie, and that you haue receiued the letters sent by them, by the hands of Francis Cherie, one from our Lord and great King of all Russia his Maiesty, vnto your Queenes most excellent Maiesty, and one from me to her Highnesse, and one from my selfe to you: and the contents thereof you haue caused to be read and well vnderstood at large. And whatsoeuer is therein written concerning Ierome Horsey, you haue sought out the ground thereof, and that he is in great displeasure. And her Highnesse hath written in her letter concerning her Maiesties merchants, that whereas I haue taken them into protection, she taketh it very louingly and kindely, that for her sake they haue receiued so great kindnesse.

And touching the damages and hinderances which your merchaunts haue sustained by meanes of the Emperours authorised people and officers, and that they were not permitted to traffike at libertie at the Sea port in the yeere 1589, for the space of three weekes, it hath beene against the Emperours Maiesties will and pleasure, as also against mine. Where you desire and wish that betweene our Emperours Maiestie, and your Queenes

Maiestie, their loue and amitie may not bee seperated at any time, but to continue: and you request mee that I should be good vnto the English Merchants, and to defend them from all such domages hereafter: your honours louing letter I haue therein throughly considered: and as I haue bene heretofore, so I will still continue to be a meane betwixt our Lorde and kings Maiestie, and your great Lady the Queene her hignesse, for the mainteyning of brotherly loue and amitie, most ioyfully and willingly, as God knoweth, aswel hereafter as I haue been heretofore: praying you to doe the like also. Mine onely desire is for your most excellent Princesse sake, to do all that lyeth in mee for the ayding, helping and protecting of her Maiesties merchants, by the order and commaundement of our Lord and king his Maiestie.

And to that ende I haue giuen order to all our authorised peopie to bee careful ouer them, and to defende them in all causes, and to giue them free libertie to trafficke at their owne willes and pleasures. It may bee that your merchants doe not certifie you the trueth of all things, nor make knowen vnto your honour my readinesse to protect them: And howe my Letters and Commissions are sent to all authorised people for them, that they shoulde ayde and assist them, according to the tenour of my Letters, to all others that bee in authoritie vnder the said Officers or otherwise.

Also your honour writeth of the debarring of your merchants at the sea port from their accustomed libertie of enterchangeable trafficke and bartar. Touching which complaint search and inquisition hath bene made, and commaundement giuen, that your Queenes Maiesties merchants at the Sea side, and in all places where the trade is, doe not sustaine any domage or hinderance hereafter, but that they shalbe at libertie without any hindering or haue departed out of your maiesties Realme secretly without licence, that we should giue order to send them home: concerning such your subiects for which you haue written vnto our Maiestie by letters, we will cause search to be made, and such as are willing to goe home into your kingdome, we will command forthwith to be deliuered vnto your merchants Agent, and so to passe. And such of your Maiesties people as haue giuen themselues vnder our gouernment as subiects, we thinke it not requisite to grant to let them passe.

And further, where you haue written vnto vs concerning the goods of Iohn Chappell, we haue written heretofore the whole discourse thereof, not once, but sundry times, and therefore it is not needful to write any more thereof. And such goods as were found out of the goods of the sayd Chappell, the money thereof was restored to your Maiesties people William Turnbull and his fellowes. [Sidenote: M. Thomas Lind.] Your Maiesties seruant Thomas Lind we haue sent with our letters the same way whereby he came into our kingdome. The long abiding heere of your Maiesties seruant in our kingdome, was for the comming of your people from the Sea port. [Sidenote: 1592.] Written in our princely court and royall seat in the city of Mosco in the yeere from the beginning of the world 7101, in the moneth of Ianuary.

* * * * *

To the Queenes most excellent Maiestie from the Lord Boris Pheodorouich Godonoua.

By the grace of God great Lord and great Duke Theodore Iuanouich gouernour of Russia, Volodimer, Mosco, and Nouogrod, King of Cazan and Astracan, Lord of Vobsko, and great Duke of Smolensco, Otuer, Vgbori, Perme, Viatsky, Bulgary, and other regions, Lord and great Duke of Nouogrod in the low countrey, of Chernigo, of Rezan, Polotsko, Rostoue, Ieroslaue, Bealozera, and of Lifland, of Vdorsky, Obdorsky, Condinsky, and all the countrey of Sibery, and commander of all the North parts, and Lord ouer the countrey of Iuersky, and King of Grusinsky, and of the countrey of Kabardinsky, Cherchasky, and duke of Igorsky, Lord and ruler of many countreys more, &c.

Most resplendent Queene Elizabeth of England, France, and Ireland, &c. his princely Maiesties seruant, Lord and Master of his horses, and high Steward of his house, and President of the territories of Cazan and Astracan, Boris Pheodorouich Godonoua, vnto your most excellent Maiesty, great Ladie Queene Elizabeth, send my humble commendations. [Sidenote: The Empresse Irene deliuered of a daughter.] It hath pleased your Maiestie to write vnto me your gracious and princely letter by your seruant Thomas Lind: which letter I receiued with all humblenesse. During the time of the abode of your Messenger Thomas Lind here in the Mosco, it pleased God of his mercifulnesse, and our Lady the mother of God, and holy Saints, by the prayers of our lord and king his Maiestie Theodore Iuanouich ouer all Russia gouernour, the right beleeuer and louer of Christ, to send our Queene and gracious Lady Irene a yoong Princesse, to the great ioy and comfort of our kingdome, named Pheodocine. Wherefore we giue all honour and glory to the almightie God vnspeakable, whose giftes had beene manifolde with mercie vnto vs: for which all wee Christians laud and praise God.

After all this your seruant was occasioned to stay vntill the comming of your merchants from the sea port.

Touching the letters which you haue receiued from your louing qbrother our Lord and Master by your ambassadour, therein you perceiue sufficiently my good meaning, in trauailing for the continuance of amitie and friendship betwixt you mighty great princes, in the which I will continue mine endeauour. Also your merchants I haue taken into my protection for to defend them for the loue I beare to your Maiestie. As heeretofore I haue done it willingly, and with great care of their good, so I meane to continue so farre as God will giue me leaue: to the end that brotherly loue be holden betweene you princes without disturbance.

As I haue beene to your merchants in times past, so now by the permission and commandement of our Lord and Master, I will be their defendour in all causes: and will cause all our authorised people to fauour them and to defend them, and to giue them free liberty to buy and sell at their pleasure. The merchants doe not certifie your princely Maiestie of all our friendship and fauour shewed vnto them from time to time. And whereas your Maiestie hath now written to our Lord and Master for the debts which your merchants ought to haue of William Turnebull lately disceased, I hauing perused your Maiesties letter, whereby I am requested to be a meane for the recouerie and obtaining of their sayd debts, I haue moued it to our Lord and King his Maiestie, that order may be giuen therein: and that his kinseman Rainold Kitchin with three persons more may be sent ouer together with company to sell or barter away their owne commodities in change or otherwise, for or at their pleasure as they will. And whensoeuer the said merchants or any of them come into our territories of great Nouogrod or Plesco, or to any other parts of our kingdome with their wares, by virtue of these our maiesties letters we straitly charge and command you our Captaines, generals, and all other that be authorised or in office, to suffer the aforesaid merchants to passe and repasse, and to take no kinde of custome or dutie of them, or any of their goods, howsoeuer it may haue name: nor in no place else where they shall come in all our kingdome. Likewise if they sell not nor buy no wares, you shall take no custome, but suffer them quietly to passe where they will with their goods. Of our gratious goodness and meere goodwill haue giuen the said merchants leaue to trafficke, throughout all our kingdomes, and in all townes and cities with all maner of wares and commodities without paying any custome or dutie. Wheresoeuer they shal happen to sel or barter away any of their commodities to our subiects, they are to barter or sell by wholesale, and not by retalie, as by the yard or by the ounce in their houses or elsewhere: but by the packe or whole clothes, veluets, damasks, taffaties by the piece, and not by the yard: and al other wares that are to be sold by weight, they are to be sold not by the ounce, but by great sale. Your wines shalbe solde by hogs heads, pipes or buttes, but not by quartes nor pintes.

The said English merchants are to sel or barter away their owne commodities themselues, and not to suffer any Russes to buy or sell for them: nor to cary or tranport any wares of strangers in stead of their owne in no wise. And if the saide English merchants shall be desirous to sell any of their commodities at Colmogro, or vpon the Riuer of Duina, or at Vologhda or at Yeraslaue: when as the saide merchants haue solde in any of the saide Townes, Cities or territories, then you our officers and authorised people by vertue of this our gratious letter wee will and straitly commaund not to take any custome of the aforesaid merchants, howsoeuer it may be named.

Also whensoeuer the saide English merchants or any of their factours shalbe desirous to hire carriers to carry their wares to any place of our dominions or Cities, it shalbe at their choyse and pleasure to hier them the best they can, and where they will, either watermen to rowe, or vessels.

Also when any of the said merchants themselues, or any of theirs are desirous to trauel into any part of our dominions, or into any other kingdomes, or into their owne kingdome if any of our treasure be deliuered to them, they to take it with them, and to sel it in bartar or otherwise for such wares as are most requisit and necessary to be brought into our kingdome and to be deliuered into our treasury. You our nobilitie, generals & al others in authority suffer them to passe through al our cities, towns & countries without taking any custome of them. And when the said merchants haue done their traffick in any place & come to the Mosco, they shal make it knowen at their arriual at the house of Chancery and Secretariship to Vasili Shalcan. And further when there come any English Merchants with their ships or vessels by sea, that by mishap shalbe cast away vpon any of our shoars or costes, we wil and command you to ayde & helpe them, and to seeke for their goods so perished by any casualtie, and to be restored againe to the saide English merchants or their assignes without any prolonging or detayning. As also if any of the aforesaide merchants goods be found in any part of our coastes or streames and they not present themselues, let the sayd goods be taken and layd vp in safetie in some place or other, and be deliuered to the aforesaid merchants or their factors, vnder penaltie of our displeasure.

Furthermore we King, Lord and great duke of all Russia, of our gracious goodnesse giue vnto the English merchants and their company, their house in the Citie of Mosco lying hard by the Church of S. Marke behinde the market place: which they shall keepe and remaine therein after their old accustomed vse. Prouided always that they shall keepe one Russe porter or one of their owne people, & may keepe any other Russe seruant at their discretion. Also their houses in sundry places, as at Ieraslaue, Vologhda, Colmogro, and at S. Michael Archangel, all these houses they shall keepe and vse at their owne pleasure, according to our former letters patents without paying any dutie, rent, or custome. Nor you the communaltie of the said townes shal take any thing of them or theirs for any duetie that should belong to you, especially of the houses aforesaid: but the said

English merchants shal enioy them peaceably for themselues and their families, but shall not suffer any other strangers Russes or others to vse the aforesaid houses. Also you shall suffer them to lay their wares and commodities in their warehouses, and to sell their commodities to whom they please without let or hindrance, by vertue of this our gratious letter.

Their housekeeper being a Russe shall not vndertake to meddle, or sell any of their wares without they themselues be present, nor to buy any thing for them.

Also it shalbe lawfull for the said merchants when they shal arriue at their port to lade and vnlade their merchandises as in times past they haue done at their pleasure. And when they lade their ships with Russe commodities or vnlade them, it shalbe lawfull for them to hire any of our subiects to helpe them for the present time, and for them to carry their goods to and fro with their owne vessels to S. Michael Archangel, or elsewhere.

Also we command you our authorised people at the sea side as wel Customers as others to take of the foresaid merchants a note, or remembrance, what goods they bring in and ship out: whereby it may be knowen what goods come in and go out. But in no wise shall you open or vnpacke any of their wares or merchandises.

In like maner when as they ship or sende away any of their countrey commodities from S. Michael Archangel to any other place, or to our royall Citie of Mosco yee shall not hinder nor let them any maner of wise for the shipping of their merchandises in or out by vertue of these our gratious letters of priuiledge giuen them.

And whensoeuer any of the said English merchants haue any occasion to send ouer land out of our dominions into their own countrey any of their seruants or factors, by vertue of this our gratious letter we command you to giue them their passeport out of the office of our Secretariship.

And whensoeuer any of our subiects hath any thing to do with any of the foresaid merchants by way of contentions: or that they be damnified or hindered by any of our subiects: then we appoint and ordeine our Chanceller and Secretary Vasili Shalcan to heare their causes, and finally to determine on both sides according to equitie and iustice: and that he shall search the trueth betweene both parties.

And when the trueth cannot be proued or found out, then to cast lots by order of the foresaide Iudge, and he to whom the lot shall fall to take his othe.

Furthermore whensoeuer any of the English merchants or their factors shall come into any parts of our dominions or Cities, and shalbe wronged any kinde of wayes in trading, or otherwise by any abused, or haue any occasion of contention with any by way of trade in merchandise or otherwayes: we straightly charge and commaund you our gouernours, and authorised subiects within all our realme and territories of the same, to minister iustice vnto the aforesaid merchants, or to their deputies, and to search the trueth of the contention: and for want of sufficient proofe cast lots who shall take his oath for the more ready triall of the cause: And in no wise to take any fee or duetie of the aforesaid English merchants for the said iudgement in Lawe.

We wil and commaund all this to be obserued and kept in all parts of our dominions by all our subiects and authorised people by vertue of these our royal letters patents: And the said letters not to be diminished in any part or parsell thereof by any persons howsoeuer they be named. And whosoeuer shall withstand and not regard these our gracious letters shalbe in our high displeasure, and shal incurre the losse of his life. [Sidenote: After our accompt 1596.] This our gracious letter was giuen in our kingdom and royal City of Mosco, in the yere from the beginning of the world 7104. in the moneth of May.

Subscribed by the Emperours Chancellour and Secretarie Vasili Shalean.

* * * * *

The contents of M. Garlands Commission vnto Thomas Simkinson for the bringing of M. Iohn Dee to the Emperour of Russia his Court.

Friend Thomas Simkinson I pray you goe to Brounswik or Cassil and inquire if Master Iohn Dee be there or where he is, and when you finde him, certifie him howe that I haue sent you purposely to knowe where hee doeth remaine, and at your returne I will come and speake with him my selfe. Also you may certefie him that the Emperour of Russeland hauing certaine knowledge of his great learning and wisdome is marueilous desirous of him to come into his Countrey. And hath giuen me his letter with his hand and golden seale at it for to bring him into the Countrey with mee if it be possible, and for his liuing shewe him that he shall be sure of 2000 pound yeerely, and also all prouision for his table out of the Emperours kitching free: and if he thinke this too little, I will assure him that if he aske asmuch more hee shall haue it, and for his charges into the Countrey, I haue sufficient of the Emperours allowance to bring him and all his royally into the Countrey. And because hee may doubt of these proffers, he shall remaine at the borders vntill the Emperour be certified of him, and of his requests, which he would haue. And I am sure he shall be conueyed through the land with fiue hundred horses, and he shallbe accompted as one of the chiefest in the land next the Emperour. Also shew him howe that my Lord Protectour at my comming away did take me in his armes, and desired me as hee should be my friend to bring him with me and he would giue him of his owne purse yeerly 1000. rubbles besides the Emperours allowance. All these foresaide grauntes and demaunds doe I Thomas Simkinson acknowledge to be spoken by Edward Garland to mee, and to be sent to declare the same vnto Master Iohn Dee. And in witnesse that this is of a trueth I haue written the same with my owne hand, and thereunto set my name, in Wittingaw, otherwise called Trebona, the 18. of September, Anno 1586.

By me Thomas Simkinson of Hull.

* * * * *

A letter to the right worshipfull M. Iohn Dee Esquire, conteyning the summe and effect of M. Edward Garland his message, deliuered to Master Dee himselfe, (Letterwise) for a more perfect memoriall thereof. Anno 1586.

Right worshipfull, it may please you to vnderstand, that I was sent vnto you from the most mightie Prince Feodor Iuanowich, Lord, Emperour and great duke of Russia, &c. As also from the most excellent prince Boris Feodorowich, Lord Protector of Russia: to giue your worship to vnderstand the great good will and heartie desire they beare vnto you; for that of long time they haue had a great good report of your learning and wisedom, as also of your good counsel vnto Princes: whereupon his Maiesties most earnest desire and request is vnto you; that you would take the paines to come vnto his Citie of Mosco, to visite his Maiesties Court: for that hee is desirous of your company, and also of your good counsell in diuers matters that his Maiestie shall thinke needfull. And for the great goodwill that his Maiestie beareth vnto you, he will giue you yeerely toward your mainteinance 2000. pound starling; and the Lord Protectour will giue you a thousand rubbles, as also your prouision for your table you shall haue free out of his Maiesties kitchin: And further whatsoeuer you shall thinke needefull or conuenient for you, in any part or parts of his dominion, it shall be at your worships commaundement. And this is the summe and effect of my message and commandement guien me by his Maiestie and the Lord Protectour.

In witnesse whereof I haue written this with my owne hand, the 17. of December 1586.

By me Edward Garland.

In Trebona Castell otherwise called, Wittingaw in BoŮmia to which place this M. Edward Garland, came to M. Dee with two Moscouites to serue him, &c. He had sixe more which by M. Dees counsell were sent backe.

Witnesse M. Edward Kelley, and M. Francis
  Garland, brother to foresaid Edward,
    and diuers others.

It seemeth that this princely offer of the Emperour Pheodor Iuanowich, and of the L. Boris Pheoilorowich Protectour to his Maiestie, was made vnto the learned and famous Mathematitian M. Iohn Dee, partly to vse his counsell and direction about certaine discoueries to the Northeast; and partly for some other, weighty occasions: but because their conquest to Siberia was not as then fully settled, and for diuers other secret reasons, it was for that time with al thankfulness refused.

* * * * *

A branch of a letter from M. Iohn Merick, Agent vnto the Moscouie company in Russia, closed vp in the Mosco the 14. of March, Anno 1597. touching the death of Pheodor Iuanowich late Emperour of all Russia, &c.

[Sidenote: Febr. 1597.] Hauing thus farre proceeded with this my answere vnto the chiefest points of your worships letters receiued, my desire was to haue sent one vnto you long since, as you may perceiue, by the first date: but by reason I could not get leaue, I haue deferred it of till this instant, for that there was none suffered to passe out of the land. The causes may be iudged, for that it pleased God to call out of this world, the Emperour his Maiestie, who departed about the 7. of Ianuary: and euer since hath bene a mourning time, and no suites for any matter could be heard. But it hath bene a very dead season. Yet (thankes be to God) through the wise gouernment of Lord Boris Pheodorowich the Lord Protector vnto the saide late Emperour, since his death all things haue bene very quiet without any dissention; as the like in such a great kingdome I haue not heard of. [Sidenote: Prince Boris Pheodorowich by generall consent chosen Emperour of Russia.] And now through the prouidence of Almighie God, and by surrender of the late Empresse Irenia Feodoruna, and the common consent of the Patriarch, Nobles, Bishops, and the whole Cleargie, with the whole Commons besides, choise is made of none other but of the said Lord Protector, L. Boris Pheodorowich to be Emperour, and great duke of all Russia, who was most vnwilling to receiue the kingdome, but the people would make no other choise, nor haue any other. So that with much adoe and entreatie, it hath pleased his Maiestie to take vpon him the kingdome, and he is absolute Emperor to him and his heires. And certainly God hath done much for this Countrey, and hath made the people greatly happy, in that he hath prouided and, appointed so famous and worthy a Prince: whose excellent gouernment and experience these foureteene yeeres hath bene manifest to all Russia. God graunt his highnesse a most prosperous and long raine, with his Lady the Empresse, the Prince his sonne, and the

Princesse his daughter. All men do reioyce both Russe and strangers for this most famous Emperour. The Coronation is thought shalbe on the Assension day next, til which time I cannot depart from Mosco: which is a litle before the time that ordinarily I doe take my iourney from hence. And touching his Maiesties fauour towards me on your behalfe, especially for her Maiesties sake, as in foretime it was extraordinary, and so specially shewed to mee, as to none the like: so hath his highnesse promised the continuance thereof, with, further fauour as shalbe desired. Whereof I haue no doubt: for dayly I do finde the same.

* * * * *

A learned Epistle written 1581. vnto the famous Cosmographer M. Gerardus Mercator concerning the riuer Pechora, Naramsay, Cara reca, the mighty riuer of Ob, the place of Yaks Olgush in Siberia, the great riuer Ardoh, the lake of Kittay called of the borderers Paraha, the Countrey of Carrah Colmak, giuing good light to the discouery of the Northeast passage to Cathay, China and the Malucaes.

Inclyto et celebri Gerardo Mercatori, domino et amico singulari in manus proprias Duisburgi in Cliuia.

Cum meminissem, amice optime, quanta, cum vnam ageremus, delectatione afficerere in legendis Geographicis scriptis Homeri, Strabonis, Aristotelis, Plinij, Dionis et reliquorum, lŠtatus sum eo quod incidissem in hunc nuncium, qui tibi has literas tradit, quem tibi commendatum esse valde cupio, quique dudum Arusburgi htc ad Ossellam fluuium appulit. Hominis experientia, vt mihi quidem videtur, multum te adiuuerit in re vna, eaque summis Ó te votis expetita, et magnopere elaborata, de qua tam varie inter se dissentiunt Cosmographi recentiores; patefactione nimirum ingentis illius Promontorij Tabin, celebrisque illius et opulentŠ regionis sub Cathayorum rege per Oceanum ad Orientem brumalem. [Sidenote: DuŠ naues ŠdificatŠ in Duina fluuio ad patefactionem Orientalem.] Alferius is est natione Belga, qui captiuus aliquot annos vixit in Moscouitarum ditione, apud viros illic celeberrimos Yacouium et Vnekium; Ó quibus Antuerpiam missus est accersitum homines rei nauticŠ peritos, qui satis amplo proposito prŠmio ad illos viros se recipiant; qui Sueuo artifice duas ad eam patefactionem naues Šdificarunt in Duina fluuio. Vt ille rem proponit, quamquam sine arte, apposite tamen, et vt satis intelligas, quod quŠso diligenter perpendas, aditus ad Cathayam per Orientem procul dubio breuissimus est et almodum expeditus. Adijt ipse fluuium Obam tum terra per Samoedorum et Sibericorum regionem, tum mari per littus PechorŠ fluminis ad Orientem. Hac experientia confirmatus cert apud se statuit nauim mercibus onustam, cuius carinam non nimium profundŘ demissam esse vult, in Sinum S. Nicolai conducere in regione Moscouitarum, instructam illam quidem rebus omnibus ad eam patefactionem necessarijs, atque illic redintegrato commeatu, Moscouitis̄ nationis notissimos iusta mercede asciscere: qui et Samoedicam linguam pulchre teneant, et fluuium Ob exploratum habeant, vt qui quotannis ea loca ventitant. Vnde Maio exeunte constituit pergere ad Orientem per continentem Vgoris̄ ad Orientales partes Pechors̄, Insulamque cui nomen est Dolgoia. [Sidenote: Dolgoia Insula.] Hic latitudines obseruare, terram describere, bolidem demittere, locorumque ac punctorum distantias annotare, vbi et quoties licebit. Et quoniam Pechors̄ Sinus vel euntibus vel redeuntibus commodissimus est tum subsidij tum diuersorij locus propter glaciem et tempestates, diem impendere decreuit cognoscendis vadis, facillimoque nauium aditu inueniendo: quo loco antehac aquarum altitudinem duntaxat ad quinque pedes inuenit, sed profundiores canales esse non dubitat: [Sidenote: Insula Vaigats.] deinde per eos fines pergere ad tria quatuorve milliaria nautica, relicta Insula quam Vaigats vocant, media ferR̄ via inter Vgoriam et Nouam Zemblam: [Sidenote: Sinus inter Vaigats et Obam vergens per meridiem.] tum Sinum quendam ps̄terire inter Vaigats atque Obam, qui per Meridiem vergens pertingit ad terram Vgoris̄, in quem confluunt exigui duo amnes Marmesia atque Karah [Marginal note: Vel Naramsey et Cara reca.], ad quos amnes gens alia Samoedorum accolit immanis et efferata. Multa in eo tractu loca vadosa, multas cataractas inuenit; sed tamen per quas possit Nauigari. [Sidenote: Littus Obs̄ incolitubar Ostijs trium dierum itinere.] Vbi ad fluuium Obam peruentum fuerit, qui quidem fluuius (vt referunt Samoedi) septuaginta habet ostia, qus̄ propter ingentem latitudinem multas magnasque concludentem Insulas, quas varij incolunt populi, vix quisquam animaduertat, ne temporis nimium impendat, constituit ad summum tria quatuorve tentate ora, ea prs̄sertim qus̄ ex consilio Incolarum, quos in itinere aliquot habiturus est, commodissima videbuntur, triaque quatuorve eius regionis nauigiola tentandis Ostijs adhibere, quÓm fieri potest ad littus proxime, (quod quidem sub itinere trium dierum incolitur) vt quo loco tutissime nauigan possit, intelligat.

[Sidenote: Yaks Olgush locus super Obam fluuium duodecim dierum itinere a mari.] Quod si nauim per fluuium Obam aduerso amne possit impellere, prima si poterit cataracta, eaque, vt verisimile est, commodissima, ad eumque locum appellere, quem aliquando ipse cum suis aliquot per Sibericorum regionem terra adijt, qui duodecim iuxta dierum itinere distat Ó Mari, quÓ influit in mare flumen Ob, qui locus est in continente, propR̄ fluuium Ob cui nomen est Yaks Olgush, nomine mutuato ab illo magno Profluente flumini Ob illabente, tum certR̄ speraret maximas se difficultates superasse. Referunt enim illic populares, qui trium duntaxat dierum nauigatione ab eo loco abfuerunt (qu͡d illic rarum est, eo qu͡d multi ad vnum duntaxat diem cymbas pelliceas Ó littore propellentes oborta tempestate perierunt, c¨m neque Ó sole neque Ó syderibus rectionem scirent petere) per transuersum fluminis Ob, vnde spaciosum esse illius latitudinem constat, grandes se carinas prŠciosis onustas mercibus magno fluuio delatas vidisse per Nigros, puta Äthiopes. [Sidenote: Ardoh flumen influens in lacum Kitthaym: de quo in itinere ad Boghariam scribit Antonius Ienkinsonus.] Eum fluuium Ardoh illi vocant, qui influit in lacum Kittayum, quem Paraha illi nominant, cui contermina est gens illa latissimŘ fusa, quÓm Carrah Colmak appellant, non alia certŘ quÓm Cathaya. Illic, si necessitas postulabit, opportunum erit hybernare, se suosque reficere, resque omnes necessarias conquirere. Qu d si acciderit, non dubitat interim plurim¨m se adiutum iri, plura illic quŠrentem atque ediscentem. Veruntamen sperat Šstate eadem ad Cathayorum fines se peruenturum, nisi ingenti glaciei mole ad os fluuij ObŠ impediatur, quŠ maior interdum, interdum minor est. Tum per Pechoram redire statuit, atque illic hybernare: vel si id non poterit, in flumen DuinŠ, quo mature satis pertinget, atque ita primo vere proximo in itinere progredi. Vnum est qu d suo loco oblitus sum. [Sidenote: Carrah Colmakest Cathaya.] Qui locum illum Yaks Olgush incolunt, Ó maioribus suis olim prŠdicatum asserunt, se in lacu Kitthayo dulcissimam campanarum harmoniam audiuisse, atque ampla Šdificia conspexisse: Et c¨m gentis Carrah Colmak mentionem faciunt (Cathaya illa est) ab imo pectore suspiria repetunt manibusque proiectis suspiciunt in coelum, velut insignem illius splendorem innuentes atque admirantes. Vtinam Alferius hic Cosmographiam melius saperet, multum ad illius vsum adiungeret, qui sanŘ plurimus est. Multa prŠtereo, vir amicissime, ipsumque hominem te audire cupio, qui mihi spospondit se in itinere Duisburgi te visurum. Auet enim tecum conferre sermones, et procul dubio hominem multum adiuueris. Satis instructus videtur pecunia et gratia, in quibus alijsque officijs amicitiŠ feci illi, si vellet, mei copiam. Deus Optimus maximus hominis votis atque alacritati faueat, initia secundet, successus fortunet, exitum foelicissimum concedat. Vale amice ac Domine singularis.

Arusburgi ad Ossellam fluuium 20. Februarij 1581.

Tuus quantus quantus sum
 Ioannes Balakus.

The same in English.

To the famous and renowned Gerardus Mercator, his Reuerend and singular friend at Duisburgh in Clieueland, these be deliuered.

Calling to remembrance (most deare Friend) what exceeding delight you tooke at our being together, in reading the Geographicall writings of Homer, Strabo, Aristotle, Plinie, Dion, and the rest, I reioyced not a little that I happened vpon such a messenger as the bearer of these presents, (whom I do especially recommend vnto you) who arriued lately here at Arusburg vpon the riuer of Osella. This mans experience (as I am of dpinion) will greatly auaile you to the knowledge of a certaine matter which hath bene by you so vehemently desired, and so curiously laboured for, and concerning the which the late Cosmographers do hold such varietie of opinions: namely, of the discouerie of the huge promontorie of Tabin, and of the famous and rich countreys subiect vnto the Emperor of Cathay and that by the Northeast Ocean sea. [Sidenote: Two ships built vpon the riuer of Dwina for the Northeast discouerie.] The man is called Alferius [Marginal note: Or Oliuer.] being by birth a Netherlander, who for certaine yeeres liued captiue in the dominions of Russia vnder two famous men Yacouius and Vnekius, by whom he was sent to Antwerp to procure skilfull Pilots and Mariners, (by propounding liberall rewards) to go vnto the two famous personages aforesayd, which two had set a Sweden Shipwright on worke to build two ships for the same discouerie vpon the riuer of Dwina. The passage vnto Cathay by the Northeast (as he declareth the matter, albeit without arte, yet very aptly, as you may well perceiue, which I request you diligently to consider) is without doubt very short and easie. This very man himselfe hath trauelled to the riuer of Ob, both by land, through the countreys of the Samoeds, and of Sibier, and also by Sea, along the coast of the riuer Pechora Eastward. Being encouraged by this his experience he is fully resolued with himselfe to conduct a Barke laden with merchandize (the keele whereof hee will not haue to drawe ouer much water) to the Baie of Saint Nicholas in Russia, being furnished with all things expedient for such a discouerie, and with a new supply of victuals at his arriuall there, and also to hire into his companie certaine Russes best knowen vnto himselfe, who can perfectly speake the Samoeds language, and are acquainted with the riuer of Ob, as hauing frequented those places yeere by yeere.

[Sidenote: The Island of Dolgoia.] Whereupon about the ende of May hee is determined to saile from the Baie of S. Nicholas Eastward, by the maine of Ioughoria, and so to the Easterly parts of Pechora, and to the Island which is called Dolgoia. And here also hee is purposed to obserue the latitudes, to suruey and describe the countrey, to sound the depth of the Sea, and to note the distances of places, where, and so oft as occasion shall be offered. And forasmuch as the Baie of Pechora is a most conuenient place both for harbour and victuall, as well in their going foorth as in their returne home in regard of Ice and tempest, he is determined to bestow a day in sounding the Flats, and in searching out the best entrance for ships: in which place heretofore he found the water to be but fiue foote deepe, howbeit he doubteth not but that there are deeper chanels: [Sidenote: The Island of Vaigats. A Baie betweene Vaigats and Ob trending Southerly.] and then hee intendeth to proceed on along those coasts for the space of three or foure leagues, leauing the Island called Vaigats almost in the middle way betweene Vgoria and Noua Zembla: then also to passe by a certaine Baie betweene Vaigats and Ob, trending Southerly into the land of Vgoria, whereinto fall two small riuers called Marmesia and Carah [Marginal note: Or, Naramsey and Cara Reca.], vpon the which riuers doe inhabite an other barbarous and sauage nation of the Samoeds. He found many Flats in that tract of land, and many cataracts or ouerfals of water, yet such as hee was able to saile by. When hee shall come to the riuer of Ob, which riuer (as the Samoeds report) hath seuentie mouthes, which by reason of the huge breadth thereof containing many and great Islands, which are inhabited with sundry sortes of people, no man scarcely can well disouer, because he will not spend too much time, he purposeth to search three or foure at the most of the mouthes thereof, those chiefly which shall be thought most commodious by the aduise of the inhabitants, of whom hee meaneth to haue certaine with him in his voyage, and meaneth to employ three or foure boates of that Countrey in search of these mouthes, as neere as possibly he can to the shore, which within three dayes iourney of the Sea is inhabited, that he may learne where the riuer is best nauigabie. [Sidenote: The place vpon the riuer Ob, where he was but 12. dayes iourney from the mouthes thereof and is called Yaks Olgush.] If it so fall out that he may sayle vp the riuer Ob against the stream, and mount vp to that place which heretofore accompanied with certaine of his friends, he passed vnto by land through the countrey of Siberia which is about twelue dayes iourney from the Sea, where the riuer Ob falleth into the Sea, which place is in the Continent neere the riuer Ob, and is called Yaks Olgush, borowing his name from that mightie riuer which falleth into the riuer Ob, then doubtlesse hee would conceiue full hope that hee had passed the greatest difficulties: for the people dwelling thereabout report, which were three dayes sayling onely from that place beyond the riuer Ob, whereby the bredth thereof may be gathered (which is a rare matter there, because that many rowing with their boates of leather one dayes iourney onely from the shore, haue bene cast away in tempest, hauing no skill to guide themselues neither by Sunne nor Starre) that they haue seene great vessels laden with rich and precious merchandize brought downe that great riuer by blacke or swart people. [Sidenote: M. Ienkinson in his voyage to Boghar speaketh of the riuer Ardok.] They call that riuer Ardoh, which falleth into the lake of Kittay, which they call Paraha, whereupon bordereth that mighty and large nation which they call Carrah Colmak, which is none other then the nation of Cathay. There, if neede require, he may fitly Winter and refresh himselfe and his, and seeke all things which he shall stand in need of: which if it so fall out, he doubteth not but in the meane while he shall be much furthered in searching and learning out many things in that place. Howbeit, he hopeth that hee shall reach to Cathaya that very Sommer, vnlesse he be hindered by great abundance of Ice at the mouth of the riuer of Ob, which is sometimes more, and sometimes lesse. If it so fall out, he then purposeth to returne to Pechora, and there to Winter: or if he cannot doe so neither, then hee meaneth to returne to the riuer of Dwina, whither he will reach in good time enough, and so the next Spring following to proceed on his voyage. One thing in due place I forgate before.

The people which dwell at that place called Yaks Olgush, affirme that they haue heard their forefathers say, that they haue heard most sweete harmonie of bels in the lake of Kitthay, and that they haue seene therein stately and large buildings: and when they make mention of the people named Currah Colmak (this countrey is Cathay) they fetch deepe sighes, and holding vp their hands, they looke vp to heauen, signifying as it were, and declaring the notable glory and magnificence of that nation. I would this Oliuer were better seen in Cosmographie, it would greatly further his experience, which doubtlesse is very great. Most deare friend, I omit many things, and I wish you should heare the man himselfe which promised mee faithfully that he would visite you in this way at Duisburg, for he desireth to conferre with you, and doubtlesse you shall very much further, the man. He seemeth sufficiently furnished with money and friends, wherein and in other offices of curtesie I offered him my furtherance if it had pleased him to haue vsed me. The Lord prosper the mans desires and forwardnesse, blesse his good beginnings, further his proceedings, and grant vnto him most happy issue. Fare you well good sir and my singular friend. From Arusburg vpon the riuer of Ossella, the 20. of February, 1581.

Yours wholly at commandement,

Iohn Balak

Master Anthonie Ienkinson in a disputation before her Maiestie with sir Humfrey Gilbert for proofe of a passage by the Northeast to Cathaya, among other things alleageth this: videlicet, that there came a continuall streame or currant through Mare glaciale, of such swiftnesse as a Colmak told him, that if you cast any thing therein, it would presently be caried out of sight towards the West, &c.

* * * * *

A testimonie of the Northeasterne Discouerie made by the English, and of the profite that may arise by pursuing the same: taken out of the second volume of Nauigations and Voyages, fol. 17. of the notable Cosmographer M. Iohn Baptista Ramusius, Secretaire to the State of Venice: Written in Italian in the yeere, 1557.

D'alla parte poi di sotto la nostra Tramontana, che chiascuno scrittore et Cosmographo di questi et de passati tempi fin'hora vi ha messo e mette mare congelato, et che la terra corra continuamente fino a 90. gradi verso il Polo: sopro questa mappa-mondo all' incontro si vede che la terra vÓ solamente vn poco sopra la Noruega et Suetia, e voltando corre poi Greco e Leuante nel paese della Moscouta et Rossia, et vÓ diritto al Cataio. Et che cio sia la veritÓ, le nauigationi che hanno fatte gl' Inglesi con le loro naui, volendo andare Ó scoprire il Cataio al tempo del Re Odoardo Sesto d'Inghilterra, questi anni passati, ne possono far vera testimonianza: perche nel mezzo del loro viaggio, capitate per fortuna a i liti di Moscouia doue trouarano all' hora regnare Giouanni Vasiliuich Imperatore della Rossia e gran Duca di Moscouia, il quale con molto piacere e marauiglia vedutogli, fece grandissime carezze, hanno trouato quel mare essere nauigabile, e non agghiacciato. La qual nauigatione (ancor che con l'esito fin hora non sia stata bene intesa) se col spesso frequentarla et col lungo vso et cognitione de que' mari si continuerÓ, Ŕ per fare grandissima mutatione et riuolgimento nelle cose di questa nostra parte del mondo.

The same in English.

Moreouer (hauing before spoken of diuers particularities, in an excellent Map of Paulus Venetus) on that part subiect to our North pole, where euery writer and Cosmographer of these and of former times hitherto, haue, and doe place the frozen Sea, and that the land stretcheth continually to 90. degress, towards the pole: contrarywise, in this mappe is to bee seene, that the land extendeth onely a litle aboue Norway and Swethland, and then turning it selfe trendeth afterwards towards the Southeast and by East, vnto the countrey of Moscouie and Russia, and stretcheth directly vnto Cathay. And that this is true, the nauigations which the English men haue of late made, intending to discouer Cathay, in the time of Edward the sixt, king of England, are very sufficient witnesses. For in the mids of their voiage, lighting by chance vpon the coast of Moscouie (where they found then reigning Iohn Vasiliwich Emperor of Russia, and great Duke of Moscouia, who after he had, to his great delight and admiration, seene the English men, entertained them with exceeding great curtesies) found this sea to be nauigable, and not frozen.

[Sidenote: The great hope of the Northeastern dicouerie.] Which nauigation to Cathay, although it be not as yet throughly knowen, yet if with often frequenting the same, and by long vse and knowledge of those seas it bee continued it is like to make a wonderfull change and reuolution in the state of this our port of the world.

* * * * *

The testimonie of Gerardus Mercator in his last large Mappe of Europe, touching the notable discoueries of the English, made of Moscouie by the Northeast.

Magnam occasionem certamque rationem emendandŠ EuropŠ nobis attulit celeberrima Angloram per Cronium mare nauigatio: quŠ littora

Septentrionalia Finlappie MoscouiŠque iuxta coeli situm, mundÝque plagas digesta habet. Exacta etiam vrbis MoscuŠ latitudo ab Anglis obseruata, interiorum Regionum emendati¨s describendarum infallibilem legem prŠscripsit: Quibus oblatis adminiculis pulcherrimis, iniquum putaui tabulam hanc castigatiorem non reddere.

The same in English.

The most famous nauigation of the English men by the Northeast sea hath offered vnto me a great occasion, and certaine direction for the reformation of the mappe of Europe: which discouerie hath the Northerne parts of Finmarke, Lapland, and Moscouie, laied out according to the iust eleuation and the quarters of the world. And further, the true obseruation of the latitude of the city of Mosco, made by the foresaid Englishmen, hath yeelded me an infallible rule, for the correcting of the situation of the inland countries: which notable helps being ministred vnto me, I thought it my duetie to exhibit to the world this Mappe, more exact and perfect then hitherto it hath bene published.

* * * * *

Another testimonie of Ioannes Metellus Sequanus concerning the same Nauigation and Discouerie in his preface prefixed before Osorius de rebus gestis Emanuelis Regis PortugalliŠ. written about the yeere, 1574.

At ne omnis, vnis Hispanis, Oceani maris gloria totßque concederetur, Britanni Septentriones noua in Moscouiam nauigatione, ab hinc annis viginti plus min¨s illustrarunt. Nam bellis Sueticis Ó Moscouitarum, NaruŠque LiuoniŠ exclusi commercio, iter ad illos Oceano, hinc NoruegiŠ, FinmarchiŠ, LappiŠ, ScricfinniŠ, BiarmiŠque; illinc GroenlandiŠ littora prŠteruecti, vltrÓ Septuagesimum latitudinis Aquilonaris gradum sibi patefaciunt. Quam nauigationem BelgŠ posteÓ, non sine tamen cum ijsdem Britannis velitatione, sunt secuti. E͜ vehunt argenti veteris fragmenta, lineßsque vestes proprŘ detritas, omnÝsque generis minutiores merces, ad vsum, cult˙mque corporis hominum vtriusque sexus, veluti lintea et byssea cingula, periscelides, crumenas, cultros, et id genus sexcenta. A Moschis autem pelles omnis generis pretiosas adferunt, et salmones salitos, fum˘que duratos.

The same in English.

But least all and the whole glory of discouering the Ocean sea should be ascribed to the Spaniards, the Englishmen about twentie yeeres past, by a new nauigation into Moscouie, discouered the Northeast partes. For they by reason of the warres of Swethland being hindered from the traffique of the Moscouites and of the Narue in Liefland, opened a passage for themselues by the Ocean sea, beyond the Northerne latitude of 70. degrees:

hauing in their course on the one side the coastes of Norway, Finmark, Lapland, Scrickfin and Biarmia: On the other side the coast of Gronland. Which voyage the Hollanders afterwarde entred into, but not without some conflict with the English. They cary thither old plate and course linnen cloth, and all kind of small Mercerie wares, seruing for the apparelling of men and women, as linnen, and silke girdles, garters, purses, kniues, and many such like things. And they bring away from the Moscouites, all kinde of precious Furres, and Salmons salted and dried in the smoke.

END OF VOL. IV.

Milton Keynes UK
Ingram Content Group UK Ltd.
UKHW030718041024
449263UK00004B/401